D1420502

Studies in the History of Medieval Religion

VOLUME XII

THE CONVENT AND THE COMMUNITY IN LATE MEDIEVAL ENGLAND

Female Monasteries in the Diocese of Norwich, 1350–1540

Studies in the History of Medieval Religion

ISSN 0955-2480

General Editor
Christopher Harper-Bill

Previously published volumes in the series
are listed at the back of this volume

THE CONVENT AND THE COMMUNITY
IN LATE MEDIEVAL ENGLAND

Female Monasteries in
the Diocese of Norwich, 1350–1540

MARILYN OLIVA

THE BOYDELL PRESS

First published 1998
The Boydell Press, Woodbridge

Transferred to digital printing

ISBN 978-0-85115-576-0

The Boydell Press is an imprint of Boydell & Brewer Ltd
PO Box 9, Woodbridge, Suffolk IP12 3DF, UK
and of Boydell & Brewer Inc.
668 Mt Hope Avenue, Rochester, NY 14620, USA
website: www.boydellandbrewer.com

A CiP catalogue record for this book is available
from the British Library

This publication is printed on acid-free paper

Contents

Tables

In memory of my parents, and for my sisters

Acknowledgements

Many, many people helped with this project. Maryanne Kowaleski, my dissertation advisor at Fordham University, has been a steadfast supporter and friend. Her careful reading of this book in all of its stages helped to refine my writing and clarify many points of analysis. I also owe a great deal to Albert Loomie, S.J., who encouraged my initial interest in the topic of medieval English nuns and continues to do so.

Without the support and co-operation of the archivists and staffs of the Public Record Office, British Museum, and especially the Norfolk and Suffolk County Record Offices this book could never have been done. I would especially like to thank Rachel Farmer, Joan Kennedy, Frank Meeres, and Paul Rutlege of the Norfolk Record Office who accommodated my research in every way possible. The staff of the Suffolk Record Office graciously allowed me to examine the Elveden Collection before it had been fully catalogued. The people associated with the Centre for East Anglian Studies, especially Hassell Smith, Mavis Wesley, and Richard Wilson, have also been helpful, as was Roger Virgoe who advised me early on to look at wills for information about nuns' social backgrounds as well as gift-giving patterns. Thanks also to Linda Campbell, Jane Key, and Phillip Judge, who drew the map.

Other scholars have also encouraged me in untold ways. T. A. Heslop, Peter Northeast, Judith Middleton-Stewart, and Nesta Evans generously shared references and insights. Discussions over the years with Judith Bennett, Heath Dillard, Mary Erler, Jo Ann McNamara, Steve Rappaport, and Suzanne Wemple have always been fruitful. Special thanks are due to Joan Greatrex, Joel Rosenthal, and John Tillotson. Along with Christopher Harper-Bill, they remain unending sources of inspiration.

My greatest debts, however, are to Rachel Farmer, Elizabeth Garity of the Fordham University Library, and Roberta Gilchrist. Their help, hospitality, and enduring friendships were as essential to the completion of this book as their tireless document retrievals, processing of inter-library loan requests, and conversations about the nature of female monastic life in the Middle Ages. Roberta and Alex West also never tired of driving me around the Norfolk and Suffolk countryside to look at the convents' remains.

Finally, I would like to acknowledge the nuns who built and run the mission of La Labore in Guatemala, who, like their sisters all over the world, continue to educate, minister to, and welcome all those who cross their paths.

Abbreviations

Sources:

ANF	Archdeaconry of Norfolk
ANW	Archdeaconry of Norwich
ASD	Archdeaconry of Sudbury
ASF	Archdeaconry of Suffolk
NCC	Norwich Consistory Court
PCC	Prerogative Court of Canterbury
CFR	*Calendar of Fine Rolls*
CCR	*Calendar of Close Rolls*
CPR	*Calendar of Patent Rolls*
IPM	Inquisitions Post Mortem
Letters and Papers	*Letters and Papers, Foreign and Domestic, of the Reign of Henry VIII*
Papal Letters	*Calendar of Entries in the Papal Registers Relating to Great Britain and Ireland*
VCH	*Victoria County Histories*
VE	*Valor Ecclesiasticus*

Journals and Series:

AHR	*American Historical Review*
EcHR	*Economic History Review*
EHR	*English Historical Review*
EETS	*Early English Text Society*
NA	*Norfolk Archaeology*
PSIA	*Proceedings of the Suffolk Institute of Archaeology and Natural History*
TRHS	*Transactions of the Royal Historical Society*

Record Repositories:

BL	British Library
CUL	Cambridge University Library
NRO	Norfolk Record Office
PRO	Public Record Office
SRO	Suffolk Record Office

NORTH SEA

NORFOLK

KINGS LYNN

BLACKBOROUGH

CRABHOUSE

NORWICH

MARHAM

SHOULDHAM

CARROW

CAMBRIDGESHIRE

BUNGAY

FLIXTON

THETFORD

REDLINGFIELD

BURY ST EDMUNDS

BRUISYARD

SUFFOLK

CAMPSEY ASH

IPSWICH

★ Female Monasteries
• Male Monasteries
▲ Friaries

0   km   15

0   miles   10

ESSEX

Sites of female and male monasteries in
the diocese of Norwich, 1350–1540

Introduction

This book is about the eleven female monasteries in the diocese of Norwich from 1350 until their dissolutions in the 1530s. Located within a single episcopal jurisdiction, whose boundaries were coterminous with those of the counties of Norfolk and Suffolk, these religious houses present a convenient and well-documented group to study. Though smaller in size, wealth, and number than their male counterparts, these religious communities for women nevertheless repay historical investigation for what they can tell us about a significant but understudied aspect of medieval monastic life.

Despite recent interest in medieval female monastic houses in continental Europe and Ireland, English nuns – particularly those of the later medieval period – have largely been ignored.[1] While numerous aspects of English monastic life in the later Middle Ages have been analyzed – monasteries' abilities to maintain their own and the Church's authority, their changing financial status, their integrity as holy houses of prayer, and the various attempts at reform – scholars have focused almost exclusively on the male monasteries, and have paid scant attention to the female houses of medieval England.[2]

[1] For works on nuns in places other than medieval England, see for example: Lisa Bitel, "Women's Monastic Enclosure in Early Ireland. A Study of Female Spirituality and Male Monastic Mentalities," *Journal of Medieval History* 12:1 (1986), pp. 15–36. To a lesser degree Bitel deals with nuns in her more recent *Isle of Saints: Monastic Settlement and Christian Community in Early Ireland* (Ithaca, 1990). Jeffrey F. Hamburger, "Art, Enclosure and the *Curia Monialium*: Prolegomena in the Guise of a Postscript," *Gesta* XXX1/2 (1992), pp. 108–34; Penny Johnson, *Equal in Monastic Profession. Religious Women in Medieval France* (Chicago, 1991); K. J. P. Lowe, "Patronage and Territoriality in Early Sixteenth-Century Florence," *Renaissance Studies* 7:3 (1993), pp. 258–71; the collection of essays edited by Andrew MacLeish, *The Medieval Monastery* (Minnesota, 1988). Another good collection is edited by Craig Monson, *The Crannied Wall: Women, Religion and the Arts in Early Modern Europe* (Ann Arbor, 1992); Dominique Rigaux, "The Franciscan Tertiaries at the Convent of Sant'Anna at Foligno," *Gesta* XXX1/2 (1992), pp. 92–8; and Jane Schulenberg, "Women's Monastic Communities, 500–1100: Patterns of Expansion and Decline," in *Sisters and Workers in the Middle Ages*, ed. Judith Bennett, et al. (Chicago, 1989), pp. 208–39. For other recent works on early medieval nuns, see: John Nichols and Lillian Shank, eds., *Distant Echoes 1: Medieval Religious Women*, Cistercian Studies Series: No. 71 (Kalamazoo, Michigan: Cistercian Publications, 1984); and Lillian Shank and John Nichols, eds., *Medieval Religious Women: Peaceweavers*, Cistercian Studies Series: No. 72 (Kalamazoo, Michigan: Cistercian Publications, 1987).

[2] Studies which touch on these particular aspects of medieval English monasticism include: R. B. Dobson, *Durham Priory, 1400–1450* (Cambridge, 1973); F. R. H. Du Boulay, *The Lordship of Canterbury: An Essay on Medieval Society* (London, 1966); Christopher Dyer, *Lords and Peasants in a Changing Society: The Estates of the Bishopric of Worcester* (Cambridge, 1980); Eleanor Searle, *Lordship and Community: Battle Abbey and*

The most comprehensive work on medieval English nuns remains Eileen Power's *Medieval English Nunneries*, a book which in many ways set the standard for subsequent views of medieval English convent life for women.[3] Drawing on a wide range of sources – account rolls, episcopal visitation records, monastic inventories, and a miscellany of wills, letters and cartularies – she presented a largely anecdotal picture of female monastic life, one beset by chronic misman-agement and debt and devoid of true religious vocation. A handful of examples of superiors accepting very young girls as novices, or of taking exorbitant entry fees, for example, led Power to generalize about all of the convents' practices and to conclude that they contributed to the decline of female monastic life from a pre-Conquest heyday.[4]

Though Power's book suffers from a lack of critical analysis, her marshalling of sources at least provided fertile ground for further studies of medieval nuns and their monasteries.[5] But few followed suit.[6] And those who did deal with

   its Banlieu (Toronto, 1974). For financial aspects of male monasteries, see for example: Ian Kershaw, *Bolton Priory: The Economy of a Northern Monastery, 1286–1325* (Oxford, 1973); Mavis Mate, "Property Investment by Canterbury Cathedral Priory, 1250–1400," *Journal of British Studies* 23 (1984), pp. 1–21; R. A. L. Smith, "The Central Financial System of Christchurch, Canterbury, 1186–1512," *EHR* 55 (1940), pp. 353–69. For male monastic charity services, see: Harvey Bloom, ed., *Liber Elemosinarii: The Almoner's Book of the Priory of Worcester* (Worcester Historical Society, 1911), esp. Bloom's introduction; P. I. King, ed., *The Book of William Morton, Almoner of Peterborough Monastery, 1448–1467* (Northampton Record Society, xvi, 1954); David Knowles, *The Religious Orders in England*, 3 vols. (Cambridge, 1948–59), esp. vol. 3, pp. 260–7; H. W. Saunders, *Introduction to Obedientiary and Manor Rolls of Norwich Cathedral Priory* (Norwich, 1930), pp. 29–38. For attempts at reform, see: Knowles, *The Religious Orders*, vol. 2, pp. 309–30, and ibid., vol. 3, pp. 62–88, 241–59.

3 Eileen Power, *Medieval English Nunneries* (Cambridge, 1922). Other works on late medieval English nuns: Anne Bourdillon, *The Order of Minoresses in England* (Manches-ter, 1926); Mary Byrne, "The Tradition of the Nun in Medieval England" (Ph.D. diss., Catholic University, 1932), are limited in scope because they concentrate on specific orders. Byrne's Ph.D. dissertation is the basis for the unfortunate Graciela Daichman, *Wayward Nuns in Medieval Literature* (New York, 1986). Studies of female monasticism which include the English scene are: Lina Eckenstein, *Women under Monasticism: Chapters on Saint Lore and Convent Life AD 500–1500* (Cambridge, 1896); Stephanus Hilpisch, *A History of Benedictine Nuns* (Collegville, 1958). These works are very general and tend to focus on the twelfth and thirteenth centuries.

4 Power, *Medieval Nunneries*, pp. 22–7, cites four instances of convents in the diocese of Lincoln which accepted girls younger than 13, and one example from Yorkshire. For expensive entry fees Power cites examples of this policy at work in nine convents also in the diocese of Lincoln, at least two of which do not hold up under close scrutiny. She finds further evidence of this practice in the wills of society's most elite groups, those who had the money to make large donations to a convent when a daughter became a nun.

5 For a non-critical assessment of Power as an historian, see: N. Z. Davis, "Histories Two Bodies," *AHR* 93:1 (1988), p. 21.

6 Major studies of English monasticism, published both before and after Power's book, include: Geoffrey Baskerville, *English Monks and the Suppression of the Monasteries* (New Haven, 1937); Giles Constable, *Medieval Monasticism: A Select Bibliography* (Toronto, 1976), covers European monasticism, but devotes only pp. 56–60 to religious women,

nuns in their studies of English monasticism in the Middle Ages echoed Power's negative views and described nuns in ways which at once trivialized their functions and diminished their significance to other medieval women or to secular society. Though critical of monasticism in general, G. G. Coulton reserved particular bite for nuns when he stated that their gender made business management more difficult for them than it was for monks.[7] Several other historians reduced English convents to inns for travelers or quaint retirement homes for the tossed-off female kin of wealthy landowning families.[8]

Such casual assessments of medieval English nuns have in part discouraged any further interest in them as a topic worthy of analysis. Even David Knowles, in many ways the authority on English monastic history, omitted any mention of nuns in the first volume of his three-volume work, *The Religious Orders in England*. When criticized for his oversight he replied that evidence for the female monasteries was non-existent.[9] While documents are less plentiful for the female houses, had Knowles picked up a copy of Eileen Power's book – written some thirty years earlier – he would have realized that sources do exist which illuminate the status and condition of the female houses during the Middle Ages.[10] But what is even more curious about Knowles' omission of nuns

---

while pp. 62–8 covers the British Isles. The rest of the bibliography focuses on various aspects of male monasteries. G. G. Coulton, *Five Centuries of Religion*, 4 vols. (Cambridge, 1927–1950) also includes all of Europe, but references to England are scattered throughout; J. C. Dickinson, *The Later Middle Ages: from the Norman Conquest to the Eve of the Reformation* (London, 1979); J. C. Dickinson, *Monastic Life in Medieval England* (New York, 1961); H. O. Evennett, "The Last Stages of Medieval Monasticism," *Studia Monastica* 2 (1960), pp. 387–419; F. A. Gasquet, *The Eve of the Reformation* (London, 1919); F. A. Gasquet, *Henry VIII and the English Monasteries* (London, 1925); P. Hughes, *The Reformation in England* (New York, 1951), esp. pp. 31–86; M. D. Knowles, "English Monastic Life in the Later Middle Ages," *History*, n.s., 39 (1954), pp. 26–38; M. D. Knowles, *The Religious Orders*, passim; W. A. Pantin, *The English Church in the Fourteenth Century* (Cambridge, 1955); R. H. Snape, *English Monastic Finances in the Later Middle Ages* (New York, 1926); A. H. Thompson, *The English Clergy and their Organization in the Later Middle Ages* (Oxford, 1947), pp. 161–86; K. L. Wood-Legh, *Studies in Church Life in England Under Edward III* (Cambridge, 1934), pp. 1–37.

7 Coulton, *Five Centuries*, vol. 4, p. 121.
8 See for example: Coulton, "The Truth about the Monasteries," in his *Ten Medieval Studies*, 3rd ed. (Cambridge, 1930), pp. 90–2; Coulton, *Five Centuries*, vol. 4, p. 222. See also: Power, *Medieval English Nunneries*, pp. 74–8 for nuns as wasteful and poor, but always daughters and widows of the upper ranks of society who by the late Middle Ages had become simply 'paying guests' at the convents; Baskerville, *English Monks*, p. 205 for female monasteries as "inns for ladies on their travels." See also: F. A. Gasquet, *English Monastic Life* (London, 1905), pp. 177–78; see also ibid., pp. 174–75, p. 179 for nuns as dotty but happy residents of retirement institutions.
9 Knowles, *The Religious Orders*, vol. 2, p. viii. True to his word, Knowles makes no mention of nuns in this second volume of his opus. In the 500 pages of vol. 3, he devotes in total one page to nuns in the Tudor period: a small paragraph on p. 75, and a large one on p. 311.
10 Power included a bibliography of primary sources in *Medieval English Nunneries*, pp. 693–99. In addition there were in print at the time of Knowles' writing: L. J. Redstone, ed., "Three Carrow Account Rolls," *NA* 29 (1946), pp. 41–88; E. Crittall, ed.,

from his study of English monasticism is that a great deal of evidence exists about most of the female houses in the very same documents he and others used to study male monasteries.[11]

More abundant sources make male religious houses unquestionably easier to study, but the treatment of nuns by Knowles and others betrays an active lack of interest in them.[12] Despite the fact that evidence exists for and about the female religious which can be exploited in the same manner as the sources for the male religious, the history of English female monasticism has been dismissed as unimportant by too many historians in the past.

This emphasis on the male religious and their houses perhaps reflects historians' fascination with power and authority, social forces most often wielded by men.[13] Monastic history is replete with examples of abbots, monks, and friars who exercised considerable power both locally and on a more national scale. But for the most part female monastic superiors and nuns did not attain high public visibility; their focus was more on local conditions and concerns. Perhaps it is historians' high regard for this kind of public profile – and those who enjoyed it – that better explains their focus on male monasticism and their consequent lack of interest in nuns and their houses. Whatever the reasons, the result of this gender bias is twofold: one, a negative assessment of medieval nuns remains the standard; and two, we know a great deal less about them than we do about their male counterparts.

This legacy is revealed in the assumptions about medieval English nuns which historians continue to make. Religious women, for example, are typically characterized as coming exclusively from the upper echelons of late medieval society, their religious vocations being compromised by the worldliness associated with their elevated social status.[14] In addition, scholars

"Fragment of an Account of the Cellaress of Wilton Abbey, 1299," *Wiltshire Record Society, Publications* 12 (1956), pp. 142–256. For problems with sources for nuns, see: Janet Burton, *The Yorkshire Nunneries in the Twelfth and Thirteenth Centuries* (York: Borthwick Paper no. 56, 1979).

11 Especially in documents housed in the Public Records Office in London such as: E 101, E 179, E 315, SC 5, SC 6, SC 12, and SP 5. Numerous documents are also printed in: William Dugdale, ed., *Monasticon Anglicanum* (London, 1817–1840); J. Gairdner and R. H. Brodie, eds., *Letters and Papers, Foreign and Domestic, of the Reign of Henry VIII, 1509–1547* (London, 1862–1910); A. H. Jessopp, ed., *Visitations of the Diocese of Norwich, 1492–1532* (Camden Society, n.s., 43, 1888); A. H. Thompson, ed., *Visitations of Religious Houses in the Diocese of Lincoln* (Canterbury and York Society, London, vols. 17, 24, 33, 1915–27); and A. H. Thompson, ed., *Visitations of the Diocese of Lincoln, 1517–1531* (Lincoln Record Society Publications, 33, 35, 37, 1940–7).

12 See for example Mary Bateson's comments on historians' misleading readings of episcopal visitations of female monasteries in the diocese of Canterbury in her article, "Archbishop Warham's Visitation of Monasteries, 1511," *EHR* 6 (1891), p. 18.

13 See Richard Southern, *Western Society and the Church in the Middle Ages* (Harmondsworth, 1970), p. 310 for his comment that "as society became more right-minded, the necessity for male dominance began to assert itself."

14 C. R. Councer, "The Dissolution of the Kentish Monasteries," *Archaeologia Cantiana* 47

continue to view the nuns' small convents as ever on the brink of collapse because of meager endowments and financial mismanagement.[15] Hence they maintain that by the end of the Middle Ages the female houses had become unimportant and moribund institutions.[16]

Some recent studies have ventured beyond the confining parameters set up by Power and so readily maintained by others. Both Joan Greatrex and John Tillotson, for example, re-evaluate the success of nuns' household management, and the vitality of the convents as houses of prayer in the later medieval period.[17] Sharon Elkins and Roberta Gilchrist offer especially fresh perspectives on medieval English nuns by using gender as a category of analysis to explore female monastic foundations and architecture.[18] By not repeating the tired assumptions about medieval English nuns, the contributions of these scholars mark new and important directions in a remarkably stubborn area of medieval English history, and present the first real challenges to the stereotypes established by Powers in 1922.

This book also questions the prevailing views and examines the internal operations of the eleven female priories and abbeys of the diocese of Norwich, and how they functioned within the context of their local communities.[19] The

(1935), p. 128; Claire Cross, "Monasticism and Society in the Diocese of York, 1520–1540," *TRHS*, 5th ser., 38 (1988), pp. 131–45; Gasquet, *English Monastic Life*, pp. 438–39; G. A. J. Hodgett, "The Dissolution of Religious Houses in Lincolnshire and the Changing Structure of Society," *Lincolnshire Architectural and Archaeological Society, Reports and Papers*, 4th ser., pt. 1 (1951), pp. 83–99; Knowles, *The Religious Orders*, vol. 3, p. 75; L. J. Lekai, *The Cistercians: Ideas and Reality* (Ohio, 1977), p. 353; Power, *Medieval English Nunneries*, pp. 4–6, and pp. 25–30; G. W. O. Woodward, *The Dissolution of the Monasteries* (London, 1956), passim.

15 Coulton, *Five Centuries*, vol. 3, p. 551; Coulton, *Five Centuries*, vol. 4, p. 121; Dickinson, *The Later Middle Ages*, pp. 120–21; Gasquet, *English Monastic Life*, pp. 161–212; Power, *Medieval English Nunneries*, pp. 161–236; A. Savine, *English Monasteries on the Eve of the Reformation* (Oxford, 1909), pp. 221–22; Snape, *English Monastic Finances*, pp. 149–50; Sally Thompson, *Women Religious. The Founding of English Nunneries after the Norman Conquest* (Oxford, 1991). See also her "The Problem of the Cistercian Nuns in the Twelfth and Early Thirteenth Centuries," in *Women in the Church*, ed. Derek Baker, *Studies in Church History*, vol. 1 (Oxford: Blackwell, 1978), pp. 227–52.

16 Diana Coldicott, *Hampshire Nunneries* (Chicester, 1989). See also Janet Burton, *Monastic and Religious Orders in Britain, 1000–1300* (Cambridge, 1994), pp. 85–108 where she restates the standard historiography of medieval English nuns.

17 Joan Greatrex, "On Ministering to 'Certayne Devoute and Religiouse Women': Bishop Fox and the Benedictine Nuns of Winchester Diocese," in *Women in the Church*, ed. W. J. Sheils and Diana Wood, *Studies in Church History*, vol. 27 (Oxford, 1990), pp. 223–36; John Tillotson, *Marrick Priory: A Nunnery in Late Medieval Yorkshire* (York: Borthwick Paper no. 75, 1989).

18 Sharon Elkins, *Holy Women of Twelfth-Century England* (Chapel Hill, 1988); Roberta Gilchrist, *Gender and Material Culture. The Archaeology of Religious Women* (London, 1993); R. B. Dobson and Sara Donaghey, *The History of Clementhorpe Nunnery*, ed. P. V. Addyman, *The Archaeology of York*, vol. 2 (London, 1984).

19 This approach has been fruitfully taken for two male monasteries by: Dobson, *Durham Priory*; and John Tillotson, *Monastery and Society in the Late Middle Ages: Selected Account Rolls from Selby Abbey, Yorkshire, 1398–1537* (Woodbridge, 1988).

first chapter surveys the origins of the six houses in the county of Norfolk and the five located in Suffolk, and how certain factors of their foundations conditioned their later histories. Chapter 2 focuses on the nuns themselves: their numbers, social ranks, level of literacy, and other aspects of their lives which affected the quality of their religious vocations. A discussion of the nuns' household management, administrative practices, and of their finances – factors crucial to the proper functioning of these convents – is the subject of Chapter 3. With Chapters 4, 5, and 6 the scope of this study broadens to encompass the range of relations between the nuns and secular society. Non-cloistered residents – the priests, servants, and lay boarders – who also lived within the monastic precincts are discussed in Chapter 4. Their presence in these houses helps to illuminate some of the contributions convents made to secular society. Chapters 5 and 6 look at the services the houses provided in their local parish and county communities, and the patronage such services garnered.

The variety of sources which enabled this study of medieval English nuns and their communities includes a rich combination of published and unpublished antiquarian materials. These supplement the regional histories, like the *Victoria County Histories*, to provide the local historical, geographic and social contexts within which these female religious houses flourished.[20] Royal and monastic administrative documents also help to identify, among other things, papal and royal patronage of these convents, and show the organization and population of the nuns' extended households, the physical state of their precincts, and the success with which the nuns lived up to the monastic ideals of prayer, poverty, and obedience.[21]

These records have been used in conjunction with wills which in many ways form the center piece of this study. Those enrolled in the four archdeaconry probate courts in the diocese, in the episcopal probate court, and in the Prerogative Court of Canterbury, can reveal the social rank of a testator.[22] Though exceptions exist, as a general rule – and one that I follow here – social rank can be determined by place of probate.[23] People of relatively minor wealth

---

[20] In addition to William Page, ed., *The Victoria County History of Norfolk*, 2 vols. (Westminster, 1906); and William Page, ed., *The Victoria History of the County of Suffolk*, 2 vols. (London, 1911), hereafter VCH, see: Francis Blomefield, *An Essay toward a Topographical History of the County of Norfolk*, 11 vols. (London, 1805–10); Walter Copinger, *The County of Suffolk . . . Index nominum et locorum . . .* (London, 1904–5), and Copinger, *The Manors of Suffolk: Notes on their History and Devolution*, 11 vols. (London, 1905–11); and Alfred Suckling, *The History and Antiquities of the County of Suffolk*, 2 vols. (n.p., 1864–48.)

[21] J. Caley and Joseph Hunter, eds., *Valor Ecclesiasticus*, 7 vols. (London, 1810–34), hereafter VE; *IPM, CFR, CPR, CCR*; and *Feudal Aids* (London, 1908–21). For monastic sources: Dugdale, *Monasticon Anglicanum*; Jessopp, *Visitations*; and R. C. Taylor, ed., *Index Monasticus: or the Abbeys and Other Monasteries, Alien Priories, Friars, etc., in the Diocese of Norwich* (London, 1821).

[22] The wills and registers are discussed fully in Appendix 4.

[23] J. S. W. Gibson, *Wills and Where to Find Them* (Chichester, 1974), pp. 93–5 for Norfolk

who held land in only one archdeaconry had their wills probated in the archdeaconry courts; those who owned more extensive estates in the two counties came under the purview of the bishop's Consistory Court. The very wealthy, whose lands were dispersed throughout the realm, enrolled their last testaments in the Prerogative Court of Canterbury.

Combined with pedigrees and royal administrative documents like the *Inquisitions Post Mortem*, for example, wills registered in all of these courts provided the basis for a prosopographical analysis, or group biography, of all of the nuns who lived in the diocese from 1350 to 1540.[24] Reconstructing the social composition of the female monasteries indicates that contrary to what previous historians have thought, the vast majority of nuns came not from the aristocracy, but rather from medieval society's middling social ranks. This prosopography also discloses a hitherto unknown aspect of female monastic household administration: an officeholding pattern which included a career ladder which was based more on merit than on a nun's social status.[25]

Wills also proved invaluable for identifying patterns of patronage among the various ranks of the counties' societies. Quantifying bequests to all of the diocese's religious houses showed that while people from all social ranks made gifts of land and money to the nuns, parish gentry and yeoman farmer groups overwhelmingly favored the female religious over their male monastic coun-terparts. And in addition to bequeathing money and goods, local people also frequently requested burial in the nuns' cemeteries and churches. This form of patronage, typical in the Middle Ages, indicates that to the people of late medieval Norfolk and Suffolk the female houses were not the frivolous and moribund institutions historians have described. Such strong patronage also in part explains how the nuns balanced their budgets and kept at bay the kind of crippling debt that so often spelled the ruin of other monasteries of similar size and wealth.

Quantitative analysis of the data from the extant household and manorial accounts, cartularies, scattered charters, Exchequer and Court of Augmenta-tion records, and Suppression Papers reveals the economic policies pursued by the nuns and their stewards, and shows fluctuations in the convents' economic stability over time. The analysis indicates that while none of the monasteries were rich, most of the superiors and their obedientiaries skillfully managed their slim resources. Only three of the eleven houses in the diocese, Blackbor-ough, Redlingfield, and Thetford Priories, were in debt at the time of the Dissolution. The relative solvency of the majority of the female houses in the

---

wills; ibid., pp. 124–27 for Suffolk ones. See also: Henry Harrod, "Extracts from Early Norfolk Wills," *NA* 4 (1849), p. 111; and Norman Tanner, *The Church in Late Medieval Norwich* (Toronto, 1984), p. 115.

[24] Appendix 3 explains this analysis and its methodology.

[25] See my "Aristocracy or Meritocracy? Office-holding Patterns in Late Medieval English Nunneries," in *Women in the Church*, ed. W. J. Sheils and Diana Wood, *Studies in Church History*, vol. 27 (Oxford, 1990), pp. 197–208.

diocese of Norwich in the later Middle Ages then makes them anomalies in an age traditionally characterized as one of monastic decline and decay.[26]

This great mix of both the monastic and secular administrative sources discloses the wide variety of services – both spiritual and secular – which bound the monasteries to their local parishes and county communities throughout this later period. At least two of the female houses probated wills, for example, in addition to providing education for local children, and room and board for temporary as well as permanent lodgers. Most of the monasteries also accommodated local parishioners in their conventual churches both for regular services, and also for the establishment of guilds. While historians have acknowledged some of these activities, the impact of female monasteries on local society, and the extent of that impact, have never been fully explored. Scholars have mostly commented that such interactions were detrimental to the proper functioning of the female houses, suggesting, for example, that the nuns' acceptance of lay boarders was not only a financial drain, but was also a distraction from their spiritual duties, which thereby compromised the quality of religious life within the cloisters.[27] Evidence for the Norwich diocese's houses, however, indicates that nuns' interactions with lay society did not undermine their spiritual viability, but rather increased their prestige among secular neighbors as holy women devoted to both the active and passive aspects of monastic life. Such activities also serve to remind us that while these houses were fundamentally religious foundations, they were nevertheless vital social institutions as well.

The sources which allowed this analysis and illuminated its conclusions vary in quantity and quality from house to house. Bruisyard Abbey and Shouldham Priory, for example, are the least well-documented female monasteries in the diocese. Neither manorial nor household accounts survive for either, and their monastic affiliation – Bruisyard was a house of Poor Clares, and Shouldham a Gilbertine priory – exempted them from episcopal visitations. With only the *Valor Ecclesiasticus* and the Suppression Papers available for each, much less is known about these two convents. Carrow Priory, by contrast, has received a great deal of attention from Walter Rye, one of Norfolk's most prolific antiquarians; and cartularies survive for Blackborough and Crabhouse, and Marham Abbey, which help to recover their histories.[28] The range and

---

26 Coulton, "The Truth," pp. 88–106; Dickinson, *The Later Middle Ages*, pp. 279–310; Gasquet, *Henry VIII and the English Monasteries*, pp. 1–10; Hughes, *The Reformation in England*, pp. 39–41; Knowles, *The Religious Orders*, vol. 2, pp. 1–13, 90–115; ibid., vol. 3, pp. 1–14; Power, *Medieval English Nunneries*, pp. 161–63; Thompson, *The English Clergy*, pp. 161, 173–74, 182; Woodward, *The Dissolution*, pp. 40–5, 66–9.

27 Coulton, "The Truth," pp. 88–90; Power, *Medieval English Nunneries*, pp. 188, 197, 409–14.

28 Walter Rye and Edward Tillet, *An Account and Description of Carrow Abbey, Norwich, together with an Appendix of Charters* (Norwich Antiquarian Miscellany, 1884); and Walter Rye, *Carrow Abbey, otherwise Carrow Priory; near Norwich, in the County of Norfolk; its Foundation, Buildings, Officers, and Inmates with Appendices* (Norwich, 1889).

quantity of sources available not only belie historians' claims to the contrary, but also enable us to test prior assumptions about the nuns and their monasteries.

Differences between the female monastic experience and that of the monks, canons, and friars in the diocese are examined throughout this study whenever comparisons are appropriate. Contrasting female and male houses allows us to discern the extent to which gender might account for differences in the kinds of services or activities female and male religious houses provided and sustained in their local communities. Incorporating gender as a tool of analysis also exposes the extent to which historians might exaggerate abuses in female houses, while down-playing similar problems when they appear in the male monasteries. Comparison is also made throughout between the nuns in the diocese of Norwich and those in other parts of England. References to other female houses show how representative those in the diocese of Norwich might have been. This study, then, not only views the female monasteries of Norwich diocese in the wider context of their local lay communities of the parish and county, but it also places these particular eleven houses in a broader monastic setting.

Finally, this study proposes an alternative to the standard views commonly held about nuns and their communities in the later Middle Ages. Rather than interpret small initial foundations, marginal property holdings, and relative poverty as negative attributes, for example, these aspects, so common to female houses throughout medieval England, can perhaps be better understood as integral parts of a gender-specific female monasticism, piety, and spirituality. Recent studies, particularly those by Caroline Walker Bynum, show that poverty, physical denigration, and isolation defined a specifically female spirituality in the later Middle Ages.[29] Such qualities are reflected in the devotional literature written specifically by and for women, in various spiritual exercises

For Blackborough: BL, Egerton 3137; parts of the cartulary have been extracted in NRO, BL vi b (viii). Mary Bateson, ed., "The Register of Crabhouse Nunnery," NA 11 (1892); Marham Abbey's cartulary was included in the subject of John Nichols, "The History and Cartulary of the Cistercian Nuns of Marham Abbey" (Ph.D. diss., Kent State University, 1974). See also John Ridgard, "The Social and Economic History of Flixton in Southelmham, Suffolk, 1300–1600" (M.A. thesis, University of Leicester, 1970), for certain aspects of Flixton Priory.

29 For example see: Carolyn Walker Bynum, "The Female Body and Religious Practice in the Later Middle Ages," in Zone 3; Fragments for a History of the Human Body, ed. Michel Feher with Ramona Naddaff and Nadia Tazi (New York: Urzone, 1989), pp. 160–219; and her Holy Feast, Holy Fast: The Religious Significance of Food to Medieval Women (Berkeley, 1987); Walker Bynum, "Religious Women in the Later Middle Ages," in Christian Spirituality: High Middle Ages and Reformation, ed. Jill Raitt, Bernard McGenn and John Meyendorff (London, 1987), pp. 273–77. Karma Lochrie, Margery Kempe and Translations of the Flesh (Philadelphia, 1991), and Jocelyn Wogan-Browne, "Saints' Lives and the Female Reader," Forum for Modern Language Studies 27 (1991), pp. 314–32, both include excellent explorations of how physical deprivation and social isolation as prominent characteristics of female piety in the Middle Ages were translated through women's writings, as well as through writings for women.

religious women practiced, and in the iconography of certain female saints. As such, poverty and isolation may well have been the qualities of religious life which nuns consciously desired and actively pursued; after all, the basic tenets of medieval monasticism called for precisely such conditions.[30]

The evidence presented here – on matters which vary from the steady number of recruits and the quality of their religious vocations, to the financial solvency of their convents and the able administration of limited resources, to the continuing patronage of both secular society and many priests and monks – suggests this more positive and nuanced view of English nuns and their communities in the later Middle Ages.

---

[30] This interpretation of medieval religious women in general is also explored in Roberta Gilchrist and Marilyn Oliva, *Religious Women in Medieval East Anglia* (Norwich, 1993).

1

The Early Histories of the Female Monastic Communities in the Diocese of Norwich

Circumstances surrounding a monastery's foundation could have enduring effects on its subsequent history. Margery de Creyk, founder of Flixton Priory in Suffolk, prescribed the number of nuns her foundation was to support.[1] Other factors, like the geographic location of a convent and the size of its initial grants of lands, could heavily influence a monastery's economic resources and the social rank of its recruits and patrons. Though the foundation details of the female houses in the diocese of Norwich have been rehearsed elsewhere – in the *Victoria County Histories*, for example – the connections between aspects of the convents' foundations and their later histories have never been fully explored.

A survey of the foundation details can also establish the convents within the larger contexts of both female houses in other parts of England and also male monastic communities in the diocese. In many significant ways conditions of the foundations of the female monasteries in Norfolk and Suffolk were similar to those of the majority of nuns' houses instituted elsewhere, indicating a pattern of female monastic piety which has for the most part gone unnoticed.[2]

Foundations

The diocese was home to eleven female monasteries, sixty-three houses of monks and canons, and twenty-three friaries. The majority of the female houses were founded in the mid- to late twelfth century, the period during which the greatest number of religious houses for women were founded in medieval England.[3] Six of the convents were founded between 1146 and 1200. Most of the male houses – 46 per cent – had already been established by this

---

[1] The number was limited to eighteen: Dugdale, *Monasticon*, vol. 6:1, p. 593.
[2] Gilchrist, *Gender and Material Culture*, passim, delineates this pattern as well.
[3] Elkins, *Holy Women*, pp. 45, 118. Male monasticism entered its period of expansion in the first third of the twelfth century. Female monasticism did not begin a similar increase until 1130. Between 1130 and 1165 especially, more female houses were being founded than were male houses. See also: Schulenberg, "Women's Monastic Communities," pp.

time; their greater number can be explained in part by the longer history of male monastic foundations, which spanned from before the Norman Conquest to the mid-thirteenth century. The smaller number of women's religious communities and their later dates of foundation reflect a change in the style of monastic foundation and the social standing of their founders. Most of the male houses were aristocratic foundations; by the twelfth century, members of the gentry – the social group which was largely responsible for the female foundations – had begun to endow monastic communities which better served their spiritual and social needs.[4] Tables 1–3 list the foundation dates, the names of their founders, and the monasteries' assessed wealth in 1536.

Several of the founders of the diocese's female houses were, like their counterparts in other dioceses in medieval England, lay people of relatively minor social standing with limited resources.[5] Three of the nine lay founders of the female houses in the diocese of Norwich were women from the middle ranks of local county society. Emma, the daughter and heir of the local lord of Redlingfield, endowed Redlingfield with part of her inheritance; Margery de Creyk, also the daughter of a local landowner, founded Flixton Priory. Blackborough was also founded by a woman of middling social standing and modest means. In some cases, a founder's social status influenced a convent's architecture: the moated precincts of Flixton, for example, as well as the layout of some of the other priories' inner courtyards, were architectural features characteristic of twelfth-century gentry manorial designs which emulated earlier aristocratic ones.[6]

Founders of other female houses in the diocese were people higher on the social ladder. Isabel, widow of the Earl of Arundel, founded Marham Abbey; Bruisyard Abbey, the last female house founded in the diocese, was instituted by the Duke of Clarence; and King Stephen founded Carrow Priory in Norwich. Bungay Priory was the creation of the Countess Gundreda, daughter of William of Warenne, and wife of Hugh of Bigod, first Earl of Norfolk, and later of Roger de Glanvill, brother of King Henry II's famous justiciar, Ranulph.

To a certain degree, founders' social standing determined the properties with which they endowed their convents.[7] And, like the majority of female monasteries in medieval England, most of those in Norfolk and Suffolk were

---

238–39 for reasons why certain times facilitated the foundation of female houses more than others.

4   Gilchrist, *Gender and Material Culture*, pp. 48, 61; see also below, p. 22.
5   Elkins, *Holy Women*, pp. 95–7 finds that most of the 136 English female houses were founded by lay people of minor social status.
6   Roberta Gilchrist and Marilyn Oliva, *Religious Women in Medieval East Anglia* (Norwich, 1993), pp. 33–45, 66.
7   Benjamin Thompson, "Monasteries and their Patrons at Foundation and Dissolution," *TRHS*, 6th series, vol. 4 (1994), p. 106 and the table on pp. 124–25 for the patrons of the Norfolk female monasteries. See also: Hugh M. Thomas, *Vassals, Crusaders, and Thugs: The Gentry of Angevin Yorkshire, 1154–1216* (Philadelphia, 1993), p. 149 for the gentry in that region who founded religious houses they could afford.

Table 1. *Female Monasteries in the Diocese of Norwich, 1350–1540*

Monastery[a]	Founder	Dates Fnd	Diss	Order[b]	County[c]	Value in £
Redlingfield P	Emma of Redlingfield	1120	1537	Ben	S	67
Carrow P	King Stephen	c.1146	1536	Ben	N	64
Shouldham P	Geof Fitz Peter	1148	1539	Gilb	N	138
Thetford P	Abbot Hugh, Bury St Edmunds	c.1160	1537	Ben	N	40
Bungay P	Countess Gundreda of Glanville	1160	1536	Ben	S	61
Crabhouse P	Leva of Lynn	1181	1537	Aust	N	24
Campsey Ash P	Agnes & Joan de Valoine	1195	1536	Aust	S	182
Blackborough P	Muriel & Rbt de Scales	c.1200	1537	Ben	N	42
Marham A	Isabel of Arundel	1249	1536	Cist	N	33
Flixton P	Margaret de Creyk	1258	1536	Aust	S	23
Bruisyard A	Lionel, Duke of Clarence	1366	1539	PC	S	56

Sources: *Valor Ecclesiasticus*; Knowles and Hadcock, *Religious Houses of England and Wales*; VCH, *Norfolk*, vol. 2; VCH, *Suffolk*, vol. 2.

a P = Priory; A = Abbey.
b Ben = Benedictine; Gilb = Gilbertine; Aust = Augustinian; Cist = Cistercian; PC = Poor Clares.
c S = Suffolk; N = Norfolk.

endowed with small, localized properties.[8] Redlingfield Priory in Suffolk was endowed with the manor of Redlingfield and the local parish church.[9] Flixton Priory was founded with comparable properties: Flixton manor and the advowson of the local church.[10] Neither manor was very large; nor were any of the original endowments accompanied by much land outside the priories' respective parish boundaries. Similarly, the initial endowments of Blackborough and

8 See for example: Tillotson, *Marrick Priory*, p. 9 for the small initial endowment of this Yorkshire house.
9 Dugdale, *Monasticon*, vol. 4, p. 26; VCH, *Suffolk*, vol. 2, p. 83; Elkins, *Holy Women*, p. 14.
10 Dugdale, *Monasticon*, vol. 6:1, p. 593; VCH, *Suffolk*, vol. 2, p. 115.

Table 2. Male Monasteries in the Diocese of Norwich, 1350–1540

Monastery[a]	Founder	Dates Fnd	Dates Diss	Order[b]	County[c]	Value in £
St Benedict of Holme A	Wulfric	c.800	1539	Ben	N	583
Bury St Edmunds A	Bishop Aelfwine & Cnut	1020	1539	Ben	S	1656
Rumburgh P	Bishop Ethelman of Elmham	c.1060	1528	Ben	S	30
Mullicourt P	Ely Abbey	−1066	c.1539	Ben	N	6
Eye P	Rbt Malet	c.1080	1537	Ben	S	161
Castle Acre P	Earl of Warenne	1087	1537	Clun	N	306
Binham P	Albreda & Peter de Valoine	1093	1539	Ben	N	101
St Leonard P	Norwich Cathedral Priory	c.1094	1538	Ben	N	48
Norwich Cathedral P	Bishop Losinga	1096	1538	Ben	N	874
Aldeby P	Bishop Losinga	c.1100	1538	Ben	N	25
Felixstowe P	Rog Bigod	c.1100	1528	Ben	S	40
Ixworth P	Gilb Bluntis	c.1100	1537	Aust	S	82
King's Lynn P	Bishop Losinga	1100	1539	Ben	N	25
Yarmouth P	Norwich Cathedral Priory	−1101	1539	Ben	N	31
Thetford, St Mary P	Cluny	1104	1540	Clun	N	312
Horsham St Faith P	Sybil & Rbt Fitzwalter	1105	1536	Ben	N	162
Wymondham A	Wm d'Albini	1107	1538	Ben	N	211
Bromholme P	Wm de Glanville	1113[d]	1536	Clun	N	100
Bricett P	Nobiliac Priory	c.1114	1444	Aust	S	x

Sources: Valor Ecclesiasticus; Knowles and Hadcock, *Religious Houses of England and Wales;* VCH, *Norfolk,* vol. 2; VCH, *Suffolk,* vol. 2.

[a]   A = Abbey; P = Priory.
[b]   Ben = Benedictine; Clun = Cluniac; Aust = Augustinian; Cist = Cistercian; Prem = Premonstratensian; Trin = Trinitarian.
[c]   N = Norfolk; S = Suffolk.
[d]   Lilian Redstone, "The Cellarer's Account for Bromholme Priory, Norfolk, 1415–16," *Norfolk Record Society* xvii (1944), p. 47.

Monastery	Founder	Dates Fnd	Dates Diss	Order	County	Value in £
Sudbury P	Wesminster Abbey	c.1115	1538	Ben	S	9
Hoxne P	Norwich Cathedral Priory	1130	1538	Ben	S	18
Holy Trinity P, Ipswich	Gastrode, son of Egnostri	c.1133	1537	Aust	S	82
Blythburgh P	St Osyth Abbey, Essex	–1135	1537	Aust	S	48
Hempton P	Rog de St Martin & Rch Ward	–1135	1537	Aust	N	32
Pentney P	Rbt de Vaux	–1135	1537	Aust	N	170
West Acre P	Ralph de Toni	temp.Hnr I	1538	Aust	N	260
Thetford P, St Sepulchre	King Stephen	1139	1536	Aust	N	39
Coxford P	Wm Cheney	1140	1536	Aust	N	121
Sleves Holm P	Castle Acre Priory	c.1140	1537	Clun	N	1
Old Buckenham P	Wm d' Albini	c.1146	1536	Aust	N	108
Sibton A	Wm de Cadomo[e]	1150	1536	Cist	S	250
Mendham P	Wm de Huntingfield	–1155	1537	Clun	S	x
Snape P	Albreda & Wm Martel	1155[f]	1528	Ben	S	99
Wangford P	Ansered of France	–1159	1540	Clun	S	30
Walsingham P	Richeldis	1169	1538	Aust	N	391
Butley P	Sir Ranulph de Glanville & Bertha	1171	1538	Aust	S	318
Leiston A	Sir Ranulph de Glanville	1182	1537	Prem	S	18
Coddenham P	Royston Abbey	–1184	1537	Aust	S	8
Hickling P	Theobald de Valoine	1185	1536	Aust	N	100
Dodnash P	Wimer the Chaplain[g]	c.1188	1525	Aust	S	4

[e]   A. H. Denny, ed., *The Sibton Abbey Estates; Selected Documents, 1325–1509* (Suffolk Record Society Publications, 1960), p. 11.
[f]   William Filmer-Stanley, "The Dissolution Survey of Snape Priory," *PSIA* 35 (1983), p. 213.
[g]   C. Harper-Bill, ed., *Dodnash Priory Charters* (Suffolk Charters xv, forthcoming).

Monastery	Founder	Dates Fnd	Dates Diss	Order	County	Value in £
West Dereham P	Herbert Walter, Dean of York	1188	1536	Prem	N	61
Sts Peter and Paul P, Ipswich	Alice & Thos Lacy	−1189	1528	Aust	S	x
Wormegay P	Sir Wm de Warenne	1189	1537	Aust	N	35
Mountjoy P	Wm de Gyney	c.1190	1539	Aust	N	x
Woodbridge P	Ernald Rufus	1193	1537	Aust	S	5
Langley A	Sir Rbt Fitz Roger	1195	1536	Prem	N	104
Weybourne A	Sir Ralph Mainwaring	1199	1536	Aust	N	28
Peterstone P	?	−1200	1449	Aust	N	47[h]
Normansburgh P	Wm de Liseurs	1200	1537	Clun	N	6
Bromehill P	Sir Hugh de Plaiz	+1200	1528	Aust	N	x
Creake A	Alice, wife of Rbt Nerford	c.1206	1506	Aust	N	x
Letheringham P	Sts Peter & Paul Priory, Ipswich	1210	1537	Aust	S	26
Flitcham P[i]	No single Founder	c.1215	1538	Aust	N	55
Alnesbourne P	Albert de Neville	c.1216	1539	Aust	S	7
Beeston P	Isabella de Cressy	c.1216	1539	Aust	N	43
St Olave's P	Rog Fitz Osbert	c.1216	1537	Aust	S	49
Kersey P	?	c.1218	1443	Aust	S	x
Chipley P	?	−1235	1468	Aust	S	x
Great Massingham P	Nich Le Syre	−1260	1538	Aust	N	x
Wendling A	Sir Wm de Wendling	c.1267	1536	Prem	N	55
Weybridge P	Hugh Bigod, Earl of Norfolk	−1272	1536	Aust	N	7
Modney P	Ramsey Abbey	−1291	c.1539	Ben	N	2
Ingham P	?	1360	1536	Trin	N	

[h]   Value at Dissolution in 1449.
[i]   *Historical Manuscripts Commission, Various*, vol. iv, 316.

Table 3. *Friaries in the Diocese of Norwich, 1350–1540*

| Friary | Founder | Dates | | Order[a] | County[b] |
		Fnd	Diss		
Norwich	?	1226	1538	Dom	N
Norwich	John de Hastings	1226	1538	Fran	N
Yarmouth	Sir Wm Gerbrigge	1226	1538	Fran	N
Burnham Norton	Sir Wm Calthorp & Sir Ralph Hemenhale	1241	1538	Carm	N
Clare	Rich de Clare, Earl of Gloucester	1248	1538	Aust	S
Sudbury	Baldwin de Shipling & Chabil	−1249	1538	Dom	S
Dunwich	Sir Rog de Holish	−1256	1538	Dom	S
King's Lynn	Thos Gedney	−1256	1538	Dom	N
Norwich	Philip, son of Warin, Norwich merchant	1256	1538	Carm	N
Bury St Edmunds	King Henry III Holish	1257	1538	Fran	S
King's Lynn	Thos Feltham	c.1260	1538	Fran	N
King's Lynn	Lord Bardolf	−1261	1538	Carm	N
Ipswich	King Henry III	1263	1538	Dom	S
Yarmouth	Godfrey Pilgrim, burgess of Yarmouth & Thos Fastolf	1267	1538	Dom	N
Norwich	Rog Minot	c.1272	1538	Aust	N
Welnetham	?	1274	1538	Crutch[c]	N
Yarmouth	King Edward I	1276	1538	Carm	N
Ipswich	Provincial Chapter[d]	1278	1538	Carm	S

Sources: Knowles and Hadcock, *Religious Houses of England and Wales*; VCH, *Norfolk*, vol. 2; VCH, *Suffolk*, vol. 2.

[a] Dom = Dominican; Fran = Franciscan; Carm = Carmelite; Aust = Augustinian.
[b] N = Norfolk; S = Suffolk.
[c] Crutched Friars. Knowles, p. 17 is the only source for this citation. This house does not appear in the Norfolk VCH.
[d] There is a disagreement about the founders of this Carmelite friary: V. B. Redstone, "The Carmelites of Ipswich," *PSIA* 10 (1898–1900), p. 189, says the founders were either Sir Thomas of Loudham, as Dugdale claims, or Lord Bardesley, Sir Jeffrey Hadley, and Sir Robert

Friary	Founder	Dates Fnd	Diss	Order	County
Dunwich	Rich Fitz John	c.1289	1538	Fran	S
King's Lynn	?	–1295	1538	Aust	N
Orford	Rbt de Herwell	1295	1538	Aust	S
Blakeney	Sir Wm Roos & Maud	1296	1538	Carm	N
Ipswich	Sir Rbt Tiptot & Una	–1298	1538	Fran	S
Gorleston	Margaret & Wm Woderowe	–1311	1538	Aust	S
Thetford	Henry, Duke of Lancaster	1335	1538	Dom	N
Walsingham	Elizabeth de Burgh, Countess of Clare	1347	1538	Fran	N
Thetford	John of Gaunt, Earl of Lancaster	c.1387	1538	Aust	N

Norton. But see: B. Zimmerman, "The White Friars at Ipswich," *PSIA* 10 (1898–1900), p. 196, who says the foundation was decided on by the provincial chapter. Knowles follows this assignment, as does the Suffolk VCH.

Bungay Priories consisted of small manors, local parish churches, and plots of rather unproductive land.[11] And though the convents acquired more parcels of land throughout the period, these small initial endowments remained their primary resources and sources of revenue, and helped to define the nuns' spheres of influence.

Despite the higher social standing and greater wealth of the founders of Bruisyard, Bungay, Carrow, and Marham, these houses were likewise locally endowed with properties similar in size and quality to those endowed by Emma of Redlingfield, Margery de Creyk, and Muriel de Scales.[12] In fact, none of the aristocratic foundations ever attained more than marginal wealth. The *Valor*

[11] For Blackborough, see: Blomefield, *An Essay*, vol. 9, pp. 32–4; Dugdale, *Monasticon*, vol. 4, p. 206; and VCH, *Norfolk*, vol. 2, p. 350. For Bungay, see: Dugdale, *Monasticon*, vol. 4, p. 338; and VCH, *Suffolk*, vol. 2, p. 81. For Marham Abbey, see: Blomefield, *An Essay*, vol. 7, pp. 386–89; Dugdale, *Monasticon*, vol. 5, p. 743; VCH, *Norfolk*, vol. 2, p. 369.

[12] For Bruisyard Abbey's foundation properties, see: Bourdillon, *The Minoresses*, p. 25; VCH, *Suffolk*, vol. 2, p. 131. For Carrow's foundation, see: Elkins, *Holy Women*, pp. 113–14; Rye and Tillet, "Carrow Abbey," pp. 465–66; VCH, *Norfolk*, vol. 2, p. 351; Blomefield, *An Essay*, vol. 4, p. 525; Dugdale, *Monasticon*, vol. 4, pp. 68–9 reprints the foundation charters and cites a cartulary which is no longer extant. Marham was endowed with a manor and other small parcels of land in the village of Marham: Blomefield, *An Essay*, vol. 7, pp. 386–89; Dugdale, *Monasticon*, vol. 5, p. 743; Nichols, "The History and Cartulary," pp. 15–18; VCH, *Norfolk*, vol. 2, p. 369.

Table 4. Female Monasteries in the Diocese of Norwich Ranked According to Wealth

Monastery	Value			Fndn Date	Social Rank of Fnder	Site of House
	£	s	d			
Campsey Ash Priory	182	5	5¼	1195	Nobility	Rural S[a]
Shouldham Priory	138	18	1	1148	Nobility	Rural N
Redlingfield Priory	67	–	1½	1120	Local Gentry	Rural S
Carrow Priory	64	10	6½	1146	Royalty	Urban N
Bungay Priory	61	11	9¼	1160	Nobility	Mkt Twn S
Bruisyard Abbey	56	12	6	1366	Nobility	Rural S
Blackborough Priory	42	6	7½	1150	Local Gentry	Rural N
Thetford Priory	40	11	2½	1160	Ecclesiastic	Urban N
Marham Abbey	33	13	5	1294	Nobility	Rural N
Crabhouse Priory	24	19	6	1181	Local Gentry	Rural N
Flixton Priory	23	4	1½	1258	Local Gentry	Mkt Twn S

Sources: Valor Ecclesiasticus.

[a]   S = Suffolk; N = Norfolk.

Ecclesiasticus – the sixteenth-century audit of all religious houses upon which most historians rely for the economic status of the religious houses in medieval England – valued Carrow Priory at roughly £64, Bungay at about £61, Bruisyard around £56, and Marham at a little more than £33.[13] Compared to the diocese's other female houses, Carrow ranked fourth in wealth; Bungay ranked fifth; Bruisyard ranked only sixth; and Marham was one of the poorest as it ranked ninth in wealth (Table 4). The higher social status of the founders of these houses thus had little impact on their financial status.

Only two of the diocese's female monasteries were endowed with extensive properties by socially prominent founders. Campsey Ash Priory was founded by two sisters, whose brother, a Norman baron, donated a sizeable estate for their community.[14] His initial grants of lands were considerably greater than those of most of the other female houses. Shouldham Priory also was founded

---

13 VE, vol. 3, pp. 305–6 for Carrow, and ibid., vol. 3, pp. 442–43 for Bruisyard; ibid. vol 3, p. 340 for Bungay; ibid., vol. 3, p. 379 for Marham. Historians use the *Valor* to gage the economic status of English monasteries despite the uncertainties about the commissioners' accounting procedures. See: Snape, *English Monastic Finances*, pp. 71–119; Savine, *English Monasteries on the Eve of the Reformation*, passim; and Chapter 3 of this book.

14 Dugdale, *Monasticon*, vol. 6:1, p. 583; Elkins, *Holy Women*, p. 123; VCH, *Suffolk*, vol. 2, p. 112.

with a large manor, extensive lands in the parish of Shouldham, and a number of shops in London by its founder, Geoffrey Fitz Peter, Earl of Essex.[15] These more substantial endowments in part explain the greater wealth of these two houses; on the eve of the Dissolution, Campsey Ash was worth about £182, and Shouldham nearly £139.[16] And these two female houses were the only ones founded in the diocese with more than one small manor and its outlying properties.

Most of the diocese's female convents then were worth less than £100; the majority of female houses in other parts of England were also valued under £100. Only a small percentage of female monasteries in other counties were worth more; the majority, in fact, were valued under £50.[17] By contrast, many of the male houses in the diocese were much wealthier. While the majority of male houses were valued in 1536 between £25 and £50, 36 percent of them were valued well above £100. Table 5 shows a comparison of the values of the female houses in the diocese of Norwich to their male counterparts, and to the female houses in other dioceses.

Most of the male monasteries in the diocese – and indeed most of the male houses elsewhere in England – were founded with considerable properties by men from the highest social groups.[18] Among those who established the male houses in Norwich diocese, for example, were William de Albini, Henry I's chief butler, as well as Countess Gundreda's brother-in-law, Ranulph de Glanville.[19] These royal and aristocratic benefactors founded their houses with considerable lands, thus ensuring later economic vitality. A correlation existed between large endowments, socially prominent founders, and financial stability, in a significant number of male houses, but it did not necessarily pertain to the female monasteries.

While the overall greater wealth of the male monasteries undoubtedly reflected the higher social status of their founders, the male houses' stronger economic standing also suggests differences in founders' perceptions between male and female religious. King Stephen, for example, endowed his numerous male monastic foundations with considerably more lands than he gave to either Carrow Priory or his only other only female foundation, Higham Priory in Kent.[20] He may have considered his male foundations more valuable in the

15 Blomefield, An Essay, vol. 7, pp. 414–15; Elkins, Holy Women, p. 122; VCH, Norfolk, vol. 2, p. 412.
16 VE, vol. 3, pp. 415–17, for Campsey, and ibid., vol. 3, p. 378 for Shouldham.
17 These percentages are based on David Knowles and R. Neville Hadcock, eds., Medieval Religious Houses in England and Wales (London, 1971), pp. 171–233.
18 Elkins, Holy Women, pp. 95–7. Though she is specifically talking about the founders of the male monasteries in the north of England, her point is valid for the founders of the male houses in southern England as well.
19 William de Albini founded Wymondham and Old Buckenham Priories in Norfolk; see VCH, Norfolk, vol. 2, pp. 336, 376. Ranulph of Glanville founded Butley and Leiston Priories in Suffolk; see VCH, Suffolk, vol. 2, pp. 95, 117.
20 R. H. C. Davis, King Stephen (New York, 1967), pp. 70–3. For the values of Stephen's male house foundations, see: Thomas Tanner, Notitia Monastica (London, 1744), p. 128

Table 5. Values at the Dissolution of Norwich Diocesan Monasteries
and all other English Female Monasteries

Type of Monastery[a]	Value in £							
	1–25 (No.) %	25–50 (No.) %	50–100 (No.) %	100–50 (No.) %	150–200 (No.) %	200–300 (No.) %	300–400 (No.) %	+500 (No.) %
NF	(2) 18	(3) 27	(4) 36	(1) 9	(1) 9	—	—	—
NM	(11) 20	(16) 30	(7) 13	(4) 7	(5) 9	(4) 7	(4) 7	(3) 6
AF	(33) 24	(32) 23	(30) 22	(10) 7	(7) 5	(9) 7	(9) 7	(3) 2

Source: Valor Ecclesiasticus. The values of five of the Norfolk male houses and the values of four of the Suffolk male houses are unknown.

a NF = Norwich Female Monasteries; NM = Norwich Male Monasteries; AF = All Female Monasteries.

struggle to consolidate his power and substantiate his claim to the throne.[21] The greater wealth of the male houses might also reflect the general subordinate status accorded to women by both the medieval Church and by secular society. The nuns' inability to perform the sacraments may also have diminished their attraction to those who wished to establish a foundation which would intercede for them and their predecessors after their deaths.[22] Consider, for example, that one person founded several male houses, but no female

for Coggeshall, a Cistercian house in Essex valued in 1535 at £251; ibid., p. 214 for Feversham, a Benedictine male house founded Kent, valued at £268; ibid., p. 230 for Furness Abbey, another Cistercian house in Lancashire, worth £805; ibid., p. 259 for the Austin male house of Thornholme in Lincoln, valued at £105; ibid., p. 319 for Westminster Abbey, worth over £1000 in 1535; ibid., p. 642 for his foundation for secular canons in York, St Leonards, valued in 1535 at £500. Compare these figures with the values of his female monastic foundations: Carrow, £64, and Higham, £26. For the female monastic values, see: Knowles and Hadcock, Medieval Religious Houses, pp. 213, 217.

21 Gilchrist, Gender and Material Culture, p. 41 for the political and economic reasons why other aristocratic men, especially Norman lords, founded male houses.

22 See: Francine Cardman, "The Medieval Question of Women and Orders," Thomist 42 (1978), pp. 582–99 for a survey of the development of the Church's stance on the inviability of women to take Holy Orders. See also: Caroline Walker Bynum, Jesus as Mother: Studies in the Spirituality of the High Middle Ages (Berkeley, 1982), pp. 9–21 for her discussion of how monks became legitimate conduits of God's grace and messages to the laity and women, and began to become priests. She also describes how the twelfth and thirteenth centuries saw the increasing power of the (male) clergy as the necessary intermediaries between God and humanity, a role enhanced by their sole authority to perform the sacraments. See also: Giles Constable, Monastic Tithes from their Origins to the Twelfth Century (Cambridge, 1964), pp. 164–66 for a discussion of the increasing identification of monks as priests who could perform these intercessory prayers for patrons, thus making the foundation of a male house more valuable.

ones.[23] Founders of female houses, on the other hand, founded only one house each, illustrating the changing style of monastic foundations whereby people of lesser wealth and social status could institute a foundation which better accommodated their needs.[24]

The relative poverty of nuns compared to monks is one of the characteristics – usually cited as a negative one – of female monasticism in the Middle Ages. But poverty was an important aspect of these convents, as well as other female houses, from their very inceptions. As Roberta Gilchrist has recently shown, poverty could not only reflect a founder's resources and social status, it also constituted a significant part of a specifically female religious asceticism which embraced poverty as an active ideal.[25]

Just as poverty appears to have been an important factor in the foundation of the convents in the diocese, so too was physical separation from society. And while founders' decisions about where to site their new institutions often reflected territorial interests, these original patrons, including the aristocratic ones, chose to locate their religious foundations in geographically marginal areas, or in places that were considered to be outside of or removed from society. As the map of monasteries (p. xiii) illustrates, while male houses could be found in virtually all parts of the diocese, the female houses tended to be clustered in three main regions of Norfolk and Suffolk.

Blackborough, Crabhouse, Marham, and Shouldham were located in the fens and Brecklands of western Norfolk, and poor soil and seasonal flooding made these areas sparsely populated and relatively poor.[26] While late

---

[23] Bishop Losinga founded Aldeby, King's Lynn, and Norwich Cathedral Priories; William de Albini founded both Buckenham and Wymondham Priories.

[24] There was one instance of a relationship between the founders of a male and female house. The niece of Agnes and Joan de Valoine, founders of Campsey Ash Priory, was married to Ranulph de Glanville, who with his wife, Bertha, founded Butley Priory.

[25] Gilchrist, Gender and Material Culture, pp. 61, 64–9 for this attribute and female monastic foundations.

[26] Francis Blomefield, An Essay, vol. 8, p. 449 (Blackborough); ibid., vol. 9, p. 173 (Crabhouse); ibid., vol. 7, p. 384 (Marham Abbey); ibid., vol. 7, p. 414 (Shouldham Priory). See also: Christobel Hood, ed., The Chorography of Norfolk (Norwich, 1938), p. 126 (Marham); ibid., p. 153 (Shouldham). For the poverty of the fens and Brecklands, see: Eric Kerridge, The Farmers of Old England (London, 1973), pp. 20, 80–1; Joan Thirsk, "The Farming Regions of England," in The Agrarian History of England and Wales, 1500–1640, ed. Joan Thirsk (Cambridge, 1967), vol. 4 of The Agrarian History of England and Wales, pp. 41–4. For the sparse population, see: Alan Baker, "Changes in the Later Middle Ages," in A New Historical Geography of England before 1600, ed. H. C. Darby (Cambridge, 1973), p. 191; John Patten, "Population Distribution in Norfolk and Suffolk During the Sixteenth and Seventeenth Centuries," in Pre-Industrial England: Geographic Essays, ed. John Patten (Folkestone, 1979), p. 79. But see also: Roger Virgoe and David Dymond, "The Reduced Population and Wealth of Early Fifteenth-Century Suffolk," PSIA 36:2 (1986), pp. 73–100. For continuous flooding, for Blackborough, see: NRO, Phi/451 577x8. For Crabhouse, see: Bateson, "The Register," pp. 38–9, and Augustus Jessopp, "Ups and Downs of a Norfolk Nunnery," in Frivola, Simon Ryan and Other Papers, ed. Augustus Jessopp (London, 1896), pp. 28–9. For Marham, see: Nichols, "The History and Cartulary," pp. 46–7.

twelfth-century efforts to drain the fens helped make the region more habitable and prosperous over time, sporadic flooding nevertheless kept it under-populated and fairly isolated. Bruisyard, Campsey Ash, and Redlingfield were sited in High Suffolk, an area known for its large population of small and relatively prosperous freeholders.[27] These Suffolk houses were therefore sited in more populated and wealthier areas than their counterparts in the Norfolk fens and Brecklands.[28]

Four of the diocese's female monasteries were more urban foundations, located in small market towns or on the outskirts of the larger cities of Norwich and Thetford. Bungay Priory was founded in the market town of Bungay, near the smaller town of Flixton where Flixton Priory lay close to the county boundary.[29] Carrow and Thetford Priories were in larger urban areas: Carrow just outside the city walls of Norwich, the diocesan seat and the region's main urban center;[30] and Thetford in the old episcopal seat of the town of Thetford, also near the Norfolk/Suffolk county border.[31] Second only to London in population size and wealth, Norwich and its environs prospered from a flourishing industry in worsted cloth and the New Draperies throughout the later Middle Ages.[32] Carrow then was close to a fairly wealthy and large

---

[27] For Campsey Ash, see: D. N. J. MacCulloch, ed., The Chorography of Suffolk (Suffolk Record Society, vol. 19, 1976), p. 68. See Taylor, Index Monasticus, p. 105 for Bruisyard; and ibid., p. 88 for Redlingfield.

[28] For the economy and population settlement of this area of Suffolk, see: Baker, "Changes," p. 191; D. C. Douglas, The Social Structure of Medieval East Anglia (Oxford, 1927), pp. 3–4; Kerridge, The Farmers, pp. 17, 86–7; J. B. Mitchell, "Suffolk Agriculture in the Middle Ages," Report of the British Association, 1938, p. 445; M. M. Postan, The Medieval Economy and Society (Berkeley, 1972), pp. 163–64; J. C. Russell, British Medieval Population (Albuquerque, 1948), p. 313; Thirsk, "The Farming Regions," pp. 46–8; VCH, Suffolk, vol. 1, pp. 632–33.

[29] Maurice Beresford and H. P. R. Finberg, English Medieval Boroughs: A Handlist (Devon, 1973), p. 165 for Bungay's status as a borough in 1228. See also for Bungay: MacCulloch, The Chorography, pp. 20, 23, 33; and Ethel Mann, Old Bungay (London, 1934), p. 136; and Suckling, The History and Antiquities, pp. 119–67. For Flixton, see: MacCulloch, The Chorography, p. 20; and Suckling, The History and Antiquities, pp. 189–211.

[30] Blomefield, An Essay, vol. 4, p. 524.

[31] The editor of the VCH for Norfolk and Suffolk included Thetford Priory in both counties' volumes, uncertain of this priory's exact location. Its reference on the Ordnance Survey Map makes it clear that the priory was in Norfolk, not Suffolk: Director-General of the Ordnance Survey, Map of Monastic Britain (Southampton, England, 1954), South Sheet 50/8884.

[32] K. J. Allison, "The Norfolk Worsted Industry in the Sixteenth and Seventeenth Centuries: 1. The Traditional History," Yorkshire Bulletin of Economic and Social Research 12 (1960), pp. 73–83; John Patten, "Patterns of Migration and Movement of Labour to 3 Pre-Industrial East Anglian Towns," in Pre-Industrial England, p. 144; John Patten, "Changing Occupational Structures in the East Anglian Countryside, 1500–1700," in Change in the Countryside: Essays on Rural England, 1500–1900, ed. H. S. A. Fox and R. A. Butlin (London, 1979), p. 107; Thirsk, "The Farming Regions," pp. 45, 48.

population.[33] Though nowhere near the size or wealth of the city of Norwich, Thetford was also a busy town on the main route from London to Norwich.[34]

Geographic settings were important factors in the histories of these religious houses. Founded in sparsely populated and difficult agrarian regions of the fens, for example, Blackborough, Crabhouse and Marham did not enjoy the economic resources or kinds and amounts of testamentary bequests or land grants bestowed on Carrow Priory.[35] Carrow's suburban location meant potentially more profitable land holdings, and a more socially diverse population whose greater wealth enabled more frequent and larger bequests.[36]

In addition to affecting resources and patronage, these locations carried a certain psychological significance. Isolated rural outposts and suburban settings outside town walls were considered marginal spaces, the closest the nuns in medieval England could ever come to the desert sites of the first cenobitic communities.[37] Such settings were appropriate for the foundations of these female monasteries because a physical and psychological remove from secular society was an essential part of a nun's vocation. Most of the female houses in the country, in fact, were founded in the same types of liminal places, suggesting a pattern of foundation for religious women which purposefully included isolated settings and the poverty that frequently accompanied them.[38] As such, these qualities can be seen not simply as unfortunate circumstances of monastic life for women but rather as significant and positive aspects of it.[39]

The positive attribution of isolation and poverty can also be seen in a monastery's order affiliation which could, like a founder's social status and wealth, affect a religious community's geographic location and the type or size of initial endowment. Most of the female houses in the diocese followed the Benedictine or Augustinian Rule, the two most popular monastic orders in medieval England.[40] As both rules stressed moderation and discouraged ascetic

---

[33] William G. Hoskins, "English Provincial Towns in the Early Sixteenth Century," *TRHS*, 5th ser., 6 (1956), pp. 4–5; but see also: Russell, *British Medieval Population*, p. 285.

[34] Beresford and Finberg, *English Medieval Boroughs*, p. 140 notes that Thetford had borough status as early as 952. See also: Blomefield, *An Essay*, vol. 2, pp. 89, 126–44; and Patten, "Population Distribution in Norfolk and Suffolk," p. 79.

[35] J. N. L. Myers, "Notes on the History of Butley Priory, Suffolk," in *Oxford Essays in Medieval History Presented to Herbert E. Salter* (Oxford, 1934), p. 190 explains that the remote location of this male house kept it from ever attaining high visibility.

[36] See Chapter 6 for more about the testamentary bequests to these houses.

[37] Gilchrist, *Gender and Material Culture*, pp. 64–8 for the psychological implications of these geographic settings.

[38] Ibid., pp. 90–1.

[39] Caroline Walker Bynum, " '. . . And Woman His Humanity': Female Imagery in the Religious Writing of the Later Middle Ages," in *Gender and Religion: On the Complexity of Symbols*, ed. Caroline Walker Bynum, Stevan Harrel, and Paula Richman (Boston, 1986), pp. 259, 273–77; and her *Holy Feast and Holy Fast*, passim, for the emphasis on physical separation and denigration as qualities of religious life for medieval women; Gilchrist, *Gender and Material Culture*, pp. 89–91.

[40] Blackborough, Bungay, Carrow, Redlingfield, and Thetford Priories were Benedictine houses, and Campsey Ash, Crabhouse, and Flixton Priories followed the Augustinian

extremes, they had little impact on where a monastery might be founded. But, as a Cistercian house, Marham Abbey was located in a desolate setting consistent with the isolated, contemplative, and individualistic ascetic which characterized the Cistercian order.[41] The Poor Clares at Bruisyard Abbey, on the other hand, followed the Isabella Rule which emphasized poverty in a modified version of the Rule of St Clare.[42] The spiritual ideal of poverty intrinsic to this order must have been especially significant to the nuns who entered this house; the ideal of poverty might also explain Bruisyard's rather modest economic status despite its relatively large initial foundation.

The foundations of Crabhouse and Thetford Priories also suggest that poverty and isolation were qualities of monastic life acknowledged by founders of female religious communities and sought after by the nuns who entered them. Crabhouse Priory was originally founded by a hermitess, Leva, who desired to live in a deserted place: "all wild and far around on every side there was no human habitation."[43] After being joined by other women, Leva and her followers were harassed by the prior and monks of Castle Acre, who claimed to own the land on which Leva had established her hermitage. The women, further disturbed by a flood which destroyed their house, moved to another similarly isolated and barren site in Crabhouse, where they helped to drain the surrounding marshes and stayed, despite the nuns' constant use as pawns in on-going property disputes between the monks of the priory of Castle Acre and the canons of the priory of Raynham. Leva's original intention to found an isolated hermitage remained a significant characteristic of Crabhouse Priory after her initial foundation.[44]

Thetford Priory, on the other hand, began as an eleventh-century cell of the great Benedictine male monastery in Suffolk, Bury St Edmunds. By 1160 though, only two monks remained, and they asked to be moved because of

Rule. The three remaining female monasteries in the diocese of Norwich were Bruisyard Abbey, a house of Poor Clares, Marham Abbey, a Cistercian foundation, and Shouldham Priory, a house of Gilbertine canonesses. Table 1 notes the convents' orders. This distribution according to order is representative of the female convents in the rest of medieval England. See Knowles and Hadcock, *Medieval Religious Houses*, pp. 171–232; Power, *Medieval English Nunneries*, p. 1.

41 Lekai, *The Cistercians*, pp. 347–63 are specifically about Cistercian nuns. See also Jordan, "The Cistercian Nunnery," p. 313 where he talks about how most Cistercian female houses had very small endowments on marginal land.

42 For the following discussion of the Poor Clares at Bruisyard Abbey, see: Bourdillon, *The Minoresses*, pp. 8–9. Bourdillon includes details of the modifications of Clare's Rule by Isabella of Longchamp and by Urban IV. The Isabella Rule was never adopted outside of England and it was eventually superseded in later European foundations of Poor Clares by the Urbanists who adopted the modifications to Clare's rule made by Urban IV. See also W. W. Seton, ed., *Two Fifteenth-Century Franciscan Rules* (Early English Text Society, o.s. no. 148, 1914), p. 71 for the history of both modifications.

43 Bateson, "The Register," pp. 12–13; Blomefield, *An Essay*, vol. p. 9, 173; *VCH, Norfolk*, vol. 2, p. 408, for this account of the priory's foundation.

44 Thompson, *Women Religious*, pp. 25, 66–7 for a slightly different version of this foundation.

ruinous buildings and great poverty.[45] The bishop of Norwich suggested that the house be turned over to a group of hermitesses who lived outside of the town of Thetford in nearby Ling. The women, numbering at least ten, became Benedictine nuns and moved into this site, whose buildings and revenues were insufficient for the two monks of Bury St Edmunds.[46] Nevertheless, the nuns continued to make annual payments to the abbey which claimed jurisdiction over them. Like Crabhouse, Thetford's later history was disrupted by disputes with the abbot of Bury St Edmunds over property rights and annual payments. But what makes Thetford's switch from a cell of monks to a priory of nuns notable is that the poverty which so distressed the male religious did not present an obstacle to the bishop or to the women who took up residency there and created a small but active community of nuns.

Features of these two foundations also indicate a certain flexibility in the nature of religious life for women. Both had non-monastic beginnings, as each started out as a group of hermitesses; similarly, Carrow Priory began not as a convent for women, but rather as a hospital.[47] In these three cases, already existing groups of religious women were regularized into religious orders. Such informal beginnings appear to have been fairly common among female monasteries; and while adaptability of female groups from informal to formal communities was characteristic of monastic foundations for women, it appears to have been less so for men.[48]

These characteristics of female monasteries, both within the diocese of Norwich and also elsewhere in medieval England, demonstrate a pattern of female monastic piety which has hitherto been seen by historians as strictly negative, particularly when compared to the circumstances surrounding foundations of male houses. But poverty and isolation for nuns represented significant and conscious concerns of their founders and patrons. Regardless of their social rank, founders of female religious houses tended to give small localized properties, suggesting that they may never have intended their foundations to attain the wealth or worldly status characteristic of so many of the male houses. Rather, poverty and physical isolation from worldly affairs, and the kind of dependence on the patronage of secular society which these factors necessitated, were integral parts of religious life for women. The prevalence of

---

[45] Blomefield, An Essay, vol. 2, p. 89; Dugdale, Monasticon, vol. 4, pp. 477–78; Elkins, Holy Women, p. 48; VCH, Norfolk, vol. 2, p. 354 for Thetford's history.

[46] Thompson, Women Religious, p. 64 fails to mention in her account of Thetford's foundation that the monks complained to the abbot of Bury about their poverty and so were moved.

[47] Elkins, Holy Women, pp. 113–14; Thompson, Women Religious, p. 49 for Carrow.

[48] Bynum, "Religious Women," p. 130; Elkins, Holy Women, passim, for examples of informal communities of women being regularized into formal houses throughout medieval England; Thompson, Women Religious, p. 161. See also: Carol Levin, "Introduction," in Ambiguous Realities: Women in the Middle Ages and the Renaissance, ed. Carol Levin and Jeanie Watson (Detroit, 1987).

anchoresses in the diocese of Norwich – women who sought complete separation from society to lead their lives of prayer – and of informal religious communities of women who relied exclusively on lay society for support, throughout the Middle Ages, further indicates that these were dynamic aspects of female spirituality.[49] Instead of viewing small endowments, the meager revenues they generated, and unconventional foundations as negative attributes of female religious life in medieval England, they may well have been just what religious women sought in leading lives of prayer and devotion.

Seigneurial Rights and Privileges

Whatever their location, size, or order, the nuns' original endowments included the seigneurial rights and privileges common to all manorial lords. All of the female houses in the diocese of Norwich had the right to hold manor courts. In addition, both Carrow and Marham held leet courts for their bond and free tenants, and had the rights to the view of frankpledge and the assizes of bread and ale.[50] The prioress of Carrow was also exempt from municipal jurisdiction as she held special rights over her lands inside and outside Norwich city walls. Her peculiar jurisdiction allowed her, among other things, to prove wills, and maintain gallows.[51] In addition to these privileges, the abbess of Marham could also bury people in the abbey's cemetery.[52] Both Marham and Blackborough, moreover, were legal sanctuaries for accused wrongdoers.[53]

These seigneurial rights carried certain economic privileges. Carrow, for example, had the right to hold a four-day fair on the vigil, day, and the two days following the Nativity of the Blessed Virgin.[54] Shouldham held a weekly market at Stoke Ferry, as well as an annual fair there on the feast of St Nicholas.[55] Blackborough also had a fair.[56] In addition, Campsey Ash, Crabhouse, and Flixton collected revenues from water mills, and Marham had both

49 For anchoresses in medieval England, see: Ann Warren, *Anchorites and their Patrons in Medieval England* (Berkeley, 1985). For anchoresses and informal religious communities of women in the diocese in the Middle Ages, and the quality of such spiritual paths, see: Gilchrist and Oliva, *Religious Women*, pp. 68–80.
50 Frederick Pollock and Frederick Maitland, *The History of English Law before the Time of Edward I* (Cambridge, 1898), vol. 1, pp. 580–82, 592. For Carrow, see: Rye and Tillet, "Carrow Abbey," p. 2; for Marham, see: Nichols, "The History and Cartulary," p. 100.
51 Blomefield, *An Essay*, vol. 4, pp. 526–27; VCH, *Norfolk*, vol. 2, p. 352, for this discussion of Carrow Priory's jurisdictional rights.
52 Blomefield, *An Essay*, vol. 7, pp. 370, 374–75; Nichols, "The History and Cartulary," pp. 99–109.
53 For Marham Abbey, see: Blomefield, *An Essay*, vol. 7, p. 375; Nichols, "The History and Cartulary," p. 123. For Blackborough, see: Blomefield, *An Essay*, vol. 7, p. 449.
54 Rye and Tillet, "Carrow Abbey," pp. 466–67; VCH, *Norfolk*, vol. 2, p. 352.
55 Ibid., p. 412.
56 Blomefield, *An Essay*, vol. 8, p. 33.

a water mill and a fulling mill.[57] Crabhouse also maintained a fishery which supplied both the nuns and their neighbors.[58]

All of these secular rights and privileges added to monastic incomes and integrated these female houses into the lives of local people. Those who served as jurors or litigants in the manor and leet courts would have dealt with the counselors and bailiffs who dispensed justice and levied fines in the name of an abbess or prioress. People who used the monastic mills to grind their grain and full their cloth, and participated in the markets and fairs the nuns were allowed to hold, also would have come into frequent contact with the stewards and collectors who represented the nuns' temporal authority.

While seigneurial and economic privileges were common to most female and male monastic foundations, the ways in which nuns and monks executed these rights could differ significantly. Many of the diocese's male monasteries had frequent disputes with their neighbors over the monks' abuses of various lordly privileges. Several priors of Walsingham in Norfolk interfered with the town's right to hold a weekly market by exacting tolls which were not rightly the monks' to collect.[59] The monks at Hempton Priory, also in Norfolk, had problems with the local people because the priors continually over-charged for use of the priory's mill, and because the monks shirked their duty to maintain the nearby main road.[60]

Chronic infringements on others' rights, and surreptitious extensions of their own, moreover, made many of the diocese's male monasteries targets in the Peasants' Revolt of 1381.[61] Norwich Cathedral Priory and Bury St Edmunds Abbey were both stormed and pillaged.[62] Indeed, the rioters beheaded Bury's prior before moving on to attack some of the smaller male houses in the nearby countryside.[63] It is no surprise that these male houses were among the objects of the rebels' wrath: abuses of seigneurial powers would have been glaring in a region known for its lack of strong manorial lordship.[64]

---

57 For Campsey Ash, see: VE, vol. 3, p. 415; Crabhouse: Bateson, "The Register," pp. 31, 35, 40; Flixton: VE, vol. 3, p. 446; Marham: Blomefield, An Essay, vol. 7, p. 393.
58 Ibid., vol. 9, p. 175.
59 VCH, Norfolk, vol. 2, p. 395.
60 Ibid., p. 382. See also: Richard Mortimer, ed., Leiston Abbey Cartulary and Butley Priory Charters (Woodbridge, 1979), p. 6 where Mortimer describes the unhappy relations Leiston Abbey had with its neighbors in Dunwich over the rights to take tolls from ships landing at Minsmere, and the houses' many oppressive superiors.
61 Edgar Powell, The Rising in East Anglia in 1381 (Cambridge, 1896), p. 34.
62 Ibid., p. 11; for the Cathedral Priory, see: VCH, Norfolk, vol. 2, p. 319, and ibid., p. 320 for the 1442 uprising against the Cathedral Priory known as "Gladman's Insurrection," when a crowd of 3,000 stormed and besieged the priory for four days in a dispute over rights to Norwich city's mills. See also, William Hudson and John Tingey, eds., The Records of the City of Norwich (Norwich, 1906–10), vol. 1, pp. xc–xci, 340–41, 321–22, 325–26, and vol. 2, pp. 368–78 for other disputes between the Cathedral Priory and the town. For Bury St Edmunds, see: Powell, The Rising, pp. 16, 34. See also VCH, Suffolk, vol. 2, pp. 62–3 for other earlier disputes between the abbey and the townspeople.
63 Powell, The Rising, pp. 17–21, 34.
64 D. C. Douglas, The Social Structure of Medieval East Anglia (Oxford, 1927), passim; Joan

Most of the diocese's female houses, by contrast, were not in constant ligation with their tenants, nor were the nuns victims in the riots of 1381. Occasionally, Carrow's prioresses clashed with tenants, and in fact the nuns there were confronted in 1381 by a disgruntled group who demanded and burned some of the prioress's court rolls.[65] Though in most of its disputes Carrow was found not guilty of abusing its privileges, as a semi-urban monastery and holder of extraordinary jurisdiction the priory was a likely target of local unrest, as were some of the diocese's male urban foundations noted above.[66]

The generally good relations which the female houses maintained with their neighbors were not, however, a result of the nuns' failure to exercise their seigneurial rights. Margery Howell, prioress of Flixton, convened an extraordinary court in 1377 to assert her rights over Robert Borel, a peasant who had denied his servile condition, married without her permission, taken some of her sheep, and wasted his holding.[67] During the proceedings, he admitted he was a serf and agreed to observe the old customs.

The relative peace between the female houses and their local communities was no doubt due to the nuns' small property holdings which rendered futile any attempts to unjustly extend their temporal power and authority. The nuns had neither the money nor the personnel to encroach upon others' rights. Many of the female houses, in fact, spent a great deal of effort defending their own properties and manorial rights against the encroachments of others. Recall the constant battles Crabhouse and Thetford Priories had with nearby male monasteries over property rights. Even Carrow occasionally had to fight off infringements from both neighboring male houses and also the city of Norwich.[68]

Thirsk, "The Farming Regions," p. 42. See also: Christopher Dyer, "The Social and Economic Background to the Rural Revolt of 1381," in *The English Rising of 1381*, ed. R. Hilton and T. H. Aston (Cambridge, 1984), p. 32 for weak seigneurial courts.

[65] Hudson and Tingey, *The Records*, p. 320; Powell, p. 32; Rye, *Carrow Abbey*, pp. xi–xii; Rye and Tillet, "Carrow Abbey," pp. 3, 6, 20, 507–8 and passim; *VCH, Norfolk*, vol. 2, p. 352.

[66] For Carrow, see: Hudson and Tingey, *The Records*, vol. 2, pp. 62, 71. See also: Postan, *The Medieval Economy and Society*, pp. 171–72 where he argues that especially in Norfolk and Suffolk the 1381 revolt was not a rural phenomenon, but rather an urban one wherein the rebels, mostly freeholders, resented any vestige of old powers, and so moved against many who held jurisdictions in the towns, as well as against those rural land owners who abused their tenants' rights.

[67] SRO, HA 12/C3/7; Christopher Dyer, "The Social and Economic Background," p. 32 cites this document also. I am grateful to Roger Virgoe for pointing this reference out to me.

[68] Hudson and Tingey, *The Records*, vol. 1, p. 139; Rye and Tillet, "Carrow Abbey," passim; and NRO, DCN 88/9, NRO, DCN 88/10, NRO, DCN 88/11, NRO, DCN 88/12, NRO, DCN 88/14, NRO, DCN 88/15 for Carrow's disputes with the Cathedral Priory over Carrow's rights to collect certain tithes within the town walls, to bury local parishioners, and to hold leet court and the view of frankpledge.

Spiritual Properties and Ecclesiastical Authorities

In addition to temporal properties and privileges, monasteries' original foundations included certain spiritual properties – churches, chapels, and rectories – from which the houses received revenues.[69] Both Blackborough and Bungay Priories, like many other female and male houses, took in more from their spiritual properties than they did from their temporal holdings.[70] The most common type of spiritual property was the right of advowson or patronage of a local parish church or chapel. As a patron of the church of All Saints in the parish of Mettingham, and of St Margaret, St Andrew, and St Lawrence in the Ilketshall parishes, the prioress of Bungay held the right to appoint these parishes' priests.[71] In return for this privilege of appointment she received tithes from each – usually a tenth of the churches' yearly income. In exchange, she was responsible for the upkeep of these parish churches.

Individual monasteries could acquire other types of patronage of religious properties.[72] The appropriation of a church or chapel by a monastic house increased its rights as patron from simply collecting an annual tithe to more extensive control over the entire property. An appropriated church was thus considerably more lucrative than a simple advowson. Shouldham Priory had the advowsons of five local churches from which it received a total of £8 6s 8d annually.[73] The priory also had the appropriations of three others: one alone yielded £8.[74] The abbess of Bruisyard collected alms, tithes from individual tenants, as well as bushels of barley, wheat and corn, sheep, and hens from the parish church of Bruisyard which was appropriated to the abbey.[75]

The widespread practice among monastic houses of appropriating parish churches or chapels is frequently viewed as an abuse of spiritual patronage. Examples are frequently cited of both female and male monasteries which did not appoint a vicar in order to reap the financial benefits of a vacant post.[76] Undoubtedly some houses kept livings vacant for less than justifiable reasons,

---

69   For a discussion of the 'spiritualities' of female monasteries in other dioceses, see: Power, *Medieval English Nunneries*, pp. 113–17. For the spiritualities of the male houses in the Norwich diocese, see: VCH, *Norfolk*, vol. 2, passim; and VCH, *Suffolk*, vol. 2, passim. See also: Savine, *English Monasteries on the Eve of the Reformation*, pp. 110–14.

70   VE, vol. 3, pp. 395–96 for Blackborough; ibid., p. 352 for Bungay. For other female monasteries, see: Power, *Medieval English Nunneries*, pp. 113–14. For male houses, see: Christopher Harper-Bill, ed., *Blythburgh Priory Cartulary*, 2 vols. (Woodbridge, 1980–81), vol. 1, p. 16 where he points out that most small houses of Augustinian canons derived a considerable amount of their revenues from their parish churches. See also: Savine, *English Monasteries on the Eve of the Reformation*, pp. 101–11.

71   VCH, *Suffolk*, vol. 2, p. 81.

72   Power, *Medieval English Nunneries*, p. 113; and Snape, *English Monastic Finances*, pp. 77–81.

73   VE, vol. 3, p. 378.

74   Ibid.

75   Ibid., p. 443.

76   Power, *Medieval English Nunneries*, pp. 114–17; Snape, *English Monastic Finances*, pp. 81–4.

but sometimes both female and male monasteries had legitimate cause to leave positions unfilled.[77] The nuns at Blackborough Priory, for example, asked the bishop of Ely for permission to retain one of their appropriated churches when the position became vacant because they needed the revenues to help rebuild part of the cloister after a series of damaging floods.[78]

Leasing out or farming appropriated churches in return for a fixed annual fee is also cited as an abuse, one which weakened the ties between parishioners and the monasteries, and often left the vicars and priests ignored and unpaid.[79] But while farming tithes could lead to neglect, it did not necessarily do so. The fifteenth-century manorial accounts of Bungay Priory show that while the house began to farm out some of its spiritual properties early in the century, the nuns did not stop paying the priests and chaplains who served therein.[80] The manorial accounts from Marham Abbey and the cellarers' accounts from Carrow Priory also indicate that these houses almost always farmed their spiritual properties out to the vicars and priests who served there.[81] And the sixteenth-century Carrow cellarers' accounts show specific entries for money paid to the vicars of the priory's appropriated churches to augment their incomes.[82] Few of the diocese's female houses, in fact, appear to have ignored their appropriated religious properties; the Valors show that the nuns annually paid the clerics of the churches and chapels of which they were patrons.[83]

These abuses, the non-payment of a cleric's pension and the neglect of a vacancy altogether, seem to have been more widespread among male

---

[77] For the male houses, see: Knowles, The Religious Orders, vol. 2, pp. 290–91.

[78] NRO, Phi/451 577x8.

[79] Power, Medieval English Nunneries, pp. 114–15; Savine, English Monasteries on the Eve of the Reformation, pp. 110–13.

[80] See SRO, HD 1538/156/2, the collector's account for 1383/84, and SRO, HD 1538/156/3, the collector's account for 1398/99, when the priory did not farm out its spiritual property. The fifteenth-century bailiffs' accounts all show that the priory farmed out most of its spiritual properties, and paid the pensions of the clerics who held the benefices of them. See the following bailiffs' accounts: SRO, HD 1538/156/4 (1402/03) when the farming practice first becomes evident; SRO, HD 1538/156/5 (1403/04); SRO, HD 1538/156/8 (1443/44); SRO, HD 1538/156/9 (1436/37); SRO, HD 1538/156/10 (1437/38); and SRO, HD 1538/156/11 (1438/39).

[81] The Marham manorial accounts are: NRO, Hare 2201 194x5 (1405/06); NRO, Hare 2202 194x5 (1409/10); NRO, Hare 2203 194x5 (1419/20); NRO, Hare 2204 194x5 (1426/27); and NRO, Hare 2205 194x5 (1446/47). The Carrow cellarers' accounts are: NRO, NRS 26882 42 E8 (1455/56); NRO, NRS 26883 42 E8 (1484/85); NRO, Hare 5954 227x1 (1503/04); NRO, Hare 5955 227x1 (1520/21); and NRO, NRS 26884 42 E8 (1529/30).

[82] NRO, Hare 5954 227x1 (1503/04); NRO, Hare 5955 227x1 (1520/21); and NRO, NRS 26884 42 E8 (1529/30).

[83] VE, vol. 3, pp. 395–96 for Blackborough Priory; ibid., pp. 442–43 for Bruisyard Abbey; ibid., pp. 352–54 for Bungay Priory; ibid., pp. 415–17 for Campsey Ash Priory; ibid., pp. 305–6 for Carrow Priory; ibid., p. 397 for Crabhouse; ibid., p. 446 for Flixton Priory; ibid., p. 379 for Marham Abbey; ibid., p. 478 for Redlingfield Priory; ibid., p. 378 for Shouldham Priory; and ibid., p. 313 for Thetford Priory.

monasteries.[84] And just as the exercise of temporal authority by nuns and monks affected their community relations, so too did performance of these spiritual responsibilities. The rioters in 1381, for example, wasted a number of the appropriated churches of Bury St Edmunds and St Benet of Holme because the superiors there had so flagrantly neglected their incumbent spiritual duties.[85] Indeed, many of the parish priests and vicars of the abbeys' appropriated churches joined the rebels to protest about their mistreatment at the hands of their spiritual patrons.[86]

While nuns exercised some authority over their spiritual properties, the women themselves answered to higher ecclesiastical powers. The Augustinian and Benedictine convents were under episcopal control, and were therefore obliged to obtain the bishop's approval for the election of a superior, and were subject to his tri-annual visitations.[87] Exceptions to these controls included the election of a superior at Carrow which was supervised by a male patron of the nuns' choice, and at Thetford Priory by the abbot of Bury St Edmunds.[88] The Poor Clares at Bruisyard, on the other hand, were exempt from episcopal jurisdiction by papal decree. Instead, they were under the supervision of the male superiors of their orders, the Friars Minor who appointed their confessors, approved abbesses' elections, and conducted semi-annual visitations.[89] Similarly, the exempt Marham nuns looked to the Cistercian monks at Waverley Abbey, the mother house of this Order in England, for similar procedures.[90] As a Gilbertine priory, Shouldham was also exempt from episcopal jurisdiction.[91] The Order's master general carried out this priory's visitations along with a female 'general scrutinizer', who would administer corrections when necessary.

The Significance of Local Customs and Enclosure

It is difficult to gage how prominent these orders' spiritual, administrative, and jurisdictional distinctions were, and whether or not they would have affected a woman's choice of monastery to enter, though the emphasis on the common

---

[84] G. G. Coulton, *Medieval Studies* (Oxford, 1915), pp. 6–8.
[85] Powell, *The Rising*, pp. 11–14, for Bury St Edmunds; and *VCH, Norfolk*, vol. 2, p. 334, for St Benet at Holme. See also: Bryan Burstall, "A Monastic Agreement of the Fourteenth Century," *NA* 31 (1957), pp. 211–18 where he discusses the bad relations the Norfolk male house of Binham had with local townspeople because of the priory's careless management of the parish church.
[86] For the part played by the lower clergy in the 1381 uprising, see, for example: A. Kriehn, "Studies in the Sources of the Social Revolt in 1381," *American History Review* 6 (1901), pp. 480–84.
[87] Jessopp, *Visitations*, ix. See also: Knowles, *The Religious Orders*, vol. 1, pp. 78–101.
[88] For Carrow: Blomefield, *An Essay*, vol. 4, p. 525; for Thetford: Elkins, *Holy Women*, p. 48.
[89] Bourdillon, *The Minoresses*, p. 55.
[90] *VCH, Norfolk*, vol. 2, p. 369; Nichols, "The History and Cartulary," pp. 126–27.
[91] Elkins, *Holy Women*, pp. 137–39.

life at Augustinian houses may have resonated more profoundly for some nuns than did the more individualistic, stricter life at Marham or Bruisyard.[92] Jean Leclercq suggested that a basic observance of the Divine Office, based on the Rule of St Benedict, was common to all monastic houses.[93] Most of the female religious in the late Middle Ages, in fact, followed the daily life of the Benedictine Rule despite their allegiances to other orders.[94] This daily routine revolved around praying the canonical hours in choir, with times for meals, recreation, private meditation, reading and sleep interspersed. Nuns also provided hospitality to permanent and itinerant guests, and administered both daily and occasional alms to the poor who gathered outside the convents' gates.[95] This schedule was observed with varying degrees of success by both nuns and monks.[96]

Leclercq also pointed out, however, that local customs – celebration of local saints' days, and variations on monastic diet – also distinguished one monastery from another, and that these differences may have been more widely recognized than those between particular orders and rules.[97] The ordinal of Barking Abbey details prayers for mass and the liturgies for the canonical hours which the nuns there said, as well as the saints' days they observed. The ordinal shows, for example, that in addition to regular saint's-day feasts, the nuns celebrated the feast of St Ethelburga, the abbey's first abbess, on October 11, and the feast of St Wulfilda on September 9.[98] While customaries do not survive for any of the female houses in the diocese of Norwich, we can assume that similar particular traditions marked life in each of these convents.

Leclercq and others have noted further that anthropological and cultural differences between the sexes made monastic life for women different from

92 Yvonne Parrey, " 'Devoted disciples of Christ': Early Sixteenth-Century Religious Life in the Nunnery at Amesbury," *Bulletin of the Institute of Historical Research* 67 no. 164 (1994), on p. 243 she demonstrates the existence and use of the Statutes of Fontrevault at Amesbury despite the house's denization, indicating the nuns' active interests and participation in their Order's rules.

93 Jean Leclercq, "Profession According to the Rule of St Benedict," *Cistercian Studies* 5 (1970), pp. 252–73.

94 In addition to the Gilbertines cited above, the Cistercian nuns also followed the daily routine of the Benedictine Rule: Jean Leclercq, "The Spirituality of Medieval Feminine Monasticism," in *The Continuing Quest for God: Monastic Spirituality in Tradition and Transition,* ed. William Skudlarek (Minnesota, 1982), pp. 128–29. See also: John Nichols, "The Internal Organization of English Cistercian Nunneries," *Citeaux* 30:1 (1979), pp. 24–5.

95 Jean Leclercq, "Hospitality and Monastic Prayer," *Cistercian Studies* 8:1 (1973), pp. 3–24; and Leclercq, "Monastic Life for Men and Monastic Life for Women," *Cistercian Studies* 6:4 (1971), pp. 327–33.

96 Bitel, "Women's Monastic Enclosures," p. 24. For more about the nuns' daily activities, as far as they can be known, see below, Chapter 2, pp. 61, 72–4.

97 Leclercq, "Profession," pp. 264, 272.

98 She was the first abbess after the abbey's destruction by the Danes, and its re-foundation by King Edgar in 990: John Tolhurst, ed., *The Ordinal and Customary of the Benedictine Nuns of Barking Abbey* (London: Henry Bradshaw Society, vols. 65 and 66, 1926–27), vol. 65, pp. 9, 10.

monastic life for men.[99] The most obvious example of such a culturally-determined and gender-based difference between monastic life for women and for men was enclosure, an aspect of medieval monasticism which, while suggested for both nuns and monks, was vigorously enforced on the female religious alone.[100] Enclosure was not an aspect of Benedict's Rule, nor was it part of St Augustine's Rule; and while Anglo-Saxon nuns never accepted claustration, their sisters in the later period were more forcibly cloistered.[101]

While a few early thirteenth-century councils – the Councils of Oxford in 1222, London in 1268, and Lambeth in 1281 – tried to regulate nuns' egress from monastic precincts, the canon law which legislated strict enclosure was the decree *Periculoso*, promulgated by Boniface VIII in 1298. He issued this act to curtail the scandal caused both by nuns traveling freely outside their convents, and also by allowing seculars, particularly men, to enter the cloisters. Nuns who wandered freely, begged, or administered to the poor and sick, alone or without the sanctions of the Church hierarchy, were seen as a threat to themselves – because they would be helpless to overcome their carnal natures and irrepressible sexual drives – and to the sexual purity of the male religious, as well as the virtue of men in general.[102] Indeed, it has been suggested that

99   Leclercq, "Monastic Life for Men," pp. 328, 331. See also: Bynum, "Religious Women," pp. 130–31; la Magli, "Il Problema Antropologico-Culturale del Monachesimo Femminile," *Enciclopedia delle Religioni*, vol. 3, pp. 627–41; Jane Schulenburg, "Women's Monastic Communities," p. 239 where she describes how times of invasion and reform hastened changes in society which affected the viability of monastic life for women and brought about a "pronounced gender-based disparity between religious communities"; and Karen Sinclair, "Women and Religion," in *The Cross Cultural Study of Women. A Comprehensive Guide*, ed. Margot Duley and Mary Edwards (New York, 1986), pp. 107–24.

100   James A. Brundage and Elizabeth Makowski, "Enclosure of Nuns: the Decretal *Periculoso* and its Commentators," *Journal of Medieval History* 20 (1994), pp. 149, 150; Coulton, *Five Centuries of Religion*, vol. 4, p. 121 states that nuns knew restrictions that their male counterparts did not due to "the frailty of their sex." He claims that Boniface VIII's *Periculoso*, the decree which officially enforced enclosure of nuns, was never meant to apply to monks who had in any case long abandoned claustration. Noreen Hunt, "Enclosure (II)," *Cistercian Studies* 22 (1987), pp. 127–29, 134–49 states that a tradition of cloistered monks did exist, but that in England insular influences, like Celtic monasticism which promoted perpetual exile and wandering as an ascetic ideal, combined with Gregory the Great's evangelical imperialism, led monks permanently out of their cloisters and into the world. And though nuns proselytized too, they were later forced to stay inside their monastic precincts. See also: Jane Schulenburg, "Strict Active Enclosure and Its Effects on the Female Monastic Experience (ca. 500–1100)," in *Distant Echoes: 1. Medieval Religious Women*, pp. 51–86, but esp. pp. 58–60.

101   Bitel, "Women's Monastic Enclosures," pp. 17–22; Hunt, "Enclosure," pp. 132, 136–38; Schulenburg, "Strict Active Enclosure," pp. 62, 65–67.

102   For society's negative view of women which combined with the Church's misogyny to enforce claustration of nuns, see: Brundage and Makowski, "Enclosure for Nuns," pp. 146–47; Vern Bullough, "Medieval Medical and Scientific Views of Women," *Viator* 4 (1973), pp. 487–93; Hilpisch, *A History of Benedictine Nuns*, p. 40; Hunt, "Enclosure," pp. 135–38; Penny Johnson, "The Cloistering of Medieval Nuns: Release or Repression, Reality or Fantasy?" in *Gendered Domains: Rethinking Public and Private in Womens'*

the Beguine movement in the Low Countries met with such hostility from the (male) Church hierarchy because uncloistered women roamed the streets to work, to minister to the needy, to beg: they were, in the Church's eyes, literally out of order.[103]

The law restricted women in religious orders from leaving their cloisters except in very specific cases and for limited amounts of time. Superiors could leave to deal with their monasteries' properties; rank and file nuns were permitted to go only if serious illness threatened the health of others. In either case a license was to be obtained from the local bishop.

Despite the law's intention, and the concerns of its fifteenth-century commentators, medieval nuns left their monasteries for several different reasons.[104] Just as Chaucer's Prioress, Madame Eglentyne, was on her way as a pilgrim to Thomas Becket's shrine in Canterbury, so too did her real-life contemporaries obtain permission to go on pilgrimage.[105] Though not all bishops agreed on this as a legitimate reason to leave; Bishop Longland of Lincoln reminded the nuns at Nun Cotham, for example, that if anyone desired to go on a pilgrimage, she must obtain his permission and travel with another nun.[106] Nuns might also visit sick relatives, as some of the nuns of Studley Priory, in the diocese of Lincoln, and of Arthington Priory, in the diocese of York, were allowed to do.[107]

Superiors and rank and file nuns could obtain permission to leave their cloisters to negotiate business for their houses. Joan Spalding, a prioress at Carrow, stayed at one of the priory's properties, Wroxall manor, to deal "with diverse matters concerning the estate of that manor."[108] At Nunkeeling in the early fourteenth century, the nuns received archbishop Melton's permission to

History, ed. Dorothy O. Helly and Susan M. Reverby (Ithaca, 1993), p. 38; Leclercq, "Monastic Life for Men," p. 331; Eleanor McLaughlin, "Equality of Souls, Inequality of Sexes: Women in Medieval Theology," in Images of Women in the Jewish and Christian Traditions, ed. Rosemary Ruether (New York, 1974), pp. 213–66; and Julia O'Faolain and Laura Martines, eds., Not In God's Image (New York, 1973).

103 Brenda Bolton, "Mulieres Sanctae," in Women in Medieval Society, ed. Susan Mosher Stuard (Pennsylvania, 1976), pp. 149, 152–53; Bynum, Jesus as Mother, pp. 14–15; Hunt, "Enclosure," pp. 149–50.

104 John Tillotson, "Visitation and Reform of the Yorkshire Nunneries in the Fourteenth Century," Northern History 30 (1994), pp. 10–13.

105 Schulenburg, "Strict Active Enclosure," p. 66.

106 Edward Peacock, "Injunctions of John Langland, Bishop of Lincoln, to Certain Monasteries in his Diocese," Archaeologia 48 (1882–83), p. 57. Langland said "none was to go out on pilgrimage or otherwise" without permission. For a bishop who denied pilgrimage as a good cause for egress, see: Tillotson, "Visitation and Reform," p. 11 for Bishop Melton in the diocese of York, who flatly forbade nuns to do this.

107 Peacock, "Injunctions of John Langland," p. 54; VCH, Yorkshire, vol. 3, p. 188.

108 NRO, NRS 26883 42 E8 for the 1485/86 cellarer's account wherein it is noted that she paid for the hay and oats eaten by the prioress's and her traveling servants' horses. See also: VCH, Essex, vol. 2, p. 124 for the bailiff of Wix's account where he spent 3s 3d for the prioress's stay in Colchester where she was visiting the Bishop of London.

leave their precincts to carry out certain agricultural tasks.[109] Elizabeth Burnett, a sixteenth-century nun at Moxby Priory in York, remembered how at harvest she "helped to straw and cock the hay" in closes near her convent.[110] Nuns might also visit friends or relatives if it would profit the monastery in any way.

Abbesses and prioresses left their cloisters for a variety of other reasons as well: befitting her status as the prioress of Carrow, Margaret Pygot attended the funeral of Sir John Paston;[111] and Prioress Alice Waryn paid a short visit to the prioress of Bungay.[112] These examples reveal legitimate reasons why nuns left their convents, and suggest an abiding influence of the Anglo-Saxon female monastic tradition on later medieval conventual life. As John Tillotson has recently shown, the decree Periculoso was not very well enforced by English bishops because nuns resisted it and refused to be bound by regulations which were stricter than those they had agreed to upon profession.[113]

Medieval English nuns' travels from their monasteries were not therefore evidence of moral decline or disregard for their monastic lifestyle: nuns traveled for sound reasons and with the permission of the local bishop.[114] Monks, on the other hand, could leave their cloisters for a number of reasons without infringing monastic rules. Their freedom to circulate in the world constituted then a significant difference between the daily lives of the female and male religious.[115]

The geographic locations, temporal and spiritual privileges and properties, and orders of the female monasteries in the diocese of Norwich in the later Middle Ages carried certain gender-related differences between the female houses and their male counterparts: differences which affected initial endowments as well as aspects of the monastic lifestyle; differences which, as we shall see, continued to influence both the inmates of these monasteries and their relations with the wider spheres of parish and county. This material on the houses' foundations provides the context within which to explore their social composition, their internal administration, finances, and the continued patronage shown to them by the lay communities to which they belonged.

---

[109] Tillotson, "Visitation and Reform," pp. 11–12.
[110] Claire Cross and Noreen Vickers, Monks, Friars, and Nuns in Sixteenth Century Yorkshire (The Yorkshire Archaeological Society, Record Series, vol. 105, 1995), p. 607.
[111] Rye, Carrow Abbey, p. 8.
[112] SRO, HD 1538/156/9. She was there for a day and a night in 1436/37.
[113] Tillotson, "Visitation and Reform," pp. 2, 20.
[114] P. F. Anson, "Papal Enclosure for Nuns," Cistercian Studies 3 (1968), p. 118 where he states that with the Periculoso enclosure for nuns became stricter; ibid., p. 122 where Anson suggests that, until the early fifteenth century, nearly all Benedictine nuns were free to travel with good reason, but the councils of Constance (1414) and Basel (1441) restrained nuns from traveling abroad. See Johnson, "The Cloistering," passim, for a good discussion of Church Fathers' ambivalence regarding the viability of strict cloistering of nuns, and also for several legitimate reasons why French medieval nuns exited their monastic precincts.
[115] Schulenburg, "Strict Active Enclosure," pp. 58–63.

2

The Cloistered Community: The Nuns

Calculations of numbers of nuns or monks in a diocese or particular house and investigations of their families and social backgrounds can tell us a great deal about both individual religious and also the monasteries they populated. Utilizing the extraordinary records which survive for the cathedral chapters of Durham and York, for example, R. B. Dobson presented personal profiles of the monks and canons who populated these two religious houses. The profiles included the male religious' geographic and family backgrounds, social status, and the average amount of time these men lived as monks and canons throughout the later medieval period.[1] This study also illuminated the priories' recruitment patterns. Joan Greatrex has carried out a similar study of the Benedictine monks at Ely, Norwich, and Worcester; using admission, ordination, and obituary lists for each priory in conjunction with extant household accounts, she calculated the communities' monastic populations and reconstructed biographies of the monks. Her data also allowed her to address the rather nebulous issue of religious motivation and its impact on the fluctuations of the monastic population she was studying.[2] And Barbara Harvey has mined various household officials' accounts to reveal ages of profession and mortality rates for the monks at Westminster Abbey.[3]

While these kinds of studies have been carried out for medieval English monks and canons, they have never before been applied to their female counterparts. Obstacles to applying such analyses to nuns include a lack of sources; admission, profession, and obituary lists do not survive – or have not yet surfaced – for any female houses. Without records like these, we cannot compute mortality or replacement rates, figures crucial to any demographic study of a specific section of the population.

---

[1] R. B. Dobson, "Recent Prosopographical Research in Late Medieval English History: University Graduates, Durham Monks, and York Canons," in *Medieval Lives and the Historian: Studies in Medieval Prosopography*, ed. Neithard Bulst and Jean-Phillipe Genet (Michigan, 1986), pp. 181–200.

[2] Joan Greatrex, "Some Statistics of Religious Motivation," in *Religious Motivation: Biographical and Sociological Problems for the Church Historian*, ed. Derek Baker, *Studies in Church History*, vol. 15 (Oxford, 1978), pp. 179–86.

[3] Barbara Harvey, *Living and Dying in England, 1100–1540: The Monastic Experience* (Oxford, 1993).

A considerable amount of information exists, however, about the nuns who lived in the diocese of Norwich: the names of 553 of them, for example, and their average lifespans as nuns. These details provide the data necessary for a demographic study of the nuns between 1350 and 1540. In addition, information about their families and social backgrounds allows a prosopographical analysis to be carried out which reveals the social status and family backgrounds of the nuns, and also the convents' recruitment practices.

All of this evidence comes from a variety of sources which are plentiful for some periods, but less so for others. We can be fairly certain of the names and numbers of nuns at each of the convents in the late fourteenth century – because of the Poll Tax Returns – and at the time of the Dissolution in 1540 – because of the documents generated by Henry VIII's actions. Information about the nuns in the intervening years is derived from wills and bishops' visitations, and so is less comprehensive. Estimates then of the numbers of nuns and their average lifespans are conservative.

In addition to these statistical details about the nuns, certain facets of their daily lives can be discerned which indicate that, for the most part, the nuns lived up to the monastic ideals to which they were vowed. Aspects of their religious lives, like the sermons the nuns heard, their ability to read and the kinds of books they owned, suggest a pious and literate group of women whose lives as nuns may not have attracted a great deal of worldly attention, but were nevertheless truly spiritual.

Demographic Data

The 553 nuns who can be identified by name can be divided into four fifty-year intervals, with an average population of nuns for each convent. By looking at these numbers in some detail, patterns of demographic change, and the effects of a convent's wealth on the number of nuns it supported, can be discerned. The data collected also allows a comparison between these nuns and those in other parts of England, and between the diocese's nuns and its monks and canons.

The figures in Table 6 show that between 1350 and 1400 the number of nuns declined as a result of the epidemics and recurring plagues of the later Middle Ages. In this fifty-year interval the number of nuns in the diocese dropped from 179 in 1350 to 113 in 1400. While all of the houses suffered losses of between three and five nuns each in this plague period, numbers at Blackborough, Bungay, Campsey Ash, and Shouldham fell more dramatically: Blackborough and Bungay lost eight nuns, Campsey Ash ten, and Shouldham nineteen. While the epidemics of the period certainly affected this decline in the diocese's female monastic population, the severity of the decrease in numbers also betrays the source bias which makes the number of nuns during this period less easy to know.

By 1450, this monastic population increased to at least 128 nuns; by 1536

Table 6.   Number of Nuns Known by Name
in each of the Eleven Female Monasteries in the Diocese of Norwich
in Fifty-Year Intervals, 1350–1540

Monastery	1350–1400	1400–1450	1450–1500	1500–1540	Average Size
Blackborough	11	3	8	13	8.5
Bruisyard	15	10	22	15	15.5
Bungay	18	10	13	9	12.5
Campsey Ash	23	13	25	20	20
Carrow	27	22	22	14	21
Crabhouse	11	6	4	11	8
Flixton	13	12	8	11	11
Marham	17	15	5	7	11
Redlingfield	9	9	7	13	9.5
Shouldham	23	4	3	10	10
Thetford	12	9	11	10	10.5
TOTAL:	179	113	128	133	136.75

Sources: See Appendix 3.

their numbers had risen to at least 133, indicating a slight recovery. Not all of
the convents recouped their losses simultaneously. Five of them, Blackborough, Bruisyard, Bungay, Campsey Ash, and Thetford, recovered from earlier
losses relatively quickly, by the middle of the fifteenth century. Numbers at
Crabhouse, Flixton, Marham, Redlingfield, and Shouldham did not begin to
climb until around 1500.

The populations at Campsey Ash and Carrow remained the most stable,
but despite three new recruits in 1532, Carrow appears to have lost ground by
the time of the Dissolution in 1536.[4] Between 1526 and 1536 Bungay, Campsey
Ash, Redlingfield, and Thetford had also attracted new novices who helped
this female monastic population's slow recovery.

The number of nuns in the other dioceses during the same period evidenced
similar fluctuations.[5] While all of the convents show a drop in population of
about one-third between 1350 and 1400, in some the decline was quite marked.

[4]   The novices are listed in: Jessopp, Visitations, p. 273.
[5]   J. C. Russell, "The Clerical Population of Medieval England," Traditio 2 (1944), p. 179;
and Russell, British Medieval Population, pp. 131–39 where he stated that there were about
5,000 nuns in England before 1350, but that the population dropped almost one third
after the mid-fourteenth-century plagues and famines. Cf. Knowles, The Religious Orders,
vol. 2, pp. 255–58 who says that nuns numbered 3,000 in the early fourteenth century.
Power, Medieval English Nunneries, p. 4.

Romsey Abbey, for example, housed ninety-one nuns in 1333; in 1478 there were only eighteen. The population of nuns there grew steadily in later years, however, reaching forty by 1501.[6] Such drastic changes seem to have occurred primarily in the larger and more populous pre-Conquest foundations which were not part of the female monastic landscape in the diocese of Norwich.[7] Like some of the diocese's convents, though, the female monastic population elsewhere in England also began to show an increase in numbers by the mid-fifteenth century.

Estimates of the male monastic population in the diocese of Norwich, like monks and canons elsewhere in England, suggest a higher mortality rate than was experienced by the nuns. Up to 50 percent of the canons, friars, and monks died between 1350 and 1400, with losses continuing until the mid-fifteenth century when the population of male religious began to recover.[8] Superiors of nine male houses in the county of Suffolk, for example, died, whereas only one prioress did, Alice Winter de Oxford of Redlingfield.[9] The male monasteries in Norfolk also suffered heavier losses than the nuns' houses in that county. The population of Hickling Priory was completely devastated by the plague in 1348 and again in 1349, and Wymondham Priory lost its abbot, prior, and subprior in 1348.[10]

The figures for the female monastic population in the diocese allow a comparison between the average population of each of the eleven houses and their estimated wealth (Table 7). The houses can be divided into three categories of relative wealth: rich, middle-income status, and poor. At the highest and lowest ends of this range there existed a positive correlation between wealth and monastic population: one of the two most populated female monasteries, Campsey Ash, was also the wealthiest; the least populated house, Crabhouse, was also the one of the poorest. Between these two extremes, however, the average size of a female house did not necessarily correspond to its wealth. Carrow Priory, for example, had the greatest average

---

6   H. G. D. Liveing, *The Records of Romsey Abbey* (Winchester, 1906), pp. 121, 223.

7   See Power, *Medieval English Nunneries*, pp. 179–82 for the significant losses sustained by the big houses like Shaftsbury Abbey and St Mary's Winchester as a result of plagues, pestilences, and the famines of 1314–15.

8   Knowles and Hadcock, *Medieval Religious Houses*, p. 54: friars suffered more heavily than monks. Knowles estimated that the Benedictines, Austins, and Premonstratensians lost about 30 per cent of their residents; the Cluniac houses lost about 40 per cent; and the Franciscans and Dominicans lost about 50 per cent each. Like Russell, Knowles saw an increase in the number of male monastics in the fifteenth century. See also Power, *Medieval English Nunneries*, p. 215; and Russell, "The Clerical Population," passim, where he suggests that because men suffered a higher mortality rate from the plague than women did, in general, the female monasteries suffered fewer losses than did their male counterparts. See also: Knowles, *The Religious Orders*, vol. 2, pp. 255–60. But see also: Greatrex, "Some Statistics of Religious Motivation," pp. 179–86 where she sees that the monastic population at the Cathedral Priory in Norwich had risen to its pre-plague number by the sixteenth century.

9   *VCH, Suffolk*, vol. 2, p. 19.

10   *VCH, Norfolk*, vol. 2, p. 383 (Hickling); ibid., p. 339 (Wymondham).

Table 7. Female Monasteries in the Diocese of Norwich
Ranked According to Wealth in 1536 with Average Populations of Houses

Monastery	Wealth in £	Population in 1377	Population in 1536	Average Population 1350–1540
Campsey Ash	182	23	20	20
Shouldham	138	23	10	10
Redlingfield	67	9	13	9.5
Carrow	64	27	14	21
Bungay	61	18	9	12.5
Bruisyard Abbey	56	15	15	15.5
Blackborough	42	11	13	8.5
Thetford	40	12	10	10.5
Marham	33	17	7	11
Crabhouse	24	11	11	8
Flixton	23	13	11	11

Sources: For 1377 population figures, see: PRO, E 179/45/5b; for population in 1536, see: Valor Ecclesiasticus; figures of wealth are rounded off to the nearest £.

number of nuns, but was only in the middle range of wealth. And Bruisyard Abbey, the third most populous, ranked only sixth in wealth compared to the other female houses. Wealth then could, but did not necessarily, affect the number of nuns resident in a particular house.

A similar relationship existed between the size and wealth of the rich and poor female houses in other parts of England, but not to those that fell in between. The wealthiest female houses – Syon, Shaftesbury, and Barking, for example – were also the most populous: Syon and Shaftesbury averaged fifty-five nuns in this later period, Barking thirty-four.[11] The poorest convents tended to house the fewest nuns: Brewood in Staffordshire was valued at £11 and supported only between eight and ten nuns; St Mary Ivinghoe had five in 1536 and was worth only £14. But a vast middle range, represented by Polesworth in the county of Warwick, worth £110 with 15 nuns in 1536, and Hampole and Nunappleton, each valued at £83 with an average monastic population of twenty, show that wealth did not necessarily determine numbers.

Table 8 indicates a similar relationship between wealth and average population among the diocese's male houses. Compare, for example, the average

---

[11] The values of the female houses are in: VE, passim; numbers for each are in: Dugdale, Monasticon, passim.

Table 8.   *Male Monasteries in the Diocese of Norwich Ranked According to Wealth in 1536 with Average Populations of Houses*[a]

Monastery	Wealth in £	Population in 1377	Population in 1535	Average Population
Bury St Edmunds Abbey	1656	47	43	54
Norwich Cathedral Priory	874	50	32	34
St Benet at Holme Priory	583	26	26	23
Walsingham Priory	391	20	22	20
Butley Priory	318	19	17	18
Thetford, St Mary's Priory	312	12	17	14.5
Castle Acre Priory	306	26	11	27
West Acre Priory	260	19	17	17.5
Sibton Abbey	250	11	8	8
Wymondham Abbey	211	16	10	12
Leiston Abbey	181	11	15	13
Pentney Priory	170	12	14	12
Ixworth Priory	168	16	18	18
Horsham St Faith Priory	162	6	6	7
Eye Priory	161	5	9	6.5
Coxford Priory	121	12	10	10
Buckenham Priory	108	8	12	9
Langley Abbey	104	14	15	14
Binham Priory	101	13	7	9.5
Bromholm Priory	100	19	4	19
Hickling Priory	100	11	10	10
West Dereham Abbey	61	19	17	17
Flitcham Priory	55	6	4	4
Wendling Abbey	55	8	5	6
Peterstone Priory	47	4	6	5
Felixstowe Priory	40	3	3	3
Thetford, St Sepulchre	39	7	7	7
Weybourne Priory	28	5	2	3
Mullicourt Priory	6	1	1	2

Sources: Valor Ecclesiasticus; Knowles and Hadcock, *Religious Houses of England and Wales.*

[a]   Figures are given only for the 29 male houses for which both average population and wealth are available; this information does not survive for 34 of the diocese's male monasteries. Information about the wealth and population of friaries does not survive. Figures of wealth are rounded off to the nearest £.

monastic population of twenty-three monks at St Benet at Holme, and the priory's wealth, £583, to the poorer and smaller Wendling Abbey whose wealth was estimated at £55, and whose average population totalled six. Sibton Abbey, on the other hand, was worth £250 with an average population of only eight, while West Dereham, worth £61, had seventeen monks.

The evidence available for the nuns in the diocese also allows us to calculate the number of years a woman lived as a nun, or 'nun years'.[12] Computing the average 'nun years' for this time is possible for 193 of the diocese's nuns, more than one third of the 553 who can be identified by name (35 percent). In some cases, we know exactly how long these women were nuns. Katherine Jerveys told Bishop Nyyke in 1526 that she had been professed at Carrow Priory for thirty-eight years.[13] Since Carrow was suppressed in 1536, we know that she was a nun for forty-eight years. In the same visitation Agnes Swanton said that she had been professed for twenty-one years.[14] Like Jerveys, Swanton was still at Carrow when it was dissolved in 1536, making her tenure there thirty-one years.

These 'nun years' were representative of the lengths of times other women lived as nuns, but whose exact tenures as professed religious are less precisely known. Katherine Beauchamp, for example, first appeared as a nun in her grandfather's will dated 1369.[15] She was also mentioned as a nun in her uncle's will of 1400. Beauchamp was a nun for at least the amount of time between her appearances in these wills: thirty-one years. The first time Isabella Clopton, a nun at Redlingfield, was noted was in the 1381 Poll Tax returns; since she died in 1419 we know that she was a nun for at least thirty-eight years of her life.[16] Similarly, we can trace Elizabeth Beaufeld, a nun at Bungay Priory, from her father's will, dated 1504, until 1536 when the priory was suppressed by the king's men.[17] She was a nun for thirty-two years or more.

Between 1350 and 1540, the average number of years these 193 women lived as nuns was 25, but this figure changed over time. A nun's lifespan in the fourteenth century was 28 years; for the fifteenth century it increases to 30; for the sixteenth century, the average declines to 17. These variations can in part be explained by the sources which allow these calculations, which are more abundant for the fifteenth century than for the fourteenth. Figures for the sixteenth century are compromised by the closing of the monasteries in the 1530s which artificially cut short the number of years a woman could be a nun.

In most cases we do not know how long a woman was a nun before she first appears in the records, so these figures and the estimated average 'nun years'

---

12 See Appendix 2 for more details of these calculations.

13 Jessopp, *Visitations*, p. 209; ibid., p. 273 for her residency here until the Dissolution.

14 Ibid., p. 209.

15 For Katherine's relatives' wills, see: William Dugdale, *Baronage of England* (London, 1675), pp. 233, 226 for her grandfather and uncle respectively.

16 PRO, E 179/45/5b (1381); VCH, *Suffolk*, vol. 2, p. 84.

17 Her father's will is: NRO, NCC 491–2 Popy.

of 25 are conservative.[18] And because similar data has never been calculated for nuns elsewhere in England, it is difficult to know if 25 'nun years' is applicable to the country's total female monastic population. But examples from several houses in other dioceses suggest that 25 years is a minimum number. Cecilia de Verney was elected prioress of Cannington in 1504 and still held that position in 1536 when her house was suppressed, indicating that her tenure as a nun was at least 32 years.[19] Two of the abbesses at Romsey lived as nuns for 44 and 45 years respectively in the late fourteenth and fifteenth centuries, an average of 44.5 years.[20] And the average lifespan for two generations of other nuns at Romsey was 29.5. Twenty-five 'nun years' then was less than the average lifespan of nuns elsewhere in England, and probably more a result of a problem with sources than a true indication of the length of a nun's tenure in the diocese of Norwich.[21]

At first glance, a comparison of these figures with those calculated for monks and canons suggests that they lived longer than their female counterparts. John Hatcher estimated that the average lifespan for monks in the fifteenth century was 33.12 years.[22] But his figure may be higher than an average for the total male religious population because his study focused on the monks at Christchurch Cathedral Priory in Canterbury, a house whose wealth undoubtedly ensured its residents healthier living conditions than those available to monks elsewhere. The average lifespan for male religious at other houses was probably not as high: Barbara Harvey estimated that the average life expectancy of the equally well-fed monks at Westminster Abbey was between 29 and 30 years;[23] Josiah Cox Russell estimated that the average length of a monk's life was 31 years.[24] But if 25 'nun years' is a conservative estimate, and 30 a liberal one for

---

[18] Though Nichols, "The History and Cartulary," p. 85 estimated that at Marham Abbey in Norfolk the average tenure was 24.

[19] VCH, Somerset, vol. 2, p. 111.

[20] Liveing, The Records of Romsey Abbey, p. 146: Isabella de Camoys was at the convent from 1352 to 1396, and Maud Lovell was there from 1417 to 1462.

[21] Ibid., p. 237: using Liveing's data which includes lists of nuns present at various times at Romsey Abbey, I calculated that in 1523 the average 'nun-years' of the 11 nuns resident there was 34 years; in 1538, 13 nuns had been resident there an average of 25 years. G. W. O. Woodward, The Dissolution of the Monasteries (New York, 1966), p. 45 shows that at Yeddingham Priory, the average tenure in 1536 was only 15 years. The lower figures in 1538 at Romsey and at Yeddingham in 1536, however, can be explained by the large number of novices both houses had at these times, rendering these later averages lower. Had the houses not been suppressed, presumably the nuns would have lived in them longer, making the average number of years a woman was a nun greater.

[22] John Hatcher, "Mortality in the Fifteenth Century: Some New Evidence," EHR 2nd ser. 39 (1986), pp. 24, 32.

[23] Harvey, Living and Dying in England, p. 128.

[24] Russell, British Medieval Population, pp. 191–92 suggests that the average length of a monk's life was 30.6 years in the first quarter of the fifteenth century, but rose to 33.2 between 1457–1471.

monks and canons, perhaps the lifespans of female and male monastics were more comparable than what has usually been assumed.[25]

The data rehearsed above, average number of nuns per house and average number of years a woman lived as a nun, can be used to compute the total number of nuns in the diocese between 1350 and 1540. This calculation is possible by multiplying the average number of identified nuns in each house by 190 – the number of years covered in this study – and then dividing by 25, the average number of years a woman was a nun. As the figures in Table 6 show, the average number of nuns per house totaled 136.75; multiplying 136.75 by 190 gives 25,982.5. Divide this number by 25 and the total number of nuns in the diocese in the period covered in this study was roughly 1,000.[26]

Nuns' Ages

The figures and calculations for the total number of nuns in the diocese can tell us more about this group of women than just their numbers. By adding the average number of 'nun years', 25, to the age of entry into a monastery, for example, we can determine the average age of a nun in this period. The canonical age of profession was 16, and with three exceptions, references to nuns both in the diocese and in other parts of England indicate that most novices entered a convent between 15 and 17 years of age.[27] In a grant dated 1426, Margery, widow of John Carbonell, Kt, adjusted her will so that her

[25] Coulton, *Five Centuries*, vol. 4, pp. 133–44; Coulton, "The Truth about the Monasteries," pp. 90–2; and Power, *Medieval English Nunneries*, pp. 166–74.

[26] The total figure is 1039.3. For these calculations, see Appendix 2.

[27] For the canonical age of profession: Power, *Medieval English Nunneries*, p. 25; Shulamith Shahar, *The Fourth Estate: A History of Women in the Middle Ages* (London, 1983), p. 41. But see: R. Luce, "Injunctions Made and Issued to the Abbess and Convent of the Monastery of Romsey after his Visitation by William of Wykeham, A.D. 1387," *Hampshire Field Club and Archaeology Society, Proceedings* 17 pt. 1 (1949), p. 37 where Wykeham tells the nuns that they can profess a nun after twelve years of age and a one year probation. For the diocese of Norwich the three exceptions are: Margaret and Katherine, daughters of Guy Beauchamp, Earl of Warwick, aged seven and one respectively, who were delivered to Shouldham Priory in the fourteenth century, see: Power, *Medieval English Nunneries*, p. 25. Though Margaret vanishes from the sources, Katherine is named as a nun at Shouldham in her grandfather's will in 1369, in the 1381 Poll Tax, and in her uncle's will of 1400. See above note 12 for Katherine's relatives' wills. For the 1381 Poll Tax returns, see: PRO, E 179/45/5b. Though Katherine does not appear as a nun until 1369, at which date she would have been seventeen years old, the wording of Guy's will suggests that he intended his young daughters to become nuns. We do not know, however, the age at which Katherine made her profession. Power said that Katherine's profession was very early, but there is no evidence for this claim. The other is Katherine, daughter of Michael de la Pole. The Crown issued a warning to the abbess of Bruisyard not to coerce Katherine into taking her vows at Bruisyard, or anywhere else, until the girl came of age, or until further orders from the King: CCR, *1413–19*, p. 247. Katherine's mother Isabel was already a nun there, and the King's concern may have been that, as sole surviving heir, Katherine's inheritance would go to the abbey and be

manor in Watton, Norfolk, would pass to Richard Carbonell and his wife Elizabeth, if they gave 100 marks to Margery's daughter Elizabeth when she turned 15, either as a marriage portion or payment for profession as a nun at Marham Abbey.[28] The Suppression Papers of Romsey Abbey indicate that in 1534 two novices were 14 years old, one was 15, and two were 17 years of age. But three novices were much older, 20, 23, and 31, making the average age of entry there 19, and indicating that convents accepted young adult women as well as those in their mid-teens.[29]

If 16 was the age of profession, and we allow for a year's probation, 15 can be used as an average age of entry, making 40 the average age of a nun in the diocese of Norwich between 1350 and 1540, with some slight variations over time.[30] For example, in the fourteenth century, the average age was 43; in the fifteenth century the average rose to 45; by the time of the Dissolution in the 1530s a nun's average age was 32, though it must be stressed again that these numbers are conservative and disguise some very real differences in nuns' ages. Some nuns at the time their houses were suppressed were in their fifties and early sixties.[31] Nevertheless, these numbers make it clear that most nuns were not young and hapless, but entered past the age of menarche and lived through their child-bearing years, indicating a more mature female monastic population than has been supposed.[32]

By contrast, most boys entered male monastic and mendicant houses and were professed when slightly older – between 18 and 20.[33] Despite the prohibitions of the general chapters, however, the Franciscans accepted boys as young as 5, and Dominican houses admitted novices as young as 15.[34]

The practice of accepting novices at a younger age than was permitted seems

taken out of the Crown's control. Nevertheless, Katherine did become a nun, at Barking where in 1433 she was elected abbess. VCH, Essex, vol. 2, p. 121.

[28] NRO, Microfilm Reel 124/7. There is no further evidence about Margery's daughter, so we do not know if she became a nun.

[29] Liveing, The Records of Romsey Abbey, p. 248.

[30] For a nun's probationary period, see below pp. 51–2.

[31] See below, Chapter 7, p. 191.

[32] Power, Medieval English Nunneries, pp. 26–7.

[33] Knowles, Religious Orders, vol. 1, p. 285; ibid., vol. 2, p. 229. Knowles included here boys who entered Benedictine, Cistercian, Augustinian, and Premonstratensian houses, and he said that donning a cowl at fifteen years was not uncommon by the fifteenth century. See also: H. M. Colvin, The White Canons in England (Oxford, 1951), p. 11; Dobson, Durham Priory, p. 27 found that boys entered Durham in their late teens and early twenties; Rose Graham, St Gilbert of Sempringham and the Gilbertines: A History of the Only English Monastic Order (London, 1901), p. 48. Joan Greatrex, "Prosopography of English Benedictine Cathedral Chapters: Some Monastic Curricula Vitae," Medieval Prosopography 16:1 (1995), p. 6 agrees and found age of entry 17–19. See also: Hatcher, "Mortality in the Fifteenth Century," p. 27, for estimates that the mean age of entrance between 1395 and 1505 was 16–20.

[34] For the Franciscans, see: J. R. Moorman, The Grey Friars in Cambridge, 1225–1538 (Cambridge, 1952), pp. 106–7. For the Dominican Order: William Hinnebusch, The History of the Dominican Order: Origins and Growth to 1500 (New York, 1966), vol. 1, pp. 282–83. In fact the Order encouraged this practice of accepting young boys, maintaining

to have been a chronic problem in the male houses but not in the female ones.[35] In 1366, the Commons petitioned the Crown to disallow anyone under age 21 from entering any of the four orders of friars; the king refused. Instead he issued an order which prohibited friars from accepting any child under 14 without the consent of parents or guardians.[36] Nevertheless, the last prior of the Carmelite priory in Ipswich joined the order in Norwich at age 12.[37]

In addition to young single women, older women, those who had left their husbands or been abandoned by them, and widows, could also enter medieval convents.[38] Widows joined female monastic communities either intending to be professed nuns or vowesses.[39] Vowesses were veiled and took vows of chastity; though some retained their own private residences others retired to a female monastic community.[40] At least six of the diocese's female houses supported vowesses, including Lady Dorothy Curson who had the farm of the 'ankerhouse' in the precincts of Carrow Priory in 1520.[41] Katharine Kerre bequeathed 10s to Margaret, vowess at Crabhouse Priory, in 1497.[42] Maud,

that the longer the Order had to train and educate them, the more promising they would be as preachers.

[35] Compare, for example, the instances when the Benedictine monks' general chapters legislated about this problem with the infrequent mention of it in the episcopal visitations for the female houses. For the monks, see: William Pantin, ed., *Documents Illustrating the Activities of the General and Provincial Chapters of the English Black Monks, 1215–1540*, 3 vols. (London: Royal Historical Society, 1931–37), esp. vol. 1, pp. 10, 99, 118, 234. For the extant episcopal visitations of the female houses see: Jessopp, *Visitations*, passim, where no instances of this practice in Norwich diocese are cited; and Thompson, *Visitations of Religious Houses*, vol. 2, pp. 5, 217 for the four fifteenth-century instances used by Power as cited above, note 3; and Thompson, *Visitations in the Diocese of Lincoln*, passim, where there are no instances of young girls being accepted by female houses in the sixteenth century.

[36] Moorman, *The Grey Friars*, p. 110. The Commons' concern over the age of boys accepted into mendicant orders probably reflected the competition for students between the friars' houses and the universities. Universities could admit boys as young as fourteen; if the mendicants could also, they would be seen as a threat to the universities' student recruitment pool. But the fact that the mendicant orders' general chapters, Parliament, and the general chapters of the English Benedictine monks continually legislated against accepting young boys, while the extant bishops' registers do not mention this practice in their visitations of and subsequent injunctions to the female monastic communities, suggests that taking in novices below an approved age was a bigger problem for the male religious than for their female counterparts.

[37] B. Zimmerman, "The White Friars at Ipswich," *PSIA* 10 (1891–1900), pp. 199–200 cites two more examples of boys entering the order at early ages as late as the sixteenth century.

[38] Power, *Medieval English Nunneries*, pp. 38–41 for wives and widows.

[39] For widows in other female monasteries, see: Liveing, *The Records of Romsey Abbey*, p. 166 where he mentions a vowess a this house in 1400. Bishop Henry received the vows of Elizabeth, relict of one John Forester of Romsey, veiled her, and bestowed on her the ring of chastity.

[40] There are two lists of fifteenth-century vowesses in the British Library: BL, Add. Ms. 5808, fol. 191b, and BL, Add. Ms. 29,692, fol. 138. See also: Mary Erler, "English Vowed Women at the End of the Middle Ages," *Medieval Studies* 57 (1995), pp. 155–203.

[41] NRO, Hare 5955 227x1 for the household account of Prioress Isabel Wygon.

[42] NRO, NCC 90–1 Multon.

Countess of Oxford, was a vowess at Campsey Ash in 1347; she retained her status as such when she left there to reside at her son-in-law's foundation, Bruisyard Abbey, in 1369.[43] Vowesses were also resident throughout the fifteenth century at Blackborough and Flixton Priories.[44]

Entry Requirements and Fees

Whether entrants were young or old, common practice and canon law in the later Middle Ages allowed monasteries to accept these newcomers with either small monetary fees, or with the veils, cloaks, and other garments which comprised a nun's habit, and whatever bedding they might need.[45] From the fourteenth century until the Dissolution, male monasteries required a fixed fee of £5 from incoming novices for their habits.[46] At some of the male houses a novice made additional contributions to various obedientiaries at the time of his profession – typically the barber and the tailor – who participated in his admission and in the ritual of his profession.[47] Novices at the Cathedral Priory in Norwich had to purchase their drinking cups from the refectorer.[48]

While canon law provides a general idea of what female and male monasteries could accept from incoming novices, Blackborough Priory's cartulary details exactly what a novice was to bring to this small house of Benedictine nuns. The list includes two mattresses, two pairs of sheets, two pairs of blankets, and two outer coverings; four coats (two black, two white), one outer garment made of skin or fur, two *rochets*, or outer cloaks, two cowls, two capes, and two single mantles. She had also to bring one napkin, one towel, one ewer, a drinking cup, a piece of silver, a saucer, one basin, one lavor, one wimple, at least three veils, one coffer, and a box.[49] This monastic trousseau could have

[43] Bourdillon, *The Minoresses*, p. 25; Power, *Medieval English Nunneries*, p. 39; VCH, *Suffolk*, vol. 2, p. 113.

[44] Three individual vowesses at Blackborough are beneficiaries in the following wills: NRO, NCC 130–32 Wylbey, will of Joan Bardolf, vowess Joan Blumstede; NRO, NCC 58–9 Brosyerd, will of Kathryn Brasyer, vowess Alice de Branges; NRO, NCC 329–30 Brosyerd, will of Cathryn Goodrede, vowess Dame Emma. Alice Brakenest of Halesworth was a vowess at Flixton in 1381: BL, Stowe Ch. 348.

[45] Power, *Medieval English Nunneries*, pp. 19–20; Coulton, *Five Centuries*, vol. 4, p. 121. See also: Taylor, *Index Monasticus*, p. viii who claims that, as with other orders, the Bridgettine Rule specified that each novice was to bring sufficient property with her to maintain herself in a convent.

[46] Greatrex, "English Benedictine Cathedral Chapters," p. 7; Knowles, *The Religious Orders*, vol. 1, p. 285. See also Pantin, *Documents*, vol. 2, p. 50. But cf. Dobson, *Durham Priory*, p. 62 where he says that at Durham Priory novices received their habits and bedding from the priory's chamberlain.

[47] Knowles, *The Religious Orders*, vol. 1, p. 285.

[48] Greatrex, "English Benedictine Cathedral Chapters," p. 8.

[49] BL, Egerton 3137. Parts of this cartulary have been extracted and can be found at NRO, BL vi b (viii).

cost anywhere from £5 to £7,[50] amounts which compare favorably to those calculated by Power for Lacock Abbey in the late fourteenth century, £6 13s 2d, and for Nunmonkton Priory in 1468, £3 13s 6½d.[51] Though certainly exceptions to these relatively reasonable expenses existed, those cited here of between £5 and £7 would have been within the realm of what many upper gentry, minor gentry families, and wealthy yeoman farmers in the fifteenth and sixteenth centuries could have afforded.[52] The entrance supplies and costs at Blackborough then were both in accord with canon law and attainable at a moderate cost.[53]

Several other female houses in the diocese of Norwich also kept within the limits of the law. In 1416, for example, Michael, Earl of Suffolk, paid the prioress of Redlingfield 6s 8d for one habit of black say to be made for the daughter of Margaret Chambrier when she became a nun there.[54] He paid another 23s 4d, "for diverse things bought for the daughter of Margaret

---

[50] It is possible to approximate costs of these goods in the fifteenth and sixteenth centuries. Prices of all of the items on the list are from: J. T. Rogers, A History of Agriculture and Prices in England, 7 vols. (Oxford, 1866–1902), vol. 4, 1401–1582, pp. 474–88, 551–89. In calculating these costs I have taken the highest and the lowest prices listed for the period from 1350 to 1535, thus figuring the highest and the lowest possible costs of these goods. The average cost of bedding was 25s 8d. The most one might have spent on a napkin, a towel, ewer, a drinking cup, a piece of silver, a saucer, one basin, one lavor, one coffer, and a string box, if they were made of the best quality linen and of silver, was about 13s. The least amount a person could have paid for these personal items was about 5s 6d, if the items listed were made of wood, pewter, and coarse sheeting. If we double the amount that the Earl of Suffolk spent on a habit for the daughter of Margaret Chambrier to 13s 4d (see below p. 69) – because the Blackborough list seems to specify two habits – and add the cost of four coats, which for high quality wool would have been about 48s – or £2 8s – and for mid-quality wool would have been about 44s – or £2 4s – we arrive at the most one could have paid for the entire list of personal belongings: £7. The least one could have paid would have been about £5. If we recalculate the cost of a habit made of lesser quality material than say – high quality sheeting or mid-quality linen, for example – the cost of a habit was anywhere from 1s to 3s. The total cost of this monastic trousseau drops to about £5 for lesser materials. My estimate for how much a habit might have cost is based on the yardage of the habit the Earl of Suffolk commissioned for Margaret Chambrier's daughter. He spent 6s 8d for a habit which might have cost 1s 5d per yard around 1416. If 6s 8d is divided by 1s 5d, the amount of material comes out to be about six yards.

[51] Power, Medieval English Nunneries, pp. 19–20. See also: VCH, Bedfordshire, vol. 1, p. 354 for the £6 13s 4d delivered to the abbess of Elstow by John Duffyn to cover the costs and charges of making Anne Loveday a nun at this house in 1502.

[52] For an example of a considerably greater amount of money for a nun's personal supplies, see: VCH, Essex, vol. 2, p. 118: John of Gaunt paid £51 8s 2d for the expenses of Elizabeth Chancy's admission into Barking Abbey. Christopher Dyer, The Standard of Living in the Late Middle Ages (Cambridge, 1989), pp. 31–2, 140–50.

[53] For similar items, including furniture, see: W. G. Clarke-Maxwell, "The Outfit for the Profession of an Austin Canoness at Lacock, Wiltshire in the Year 1395 and Other Memoranda," Archaeological Journal 69 (1912), p. 118.

[54] BL, Egerton Roll 8776: Receiver General Accounts of the Earl of Suffolk. I am grateful to Roger Virgoe for this reference.

Chambrier to be entered and accepted as a nun of the same place."[55] John Fox of Castleacre bequeathed the heftier sum of £10 in 1434 to his daughter Mary to be made a nun at Marham Abbey.[56]

While these houses generally adhered to custom and law, at least two others waived the requirement of entry fees or goods altogether. Carrow Priory earmarked a certain amount of money from the sale of malt for items a novice needed to enter this house.[57] And Bruisyard Abbey maintained special annuities, or "dots," for habits and other goods for women too poor to afford these personal items.[58]

The entry fees required by the diocese's female monasteries indicate that the nuns neither exploited this custom nor discriminated against a recruit because she could not afford the necessary goods. Practices at female houses in other dioceses, moreover, were similar to those of Blackborough, Carrow, Bruisyard, and Redlingfield. H. F. Chettle found no evidence that the nuns at Barking Abbey either demanded or received huge entrance fees from incoming novices.[59] And Bishop Wykeham allowed the nuns at Romsey Abbey to admit the relatives or parents of poor nuns as sisters of the abbey's hospital when their cloistered relative died, indicating that this house also accepted women who were unable to bear the costs of habits, bedding, or fees upon entry.[60]

In addition to personal belongings and/or a monetary fee, religious houses in late medieval England expected novices to meet certain criteria. These included legitimacy of birth and the physical stamina needed to undertake the rigors of a lifetime devoted to poverty and prayer.[61] A novice was also expected to have attained a certain degree of education by the time she entered a house, or to demonstrate an ability to learn to read the Latin prayers of the canonical hours.[62] If these conditions were not met, the whole community could voice

---

[55] Ibid.

[56] NRO, NCC 152–3 Surflete.

[57] NRO, Hare 5955 227x1 is the account of Isabel Wygon, prioress and cellarer for the year 1530.

[58] The Isabella Rule does not mention this practice, but it is clear from the Franciscan general chapters that special moneys were being set aside in the Order's female houses for women who could not afford to provision themselves with habits: Bourdillon, *The Minoresses*, pp. 37–8.

[59] Ernst Loftus and H. F. Chettle, *A History of Barking Abbey* (Barking, 1954), p. 55 where Chettle says that he cannot find more than very slight evidence that the house demanded huge entrance fees before a woman was admitted as a novice. He also says that he finds no evidence that the nuns at Barking treated the money or goods with which a novice entered as compulsory or as deferred dowries.

[60] Luce, "Injunctions Made and Issued," p. 41.

[61] Hinnebusch, *A History of the Dominican Order*, vol. 1, p. 283; and Knowles, *The Religious Orders*, vol. 2, pp. 232–33 for males. But see also: Raphael Huber, *A Documented History of the Franciscan Order, 1182–1517* (Milwaukee, 1944), p. 17. He says that the order required only a renunciation of a candidate's goods, and a declaration of his desire to observe the Rule. Power, *Medieval English Nunneries*, pp. 24–5 for female novices.

[62] Dobson, *Durham Priory*, p. 58 where he says that as with most other English monasteries, skill in reading and music was required. Power, *Medieval English Nunneries*, pp. 13–14.

objections as did two nuns at Thetford in 1492 when they feared the prioress was willing to accept "unlearned and even deformed persons."[63]

Novice to Nun

Having met all of these prerequisites, a novice was presented to the community she wanted to join.[64] If accepted she underwent a probationary period before becoming fully professed. Not much is known about a nun's novitiate. One of the extant profession rituals includes a brief description of a year-long trial period during which time a novice was to learn the Rule of the monastery, "be informed as religion will," and be examined by the community's superior in chapter four times within that year.[65] During that year at the houses of Poor Clares, a novice was excluded from the bi-weekly chapter meetings, and was taught by a novice mistress.[66] Though there are no specific references about what a female novice of any order was supposed to learn we can assume that, like her male counterpart, she at least studied the psalms, antiphons, and responsories of the Divine Office.[67]

We know a great deal more about what a male novice's probation entailed. His training period lasted anywhere from one to seven years, during which time he would learn the Rule of the house, the hymns and psalms which comprised the Divine Offices, sacramental prayers, and Latin grammar.[68] Those who entered a mendicant house also underwent a long period of study which

But see Bourdillon, The Minoresses, p. 78 for her comments that the Isabella Rule took it for granted that some novices would be illiterate; the Rule suggested that these women should not be taught to read or sing, but rather be instructed to say the Our Father twenty-seven times a day at prescribed hours.

63 Jessopp, Visitations, p. 33.

64 There is a description of a female novice's acceptance into a monastic community in: G. J. Aungier, The History of Syon Monastery (London, 1840), pp. 303–4; and in W. L. Bowles and J. G. Nichols, Annales and Antiquities of Lacock Abbey (London, 1835), pp. 199–213. For a description of a male novice's reception into a monastery, see: Gasquet, English Monastic Life, pp. 106–9.

65 For a female novice's probation see: Ernst Kock, Three Middle-English Versions of the Rule of St Benet and Two Contemporary Rituals for the Ordination of Nuns (EETS, o.s. 120, 1902), pp. 141–44; and Luce, "Injunctions Made and Issued," p. 37 where Bishop Wykeham confirms a one year novitiate before full profession for the nuns at Romsey.

66 Bourdillon, The Minoresses, p. 70.

67 Power, Medieval English Nunneries, p. 24. Thompson, Visitations of Religious Houses, vol. 1, p. 53 for the injunctions to Elstow Abbey that novices must have a teacher to instruct them in the Divine Office. See also: ibid., vol. 2, p. 5 for similar injunctions to the nuns at Ankerwaite Priory.

68 Gasquet, English Monastic Life, pp. 107–9 and Greatrex, "English Benedictine Cathedral Chapters," pp. 10–12. Knowles, The Religious Orders, vol. 1, p. 285 says that the novitiate for males lasted one year. But later, vol. 2, p. 233 he says that the period of training was usually seven years between the time of acceptance and when one was professed. This difference in length of time must have been contingent on the age at which a male novice entered a monastery. For what a male novice was supposed to learn, see: Alfred

included Latin grammar and rhetoric, subjects necessary to acquire preaching skills which were often viewed as the first step toward a university education.[69] By the late fourteenth century monks were also required to study these subjects and learn these skills.[70]

Female and male novices had some things in common – the fees and personality traits which monasteries required for their admission – but differed in others. Nuns were usually slightly older when admitted to a monastery, and their novitiates were shorter and less academically rigorous. These differences reflect the male religious' functions as preachers and their opportunities to attend university, and indicate another way that gender affected the female and male religious in the later Middle Ages.

After this trial period, novices took vows of obedience, chastity, and poverty which forever bound them to their monastic communities.[71] The ceremony for a nun's profession was presided over by the bishop and enacted in the conventual church.[72] After kneeling before the gathered congregation, a novice spoke her vows aloud, wrote them down, and then signed her name or made a cross on a parchment laid across the bishop's knees. He placed the signed document in the hands of the convent's superior.[73] This ceremony carried profound implications; it was a public proclamation of a nun's release from the secular world, and signaled her reception within the cloistered community of religious women with whom she would spend the rest of her life.

Family Backgrounds

The women who took these vows and lived their lives in community with others were a socially mixed group. Information about the nuns and their families culled from wills, pedigrees, and other sources allow a prosopographical

Watkin, "An English Mediaeval Instruction Book for Novices," *Downside Review* 57 (1939), pp. 477–88 for part 1, and ibid., 58 (1940), pp. 53–66, 199–210 for part 2.

[69] Maura O'Carroll, "The Educational Organisation of the Dominicans in England and Wales, 1221–1348: A Multidisciplinary Approach," *Archivum Fratrum Praedicatorum* 50 (1980), pp. 23–62.

[70] Greatrex, "English Benedictine Cathedral Chapters," pp. 12–13.

[71] For male monastic vows, see: Gasquet, *English Monastic Life*, p. 108. For female monastic vows, see Kock, *Three Middle-English Versions*, pp. 142, 144, 147; Parrey, "Devoted Disciples," p. 243 for a form of this ceremony said by the nuns at Amesbury; and M. F. Wakelin, "A New Vernacular Version of a Nun's Profession," *Notes and Queries* 229 (1984), pp. 459–61.

[72] Erler, "English Vowed Women," p. 166; Kock, *Three Middle-English Versions*, pp. 143–150; Liveing, *The Records of Romsey Abbey*, p. 167; and Tolhurst, *The Ordinal and Customary*, vol. 65, pp. 349–52. This ritual was more elaborate if the novice were a virgin: she was consecrated by the bishop with blessings and prayers which were specifically for virgins, and inapplicable to widows or married women.

[73] William Maskell, ed., *Monumenta Ritualia Ecclesiae Anglicanae* (Oxford, 1882), vol. 2, pp. 316–17; Parrey, "Devoted Disciples," p. 244; Tolhurst, *The Ordinale and Customary*, vol. 2, pp. 350–51.

analysis of the nuns in the diocese of Norwich which indicates that a substantial percentage of these women – 64 per cent – came not from the most socially elite groups, but rather from the middling ranks of medieval Norfolk and Suffolk society.[74] This analysis also suggests that while the wealth of a house was a factor for some recruits, geographic proximity appears to have been a more significant factor in deciding which of the diocese's convents to enter – more important even than whether or not a woman had relatives already resident at a particular place.

The nuns can be classified into five social groups; the highest was the aristocracy.[75] This category includes royal women, those who came from families with hereditary peerage titles, and those from powerful families who held earldoms, duchies, and baronies. This titled aristocracy enjoyed the wealth and privileges that accompanied lordship over vast estates, as well as the responsibilities of being the Crown's chief counselors in the House of Lords. Only Katherine Beauchamp, a nun at Shouldham, came from a family of this elevated group.[76] She was part of only a small percentage of the nuns of this social rank. Only seven of the 553 identifiable nuns who lived in the diocese from 1350 to 1540 belonged to this elite social group (Table 9).

Directly below the titled aristocracy in social rank were nuns from the upper gentry. While they shared certain characteristics with the titled aristocracy – the dependence for wealth and power on landed estates, and involvement in the affairs of the realm as well as in the affairs of the counties from which they came or wherein they held their titles – nevertheless, the upper gentry formed a distinct second social group.[77] Nuns in this social category came from families

---

[74] Appendix 3 explains the methodology of this study.

[75] For discussions about the problems of classifying social groups in the Middle Ages, see: Dyer, *The Standard of Living*, pp. 10–26. For my definition of the titled aristocracy, see: G. W. Bernard, *The Power of the Early Tudor Nobility: A Study of the Fourth and Fifth Earls of Shrewsbury* (New York, 1985), pp. 173, 176, 197–208; Michael Bush, *The English Aristocracy: A Comparative Synthesis* (Manchester, 1984), pp. 3–95; Mervin James, *Family, Lineage and Civil Society: A Study of Society, Politics and Mentality in the Durham Region, 1500–1640* (Oxford, 1974), p. 32; K. B. Mc Farlane, *The Nobility of Later Medieval England* (Oxford, 1973), pp. 1–18.

[76] For Katherine's family's status, see: Dugdale, *Baronage*, p. 235, and *IPM, 39–43 Edward III*, p. 307. For Maud's status see: BL, Add. Ms. 19,144, fol. 356.

[77] For the distinction between the two groups and a definition of the upper gentry, see: Christine Carpenter, "The Fifteenth-Century Gentry and their Estates," in *Gentry and Lesser Nobility in Late Medieval Europe*, ed. Michael Jones (Gloucester, 1986), pp. 36–60; J. P. Cooper, "The Social Distribution of Land and Men, 1463–1700," *EHR* 20:3 (1976), pp. 419–40; J. Cornwall, "The Early Tudor Gentry," *EcHR* 2nd ser. 17 (1965), pp. 456–75; N. Denholm-Young, *The County Gentry in the Fourteenth Century* (Oxford, 1969); G. E. Mingay, *The Gentry: The Rise and Fall of a Ruling Class* (London, 1976), esp. pp. 1–30; T. H. Swales, "The Redistribution of the Monastic Lands in Norfolk at the Dissolution," *NA* 34 (1969), pp. 14–44; Roger Virgoe, "The Crown and Local Government: East Anglia under Richard II," in *The Reign of Richard II: Essays in Honor of May McKisack*, ed. F. H. R. Du Boulay and Caroline Barron (London, 1971), pp. 218–41; and Roger Virgoe, "The Crown, Magnates, and Local Government in Fifteenth-Century

Table 9.   *Social Rank of All Identifiable Nuns*
in the Diocese of Norwich, 1350–1540

Social Rank	Numbers of Nuns in Known Social Ranks		Adjusted Numbers of Nuns in Social Ranks	
	(No.)	%	(No.)	%
Titled Aristocracy	(7)	4	(7)	1
Upper Gentry	(55)	32	(55)	10
Parish Gentry	(78)	46	(354)	64
Urban	(24)	14	(108)	20
Yeoman	(6)	4	(29)	5
Total Known	(170)	100		
Total Adjusted	(383)		(553)	100

Notes: Figures in the first column are based on information concerning 170 nuns whose social background can be clearly identified. The adjusted figures are the 170 nuns added to the remaining 383 nuns whose social rank is less positively known, but who have been assigned a social status based on the percentages of known nuns and their social rank. This adjustment redresses the source bias, and reflects the social rank of all 553 nuns identified in this study; see below, pp. 57–9. For sources and calculations of adjusted figures, see Appendix 3.

whose fathers and sons were knights and esquires, who were elected to sit in the House of Commons, or filled county offices such as sheriff and escheator. Katherine Clifton, daughter of Sir Adam Clifton, Knight, Lord of Topcroft Manor and lands elsewhere in Norfolk, and a Cistercian nun at Marham Abbey in 1367, was from this group.[78] So was Dorothy Calthorp, a sixteenth-century nun at Bruisyard Abbey. She was the daughter of Sir Philip Calthorp, Knight and Sheriff of Norfolk in 1489/90.[79] Overall, about 10 percent of the diocesan nuns came from upper gentry families.

Most of these upper gentry nuns were members of the community at Bruisyard Abbey, the last monastic foundation for women in the diocese, and also one of only three country-wide of the Order of Poor Clares. The majority of upper gentry women from the counties of Norfolk and Suffolk who decided to become nuns chose convents in dioceses other than Norwich. The female kin of Thomas Fincham, a prominent Suffolk office and land holder, for example, entered the Cambridgeshire abbeys of Chatteris and Denney in the neighboring diocese of Ely, and Elstow Priory in the diocese of Lincoln.[80] Other

East Anglia," in *The Crown and Local Community in England and France in the Fifteenth Century*, ed. J. R. L. Highfield and Robin Jeffs (Gloucester, 1981), pp. 72–87.
[78] *IPM, 39–43 Edward III*, p. 128.
[79] Rye, *The Visitation of Norfolk*, p. 64.
[80] See his will: PRO, PCC Prob 11/19/5, dated 1517.

Norfolk and Suffolk women chose Barking Abbey in Essex, where ten of the twenty-five families represented in this group had daughters or sisters.[81] Geographic proximity to Norfolk and Suffolk may have played a part in why Chatteris, Denny, and Barking were popular choices, as they were located in neighboring counties.

The wealth of a house may also have been a determining factor in where these women became nuns: Barking was the third wealthiest female house in medieval England, and the other popular choices with this socially elite group were among the twenty wealthiest houses. The fact that women from high ranking families in Norfolk and Suffolk favored wealthy monasteries outside the diocese suggests a correlation between the wealth of a female monastery and the social ranks from which it drew recruits.[82] Denny, however, was only twenty-fifth in wealth; its affiliation with the popular Order of Poor Clares may have been what appealed to these upper status women and to those who chose Bruisyard Abbey.[83]

The third social group into which the nuns in the diocese of Norwich can

---

[81] See, for example, VCH, Essex, vol. 2, p. 121 for Eleanor Chamberleyn, prioress of Barking, daughter of Ralph Chamberleyn of Suffolk and Katherine de la Pole, eldest daughter of Michael, the third Earl of Suffolk, who was elected abbess there in 1433. The next most popular convent was Denny Abbey: of the twenty-five families noted in Appendix 3, who had two or more relatives at female houses, nine families had remale kin here. St Helen's, Bishopsgate in London; Elstow in Bedfordshire; Dartford in Kent; and Shaftsbury in Dorset each had one nun from an upper gentry Norfolk or Suffolk family, and Malling Abbey, also in Kent, housed two nuns from this social group. References to these families and the convents which they preferred can be found in: Joan Corder, ed., Suffolk Visitation, 1561 (Harleian Society, n.s. pt. 1), pp. 86, 170; G. H. Dashwood, Visitation of Norfolk, in the Year 1563 taken by William Harvey, Clarenceaux of Arms (Norwich, 1878), pp. 111, 130, 234, 267; Joseph Jackson Howard, ed., The Visitation of Suffolk . . . and Other Documents (Lowestoft, 1866–1876), vol. 1, p. 250; ibid., vol. 2, pp. 117, 137; and Walter Rye, ed., The Visitation of Norfolk, Made and Taken by William Hervey, Clarenceaux of Arms, Anno 1563 (Harleian Society, 1891), pp. 175, 200. The wills include those of John Wodehouse, esq., Katherine, widow of William Godrede, Middleton, Norfolk, Isobel, Lady Morley of Higham, Norfolk, Margaret de la Pole, Geoffrey Boleyn, John Heward of London, gent., Robert Blickling, John Jernegan of Walsingham, esq., and Walter Ingham of Norwich, gent. These wills are all: NRO, NCC, except for the will of Margaret de la Pole, whose will is PRO, PCC Prob 11/6/12.

[82] Gail McMurray Gibson, Theater of Devotion: East Anglian Drama and Society in the Late Middle Ages (Chicago, 1989), pp. 20–1 notes that while most East Anglians made bequests to local religious houses, the exceptions were those from the upper ranks of society who favored very wealthy houses outside the diocese: the Charterhouse of Mount Grace in York, the Charterhouse in London, the Charterhouse at Sheen, and Syon Abbey, also in London. No doubt these houses benefitted from the largesse of many people from this social group because of their contacts with them in their travels for business and legal matters. Gibson explains the popularity of Syon by pointing out that St Bridget, the patron of the founding order of Syon, was especially popular in East Anglia where influences from Germany and the Low Countries were particularly strong.

[83] See Knowles, Medieval Religious Houses, p. 210 for Barking, whose value at the Dissolution was over £862; and ibid., p. 232 for Denny's 1535 valuation: £172. See also Paxton, "The Nunneries of London," p. 33.

be classified was the lower gentry, or parish gentry.[84] Though sometimes cadet branches of upper gentry families, the parish gentry were less well-propertied, but more involved with local parish and village affairs, holding minor county offices, like constable and bailiff, and serving as stewards for more prestigious families. Among nuns of this social group were Margaret Fincham, prioress of Blackborough from 1508 to 1514, Petronilla Fulmerston, subprioress at Campsey Ash in 1514, and Alice Crowmere, a nun at Thetford in the fourteenth century, who was executrix of her brother's will.[85]

Nuns from parish gentry families constituted by far the largest group in the diocese's female houses, 64 percent, thus considerably outnumbering those of the titled aristocracy and the upper gentry. And consistent with the majority of nuns' middling social rank were their geographic origins. Of the 170 nuns whose social status can be positively identified, 122 (71 percent) chose convents in their home counties, most frequently within a ten-mile radius of their home parishes. The majority of identified nuns in the houses founded in the western fens of Norfolk – Blackborough, Crabhouse, and Marham – for example, came from the neighboring parishes of Wiggenhall St Mary, Dereham, Outwell, and Crimplesham. Likewise, both Flixton and Bungay Priories recruited locally from the parishes of Wingfield, Homersfield, and Denham.

A correlation between social status and geographic origins prevailed for monks, canons, and friars both in the diocese of Norwich and elsewhere.[86] The Carmelite friars of Ipswich came primarily from local Suffolk villages; most of the canons of both Butley Priory and Leiston Abbey were from the vicinity of these two houses.[87]

The clearest evidence of a local recruiting pattern can be seen among the nuns who came from urban families, the fourth social group. They can be

---

[84] For use of this term and its meaning, see: P. W. Fleming, "Charity, Faith, and the Gentry of Kent, 1422–1529," in *Property and Politics*, ed. A. J. Pollard (Gloucester, 1984), p. 36; James, *Family, Lineage, and Civil Society*, p. 31; Cornwall, "Tudor Gentry," p. 460; Mingay, *The Gentry*, pp. 13–14; and Virgoe, "The Crown, Magnates," p. 73.

[85] Fincham was from a cadet branch of the Fincham family from Clacklose Outwell: Blomefield, *An Essay*, vol. 8, p. 449; Fulmerston's family was from Framlingham in Suffolk: Roger Virgoe, personal correspondence; Crowmere's status is evident from the will of her brother, Lawrence Draper of Crowmer, chaplain of Ereswell: NRO, NCC Heydon 199 dated 1382.

[86] For monks, friars, and canons see: R. B. Dobson, "The Prosopography of Late Medieval Cathedral Canons," *Medieval Prosopography* 15:2 (1995), pp. 67–92; R. B. Dobson, "Recent Prosopographical Research in Late Medieval English History," p. 189, for the monks of Durham; Knowles, *The Religious Orders*, vol. 2, p. 229; Moorman, *The Grey Friars in Cambridge*, p. 80 where he says that a majority of Cambridge friars came from East Anglia, but that many came from further away as well; David Lepine, " 'My Beloved Sons in Christ': The Chapter of Lincoln Cathedral 1300–1541," *Medieval Prosopography* 16:1 (1995), pp. 93–4, 104, 107; and Tillotson, *Monastery and Society*, pp. 23–4. Tanner, *The Church in Late Medieval Norwich*, pp. 25–6 for the male religious of the Cathedral Priory and friaries in the city of Norwich.

[87] B. V. Redstone, "The Carmelites of Ipswich," *PSIA* 10 (1898–1900), p. 193; Mortimer, *Leiston Abbey Cartulary and Butley Priory Charters*, p. 8.

distinguished from the titled aristocracy and the county and parish gentry by
their families' residence in towns, involvement with trade and industry, and
interests in civic government.[88] Most nuns from this social group entered
Carrow Priory, in the suburbs of the city of Norwich. Margaret Folcard, only
daughter of John Folcard, citizen and alderman of Norwich, for example, was
at Carrow Priory in the 1460s.[89] Isabel Barbor, alias Welan, a nun at the same
place, was from an urban family as well: her mother's second husband, William,
was a citizen of Norwich and left Isabel 5 marks in his will.[90] Nuns from urban
families comprised 20 per cent of all of the identifiable nuns, more numerous
than those from the upper gentry but considerably less than those of the parish
gentry. Though most of these women went to Carrow, other houses attracted
women from urban families too.[91] Alice Cook was a nun at Campsey Ash Priory
in the sixteenth century; her father, John Cook, draper, served as alderman,
sheriff and mayor of Norwich in the late fifteenth century.[92]

Similar in wealth and local interests to the parish gentry was the fifth group:
substantial freeholders, or yeoman farmers, members of which are more difficult to identify than the others.[93] Yeomen generally did not hold any local
offices, and had no pretense to gentility – that intangible quality often used to
distinguish the gentry from lower social ranks. Alice Fermer, a nun at Thetford
Priory in the early sixteenth century, was from a family of this fifth category.
Her father left her a brass pot in his will, one of the few items he had to bequeath
to his heirs.[94] At least 5 per cent of all of the identifiable nuns in the diocese
were part of this social group.

The percentages and figures offered here (Table 9) for the female monastic
population of the diocese are based on a group of 170 nuns whose social rank
can be definitely established by means of wills and other documents, and on a
group of 383 whose social rank is less readily identifiable. But several reasons
argue for their inclusion into the three middling social ranks rather than into
the top two elite groups of titled aristocracy and upper gentry.

The biased nature of our sources for the Middle Ages – their emphasis on
social hierarchy and the elite – makes our knowledge of aristocratic and
upper gentry families fairly complete. Both of the upper social ranks are

---

88 John Patten, "Patterns of Migration," pp. 143–62; J. Patten, "Population Distribution,"
   pp. 71–92; Colin Platt, The English Medieval Town (London, 1979); Sylvia Thrupp, The
   Merchant Class of Medieval London (Chicago, 1948).
89 Jessopp, Visitations, p. 17; for Margaret's father, see: NRO, NCC 250 Brosyerd.
90 NRO, NCC 159 Brosyard; her mother Joan's will is: NRO, NCC 206 Brosyerd. See also
   Rye, Carrow Abbey, pp. xv–xvi.
91 Lepine, " 'My Beloved Sons,' " pp. 109–10 notes that members of the urban elite of the
   city of Exeter supplied most of the Cathedral Chapters' canons as well.
92 For Alice, see: Jessopp, Visitations, pp. 36, 133, 219, 290; for her family, see her mother's
   will: PRO, PCC Prob 11/8/9.
93 For this definition, see: Cornwall, "Tudor Gentry," pp. 464–65; Cooper, "The Social
   Distribution," pp. 426–27; James, Family, Lineage, p. 38; and Mingay, The Gentry, pp. 3,
   6, 27.
94 His will is dated 1508, and is in: NRO, ANF 188 Shaw.

well-documented for Norfolk and Suffolk.[95] The plentiful sources for the aristocracy and the upper gentry, combined with our knowledge about the nuns' identities, indicate that the seven nuns who were from the aristocracy, and the fifty-five nuns from upper gentry families, were probably the only representatives of these two elite groups in the female houses in the diocese during the period from 1350 to 1540.

Members of the lower social groups, however, are generally less visible in the available sources. Some of these families can be identified through minor office-holding, or as cadet branches of upper gentry families. But aside from wills, both the parish gentry and the yeoman farmers are largely undocumented: less, then, can be known about them. Since we can be fairly certain of the two upper social groups' members and their female relatives, and because the nature of the sources renders the lower social ranks less identifiable, the 383 nuns whose social backgrounds are less easy to identify must, therefore, have come from other social groups.

This assignment of nuns who lack positive family identifications to the lower social groups is consistent with what other historians have determined about the social status of monks.[96] John Tillotson, for example, assigns the monks of Selby Abbey and the nuns of Marrick Priory in Yorkshire to the lower ends of the social scale because of the lack of information on their families.[97] In any case, the adjustment of the figures is further supported by what some of the nuns reveal about themselves in their wills.

Seven of the nuns who died after their houses were suppressed left wills which provide some insight into their social backgrounds.[98] Five of these

95   See, for example: W. J. Blake, "Fuller's List of Norfolk Gentry," NA 32 (1961), pp. 261–91; Blomefield, An Essay, passim; A. W. Clarke and Arthur Campling, The Visitation of Norfolk Made AD 1664 . . . (Norfolk Record Society, vols. 4 and 5, 1934); Copinger, The Manors of Suffolk, passim; Corder, The Visitation of Suffolk, 1561; Basil Cozens-Hardy and Ernest Kent, The Mayors of Norwich, 1403–1835 (Norwich, 1983); G. H. Dashwood, ed., The Visitation of Norfolk in the Year 1563 (Norwich, 1878); Thomas Fuller, The History of the Worthies of England, 3 vols. (London, 1952); S. J. Gunn, Charles Brandon, Duke of Suffolk c.1483–1585 (Oxford, 1988); Le Strange, Norfolk Official Lists, passim; Diarmaid MacCulloch, Suffolk and the Tudors: Politics and Religion in an English County, 1500–1600 (Oxford, 1986); Muskett, Suffolk Manorial Families, passim; Rye, Norfolk Families, passim; Virgoe, "The Crown, Magnates," passim; Virgoe, "The Crown and Local Government," passim; and J. C. Wedgewood, History of Parliament, 1439–1509, Register (London, 1936–38), passim.

96   See: Dobson's "Recent Prosopographical Research," pp. 189–90 for the monks of Durham; and Knowles, Religious Orders, vol. 2, pp. 229–30, where he states that the majority of monks and canons were sons of burgesses, or of middle or lower ranks of rural landowners and freemen, and that no male house attempted to make itself a preserve for the sons of the aristocracy. But cf. Lepine, " 'My Beloved Sons,' " p. 103 where he states that a lack of evidence should not necessarily be taken to mean middle or lower social status.

97   Tillotson, Monastery and Society, p. 24. See also: Tillotson, Marrick Priory, p. 6, where he further cautions against assuming that the high visibility of upper status nuns means that they accurately reflect the overall female monastic population.

98   These seven nuns represent six of the eleven female houses in the diocese. Barbara

women were superiors who were clearly not from the upper end of the social scale. Their bequests were insubstantial, consisting of personal belongings – beds and bedding, and clothing, for example – and while they bequeathed a few silver spoons and a bit of money, they did not have any extra items to pass on.[99] Only one of the nuns whose will survives, Jane Drury, called herself "gentlewoman," and indeed her bequests and legatees indicate that she was from an upper gentry family. She named siblings – among them a brother who can be identified as an esquire – and left them and others a variety of goods and a considerable amount of money.[100] Barbara Jernegan, ex-nun of Campsey Ash, on the other hand, had only silver plate, a gold ring, and "things belonging to my body" to bequeath.[101] She left her few things to a Katherine Woodward, "her keeper," and to a man named Thomas Bokkyng. Unlike Jane Drury, Jernegan's bequests and legatees indicate that she was not from the upper echelon of late medieval society.

The prioresses' beneficiaries also indicate that these women were not connected to upper gentry families. Barbara Mason was the only one who mentions siblings, none of whom appear to have held high social status. Cecily Fastolf remembered two nieces, and Grace Sampson left everything she owned to the Bedingfields, the family who purchased Redlingfield, the priory over which she presided. Elizabeth Dawney left what little she had to other ex-nuns of Blackborough; likewise Ela Buttery bequeathed her personal belongings to ex-nuns of Campsey Ash. Finally, if these nuns had been drawn from upper gentry families, they would probably have returned to them after the Dissolution, as Drury and others of her rank did.[102]

The small size and relative poverty of most of the female monasteries in the

Mason was abbess of Marham; Elizabeth Dawney was prioress of Blackborough; Grace Sampson presided over Redlingfield; Ela Buttery over Campsey Ash; and Cecily Fastolf over Bungay. Jane Drury was a nun at Bruisyard, and Barbara Jermingham was with Ela Buttery at Campsey Ash.

99   Barbara Mason's will is dated 1538 and is printed in Samuel Tymms, ed., *Wills and Inventories from the Registers of the Commissary of Bury St Edmunds and the Archdeaconry* (Camden Society 49, 1850), pp. 133–35; Elizabeth Dawney's will: NRO, NCC 47 Mayett, dated 1539; Grace Sampson's will: NRO, NCC 235 Bircham, dated 1561. Ela Buttery's will: NRO, NCC 261 Hyll, dated 1546. Cecily Fastolf's will: NRO, NCC 131 Lyncolne, dated 1552.

100 NRO, NCC 93–4 Cooke, dated 1540.

101 Fitch, *Suffolk Monasteries*, vol. 1, p. 235.

102 For example, Elizabeth Throckmorton, last abbess of Denny Abbey in Cambridgeshire, returned to her family's manor in Coughton with two of her fellow ex-nuns where they continued to live a religious life: *VCH, Cambridge*, vol. 2, pp. 301–2, and *VCH, Warwicks*, vol. 3, p. 78. For other examples, see: G. A. J. Hodgett, ed., "The State of the Ex-Religious and Former Chantry Priests in the Diocese of Lincoln, 1547–1574," *Lincoln Record Society* 53 (1959), passim. And see: J. Raine, ed., *Wills and Inventories from the Archdeaconry of Richmond, 1442–1578* (Surtees Society, vol. 26, 1853), p. 191, where he reprints the will of Christianne Burghe, alias Dame Prieres, who was the last prioress of Nunkeeling. She was also from an upper gentry family to which she returned after her house was dissolved. See also Chapter 7, below.

diocese argues further for a population of nuns from the middling rather than aristocratic ranks of society. Recall that the women from elite families usually sought to enter relatively wealthy convents in other dioceses. With the exception of Bruisyard Abbey, whose affiliation with the Poor Clares and the order's ideal of poverty nevertheless attracted the majority of upper gentry nuns, most of these monasteries, while accommodating a smattering of nuns from this social group, were populated overwhelmingly by nuns from the parish gentry. The founders and locations of many of these houses with their shared architectural features of gentry manors, such as moated precincts and particular courtyard layouts, render this reading of the social composition of the convents even more persuasive.[103] The predominance of local recruits also must have enhanced the relations between the monasteries and their neighbors, as Norman Tanner concluded in his work on the male religious houses in the city of Norwich.[104]

Studies of the social origins of nuns in other dioceses suggest that the social composition and geographic backgrounds of the Norwich diocese's nuns were fairly representative of nuns elsewhere.[105] Both Liveing and Chettle, for example, described the young women who entered Romsey and Barking Abbeys as county "gentle folk," and "tradesmen's daughters," suggesting middling status for the nuns of these houses.[106] The nuns of Cannington Priory in the county of Somerset also hailed from local gentry families.[107] Catherine Paxton identified a similar pattern among the nuns who populated the female houses in and around the city of London: the convents housed very few aristocratic nuns, more upper gentry ones, but mostly nuns from urban families, indicating a geographic pattern of recruitment there as well.[108] Yvonne Parrey has also recently questioned the assumption that the nuns at Amesbury Abbey, a large Benedictine house, were from aristocratic families.[109] As Barbara Harris recently found, the daughters of the English aristocracy preferred marriage over monastery.[110]

---

[103] Above, Chapter 1, p. 12.

[104] Tanner, The Church of Late Medieval Norwich, pp. 119–20. Tanner analyzed the testamentary bequests made to the diocese's religious institutions by Norwich city residents, focusing almost exclusively on bequests made to local male houses. But as Chapter 6 of this study shows the same pattern of local patronage is evident for the diocese's female houses as well.

[105] Bourdillon, The Minoresses, pp. 51–3 says Denny Abbey accommodated both aristocratic and poor sisters.

[106] Liveing, The Records of Romsey, p. 113; Loftus and Chettle, A History of Barking, p. 54. Chettle says that in the abbey's early years recruits were from the nobility, but that by the early fourteenth century the nuns were mostly from rising urban families; see also: Tillotson, Marrick Priory, p. 6.

[107] VCH, Somerset, vol. 2, p. 109.

[108] Paxton, Catherine, "The Nunneries of London and Its Environs in the Later Middle Ages," D.Phil. thesis, Lincoln College, Oxford, 1992), pp. 18–33.

[109] Parrey, "Devoted Disciples," p. 248.

[110] Barbara J. Harris, "A New Look at the Reformation: Aristocratic Women and Nunneries, 1450–1540," Journal of British Studies 32 (1993), pp. 89–113.

While geographic location and, to a lesser degree, a house's wealth influenced a woman's decision about which monastery to enter, it appears that kinship ties did not.[111] At least twenty-two Norwich nuns had female relatives who were also nuns, but only seven of them joined a convent where female relatives were already professed.[112] Far more frequently, family members entered different monasteries: the Todenham sisters Joan and Margery were nuns, Joan at Shouldham Priory, and Margery at Carrow.[113] And often women from the same families joined houses in different counties. Ellen Mortimer, for example, was a nun at Bruisyard in 1452; her relative, Isabel Asgar, was a nun at Denny in Cambridge.[114] Similarly, Anne Heveningham, a Bruisyard nun, had a sister, Katherine, at Barking in Essex.[115]

Daily Religious Life

What is known about nuns' daily activities comes mostly from prescriptive literature, rules of orders and episcopal injunctions. They detail a life focused on the set hours of communal prayer – the Divine Offices – and private reading and prayer, punctuated by eight hours of sleep, and three meals: bread and ale after Prime, a more substantial midday meal, and a final light supper after Vespers, around 5 or 6 p.m.[116] Silence was to be maintained throughout, except for weekly chapter meetings, mealtime readings, and certain recreational

---

111 Power, *Medieval English Nunneries*, pp. 25ff for her discussion of kinship as a significant factor in determining the religious community a woman chose to enter.
112 Katherine Beauchamp's great aunts were nuns at Shouldham, though they were there in 1335, and Katherine arrived about twenty years later. Dorothy Calthorp's paternal aunt was a nun at Bruisyard at the same time Dorothy was there. Margery and Elizabeth Cobbe, aunt and niece respectively, were nuns at Blackborough in the late fifteenth century. Alice Corbet and her niece Phillipa were nuns at Campsey Ash. Finally, Alice Hetherset and her niece Agnes were nuns at Carrow. For the Beauchamps, see: Dugdale, *Baronage*, vol. 1, p. 226; for the Calthorps: Rye, *Norfolk Visitations*, p. 64; for the Cobbes see the will of William Cobbe, of Sandringham: PRO, PCC Prob 11/10/4; for the Corbets, see Guy Corbet's will: NRO, NCC 130 Surflete; for the Hethersets, see: Norris, *A Collection of Pedigrees*, p. 605. There are ten more nuns who share common surnames, but for whom direct links cannot be established. Elizabeth Willoughby, for example, was a nun at Campsey in 1498. See: PRO, PCC Prob 11/11/35. In the same will a Jane Willoughby is named as a nun at Bruisyard. While they were probably related, there is no evidence to indicate how. The nuns with shared surnames do not include references to Norfolk or Suffolk nuns from wills and pedigrees who share surnames, but whose convents are unknown. A significant number of nuns also had brothers who were monks. The nuns with identifiable relatives, and those who share common surnames but for whom direct familial links cannot be established, are listed in Appendix 3.
113 Norris, *A Collection of Pedigrees*, p. 1125.
114 See the will of Robert Blickling: NRO, NCC 130 Alyn. He refers to Ellen Mortimer as his kinswoman; Isabel Asgar was his niece.
115 See the will of Margaret de la Pole: PRO, PCC Prob 11/6/12. Anne was Margaret's sister and Katherine was her niece.
116 Cardinal Gasquet, ed., *The Rule of St Benedict* (New York, 1966), esp. pp. 36–51.

purposes.[117] A books of saints' lives which belonged to the nuns of Campsey Ash bears an inscription, in fact, that says the book is for reading at meal-times.[118]

In addition to the services of the canonical hours, the nuns also confessed once every two weeks, received communion every first Sunday of the month and on important saints' feasts days, and heard two masses a day.[119] Though most monastic orders followed the Roman mass rite, the Benedictine and Austin Orders were allowed to chose another liturgy for the mass.[120] In England this freedom found expression in the development of four indigenous mass liturgies or uses: the Use of Sarum, the Use of York, and the Uses of Hereford and Lincoln, all slight variations of the Roman mass. Most of the English monasteries adopted the highly ritualized Sarum use; the nuns at Redlingfield obtained papal permission in 1452 to adopt this rite because their regular mass books were irreparably damaged, and because it was a rite with which they were already familiar.[121] It differed from other uses in the color sequences of the liturgical seasons, in the placement and recitation of certain prayers, and in its greater number of celebrants for the mass.

At mass and on feast days nuns – and monks and canons – heard sermons whose topics extolled the virtues of purity, holiness, and humility, and which usually drew on contemporary life for their exposition.[122] These homilies were delivered in English or French by a house's superior, a visiting scholar, or an itinerant preacher – usually a friar.[123] The account of Catherine Segrine, cellarer at Carrow Priory, noted that 20d was paid to the "fratri facienti sermonem" on Rogation Monday in September 1503.[124] Not many sermons for nuns have survived, but among those that have is a Middle English prose sermon, part of a fifteenth-century collection of devotional materials, which was delivered to the nuns at Carrow.[125]

---

[117] Aungier, The History of Syon, pp. 405–9 for a description of the sign language which was to be used at mealtime at Syon; Power, Medieval English Nunneries, p. 286.

[118] It is BL Add. 70513, formerly BL Loan Ms. 29/61: see Neil R. Ker, Medieval Libraries of Great Britain: A List of Surviving Books, 2nd ed. (London, 1964), p. 28. For more about this manuscript see below, pp. 66–7. For a reader's duties, see: John Henry Blunt, ed., Myroure of Oure Lady (EETS, extra series 19, 1873), p. xxxiii.

[119] Ibid.

[120] Archdale A. King, Liturgies of the Past (Wisconson, 1959), pp. 276–374.

[121] J. A. Twemlow, ed., Calendar of Entries in the Papal Registers relating to Great Britain and Ireland: Papal Letters (London, 1915), vol. 10, p. 590. Interestingly, many of the most complete extant manuscripts of the Sarum rite come from the diocese of Norwich: King, Liturgies of the Past, p. 310.

[122] G. R. Owst, Literature and Pulpit in Medieval England (New York, 1961), p. 29; and his Preaching in Medieval England (New York, 1965), pp. 144, 259.

[123] Ibid., pp. 4, 149, 259. See also: Antonia Gransden, ed., The Customary of the Benedictine Abbey of Bury St Edmunds in Suffolk (London: Henry Bradshaw Society, vol. 99, 1973), p. xvii where she reports that sermons preached there were in English and French, "for the better edification of the monks."

[124] NRO, Hare 5954 227x1.

[125] It is Cambridge University Library Ms. Hh.1.11; Veronica O'Mara, A Study and Edition

This sermon was for the feast of the Assumption of the Blessed Virgin Mary and was given to the nuns at Carrow.[126] The first section deals with God's choice of Mary as mother of His Son, emphasizing her purity of spirit, a trait which removed her entirely from the realm of both human and angelic creatures. A description follows of how the apostles and others were led to her sepulchre after her death and witnessed that her body, "raised again of our Lord, her son, to everlasting life all alive with her soul, honorably was to heaven assumed."[127]

The "seven dignities" of the Virgin Mother follow, with a detailed description of a nun's habit, specific parts of which were used as metaphors for specific religious qualities or virtues which a nun should ever strive to obtain. Her smock was contrition and confession; her kirtle, trust in God, with one sleeve signifying righteousness, the other mercy. A nun's two boots were two desires: her will to amend her sinful ways, and her will to do good deeds and abstain from evil. Her girdle represented restraint from her own will in order to do God's; the knives which hung from the girdle acted as reminders of the perpetual joy which would lead her to love of God and hatred of sin. Her surplice signified knowledge of God, revealing what she owed Him, her sisters, and the world. Her mantle was faith:

> . . . just as your mantle covers all other clothing and under garments, so in the same way will you understand all things by faith. The seams of the mantle are tokens of Christ, your spouse's charity, how in His charity he created you, redeemed and nourishes you and endows you with the Holy Ghost for salvation.[128]

A final admonition to meditate continually on these symbols and the ideas they represented and to pray to the Blessed Virgin for further edification and redemption – one of the most popular devotional themes of the later Middle Ages – closes this homily.

The nuns in the diocese also probably heard as regular fare a set of sermons now known as the Northern Homily Cycle, which included a different sermon for every Sunday and feast day from Advent through Lent.[129] A collection of

---

of Middle English Sermons (Leeds Texts and Monographs, 1987), pp. 141–223 includes an edition of this sermon with textual and explanatory notes. Citations from the sermon are from her edition; translations of sections of the sermon here are mine. See also: Alexandra Barrett, "The Revelations of Saint Elizabeth of Hungary: Problems of Attribution," *The Library*, 6th ser. 14 (1992), p. 3.

126 O'Mara's argument for Carrow as the place where this sermon was delivered, and provenance for this booklet of devotional prose, is more convincing than earlier commentators who suggested Bruisyard Abbey as the likely home of this manuscript: see *A Study and Edition*, pp. 164–72.

127 Ibid., pp. 197–99.

128 Ibid., pp. 199–203.

129 The Northern Homily Cycle is one of the better known sermon cycles in late medieval England: G. H. Gerould, *North-English Homily Collection* (Oxford, 1902), pp. 5–6; and John Small, *English Metrical Homilies from the Manuscripts of the Fourteenth Century*

rhyming sermons, this cycle is in an English east-midland dialect interspersed with French and Latin phrases, illustrated by a scriptural narrative, a legend from a saint's life, or a popular tale. The cycle begins with the New Testament story of Mary Magdalene.[130] Other tales include one which describes the public shaming and divine retribution of an archbishop who uses his authority over a convent of nuns to rape one of the sisters there.[131] Many of the stories feature the intercessory powers of the Virgin Mary, as in the tale of the monk who returned from the dead.[132] And most of the tales warn about the ever-present dangers of the devil who tricks the unwary.[133]

Communal and Individual Reading

Communal services and private reading of devotional piety or religious instruction formed the greatest part of a nun's daily life, and these exercises required books.[134] The issue of nuns' abilities to read in the later Middle Ages is a hotly debated topic. Were they illiterate, unable to read in any language? Or were they literate but not Latinate: able to read and understand some English or French but not Latin?[135] Both corporate collections and also books belonging

---

(Edinburgh, 1862), p. ii. The known manuscripts are described and collated by Gerould in his *North-English Homily Collection*, and until recently, his list was considered complete. One known manuscript remained missing: Maryanne Corbett, "An East Midland Revision of the 'Northern Homily Cycle'," *Manuscripta* 26 (1982), pp. 100–7; and Thomas Heffernan, "The Rediscovery of the Bute Manuscript of the 'Northern Homily Cycle'," *Scriptorium* 36 (1982), pp. 118–29 identified the missing piece. I am grateful to Bill Stoneman for these references. The Bute manuscript is described in: N. R. Ker, *Medieval Manuscripts in British Libraries; Supplement to the Second Edition*, ed. Andrew G. Watson (London, 1987), p. 15: Watson identified from a partially erased inscription which was visible only under ultra-violet light that this manuscript, which is in the CUL, Add. Ms. 8335, belonged to the Cambridgeshire house of Poor Clares, Denny Abbey. I suggest that the nuns in the diocese of Norwich may have heard this cycle because of the provenance of this manuscript – which was relatively close to the female houses in Suffolk and Norfolk – and because of the prevalence of this cycle in the northern and eastern parts of England. The few printed sections of the sermons only partially match what CUL, Add. Ms. 8335 contains. Citations given here are from the CUL manuscript.

130 CUL, Add. Ms. 8335, fols. 1–2.
131 Ibid., fols. 37–47.
132 Ibid., fols. 13–18.
133 See the tale about St Martin: ibid., fols. 34–37; and the story about the devil who disguises himself as a monk-physician: ibid., fols. 45–47.
134 A. I. Doyle, "Publication by Members of the Religious Orders," in *Book Production and Publishing in Britain 1375–1475*, ed. Jeremy Griffiths and Derek Pearsall (Cambridge, 1989), p. 109; Power, *Medieval English Nunneries*, p. 287.
135 Those who hold that nuns were for the most part illiterate: Baskerville, *English Monks and the Suppression*, p. 208; Power, *Medieval English Nunneries*, pp. 246–60, 277. For literate but not latinate, see: Alexandra Barrett, "Introduction," in *Women's Writing in Middle English*, ed. Alexandra Barrett (New York, 1992), p. 3; Jo Ann Hoeppner Moran,

to individual nuns in the diocese indicate that at least some, and probably most, could read some English and French, and perhaps a little Latin.[136]

Evident throughout this later medieval period are corporate female monastic collections comprised of both well-used and valuable books. Numerous books at Thetford and Campsey Ash Priories were repaired, often at great expense, and those which belonged to Blackborough Priory were worth enough to attract the attention of the monks at Norwich Cathedral Priory who purchased them after the convent's suppression.[137] Redlingfield and Marham also owned small collections of books.[138]

These collections included three types of works: service books, books of biblical material, and texts of contemplative literature. Service books – missals, antiphons, and psalters – were important parts of these corporate collections because they were used daily by the nuns in the recitation of the Divine Office, as well as in other liturgical celebrations. These books were among the most expensive in the Middle Ages; in 1425, for example, the nuns at Crabhouse spent 26 marks for two antiphons.[139] Psalters, which comprised the Book of Psalms, and usually a calendar of saints' days, and the obits of superiors and benefactors, survive from several of the diocese's houses. Two psalters survive from Campsey Ash, and three remain from Carrow, one of which is highly illuminated.[140]

"Literacy and Education in Northern England, 1350–1550. A Methodological Inquiry," *Northern History* 17 (1981), p. 5. One of the traditional ways historians have determined medieval English nuns' inabilities to read Latin has been to cite the necessity of translating episcopal injunctions into English or French because the nuns could not otherwise understand them. The diocese of Norwich's nuns seem to have understood some Latin because the bishops' injunctions to them were in that language. There is no evidence that the visitation findings were translated into English or French except for an editor's comment in the VCH, *Suffolk*, vol. 2, p. 83, that the 1472 visitation was translated for the nuns at Redlingfield; Thompson, *Visitations of Religious Houses*, vol. 3, p. 417 where the visitation and injunctions are printed in Latin, and there is no indication that they were translated. Thompson says that problems arising from nuns' inabilities to understand Latin were handled after the visitation of a house was completed by one of the bishop's agents, though he offers no evidence for this statement.

136 Scholars believe that literacy can be determined by a number of factors, primary among which is bookownership: Moran, "Literacy and Education," p. 1.

137 For Campsey Ash see: Jessopp, *Visitations*, pp. 219–20; and ibid., p. 155 for the 1514 visit of Thetford. In both cases the bishop tells the prioresses to repair the books. For the sale of the Blackborough books: NRO, DCN 29/3, 136v I am grateful to Barbara Dodwell for informing me about this reference and to Paul Rutlege for helping to locate it.

138 E. C. Walcott-Mackenzie, "Inventories and Valuations of Religious Houses at the Time of the Dissolution," *Archaeologia* 43 (1871), p. 245 for the service books purchased by Sir Edmund Bedingfield who bought Redlingfield; and VCH, *Norfolk*, vol. 2, p. 370 for the same type of books at Marham.

139 H. E. Bell, "The Price of Books in Medieval England," *The Library* 4th ser. 17 (1937), pp. 320, 322, 328; Blomefield, *An Essay*, vol. 9, p. 173.

140 Ker, *Medieval Libraries*, pp. 14, 28. One of the Campsey Ash psalters is either twelfth-

This very decorated psalter belonged to the nuns at Carrow in the mid-thirteenth century and is distinguished by its elaborately historiated initials, its exquisite decorated borders and marginalia composed of animal and human figures, as well as various plant formations.[141] The initial B, for example, is made up of six scenes from the legend of St Olaf; other miniatures include a full page portrayal of an angel giving Adam a spade and Eve a distaff. These miniatures and decorations were precursors of the fourteenth-century East Anglia School which was centered in the city of Norwich, close to where Carrow was located.[142]

Besides containing other unusual elements, including a depiction of the martyrdom of Thomas Becket, the psalter is one of only twelve thirteenth-century sources of the prayers and devotional services of the Offices of the Virgin: as Carrow was dedicated to the Virgin Mary, these services and prayers were very appropriately included in one of the priory's prayer books.[143] These twelve manuscripts make it clear that from the thirteenth century the Hours of the Virgin were read in Latin, not in the vernacular.[144]

While prayer books were crucial to the nuns' lives for readings in chapter and church, as well as for their private meditations, some of these monastic collections also included non-service books, like bibles and tracts of devotional literature. At least two convents had biblical material: Flixton Priory had a French copy of the Old Testament and Thetford had an English translation of the New Testament.[145] The existence of this material places Thetford with Barking and Syon as being among the only English female religious houses known to have owned any vernacular gospel books or bibles at this time.[146]

Both Bruisyard and Campsey Ash owned copies of contemplative literature, including French and English compilations of biblical material – like lives of

---

or thirteenth-century, the other fourteenth-century; two of the Carrow psalters are also fourteenth-century; one is mid-thirteenth-century.

[141] This psalter is in Baltimore, Maryland at the Walters Art Gallery, Walters Gallery W 34 and has been described in: M. R. James, A Descriptive Catalogue of the Second Series of Fifty Manuscripts (nos. 51–100) in the Collection of Henry Yates Thompson (Cambridge, 1902), pp. 2–11; and Nigel Morgan, Early Gothic Manuscripts (II), 1250–85 (London, 1988), pp. 88–90.

[142] David Diringer, The Illuminated Book: Its History and Production (London, 1958), pp. 262, 275.

[143] For Carrow's dedication: Rye and Tillett, "Carrow Abbey," p. 466; Nigel Morgan, "Texts and Images of Marian Devotion in Thirteenth-Century England," in England in the Thirteenth Century: Proceedings of the 1989 Harlaxton Symposium, ed. W. M. Ormrod (Woodbridge, 1991), pp. 72–4.

[144] Ibid., p. 81.

[145] The French translation was of Genesis through Job; see Ker, Medieval Libraries, 2nd ed., p. 87; it was given to the nuns of Flixton by Thomas Croftys in 1442. For the New Testament at Thetford, see ibid., p. 189; it has two dates inscribed, 1492 and 1514. The other convent in the diocese of Norwich to possess a bible was Blackborough; see below, p. 102.

[146] Margaret Deanesly, The Lollard Bible and Other Medieval Biblical Versions (Cambridge, 1920), pp. 335–36, 342 thought that only Barking and Syon had such manuscripts.

saints and *The Legenda Aurea*, a Life of Christ mixed with other biblical matter
– as well as texts of instructions for good living.[147] The nuns of Thetford, for
example, owned an English copy of *The Revelations of St Bridget*, and at
Shouldham the nuns possessed a copy of Pierre de Packham's *Lumiere as Lais*.[148]

Possession of several books, including bibles as well as works of religious
instruction and contemplation, indicates that at least two of the diocese's
houses – and probably more – maintained libraries.[149] Libraries at Campsey
Ash and Carrow are evidenced by the French and Latin *ex libris* inscription
with which each house marked their books.[150] Formal collections at these two
priories perhaps reflect Campsey Ash's relative wealth, and Carrow's proximity
to – perhaps involvement with or accommodation of – the East Anglian
School, the style of which reflected that of the illuminations in Carrow's
thirteenth-century psalter.[151]

While the existence of a library does not necessarily mean that individual
nuns read – though libraries at Bruisyard, Campsey Ash, and Carrow certainly
suggest a readership of more than one – private ownership of books by
individuals indicates that some of the nuns could read. To a certain extent, the
types of books individual nuns owned reflected those in their monasteries'
greater collections. Prayer books included a fifteenth-century psalter, possibly

---

147 The nuns at Campsey Ash, for example, owned the French collection of saints' lives
   mentioned above, p. 88: Ker, *Medieval Libraries*, 2nd ed., p. 28. David N. Bell, *What
   Nuns Read: Books and Libraries in Medieval English Nunneries*, Cistercian Studies, series
   158 (Michigan, 1995), pp. 124–25. For texts at both Bruisyard and Campsey Ash, see:
   M. Dominica Legge, *Anglo-Norman in the Cloisters. The Influence of the Orders upon
   Anglo-Norman Literature* (Edinburgh, 1950), pp. 27, 50, 113, 115; J. Wogan-Browne,
   " 'Clerc u lais, miune u dame': Women and Anglo-Norman Hagiography in the Twelfth
   and Thirteenth Centuries," in *Women and Literature in Britain, 1150–1500*, ed. Carol
   Meale (Cambridge, 1993), p. 62. F. Haslewood, "Will of Sir Walter Quyntyn, of
   Ipswich," *PSIA* 7 (1889), p. 111 for the will of Sir Walter Quyntyn who left his copy
   of the *Legenda Aurea* in 1501 to the nuns of Bruisyard.
148 Henry Harrod, "Extracts from Early Norfolk Wills," *NA* 4 (1849), p. 336 which prints
   the 1481 will of Margaret Purdens who bequeathed this book to the Thetford nuns.
   For *Lumiere as Lais* at Shouldham: Ker, *Supplement*, p. 62.
149 There is an extant account of the process by which medieval nuns borrowed books from
   their convents' libraries to read. Thomas Robert Gambrier-Parry, "Lending Books in a
   Medieval Nunnery," *Bodleian Quarterly Record* 5:55 (1927), pp. 188–89. Thomas says
   that although this particular account was composed c.1440 for the nuns at Barking
   Abbey, there are several other accounts for other female houses which are not
   accessible. He does not say where these other accounts might be or for which houses
   they existed. See also: Tolhurst, *The Ordinale*, vol. 1, pp. 67–8.
150 Formal insignia like these demonstrate the existence of a library and few female houses
   appear to have used this type of singular marking: Ker, *Medieval Libraries*, 2nd ed., p.
   xvi for the French inscription at Campsey Ash. For Carrow, see: Rye, *Carrow Abbey*,
   Appendix I, p. i, where he prints excerpts from Tanner Ms. 342, F. 149 which begins
   with a Latin *ex libris* heading; Walters Art Gallery, W 34 also has one.
151 Rye, *Carrow Abbey*, p. xliv where he cites F. S. A. Phipson's speculation that either a
   library or a scriptorium was situated above the chapter house. For the original, see: R.
   M. Phipson, "Notes on Carrow Priory, Norwich," *NA* 9 (1884), pp. 215–25.

copied and embroidered by a nun at Bruisyard named Anna Felbrigge.[152] Another Bruisyard nun, Jane Blakeney, received "a white book of prayers" from Anne Lady Scrope of Harlyng.[153] John Baret of Bury St Edmunds left Joan Stanys, a nun at Campsey Ash, a book of both English and Latin devotional texts "written in pages and closed with parchment."[154] Margery Cobbe, prioress of Blackborough, owned a bible as well as a missal.[155]

Individuals also owned works of devotional literature, including Capgrave's *Life of Saint Catherine* in English and French. In 1492, Katherine Babyngton, a subprioress of Campsey Ash, had an English copy of this popular defense of virginity.[156] *The Chastising of God's Children* and Hilton's *The Scale of Perfection*, the first two books to be printed by Wynkyn de Worde, were also owned by nuns at Campsey Ash.[157] Three Bruisyard nuns also owned works of spiritual piety: Margaret Yaxle was bequeathed a copy of *The Doctrine of the Heart*;[158] Margery Bakon owned an English translation of *The Royal Book*;[159] and a copy of *The Pilgrimage of the Soul* belonged to Jane Wentworth.[160] These books, which were among the most popular devotional texts in late medieval England, differed slightly from the contemplative works found in the corporate collections. While also focusing on contemplative life, these individually-owned texts formed part of a mystical tradition which appealed especially to women.[161] *The Chastising* and *The Scale of Perfection* were, in fact, written

152 This psalter is BL, Sloane 2400. See: Bourdillon, *The Minoresses*, 79; Mirjam Foot, *Pictorial Bookbindings* (London, 1986), p. 53. This psalter has the earliest English embroidered binding; Ker, *Medieval Libraries*, p. 14. Anne's mother Katherine Felbrigge bequeathed a large grail to the parish church of St Peter Mancroft in the city of Norwich: W. H. St John Hope, "Inventories of the Parish Church of St Peter Mancroft, Norwich," *NA* 14 (1901), p. 190 providing an example of a family of female book-owners.

153 Lady Scrope's will is: *TE* 53, p. 152.

154 Tymms, *Wills and Inventories*, p. 35: his will is dated 1463.

155 Her brother, William Cobbe, bequeathed these books to her: PRO, PCC Prob 11/10/4.

156 Ker, *Medieval Libraries*, pp. 28 and 238. Clarissa Atkinson, *Mystic and Pilgrim: The Book and the World of Margery Kempe* (Ithaca, 1983), p. 183.

157 Ker, *Medieval Libraries*, pp. 28, 238. See also: Joyce Bazire and Eric Colledge, eds., *The Chastising of God's Children and the Treatises of Perfection of the Sons of God* (Oxford, 1957); and Hilary Carey, "Devout Literate Laypeople and the Pursuit of the Mixed Life in Later Medieval England," *Journal of Religious History* 14 (1987), p. 376.

158 Harrod, "Extracts," p. 336, again by Margaret Purdens. Sister Mary Patrick Candon, R.S.M., "The Doctrine of the Herte," (Ph.D. thesis, Fordham University, 1963). Thanks to Mary Erler for this reference.

159 Ker, *Medieval Libraries*, pp. 14 and 232; Robert Raymo, "Works of Religious and Philosophical Instruction," in *A Manual of the Writings in Middle English*, vol. 7, ed. Albert E. Hartung (Connecticut, 1986), pp. 2475–477.

160 It is Cambridge, Gonville and Caius MS 124/61: Rosemary McGerr, ed., *"The Pilgrimage of the Soul." A Critical Edition of the Middle English Dream Vision* (New York, 1990).

161 Carey, "Devout Literate Laypeople," pp. 370–71; Margaret Deanesly, "Vernacular Books in England in the Fourteenth and Fifteenth Centuries," *Modern Language Review* 15 (1920), passim. See also Carey, ibid., p. 379 where she cites David Knowles in *The Religious Orders*, p. 221, for "his disparaging remarks on the 'contamination of mystical writing represented by Rolle, Hilton, and *The Cloud* author, by the emotional and

specifically for religious women.[162] It is not surprising then that these were the type of works owned by individual nuns in the diocese.

Donors of books to nuns frequently included specific instructions regarding ownership after the recipient's death. When William Brygham bequeathed a new psalter to Isabella Virly, a nun at Flixton, for example, he requested that after Virly's death, the psalter remain at the priory.[163] Katherine Babyngton inscribed a similar request when she gave her fellow nuns at Campsey Ash her copy of The Life of Saint Catherine, which also contained two poems for Easter and a poem in praise of the mass, John Lydgate's "Interpretacio misse."[164] And Elizabeth Willoughby passed on to her friend and fellow nun, Katherine Symond, her copies of The Chastising of God's Children and The Scale of Perfection, with instructions that both books stay at Campsey Ash after Symond's death.[165]

Provisions like these indicate a wider reading audience than the individual nuns to whom the bequests were made. The nuns in the diocese were more than simply passive recipients of books, as a bequest of Reginald Rous of Dennington to the nuns of Campsey Ash makes clear: he willed them "the three best french books which belong to me which they have in custody . . . "; and he requested that they return to his son the fourth book, which was also already in their possession.[166] A similar bequest was made to the nuns of Shouldham by Elizabeth Fincham who requested that all of her books be divided between her daughter Elizabeth and her fellow nuns, and Elizabeth's brother Simon.[167] Such bequests and provisions indicate an active group of readers who not only traded books with each other but also with local people whose comments signal a public perception of nuns as readers: if the nuns could not read, it seems unlikely that people would have given them books in the first place.

The texts owned collectively by the convents and by individual nuns mirror the collections of secular women who were transmitters and patrons of a specific lay piety.[168] As owners of such texts, the nuns were part of a growing

---

idiosyncratic behavior ranging from visions to tears and exclamations, of the ecstatic tradition,' a tradition he identifies with certain female saints, Ruysboeck (upon whose work The Chastising was based), and Suso."

162 Bazire and Colledge, The Chastising of God's Children, p. 41; Carey, "Devout and Literate Laypeople," p. 376; Atkinson, Mystic and Pilgrim, p. 183.

163 NRO, NCC 74 Hubert, will dated 1473.

164 Ker, Medieval Libraries, pp. 28, 238.

165 Ibid.

166 Fitch, Suffolk Monasteries, p. 21.

167 PRO, PCC Prob 11/22/33. The bronze lifting-tool used for turning pages or gold leaf found among the ruins of Shouldham further suggests an active readership: Gilchrist and Oliva, Religious Women, p. 87.

168 Susan Groag Bell, "Medieval Women Book Owners: Arbiters of Lay Piety and Ambassadors of Culture," in Women and Power in the Middle Ages, ed. Mary Erler and Maryanne Kowaleski (Athens, 1988), pp. 149–87. See also: Julia Boffey, "Women Authors and Women's Literacy in Fourteenth- and Fifteenth-century England," in Women and

number of female bookowners who often passed their books on to other women in their families – in the case of these convents, to other nuns.[169] They complemented their secular sisters then in the development and spread of vernacular literature by encouraging English translations of prayer books and saints' lives.[170] What is perhaps most interesting about book-ownership among these nuns is that the majority of them came from parish gentry families. That a significant number of women from the middle ranks of medieval society were able to read supports the work of several historians who identify a trend in this later period of increasing literacy among people of middling social status.[171]

The level of reading and the degree of intellectual activity they signal is perhaps best reflected in the activities of Anne, Lady Scrope, of Harling. She was one of many who bequeathed books to nuns in the diocese, and her piety and interest in reading and learning are well known; not only did she leave books to houses of religious women, but she also refounded a secular college in Norfolk into a grammar school.[172] In addition to her book bequests, however, Lady Scrope was a lay sister at eight female houses in the country: Blackborough, Bruisyard, Campsey Ash, Carrow, Marham, Redlingfield, Shouldham, and Syon; she also called herself kinswoman to the prioresses of Crabhouse, Redlingfield, and Shouldham.[173] Her association with Syon is understandable; the abbey's literary activities were – and still are – widely recognized, and its reputation would have attracted the attention and patronage of someone with Lady Scrope's interests. Her association with the houses in the diocese of Norwich, however, is more puzzling. Geographic proximity might partly ex-

---

Literature in Britain, 1150–1500, ed. Carol Meale (Cambridge, 1993), pp. 159–82; Felicity Riddy, " 'Women Talking about the Things of God': a Late Medieval Sub-Culture," op. cit., pp. 104–27; Vincent Gillespie, "Vernacular Books of Religion," in Book Production and Publishing in Britain, 1375–1475, p. 321; and Wogan-Browne, "Saints' Lives and the Female Reader," pp. 314–32.

169   P. J. P. Goldberg, "Lay Book Ownership in Late Medieval York: The Evidence of Wills," The Library 6th ser. 16:3 (1994), pp. 186–87, 189; Tanner, The Church in Late Medieval Norwich, p. 112 noticed a similar pattern among female testators.

170   Bell, "Medieval Women Book Owners," p. 151. See also: Rosalind Hackett, "Women in African Religions," in Religion and Women, ed. Arvind Sharma (New York, 1994), p. 92 for the changes African women have made to west African Islam through their encouragement of the use of vernacular languages.

171   J. W. Adamson, "The Extent of Literacy in England in the Fifteenth and Sixteenth Centuries," The Library 4th ser. 10 (1929–30), pp. 163–95; H. S. Bennett, "The Production and Dissemination of Vernacular Manuscripts in the Fifteenth Century," The Library 5th ser. 1 (1947), pp. 167–78; especially p. 169; William Courtney, Schools and Scholars in Fourteenth-Century England (New Jersey, 1987), p. 13; Carol Meale, "Patrons, Buyers, and Owners: Book Production and Social Status," in Book Production and Publishing in Britain, p. 217; Jo Ann Hoeppner Moran, The Growth of English Schooling, 1350–1548 (New Jersey, 1985), p. 164. See also her article: "Literacy and Education," pp. 6–7; and Owst, Literature and Pulpit, p. 8.

172   Harris, "A New Look at the Reformation," pp. 101–02.

173   Her will is: TE, vol. 4, pp. 149–54; and see Douglas I. Sugano, "Apologies for the Magdalene: Devotion, Iconoclasm, and the N-Town Plays," Research Opportunities in Renaissance Drama 33 (1994), pp. 172–73.

plain her connection to these small houses, but it is difficult not to wonder if her affiliations did not also signify a recognition of a high level of literacy among the nuns there.

Nuns elsewhere in England could also read English and French and understand Latin as well, as demonstrated by the books they owned, the depiction on both corporate and individual nuns' seals of nuns reading or holding books, and references to them in episcopal visitation records.[174] A sixteenth-century abbess's seal from the Minories in London shows a standing female figure holding a pair of pincers in her right hand, and a book in her left.[175] In 1404, Alice Henly, prioress of Godstow, compiled and annotated her house's Latin cartulary, and the nuns there were enjoined by Bishop Grey to read good books if they were unable to attend matins.[176] David Bell's recent book, *What Nuns Read: Books and Libraries in Medieval English Nunneries*, represents a step forward in recovering the books and manuscripts Godstow and other convents owned.

Perhaps, however, the biggest barrier to this line of inquiry in the past has been the equation of literacy with the ability to read Latin, something which has been applied to female monastics, but not to their male counterparts. While the decline of Latin learning has been cited as an example of decay in male religious institutional life in the late Middle Ages, it has never been suggested that the increasing disuse of Latin among monks, canons, and friars signaled an illiterate clergy.[177] Nuns' abilities to read therefore have been judged by a male monastic standard, one which even they had trouble living up to in this later medieval period.

Writing skills are usually also considered a component of literacy, and one which late medieval nuns rarely acquired.[178] But at least some of the diocese's nuns could write: recall Anne Felbrigge who possibly copied her own psalter, and Katherine Babyngton and Elizabeth Willoughby, the nuns at Campsey Ash who copied poems and inscribed their books. In addition to these, other nuns signed their names to various documents and wrote letters.[179] All of the

---

174 Among the numerous houses whose seals portray a nun holding a book or reading: Coldicott, *Hampshire Nunneries*, pp. 72–3 (Winchester St Mary's); *VCH, Kent*, vol. 2, p. 190 (Dartford), ibid., p. 150 (Minster Sheppy); *VCH, Wiltshire*, vol. 3, p. 242 (Wilton); *VCH, Cambridge*, vol. 2, pp. 219, 222–23 (St Radegund and Chatteris); *VCH, Oxford*, vol. 2, p. 79 (Studley); and *VCH, Yorkshire*, vol. 3, p. 129 (Yedingham), ibid., p. 131 (St Clements), ibid., p. 174 (Nunappleton), ibid., p. 182 (Swine). These include both corporate and individual nuns' seals and are dated from the twelfth through the sixteenth centuries.

175 *VCH, London*, vol. 1, p. 519.

176 Andrew Clark, ed., *The English Register of Godstow Nunnery* (EETS, o.s. 1905), pp. xviii–xix, lxxxiv.

177 For example, see: Baskerville, *English Monks and the Suppression of the Monasteries*, passim; Evennett, "The Last Stages of Monasticism," passim; Knowles, *The Religious Orders in England*, vol. 3, passim.

178 Power, *Medieval English Nunneries*, pp. 245–46, 260

179 While most scholars see the ability to sign one's name as evidence of the ability to write, not all do: Rosemary O'Day, *Education and Society, 1500–1800* (London, 1982), pp. 14–15.

Shouldham nuns, for example, signed the papers which closed their priory.[180] The superiors of Blackborough, Bruisyard, Marham, and Redlingfield compiled and signed the lists of their convents' furnishings when they were dissolved.[181] Mary Page, last abbess of Bruisyard, wrote a letter to Henry VIII and his ministers asking them to spare her abbey from suppression.[182] And finally, we know that at least two nuns could both write and read: Isabella Norwich and Bridget Coket ran a school together in Dunwich after their convent, Campsey Ash, was closed down.[183] Surely if they could teach others to read and write, they must have been able to do so themselves.[184]

Quality of Life

Corporate and individual bookownership and writing skills indicate a group of devout and prayerful women involved in some intellectual activities, but their degree of success in leading lives according to monastic ideals is not always easy to discern.[185] While most of the nuns in the diocese appear to have regularly and correctly observed the Daily Office and lived monastic life according to custom, a few nuns had difficulties. In 1427, Isabel Hermyte, prioress of Redlingfield, was banished for life to Wix Priory – a female house in Essex – for flagrantly ignoring earlier injunctions that she go to confession and celebrate Sundays and other feast days properly.[186] She was also found guilty of allowing one of the novices to sleep in her private chamber.[187] Nearly a century later, a nun at Crabhouse was punished for having borne a child; she had to take the lowest seat at table for a month.[188]

Subsequent episcopal visits show that monastic life at both priories had been reformed.[189] Minor problems, however, surfaced at Carrow where disregard of certain feast days, the enactment of a game called "girl abbess," and the habit among some of the younger sisters of gossiping and singing the Divine Office

---

180 Joseph Hunter, ed., A *Catalogue of the Deeds of Surrender of Certain Abbeys: The Eighth Report of the Deputy Keeper of the Public Records* (London, 1874), p. 40.
181 PRO, SP 5/4/132 (Blackborough); PRO, SP 5/3/126–27 (Bruisyard); PRO, E 117/14/22 (Marham); and PRO, SP 5/3/131–33 (Redlingfield).
182 *Letters and Papers*, vol. ix, p. 376 no. 1094.
183 We know this from the 1541 will of Thomas Roberts, mercer of Thetford, who left a bequest to these two ex-religious who rented a room from him "where they keep school": NRO, NCC 520–521 Popy. I am grateful to Diarmaid MacCulloch for this reference.
184 For other nuns' abilities to write, see Chapter 3, pp. 99–100.
185 Parrey, " 'Devoted disciples of Christ'," passim for the nuns at Amesbury Priory in the sixteenth century who very conscientiously studied their Rule and maintained services, reflecting a high quality of religious vocations among the nuns there.
186 Thompson, *Visitations of Religious Houses*, vol. 3, p. 415.
187 Ibid., pp. 415–16.
188 Jessopp, *Visitations*, pp. 108–10 (1514).
189 Ibid., pp. 224, 297 for the two subsequent visits to Redlingfield, one in 1526, the other in 1532; ibid., p. 168 for the 1526 visitation of Crabhouse.

too quickly caused some of the older nuns there to complain.[190] These issues were addressed by Bishop Nykke who enjoined the nuns to properly observe the feast days and celebrate the Divine Office, and cease the "girl abbess" celebration.[191]

The trouble at Carrow could have resulted from its suburban location, which perhaps more easily allowed secular ways of the world to infiltrate the nuns' cloistered one. The incidences at Crabhouse and Redlingfield, however, raise serious questions about the quality of religious life at those two houses. Though the problems were isolated to particular individuals, these episodes, whatever the cause or frequency, cannot be glossed over or dismissed as unimportant.

The lapses in monastic life at Carrow, Crabhouse, and Redlingfield pale considerably, however, when compared to the scandals found in several of the male monasteries. Wymondham Priory in Norfolk, for example, was notoriously lax throughout the late fifteenth and sixteenth centuries. Not only was habitual drunkenness a problem, but so apparently were fist fights.[192] At the Cathedral Priory in Norwich, the prior dressed in a peculiar fashion, and the monks kept too many dogs, and were frequently found dancing in the guesthouse.[193] At Walsingham, things were little better. The canons hunted, hawked, and drank regularly at local alehouses, while the prior dressed as a layman, kept a jester and a lover, and stole the priory's money and jewels.[194] Smaller male houses were in similar disarray. Canons at Weybridge, Woodbridge, and Butley priories caused considerable trouble, as did some of their priors whose mistresses stole from the priories' treasuries.[195]

Infractions among the nuns, though less frequent and less chronic compared to their male counterparts, have nevertheless drawn more severe criticism.[196] A celebration identical to the "girl abbess" was regularly carried out in the male monasteries, and though episcopal and provincial authorities, as well as

[190] Ibid., pp. 208–10 for the 1526 visitation at which time complaints were made that the feasts of the Name of Jesus and of St Edward went unobserved; and ibid., pp. 273–4 for the non-observance of the feast of St Benedict; ibid., p. 208 for the "girl abbess" reference. The bishop addressed all of these infractions in his injunctions. The "girl abbess" ritual entailed the election of a novice who, with the other novices and female secular borders, spent part of a feast day – at Carrow it was Christmas – acting as the prioress and nuns. Power, *Medieval English Nunneries*, pp. 311–13 for examples of "girl abbess" feasts at other female houses.

[191] Jessopp, *Visitations*, pp. 110, 273–75.

[192] Ibid., pp. 20–3, 95–101, 161–64.

[193] Ibid., pp. 1–7, 71–8, 196–206, 262–70.

[194] Ibid., pp. 57–9, 113–22, 170–72, 252–54.

[195] Ibid., p. 129 for Weybridge; ibid., pp. 180–81 for Woodbridge; ibid., pp. 258–59 for Butley.

[196] Parrey, " 'Devoted disciples of Christ'," pp. 240–41 for another example of this double standard: she found that historians have focused on Bishop Fox's descriptions of lax discipline among nuns in the diocese of Winchester without acknowledging his more positive stance toward them; Fox thought the nuns were more easily redeemable than their male counterparts.

later historians, have excused it as a festive ritual for the monks to enjoy, critics have condemned its enactment in the female houses.[197] Denouncing abuses among the nuns while lightly dismissing similar or worse offenses occurring in the male houses describes female and male monastics in unrealistic terms, and betrays a double standard in judgement.

Most of the nuns in this later medieval period appear to have lived quiet lives of prayer and devotion to the monastic vows to which they were wed. While young and old women professed at the diocese's female monasteries, most entered a local convent at around 15 years of age and lived for at least 25 years as a nun. The monasteries do not seem to have demanded costly entry fees or dowrys, and in fact some of the convents reserved special funds for women who could not afford the basic personal items the communities required of newcomers. Though a nun's year-long novitiate was less rigorous than a monk's, canon's, or friar's, she was likely taught at least the basic skills of reading; in fact, there is a significant amount of evidence to suggest that most nuns in the diocese could read English and that some could read French and even a little Latin.

The vast majority of the nuns were parish gentry women and in their social composition and local origins, the nuns were like many of their male counterparts in the diocese who were also local recruits. The convents' local recruiting patterns reflected their economic status as relatively poor houses founded by women of middling social status whose imprint on many of the convents was evident in some shared architectural features. With few exceptions, their social composition and relative poverty did not have adverse affects on the quality of the nuns' religious lives. Their monastic vocations encompassed more, however, than hours of prayer and private meditation; the nuns also were bound to be good trustees of the property and buildings which made up their foundations. What this stewardship entailed and how well the nuns executed their duties as housewives of Christ are discussed in the next chapter.

---

[197] In the male houses this festivity took place on the eve of St Innocent's Day, December 27: Power, *Medieval English Nunneries*, pp. 312–13. There are no prohibitions in the visitations or in the provincial legislations against the "boy bishop" game. For its general acceptance in the male houses, see: Neil Mackenzie, "Boy into Bishop: A Festive Role Reversal," *History Today* 37:12 (1987), pp. 10–16.

3

The Monastic Community: Organization and Administration

Monastic precincts enclosed a complex of out-buildings – granges, stables, a bakehouse, and sheds for brewing, tools and equipment – as well as more domestic spaces: kitchens, gardens, latrines, parlors, a chapel or church, and the cloistered rooms of the religious inmates. While hired manorial officials, agricultural laborers, and domestic servants acted as the nuns' agents in the temporal world, and worked in and around the outer edges of the cloistered residence, the superior and religious inmates were ultimately the stewards of the land and properties they held.[1] For the most part, the nuns' active involvement in managing their monasteries' outlying properties is difficult to discern.[2] But in the administration of the more domestic and cloistered parts of the precincts the nuns were hands-on managers of their own extended households.

Monastic household management covered a broad range of duties: supplying the food, linens, and bedding of the nuns and their often numerous guests; caring for the conventual chapel: its vestments, books, and candles; and regulating the interactions among the nuns themselves, and between the nuns and the secular world. Any number of monastic officials, known as obedientiaries, executed these responsibilities under the leadership of the house's superior, who was ultimately responsible for her household's management.

---

1 Nichols, "History and Cartulary," p. 99 for female houses. For monastic superiors as responsible for the maintenance and even extension of their houses' initial endowments, see: David A. Postles, "Heads of Religious Houses as Administrators," in *England in the Thirteenth Century: Proceedings of the Harlaxton Symposium*, ed. W. M. Ormrod (Woodbridge, 1991), p. 47.

2 Clark, *The English Register of Godstow Nunnery*, pp. xviii–xix: Alice of Henley, prioress of Godstow commissioned a "pore brodur and welwyller" to make an English language key to the Latin cartulary she worked on so that the nuns, who were "managers of their estates" could consult their own records and make decisions about leases, etc., without having to ask an outsider. See also Paxton, "The Nunneries of London," pp. 89, 251 for examples of prioresses of St Helen's Bishopsgate and Clerkenwell as active estate managers.

How she and the other monastic officials were chosen and administered their resources and expenses reveals a great deal about the internal organization and administration of these small female monasteries.

Abbesses and Prioresses as Managers

Monastic superiors were chosen by a multi-step process. A delegation of nuns notified the appropriate ecclesiastical or secular patron of a superior's death and obtained the *congé d'élire*, a license from the Crown or local bishop to elect a new superior. The nuns then announced the feast day on which the election of a new superior would take place, allowing the appropriate authority time to mediate in the event of a corrupt or disputed election.[3] At St Radegund's in Cambridge in 1487, for example, Bishop Alcock declared the nuns unfit to elect a prioress and he appointed her himself.[4]

All of the nuns had to be present for a valid election, which proceeded by unanimous vote, by compromise, or by scrutiny.[5] Compromise and scrutiny entailed the election of a committee of senior nuns who either voted for the whole community, or polled the nuns and then voted. After a nun was elected and agreed to accept her new position as superior, the results were reported to the convent's patron for confirmation.[6] A newly elected superior then took an oath of obedience to the local authority. Upon her confirmation as prioress of Arthington, a small Cluniac house in Yorkshire, Katherine Willesthorpe vowed to:

> swere and faithfully promyttis obedience unto my most Rev'nt fader in God george be the mercy of God Tharchebisshop of York, prymate of England and legate off the courte of Rome and to all his successors lawfully enteryng and too all ye officers and mynisters in all maner of commaundmentes. So God help and thies holy Evangelistez.[7]

---

3 Bourdillon, *The Minoresses*, p. 55 for the Poor Clares; and Nichols, "The History and Cartulary," p. 83 for this procedure at Marham.

4 Arthur Gray, *The Priory of St Radegund* (Cambridge Antiquarian Society, vol. 31, 1898), pp. 42–3.

5 J. Hutchins, *History and Antiquities of Dorset*, 3rd ed. vol. 3 (London, 1861–73), pp. 29–30 for the roll call of nuns at Shaftsbury Abbey for four superiors' elections in the late fifteenth and sixteenth centuries.

6 Blunt, *Myroure of Oure Lady*, pp. xxii–xxiii; Hilda Johnstone, "The Nuns of Elstow," *Church Quarterly Review* 133:265 (1941), p. 48; Charles Spencer Perceval, "Remarks on Some Early Charters and Documents Relating to the Prior of Austin Canons and the Abbey of Austin Canonesses at Canonsleigh, in the County of Devon," *Archaeologia* 60 (1866), p. 427 for the record of the election of Alice Parker in 1470; Power, *Medieval English Nunneries*, p. 43; and also Tolhurst, *The Ordinale and Customary*, vol. 66, pp. 349–52.

7 *VCH, Yorkshire*, vol. 2, p. 189. See also Elizabeth Kylburn's oath at her confirmation as prioress of Nunburnholme in 1534 in: M. C. F. Morris, *Nunburnholme: Its History and Antiquities* (London, 1907), p. 165.

The costs of these procedures were borne by the convent. Those incurred by the 1481 election of Margaret Ratcliff at Swaffham Bulbeck, a priory similar in size and wealth to most of the female houses in the diocese of Norwich, included £1 to the official of the bishop at the installment of Dame Ratcliff; 5s to a scribe for a transcription of the decree of the election; and 1s to cover the cost of the new prioress's walk to Bury St Edmunds where she was presented to the bishop's agent.[8]

Application of these procedures varied. At Carrow, for example, papal exemption from episcopal jurisdiction in this matter meant that the priory could chose their own male authority to install a newly-elected prioress. The nuns most frequently chose the archdeacon of Norfolk, in whose archdeaconry the house was located.[9] Because the abbot of Bury St Edmunds was the patron of Thetford Priory, the subprioress requested the *congé d'élire* from him. He then confirmed the election and informed the bishop of Norwich of its results.[10] At Marham, the abbot-father, a representative of Cistercian General Chapter, oversaw and ratified the election of a new abbess there who then presented herself to the abbey's patron and afterwards to the bishop of Norwich.[11]

To accede to this highest office a nun had to meet certain qualifications: she had to be born of legally married parents, be pious, honest, and of good reputation.[12] She also had to be over twenty-one years of age, though the Cistercian order fixed the age at thirty.[13] If the community's choice was too young or illegitimate, a special dispensation was necessary for the election to be valid.[14]

A superior directed the spiritual development and welfare of her nuns and was to be to them, "like a loving mother."[15] Though little direct evidence exists of what this facet of her position entailed, it surely included seeing that all the nuns attended and participated fully in the Divine Office. She also probably suggested readings or prayers to guide and enrich individuals on their spiritual paths. She was no doubt responsible for treating all of the nuns in an equal, fair, and judicious manner, setting out by her own example how the nuns themselves should act. It also fell to her to mediate and negotiate the quarrels and conflicts which often accompanied communal living.

In addition to providing spiritual and interpersonal guidance, a superior also oversaw her priory's internal affairs and while she could assemble her commu-

---

8 Dugdale, *Monasticon*, vol. 4, p. 458.
9 Blomefield, *An Essay*, vol. 4, p. 525.
10 Ibid., vol. 2, p. 91.
11 Nichols, "The History and Cartulary," pp. 82–3.
12 Power, *Medieval English Nunneries*, p. 45 for these qualifications.
13 Nichols, "The Internal Organization," p. 25.
14 Tillotson, *Marrick Priory*, p. 5 cites an example of an illegitimate nun, Alice de Ravenswathe, a local woman of unknown heritage, who, upon being elected prioress by her sisters, obtained a dispensation from the archbishop so that she could accept the office. Her lack of social standing must have been unimportant to the nuns who wanted her to be their superior.
15 Peacock, "Injunctions of John Langland," p. 56.

nity for advice in certain matters – the acceptance of a novice, for example – all final decisions were hers to make.[16] She bore the greater burden of her monastery's operating costs, collecting or receiving the revenues necessary to execute extensive administrative tasks.[17] Superiors' accounts survive from six of the diocese's eleven female houses – one each from Campsey Ash and Redlingfield, two from Blackborough and Carrow, three from Bungay, and nine from Marham – and while clearly no match for the extensive runs of household accounts which survive for many superiors of the male monasteries, those extant for these prioresses and abbesses detail the sources and amounts of revenues, how they were collected, what they purchased, and how much the superiors spent in a year.

Most of the superiors of the diocese's female houses were direct receivers of money and goods from wide ranging sources: rents from the farms of rectories, tenements and other income-generating properties, issues of their home manors if they were not leased, and various fines and moneys from any number of other assets.

The abbess of Marham's revenues are typical of those of the superiors in other female houses: rents from meadows and pastures, money from sales of wood, hides, and dairy products, mill tithes, and perquisites of courts. The abbey's lay boarders also provided her with income.[18] In addition to collecting these revenues, the prioresses of Blackborough and Carrow also received alms from their conventual chapels or churches as well as payments from some of the convents' other officeholders. In 1461/62, for example, Alice Erle, prioress of Blackborough from 1434 to 1462, received from the priory's sacrist, Margaret Brunger, 9s 9d in alms given on the feast of St Katherine, the conventual chapel's patron saint. Erle took in another 30s in alms from Brunger over the course of the year.[19] Margaret Pygot, prioress of Carrow, collected 2s 10d from "Juliana Lampet anchorista," for baking and brewing within the monastery, providing an interesting example of the resources these women culled in order to run their households.[20]

Not all of the diocese's superiors acted as direct receivers of their operating capital. The prioress of Bungay received most of her income through the hands of the priory's bailiff, while also deriving income from property rents, tithes, boarders, and pensions from appropriated churches – like the £17 the chaplain of the parish church of St Thomas paid to her annually.[21] The bailiff customarily owed the prioress the difference between his income and his expenses,

16 Nichols, "The Cartulary and History," p. 86.
17 Nichols, "The Internal Organization," p. 30.
18 For this description of the abbess's income and expenses, see for example: NRO, Hare 2207 194x5; and Blomefield, An Essay, vol. 7, p. 375.
19 Reading, Mapledurham Archives, C3 no. 39. The Blackborough prioresses' and manorial accounts are described in: A. H. Cooke, "Five Account Rolls of Blackborough Priory," NA 22 (1926), pp. 83–5.
20 NRO, NRS 26882 42 E8, dated 1455/56.
21 SRO, HD 1538/156/6–A–D for the chaplain's accounts.

which ranged anywhere from £13 10s 1d in 1375, to £57 13s 10d in 1437/38, to £22 5s 2d in the last account of 1444.[22]

Most of these superiors' total yearly receipts were never very large and fluctuated over time: Alice Erle at Blackborough took in between £85 and £87; Bungay's prioress's income increased from £35 in 1490, to £83 in 1513, to £100 in 1529; Carrow's prioresses saw a decrease in theirs, from £133 in 1455 to £98 in 1529. The abbesses at Marham for whom the most accounts survive show a decrease in revenues also, from £125 in 1405 to £58 by the end of the century.[23] Nevertheless, these prioresses were able to stretch their relatively small annual incomes to cover numerous – and often onerous – expenses common to all land holders. In 1529/30, Isabel Wygon, prioress at Carrow, used her £98 7s 4d for, among other things, customary payments like rents for leased lands, the pensions of the vicars or priests of the convent's appropriated churches, and fines to ecclesiastical or temporal lords.[24] For the abbess of Marham, such customary payments included an annual fee to the Pope for the special patronage he showed to all Cistercian houses.[25]

Superiors usually also paid the costs of the autumn harvests: of carting and carrying corn and other stock, and of the threshing and winnowing of grain.[26] Common expenses also included those associated with the maintenance of the monastic precinct buildings and grounds. For Alice Erle at Blackborough, these entailed repairs to the dykes and walls which protected her monastery's precinct from the rising waters of the fens and marshes which characterized this western region of Norfolk.[27] The costs of ditching and hedging around the outside of the priory's walls were also paid by the prioress of Bungay.[28] The prioress of Carrow paid for general repairs to the buildings and grounds, and for any new tools or repairs to old equipment which were needed: a wheelbarrow, forks, and other items necessary for the household were among her expenses.[29] The abbess of Marham covered any repairs of the abbey's mills.[30]

This kind of maintenance typically constituted between 10 and 11 percent of Alice Erle at Blackborough's and Elizabeth Stephenson at Bungay's expenses; about 8 percent of the prioresses of Carrow's costs, and for the abbesses at Marham usually less than 5 percent. But the upkeep of grounds and buildings

---

[22] See: SRO, HD 1538/156/1, SRO, HD 1538/156/10, and SRO, HD 1538/156/13.
[23] Reading, Mapledurham Archives C nos. 3, 39, 40 (Blackborough); SRO, HD 1538/156/14, HD 1538/156/17 (Bungay); NRO, NRS 26882 42 E8, NRS 26884 42 E8 (Carrow); and NRO, Hare 2201 194x5, Hare 2204–09 194x5, and Hare 2211–2212 194x5 (Marham).
[24] NRO, NRS 26884 42 E8.
[25] NRO, Hare 2201 194x5, and Hare 2204 194x5 for example.
[26] See, for example, the Blackborough prioresses' account of 1461/62: Reading, Mapledurham Archives, C3 no. 39, and the prioress of Carrow's account: NRO, NRS 26882 42 E8, 1455/56.
[27] Reading, Mapledurham Archives, C3 no. 39 and C3 no. 40.
[28] SRO, 1538/156/14, HD 1538 156/17, HD 1538/345.
[29] NRO, NRS 26884 42 E8.
[30] NRO, Hare 2205 194x5.

could turn into major projects. At least two of the diocese's prioresses undertook extensive building works in addition to the yearly repairs their houses
required. Joan Wiggenhall, prioress of Crabhouse from 1420 to 1445, tore down
and completely rebuilt the priory's main barn in the first year of her tenure as
prioress there.[31] She used timber felled on her priory's lands and re-used roofing
tiles from the old barn. She also built an extension of her quarters within the
cloister, reconstructed the convent's dorter, and contributed 20 marks to the
renovation of the convent's half of the decayed chancel of St Peter's, Wiggenhall. Two years later, she had the priory's outer walls rebuilt and began a
three-year reconstruction of the conventual church.

Members of Wiggenhall's family financed a portion of this work, and
perhaps this support in part explains her ambitious projects. But she also must
have had the vision and courage it takes to execute plans like these, qualities
Elizabeth Stephenson, prioress at Bungay from 1487 to 1520, must also have
possessed. She commissioned the construction of a new house within the
priory's walls – called "the nonnehouse" – and oversaw major repairs to the
infirmary, as well as the rehabilitation of the church roof.[32] In addition to
non-specific repairs Stephenson made to some of her priory's other properties
– to the churches of St Mary, St John, St Margaret, St Lawrence, and the
church of Metyngham, and "for diverse repairs to the houses of the abbey" –
the costs of these building works constituted her single largest expense: £7 9d.

These are just two examples of superiors who undertook sizeable construction projects, many of which were partly funded by outside sources. The *Register
of Papal Letters* includes numerous notices of indulgences for those who aided
the nuns in the diocese with various building works and grants of appropriation
to finance them. In 1414, for example, the nuns at Bruisyard received the
appropriation of the parish church of Sitton to help them fix their refectory
and their dormitory.[33] Those who gave alms to the nuns at Flixton in 1395 for
the repair of their church received a three-year indulgence.[34] It would have
been up to these superiors at Bruisyard and Flixton – as it was up to those at
Bungay and Crabhouse – to organize and collect the money and oversee these
works. These women must also have appealed to other patrons for funds, but
the significance of the prioresses' actions here is the administrative talents they
showed in planning these projects and realizing the necessary funds. Such
foresight and aptitude – qualities typically used to define the more visible male
monastic superiors – can also easily be seen among the prioresses and abbesses
of several of the small female houses.[35]

Superiors, like Alice Lampet, prioress of Redlingfield, also paid the wages

---

[31] Joan Wiggenhall's building works are detailed in: Bateson, "The Register," pp. 57–63,
and summed up in VCH, *Norfolk*, vol. 2, pp. 408–9.
[32] SRO, HD 1538/156/17 for her rebuilding program.
[33] *Papal Letters*, vol. 6, pp. 468–69, 489.
[34] Ibid., vol. 4, p. 373.
[35] For male monastic superiors, see: Postles, "Heads of Religious Houses as Administrators,"
passim.

of various seasonal laborers and household servants.[36] The abbess of Marham typically made payments to the nuns' confessor, her own chaplain, agricultural laborers, carters and carriers, and to the abbey's bailiff and auditor.[37] Wages made up anywhere between 14 and 19 percent of a superior's yearly expenses: 14 percent at Bungay, and 18 percent at Redlingfield.[38] The costs of wages at Carrow show an increase from 12 percent of Margaret Pygot's income in 1490 to more than double that percentage in Isabel Wygon's account of 1529.[39] This increase at Carrow likely began in the late fourteenth century when wages began to rise in response to a diminished work force, and also reflected the economy of the city of Norwich by the sixteenth century, where wages for all workers were high. The abbesses at Marham paid less in wages, which declined steadily from £19 in 1426 to £12 in 1497.[40] This steady decrease reflects the nuns' estate management in this period which, like that of landholders in the rest of the country, changed from direct farming to leasing out their holdings for others to work.

Most superiors, like those at Bungay and Redlingfield, also contributed to their priories' general food costs.[41] Some superiors also covered the costs of the nuns' clothing. Abbess Joanna Narburgh, at Marham, shows in her account of 1426/27 that she owed three nuns – one of whom was lately bursar – 18s for their vestments.[42] In many female houses elsewhere in England, the nuns' clothing was handled by the chamberer, as it was at Catesby Priory and at St Mary de Pre, both houses in the diocese of Lincoln.[43] In most male houses this duty was discharged by a chamberer.[44]

In addition to contributing to their houses' general expenses, most monastic

---

36 SRO, HD 1538/327 (1447/48).
37 NRO, Hare 2204 194x5.
38 Elizabeth Stephenson paid £14 for wages in 1490 when her income totalled £35, £13 in 1513 when she took in £83: SRO HD 1538/156/14, HD 1538/345. Lampet spent £14 for wages out of an income totalling £72, SRO, HD 1538/327.
39 Margaret Pygot paid £16 in wages out of £133 in revenues in 1455; in 1529 her successor paid £21 for servants' wages out of £98 in revenues: NRO, NRS 26882 42 E8 and NRS 26884 42 E8.
40 Margery Harsyk paid £19 out of an income of £125; for Joanna Narburgh these costs declined from £16 in 1446, to £15 in 1456, to £12 in 1468 and 1470; Abbess Heyham paid the same in 1497: NRO, Hare 2201 194x5, Hare 2204 194x5, Hare 2209 194x5, and Hare 2212 194x5.
41 For Bungay see: SRO, HD 1538 156/14, and HD 1538/345; for the prioress at Redlingfield, see: SRO, HD 1538/327.
42 NRO, Hare 2205 194x5.
43 For Catesby, see: George Baker, The History and Antiquities of the County of Northamptonshire (London, 1822–30), vol. 1: p. 280; for St Mary de Pre, see: Dugdale, Monasticon, vol. 3, pp. 359–60. See also: Power, Medieval English Nunneries, p. 132.
44 R. M. Thompson, "Obedientiaries of St Edmunds Abbey," PSIA 35:2 (1982), pp. 96–7; Saunders, An Introduction, pp. 114–20; Snape, English Monastic Finances, pp. 29–31; J. R. West, St Benet of Holme, 1020–1210. Introduction Essay on the Eleventh and Twelfth-Century Sections of Cott. MS Galba Eii, The Register of the Abbey of St Benet of Holme (Norfolk Record Society Publications, 1932), vol. 3, pp. 251–52.

superiors also maintained their own households.[45] The last prioress of Campsey Ash, Ela Buttery, for example, paid "for diverse expenses of the lady's house."[46] Prioress Sara Richeres' household at Bungay included Alice, the launderer, Margaret, *ancell* or maid, Katherine Gadynegge, the prioress's butler, and Alice, *camerisse* or prioress's chamberer.[47] Alice Lampet at Redlingfield paid for her personal servants' clothing, while the prioresses at Carrow paid for expensive linen and other cloth for the liveries of their many attendants.[48]

Superiors' households contained a kitchen, distinct from the one that served the convent as a whole. Food consumed by the priories' guests was prepared in "the lady's kitchen," as it appears in the accounts, and costs thus incurred were also met by the prioresses and abbesses. While the existence of "the lady's household," personal servants, chaplains, and kitchens indicates separate households, with the exception of the prioress at Flixton none of the superiors in this diocese lived in quarters which were physically separated from the existing cloister.[49] At Crabhouse, Joan Wiggenhall's addition to the prioress's rooms in the fifteenth century was an extension of the west range.[50] A similar layout existed at Carrow: the extant west range was divided into a hall and the prioress's lodgings.[51] West ranges also served to quarter any lay visitors, the costs of whom were also borne by the prioress or abbess.[52] So while these female superiors kept separate chambers, detached lodgings, more typical of male monastic superiors, were not common among the female houses in this diocese.[53] Superiors' contiguous chambers no doubt reflected their monasteries' lesser wealth; these closer quarters must also have enabled the prioresses to identify and head off any problems among the nuns more quickly than they could have if their quarters had been far removed. Perhaps this in part explains

---

[45] Dobson, *Durham Priory*, pp. 114–23 are about the prior's household there; Power, *Medieval English Nunneries*, pp. 59–60.

[46] PRO, SC6/H8/3401.

[47] These women are paid by the cellarer in whose account their names can be found: SRO, HD 1538/156/7.

[48] For Lampet: SRO, HD 1538/327; for Carrow, see the 1455/56 account of Margaret Pygot: NRO, NRS 26882 42 E8.

[49] In 1446, Baldwin Cratyng bequeathed 40s to the fabric of the house of the prioress of Flixton: NRO, NCC 126 Wilby. In addition to the information above, inventories generated by the suppression of the monasteries in the 1530s for the female houses in the diocese do not describe detached lodgings for superiors. For Bruisyard: Francis Haselwood, "Monastery at Bruisyard," *PSIA* 7 (1889/91), pp. 321–23; for Campsey Ash: PRO, SP 5/1/130; for Carrow, Rye, *Carrow Abbey*, pp. 23–4 and PRO, SP 5/1/110; for Marham: PRO, SP 5/1/120; Redlingfield: PRO, SP 5/1/131; and Thetford: PRO, SP 5/1/119.

[50] Gilchrist and Oliva, *Religious Women*, pp. 38, 86.

[51] Ibid., pp. 38, 83–5.

[52] Ibid., pp. 36–8 for guest accommodation; SRO, HD 1538/327, Redlingfield prioresses' account for the expenses of boarding guests.

[53] For the common practice of separate households for the heads of monasteries, Gilchrist, *Gender and Material Culture*, pp. 119–20 for the rarity of detached quarters in most of the country's female houses; ibid., p. 166 for abbots' and priors' detached lodgings.

the peace which seems to characterize most of the diocese's female houses in this later medieval period.

With some minor administrative idiosyncrasies, the receipts and expenses of the female monastic superiors in the diocese of Norwich were similar to those of female houses in other parts of England, as well as to those of male monasteries in Norfolk and Suffolk.[54] Abbesses, prioresses, and their male counterparts were customarily responsible for a wide range of building repairs, wages, and certain provisions for religious inmates and guests, as well as contributing to the expenses of the rest of their convents. And while few of the superiors of any of these small female houses attained any prominence outside of their parishes or counties, most must have been very able and commanding women to operate their houses within the limits of their annual incomes.[55]

Second in importance to the superior was the subprioress, or in the case of an abbess, the prioress. In the absence of the house's superior, this second-in-command assumed full authority and was in charge of discipline.[56] On the day of her installation, she gave the convent a gift – at Barking Abbey it was a pittance of fish – and on her death-bed she gave the house a donation of money.[57]

Obedientiaries

Responsibility for the daily operations of a monastic household was divided between a superior and her subprioress, and the household officers she appointed, the obedientiaries.[58] Under a prioress's guidance, these monastic officials administered individual household departments. We know how this obedientiary system worked mostly through the numerous and often extensive collections of household officials' accounts which survive from the male houses.[59] But a sixteenth-century description of the household officers and

54 For other prioresses' accounts which show similar receipts and expenses, see: Baker, *The History and Antiquities*, vol. 1, pp. 278–83 for the 1414/15 account of Elizabeth Swynford, prioress of Catesby Priory. See also: Dugdale, *Monasticon*, vol. 3, pp. 353–61 for the account of Prioress Christiane Basset, St Mary de Pre Priory, covering two years, 1423–25; and also: Gasquet, *English Monastic Life*, pp. 158–76 for a fifteenth-century prioresses' account from Grace Dieu Priory in the diocese of Lincoln. For priors' duties in male houses in the diocese of Norwich, see: A. H. Denny, *The Sibton Abbey Estates; Selected Documents, 1325–1509* (Suffolk Record Society Publications, vol. 2, 1960), pp. 12, 33–5; Saunders, *An Introduction*, pp. 13, 137; West, *St Benet of Holme*, vol. 3, p. 247.
55 Harper-Bill, *Blythburgh Priory Cartulary*, p. 4 for similar views of the superiors of this small male house.
56 Aungier, *History of Syon*, pp. 388–90; Nichols, "The History and Cartulary," p. 88; Power, *Medieval English Nunneries*, p. 131.
57 Tolhurst, *The Ordinale and Customary*, vol. 2, pp. 358, 363.
58 Aungier, *A History of Syon*, p. 292; Nichols, "The Internal Organization," p. 30.
59 Bloom, *Liber Elemosinarii*, passim; Charles Cotton, ed., "St Austin's Abbey, Canterbury Treasurer's Accounts, 1468–9 and Others," *Archaeologia Cantiana* 51 (1940), pp. 66–103; Dobson, *Durham Priory*, pp. 66–9; C. T. Flower, "Obedientiars' Accounts of Glastonbury

their duties at Syon Abbey, the last, largest, and richest religious foundation for women, shows how nuns there managed their household.[60] Scholars also draw on a fifteenth-century description of a cellarer's duties at Barking Abbey, the large and wealthy Benedictine female house in Essex where many of the upper gentry women from Norfolk and Suffolk went to be nuns.[61] While providing a general outline of obedientiaries and their duties at either male houses or large and wealthy female ones, these sources say nothing about household organization and administration in the smaller, poorer houses of nuns like those in the diocese of Norwich.

Most of these houses had individual cellarers, treasurers, and chamberers, whose responsibilities for keeping a convent's stores of cash, fuel, food, and clothing put them among the most important officials.[62] Following these, obedientiaries ranked in importance from the second prioress, to the sacrist, almoner, infirmarer, frater, circuitrix – who guided the nuns in their daily reading – to mistress of the novices, precentrix, and succentor.[63] This hierarchy was modified in many places, suggesting that monastic households were flexible and adapted this system to suit their particular needs.

Like those who became superiors, nuns chosen for monastic office had to possess certain qualities – including honesty and industry – and be in good

---

and Other Religious Houses," *Transactions of St Paul's Ecclesiological Society* 7 (1912), pp. 50–62; Joseph Fowler, ed., *Extracts From the Account Rolls of the Abbey of Durham, 1303–1541*, 3 vols. (London, Surtees Society 99, 100, 103, 1898–1901); Joan Greatrex, ed., *Account Rolls of the Obedientiaries of Peterborough* (Northamptonshire Record Society Publications, 1984); G. W. Kitchin, ed., *Compotus Rolls of the Obedientiaries of St Swithun's Priory, Winchester* (Hampshire Record Society, 1892); R. E. G. Kirk, ed., *Accounts of the Obedientiaries of Abingdon Abbey* (Camden Society, n.s. 51, 1892); James Raine, ed., *The Durham Household Book; or the Accounts of the Bursar of the Monastery of Durham, 1530–34* (London: Surtees Society 18, 1844); Saunders, *An Introduction to Obedientiary and Manor Rolls*, passim; Joseph Stephenson, ed., *Chronicon Monasterii de Abingdon* (London: Rolls Series, 1858); Eleanor Swift, ed., *The Obedientiary Rolls of Battle Abbey* (Sussex Archaeological Collections 78, 1938); Tillotson, *Monastery and Society*, passim.

60 Blunt, *Myroure of Oure Ladye*, pp. xxv–xxxii. More recently John Nichols describes female obedientiaries in female Cistercian houses in: "The History and Cartulary," p. 88.

61 The Barking Abbey document, "The Charthe Longynge to the Office of the Celeresse of the Monasterye of Barkinge," is reprinted in: Dugdale, *Monasticon*, vol. 1, pp. 442–45. Power also discusses it: *Medieval English Nunneries*, pp. 563–68. Redstone, "Three Carrow Account Rolls," uses the Barking Abbey description in her discussion of the cellarer's duties at Carrow Priory. See also: Tolhurst, *The Ordinale and Customary*, vol. 65, pp. 55–9.

62 Aungier, *History of Syon*, pp. 391–94. At male houses, these important officers were appointed by a house's superior; but in at least one male house, Canterbury Cathedral Priory, these appointments were made by the local bishop or archbishop who chose from among a list of nominees submitted to him by the priory: Greatrex, "Prosopography of English Benedictine Cathedral Chapters," p. 23.

63 Tolhurst, *The Ordinale and Customary*, vol. 2, p. 374. See also: Kate Mertes, *The English Noble Household, 1250–1600: Good Governance and Political Rule* (New York, 1988), p. 19 for a similar hierarchy among greater and lesser officials in secular households.

standing among their fellow nuns.[64] A fifteenth-century description of the sort of nun who should be appointed hosteler – or guesthouse keeper – at St Helen's, Bishopsgate in London, suggests the ideal qualities: ". . . some sadde woman and discrete of the seyde religione, honest, welle named, be assigned to the shuttyng of the cloysters dorys, and kepyng of the keyes, that non persone could get in."[65] Good manners and comportment were especially important for obedientiaries like hostelers and porters whose interactions with secular people could influence the reputation of a house and affect the patronage of its visitors.[66] Age and experience must have also come into play when a superior chose her officers: at the convents of Poor Clares, a nun had to be professed for nine years before she could be appointed to an office; at Barking a nun could only take office after she had been professed for seven years.[67]

Once a year, usually on a Sunday in Lent, superiors reviewed the obedientiaries' performances, after which they asked forgiveness for any mistakes they might have made in the course of their duties.[68] Successful obedientiaries were re-appointed; others were replaced, like the two janitrices at Swine in Yorkshire who apparently were passing more than just food and drink through the cloister kitchen grille to the canons on the other side.[69] This process of review and appointment took place in chapter in full view of the entire community.[70] Such a public procedure no doubt guarded against favoritism; it may also have allowed the nuns to voice objections to a superior's choice if they felt so inclined.

Obedientiaries, common to all monastic households, performed functions which ensured their convents' smooth running.[71] Their roles and responsibilities must have conferred a certain amount of prestige. This prestige, as well as the work load these officials carried, was reflected in their exemptions from some of the strictures of monastic life. Obedientiaries could speak freely, read

---

64 Aungier, *History of Syon*, pp. 294–96.
65 Dugdale, *Monasticon*, vol. 4, p. 553.
66 J. W. Nicholls, *The Matter of Courtesy* (Cambridge, 1985), p. 27 where he discusses the courteous behavior monks were to show.
67 Bourdillon, *The Minoresses*, p. 75; Loftus and Chettle, *A History of Barking Abbey*, p. 55.
68 Tolhurst, *The Ordinale and Customary*, vol. 1, p. 55.
69 VCH, *Yorkshire*, vol. 3, p. 179.
70 Aungier, *History of Syon*, p. 292.
71 For other female houses, see: Aungier, *History of Syon*, pp. 359–94; Critall, "A Fragment of an Account of the Cellarer of Wilton Abbey," pp. 142–56; Flower, "Obedientiars' Accounts," p. 54; Liveing, *The Records of Romsey Abbey*, pp. 224–26, 234–35; Tolhurst, *Ordinale and Customary*, vol. 65, pp. 51, 59; VCH, *Yorkshire*, vol. 3, p. 126 for Wilberfosse. For male houses in the diocese of Norwich, see: G. A. Carthew, "A Cellarer's Account Roll of Creake Abbey, 5 and 6 Edward III," *NA* 6 (1864), pp. 314–59; and G. A. Carthew, "North Creake Abbey," *NA* 7 (1871), pp. 153–68; Christopher Cheney, "Norwich Cathedral Priory in the Fourteenth Century," *Bulletin of the John Rylands Library* 20 (1936), pp. 97–8, 103; Denny, *The Sibton Abbey Estates*, passim; Howlett, "Account Rolls of Certain Obedientiaries," passim; Lilian Redstone, ed., "The Cellarer's Account for Bromholme Priory, Norfolk, 1415–16," *Norfolk Record Society* 17 (1944), pp. 45–91; and Saunders, *An Introduction*, passim.

and write in the cloister, and were often excused from the daily offices.[72] As a matter of courtesy, the hostelers of many of the female convents in Yorkshire were even allowed to eat or drink in their priories' guesthouses.[73]

As mentioned earlier, both superiors and their officers could also leave their monasteries to transact any relevant business.[74] In 1406/7, the cellarer of Bungay incurred the costs of a trip to Norwich she and the subprioress took, expenses which included feeding and stabling ten horses.[75] In 1450, the expenses of a trip to Lynn from the priory of St Radegund by the cellarer and another nun on business included the price of a ferry-crossing.[76] And the prioress there, accompanied by one of her servants, inspected her tenements in and around Cambridge on several occasions.[77] This privilege was apparently not, however, an automatic one; in 1532 the subprioress of Campsey Ash, Katherine Symond, complained to Bishop Nykke that Ela Buttery, the prioress, was not allowing the obedientiaries to leave to transact their business.[78]

Accounts which survive for cellarers from three of the diocese's female houses describe the duties of this important office, and detail the funds they received to execute them. The cellarers at Blackborough and Carrow derived their revenues from similar sources. Both collected fixed rents from tenements and leased lands, and tithes from some of their priories' rectories; they also controlled their priories' home farms, whose profits provided the goods necessary to feed their sisters. Blackborough's home farm, for example, provided Margaret Geyton, prioress acting as cellarer in 1479/80, with fowl and fish for the convent; she also kept money generated by the sale of wool, pelts and hides from the priory's stock of cattle and sheep.[79] Margery Palmer at Carrow collected fines from both the priory's manor and leet courts, money from the sale of wood, the payments from lay boarders, and the profits from brewing.[80]

From these revenues, which for Margaret Geyton totaled £66 11s 11d, the household servants' wages were paid; so were the costs of corn, grain, and other foodstuff for the convent. She also made annual payments to the priory's sacrist. In addition to paying for the priory's kitchen supplies, the cellarer at Carrow covered the costs of carting and carrying fuel. She also paid the prioress's servants – including the liveries for the bailiff, yeomen, and grooms – and for repairs to some of the precinct's buildings, probably those used to store the goods she supplied. She made numerous payments in alms, such as bearing the

[72] Knowles, Monastic Order in England, p. 438.
[73] VCH, Yorkshire, vol. 3, p. 163.
[74] Chapter 1 above, pp. 53–4; Nichols, "The Internal Organization," p. 27 for abbesses and cellarers of female Cistercian houses.
[75] SRO, HD 1538/156/7.
[76] Gray, Priory of St Radegund, p. 173.
[77] Ibid., p. 157.
[78] Jessopp, Visitations, p. 290.
[79] Reading, Mapledurham Archives, C3 no. 43.
[80] NRO, NRS 26883 42 E8.

annual costs of feeding and clothing twelve paupers.[81] As noted earlier, the cellarer of Carrow was also responsible for providing poor novices with funds to acquire the personal items they needed to enter this house.[82]

Unlike her counterparts at Blackborough and Carrow, the cellarer at Bungay received most of her operating capital from the priory's bailiff.[83] These revenues were supplemented by rents, tithes, alms from the chaplain of the chapel of St Thomas, and money from the priory's many lay boarders.[84] Her expenses included a small payment in alms to the prioress, but, like her counterparts elsewhere, her primary duty was to maintain the convent's stores of meat, grain, and dairy foods. She also paid the wages of several household laborers, including the maltsters, bakers, and housekeeper, as well as the prioress's servants: her confessor, chamberlain, laundress, and others.[85] In addition to their wages, she also paid for clothing for several of the priory's servants.

Most of the other obedientiaries in the diocese received their operating capital either directly from properties assigned specially to them, or from another monastic officer. The sacrist at Flixton secured her income from rents of nearby meadows and pastures.[86] Both the sacrist and the hosteler at Marham received income from land granted to the abbey particularly for their use: the sacrist used the profits from eleven acres of land donated specifically for this office, and the hosteler had seven acres and three and a half roods which produced revenues for her use.[87]

At two other female houses obedientiaries received some of their annual income from other officials. The sacrist at Bungay received at least some – 10s – of her annual income from the prioress.[88] With her revenues, she maintained the lights in the church of the Blessed Virgin Mary, a task in keeping with the

---

81 See, for example: NRO, Hare 5954 227x1, account of Catherine Segrime, prioress in the office cf cellarer, dated 1503/04. NRO Phi 545 577x9 is a fragment of a fifteenth-century cellarer's account which includes all of these same payments.

82 NRO, NRS 26883 42 E8, and see above, Chapter 2, p. 57.

83 SRO, HD 1538/156/7 for the cellarer's account.

84 For the sacrist's money received from the chaplain, see his accounts: SRO, HD 1538/156/6–A–D, dated 1386/87, 1402/03, 1414/15, and 1415/16.

85 The thirteenth-century cellarer at Campsey Ash made similar payments both to other obedientiaries and also to household laborers: SRO, HD 1538/174. See also: VCH, London, vol. 1, p. 465 for an account from the female priory of St Helen's Bishopsgate which details various household payments. Though not identified as a cellarer's account, the expenses are similar to those of the cellarers at both Bungay and Campsey Ash priories.

86 BL, Stowe Ch. 343, a grant of meadow given to the sacrist, dated 1356; SRO, HA 12/B2/9/29 for a grant of pasture, dated 1359.

87 Blomefield, An Essay, vol. 11, p. 64. Blomefield is quoting a now lost rental which stated the location and amounts of land which had been earmarked specifically for these obedientiaries' use. See also: Nichols, "The History and Cartulary," p. 157. For a similar arrangement at another female house, St Mary Clerkenwell, see: W. O. Hassal, ed., The Cartulary of St Mary Clerkenwell (Camden Society, 3rd ser. lxxi, 1949), p. xiv.

88 SRO, HD 1538/345–46, Prioress Elizabeth Stephenson's account dated 1516/17.

usual responsibilities of a monastery's sacrist, whose domain was the convent's church and its furnishings.[89] The sacrist at Elstow Abbey in the diocese of Lincoln, for example, oversaw the repair and maintenance of the abbeys church's books, plate, vestments, and candles.[90]

Household management and finances were much different at the Cistercian abbey at Marham, where most of the revenues and operating costs were controlled by a central receiver, or bursar, who shared most of the abbey's general expenses with the abbess and cellarer, thus constituting an executive board of administrators.[91] All three officials, for example, contributed to the cost of food served in the abbess's household, while the bursar and cellarer paid for the meat and fish consumed by the rest of the convent.[92] Throughout the fifteenth century, the abbesses and their officers met these expenses by shifting some revenues around; for example, though the abbess was customarily owed issues of the dairy, she transferred these profits to the hands of the cellarer who provided dairy products for both the abbess's household and also for the rest of the abbey.[93] The bursar and cellarer also contributed with the abbess to the repair of the precinct's buildings.[94]

This executive administrative board of abbess, bursar and cellarer at Marham constitutes the only major difference in household administration among the female houses in the diocese. The existence of a bursar at Marham is especially significant for a convent of its small size and poverty. Though we lack any of her accounts, it would not be unrealistic to suggest that this officer received all of the abbey's revenues – including the eleven acres donated specifically for the sacrist's use, for example – and then paid the money out to the individual obedientiaries.[95]

The bursar or treasurer was considered to be the most important obedientiary, and one found primarily in large, wealthy male houses whose size and wealth made household administration more complex.[96] But this office can be found both in other female Cistercian houses and also in female monasteries

---

[89] Ibid. See also: Nichols, "The History and Cartulary," p. 88 for her duties at Marham Abbey; Power, *Medieval English Nunneries*, p. 132; and Tillotson, *Marrick Priory*, pp. 33–4 where he reprints an account of Dame Agnes Gower who was sacrist at this small priory and whose similar responsibilities are detailed. At Syon Abbey in London, however, these duties were carried out by a "sexteyne": Aungier, *History of Syon Abbey*, p. 367.

[90] Flower, "Obedientiars' Accounts of Glastonbury," p. 56.

[91] Nichols, The History and Cartulary," p. 157.

[92] NRO, Hare 2207 194x5.

[93] For example, see: NRO, Hare 2212 194x5.

[94] These payments appear in all of the abbesses' accounts, for example, NRO, Hare 2211 194x5.

[95] Nichols, "The History and Cartulary," pp. 88, 157 where he also suggests that the bursar of Marham acted as a central receiver.

[96] Knowles, *The Religious Orders*, vol. 2, pp. 315–16; Power, *Medieval English Nunneries*, p. 132; Raine, *The Durham Household Book*, p. viii; Smith, *Collected Papers*, pp. 28–30; Snape, *English Monastic Finances*, pp. 39, 44–5, 52.

of other orders.[97] Syon Abbey, Elstow, Marrick, St Radegund's, St Michael's Stamford, St Mary Clerkenwell, Nunkeeling, Wroxall, and Heynings were some of the female houses of other orders which also utilized this position.[98] Wealth seems to have been the determining factor for employing a bursar at Syon Abbey, the richest female house in all of England.[99] At Elstow, Nunkeeling, Wroxall, and Heynings episcopal authorities instituted this office because of financial mismanagement, as they did at the Cathedral Priory in Norwich and Bury St Edmunds in Suffolk.[100] Marrick, St Michael's, and St Radegund's, on the other hand, were poor female houses, though none of them were bedeviled by debt or mismanagement.[101] As Marham Abbey also successfully managed only meager revenues, perhaps administrative simplicity dictated the use of a bursar at these four convents. In any case, the appearance of a bursar at this small Cistercian house in Norfolk indicates rather sophisticated household organization and management.[102]

The diocese's convents had a sufficient number of capable nuns in this later medieval period to fill most of the household offices and, as Table 10 shows, the most important ones of cellarer and sacrist were always covered, even at the poorest convents like Flixton. Much of the evidence for these obedientiaries relies on the sixteenth-century episcopal visitations, especially for Campsey Ash. The relative abundance of details for this later period reflects, however, less a lack of obedientiaries – especially at Campsey Ash, whose wealth and population of nuns would have necessitated many if not all of the offices listed

97 For other Cistercian female houses: Nichols, "The Internal Organization," pp. 30–1.
98 For Syon Abbey, see: Aungier, *History of Syon Abbey*, pp. 391–92, and Flower, "Obedientiars' Accounts of Glastonbury," p. 55. For Elstow Abbey: ibid., p. 52. For Marrick Priory, see: Tillotson, *Marrick Priory*, pp. 27–33 where he prints a fifteenth-century bursar's account. For St Radegund's Priory, see: Gray, *Priory of St Radegund*, pp. 145–79 where the three fifteenth-century extant treasurers' accounts are printed. For St Michael's, Nunkeeling, Wroxall, and Heyning, see: Power, *Medieval English Nunneries*, pp. 204–5, 223; and Hassal, *The Cartulary of St Mary*, p. xv for St Mary Clerkenwell.
99 Knowles, *Medieval Religious Houses*, p. 232.
100 Power, *Medieval English Nunneries*, pp. 204–5, 223 for the female houses. At these two male houses, the office of treasurer was imposed by bishops concerned that autocratic priors and abbots were recklessly spending their monasteries' revenues. For Bury St Edmunds: Snape, *English Monastic Finances*, p. 54. Snape notes that despite the creation of this office at Bury, the abbot there disregarded the bursar and his office in running the abbey. For Norwich Cathedral Priory, see: Cheney, "Norwich Cathedral Priory," p. 97.
101 Gray, *Priory of St Radegund*, pp. 67–8, for St Radegund; Knowles, *Medieval Religious Houses*, p. 214 for Marrick; ibid., p. 219 for St Michael's.
102 Whether or not the nuns at Marham – or anywhere else for that matter – who operated their households successfully did so without outside interference or without the help of male guardians is difficult to know. But except for an incidence at Carrow, there's no evidence that outsiders were appointed to oversee or administered the nuns' finances in the diocese. Nichols, "The Organization," p. 30 discusses episcopal appointments of masters or wardens over nuns' houses due to financial mismanagement. He suggests that at female houses where the episcopal and other documents are mute on this point, the superiors and their obedientiaries administered their finances themselves.

in Table 10 – and more of change in visitation procedures, as the obedientiaries are noted more fully when Bishop Nykke commenced his visits in 1514. As other, earlier, sources demonstrate, several household officers operated at each of the other seven houses throughout the later fourteenth and fifteenth centuries as well.

The details about most of these obedientiaries' revenues, expenses, and duties are limited, but what we do know suggests well-organized households. The monastic officers at Blackborough, Bungay, and Carrow, for example, made intra-household payments. And in addition to the existence of a bursar at Marham, the abbess there conducted the abbey's household in co-operation with the bursar and cellarer, who as an executive body dispersed funds from a central treasury and kept their own accounts. Similar payments and administration seen in male obedientiary accounts are cited as evidence of sophisticated management.[103] These organized female monastic households suggest that these nuns were also adept administrators of their monasteries.[104]

Financial Stability

While the practical administration and organization of the convents meet the standards used to judge the male monasteries, surely a truer test of the nuns' managerial skills would be the state of their finances and the degree of their indebtedness.

Like all landowners in this later medieval period, the nuns experienced financial difficulties from time to time due to declining rents and grain prices, and rising wages.[105] The depression of the late fourteenth and early fifteenth centuries hit all landholders fairly hard, and smaller ones, like the nuns at Crabhouse for example, had a difficult time regaining income in later years. The nuns at Thetford Priory, in fact, explicitly cited the high mortality rate and its effect on their holdings for their decreased revenues in the 1440s; that the nuns were still in debt at the time of the Dissolution to the amount of £17 suggests that perhaps they never recovered.[106] Marham Abbey's manorial and household accounts also show a decay of rents over the course of the fifteenth

---

103 Flower, "Obedientiars' Accounts of Glastonbury," p. 57; Fowler, *Extracts from the Account Rolls of the Abbey of Durham*, passim; Saunders, *An Introduction*, pp. 17–26; Smith, *Collected Papers*, pp. 61, 72.

104 For similar assessments of other female houses, see: Liveing, *Romsey Abbey*, p. 234ff; and Perceval, "Remarks on Some Early Charters," p. 151 for the nuns at Canonsleigh.

105 The values of five of these houses are known from the 1291 *Taxatio* and when compared to the 1536 *Valor* estimates, these figures show a decrease in taxable revenues, except for Campsey Ash. The *Taxatio* information is in VCH, *Suffolk*, vol. 2, p. 81 (Bungay); ibid., p. 112 (Campsey Ash); ibid., p. 83 (Redlingfield); ibid., p. 85 (Thetford). For Flixton the early figures are from a 1292 survey of the house's holdings: ibid., p. 115.

106 VCH, *Suffolk*, vol. 2, p. 85.

Table 10. *Obedientiaries of the Female Monasteries*
in the Diocese of Norwich, 1350–1540

Convent	Office	Name of Holder	Date
Blackborough[a]	Kitchener	Elene Burgeye	1461, 1462
	Sacrist	Margaret Brenger	1461, 1462
		Margaret Hollins	1514
		Margaret Coleman	1532
	Cellarer	Richard Call	1471
		Margaret Geyton	1479
	President	Margaret Hollins	1514
Bungay[b]	Cellarer	Margaret Cotur	1406–33
		Emma	1414
	Sacrist	Unknown	1406
		Elizabeth Clere	1513
		Elizabeth Beaufeld	c.1530
	Infirmarer	Joanna Molles	1520
		Elizabeth Duke	1532
	Praecenter	Elizabeth Nuttell	1532
Campsey Ash[c]	Cellarer	Elizabeth Wingfield	1526–32
		Petronilla Felton	1532
		Unknown	1536
	Chamberer	Margaret Bacon	1526
		Elizabeth Wingfield	1532
		Unknown	1536
	Sub-chamberer	Bridget Coket	1526
		Christina Abell	1532
	Sacrist	Margaret Harman	1532
		Unknown	1536
	Sub-sacrist	Anna Butler	1526
		Dorothea Brampton	1532
	Refectorer	Katherine Simonds	1526
		Bridget Coket	1532
	Infirmarer	Petronilla Felton	1532
		Unknown	1536
	Praecenter	Margaret Harman	1526
		Katherine Groome	1532
	Almoner	Katherine Logan	1532
		Unknown	1536
	Succenter	Alice Winter	1532

[a] Reading, Mapledurham Archives C no. 3 39, 40, 41, 43 (1461, 1462, 1471, 1479); Jessopp, *Visitations*, pp. 108, 133 (1514, 1532).

[b] SRO, HD 1538/156/7, BL, ADD CH 16563 (1406–33); SRO, HD 1538/156/8 (1433); SRO, HD 1538/156/6–C (1414); SRO, HD 1538/156 (1513); SRO, HD 1538/345 (1530); Jessopp, *Visitations*, pp. 189, 318 (1520, 1532).

[c] Jessopp, *Visitations*, pp. 219, 290–92 (1526, 1532); PRO, SC6/H8/3401 (1536).

Convent	Office	Name of Holder	Date
	Prioress' Chaplain	Katherine Bloomfield	1532
Carrow[d]	Cellarer	Sybill Fastolf,	
		Margery Enges	1350–66
		Joan Parke	1366–72
		Edith Wilton	1373–75
		Joan Parke	1378–86
		Margaret Baryngton	1386–89
		Margaret atte Parke	1389–92
		Joan Parke	1392–1404
		Margaret Baryngton	1406–10
		Agnes Garbald	1410–15
		Lettice Eton	1416–19, 1428–30
		Margaret Gappe	1436
		Agnes King	1438
		Margaret Pygot	1441
		Agnes King	1444–53
		Margery Folcard	1461–63
		Joan Spalding	1474
		Mary White	1474–80
		Margery Palmer	1480–86
		Catherine Segrime	1488–89
		Joan Green	1492–1502
		Catherine Segrime	1503
		Isabel Wygon	1505–19, 1521–34
		Joan Erend	1520
	Sacrist	Alice Pernel	1358
		Catherine Betterings	1372
		Unknown	1458
		Joan Spalding	1466–67
		Margery Folcard	1468
		Cecily Ryall	1480–81
		Agnes Swanton	1526
		Agnes Swanton	1532
	Refectorer	Anna London	1526
		Anna London	1532
	Infirmarer	Anna Marten and	
		Agnes Warner	1526
	Praecenter,		
	4th Prioress	Katherine Jerves	1526
	3rd Prioress	Katherine Jerves	1532
Flixton[e]	Sacrist	Joan Hemynhall	1356
		Unknown	1359

d   Rye, Carrow Abbey, pp. 40–2, NRO, NRS 26883 42 E8, NRO, Hare 5954 227x1, and Hare 5955 227x1 (13501534 cellarers and sacrists); Jessopp, Visitations, pp. 209–10, 273 (1526, 1532).

e   BL, Stowe Ch. 343 (1356); SRO, HA 12/B2/9/29 (1359); Jessopp, Visitations, pp. 318–19 (1532).

Convent	Office	Name of Holder	Date
		Alicia Laxfield	1532
	Infirmarer	Margaret Rouse	1532
	Praecenter	Agnes Ashe	1532
Marham[f]	Bursar	Joanne Narburgh	1405
		Elizabeth Skathowe	1409
		Joanne Narburgh,	
		Katherine Socker	1419–26
		Margery Harsyk	1426
		Joanne Narburgh	1446
		Christiane Benet,	
		Katherine Berry	1456–70
	Cellarer	Margery Harsyk	1419
		W? Atruel	1446
		Margaret Nekton	1468–70
Redlingfield[g]	Refectorer	Alicia Bedingfield	1532
	Infirmarer	Agnes Nicoll	1532
	Succenter	Margaret Poly	1532
	Sub-sacrist	Joanne Petwell	1532
	Praecenter	Isabell Allen	1526–32
	Prioress' Chaplain	Joanne Denne	1514
		Joanne Denne	1526
		Anne Drury	1532
Thetford[h]	Cellarer	Margery Gerves	1526
		Alicia Wodegate	1532
	Refectorer	Margaret Chickering	1418
		Dorothea Smith	1526–53
	Infirmarer	Alice Wesenham	1418
	3rd Prioress	Elizabeth Jenny	1390
		Juliana Bluton	1418
		Dorothea Smith	1526–1532
	Sacrist	Margery Leggete	1532
	Succenter	Rose Reeve	1532
	Praecenter	Agnes Mason	1532

[f] NRO, Hare 2201 194x5 (1405); NRO, Hare 2202 194x5 (1409); NRO, Hare 2203 194x5 (1419); NRO, Hare 2204 194x5 (1426); NRO, Hare 2205 194x5 (1446); NRO, Hare 2207 194x5 (1456); NRO, Hare 2208 194x5 (1468); NRO, Hare 2209 194x5 (1470).

[g] Jessopp, *Visitations*, pp. 138, 224, 297 (1514, 1526, 1532).

[h] Thetford: Blomefield, *An Essay*, vol. 2, p. 92 (1390, 1418); Jessopp, *Visitations*, pp. 243, 303 (1526, 1532).

century of about 47s.[107] Beginning in 1399, the nuns at Bungay Priory adjusted to the changes in population and productivity by leasing out most of the land they had previously held in their own hands, as did the nuns at Marham.[108]

The situation at both of these houses – and at most of the others in the diocese – stabilized by the mid-fifteenth century, and though this tells us little about the nuns' finances, a detailed assessment is problematic for two reasons. First, the *Valor Ecclesiasticus*, the sixteenth-century royal audit of all monasteries, traditionally the standard measure of monastic finances, provides only a limited view of sources of income, those which were taxable.[109] A quick comparison of the receipts in the household accounts with the convents' *Valor* assessments shows clearly that the *Valor* is not a reliable guide to the sources of income available to superiors or the obedientiaries. The *Valor* for Carrow Priory, for example, states that the priory's total annual income was £64 16s 6d.[110] But the account of Isabel Wygon, cellarer of Carrow in 1529 – just six years before the *Valor* was compiled – shows her income alone to be £98 7s 4d.[111] Similarly, Bungay's *Valor* lists the priory's total income at £61 11s 9d.[112] The last extant prioress's account, however – that of Elizabeth Stephenson, dated 1516/17 – reveals an annual income of £100 15s 4d.[113]

This problem is compounded by the paucity of complete runs of household accounts for these female houses, making any attempt to generalize about their finances for the 190 years covered here difficult. But manorial and household accounts survive for both Bungay and Marham for a reasonable amount of time and provide some idea of these two convents' economic status.[114] And while evidence regarding the financial stability of the other female houses is less straightforward, information from the household accounts, episcopal visitations,

107   NRO, Hare 2201–10 194x5 (1405–97).
108   SRO, HD 1538/156/3–5 (1399–1404), 8–13 (1433–38, 1442–43); 15–16 (1495–96).
109   The standard analysis of the *Valor Ecclesiasticus* is: Savine, *English Monasteries on the Eve of the Reformation*. His analysis is thorough, and though he admits that some sources of income were omitted, he maintains that overall the values given in the audit fairly represent monasteries' total income, although he does not compare the figures in the *Valor* with those given in any of the available obedientiary accounts. Knowles, *The Religious Orders*, vol. 3, pp. 244–53 acknowledges Savine's work but adds useful correctives, like figures of income and expenses from various male monastic household accounts, to show that the *Valor* underestimated monastic incomes considerably. While historians acknowledge this problem for the male monasteries, it has never been included in any discussions of female houses.
110   VE, vol. 3, p. 305.
111   NRO, NRS 26884 42 E8.
112   VE, vol. 3, p. 431.
113   SRO, HD 1538/345/46.
114   The collectors' and bailiffs' accounts cover the years 1375–1445 as follows: 1375/76, 1383/84, 1398/99, 1402/03, 1403/04, 1433/34, 1436/37, 1437/18, 1438/39, 1443/44, 1444/45, 1495/96, 1496/97. The prioresses' accounts are 1490/91, 1513/14, and 1516/17. The abbesses' accounts from Marham are dated: 1446/47, 1455/56, 1456/57, 1468/69, 1470/71, 1492/93, and 1497/98; the bailiffs' accounts are 1355/56, 1405/06, 1409/10, and 1426/27.

and suppression documents regarding debt at the time of the Dissolution, indicates that despite periodic declines in operating revenues, by adapting to economic changes and keeping a tight rein on their expenses, the nuns were nevertheless able to manage their resources successfully.

Both the collectors' and bailiffs' accounts for Bungay Priory show fairly stable incomes for this house. The collector, for example, always operated well within his income which thereby enabled him to deliver significant sums of money to the prioress. In 1383, he was able to pay the prioress only £13 5s, but in 1399 he paid her £37 17s, and by 1439 paid out over £59 to her.[115] The bailiff's position was the same: he was able to deliver sufficient sums both to the prioress and her obedientiaries, between £20 and £22 to the prioress in 1490, and between £5 and £7 to the priory's cellarer and sacrist.[116] As noted above, the accounts of both of these manorial officials show that the nuns were increasingly leasing out their lands to others to work, instead of directly farming them themselves. This change in estate management in this later period, adopted by landlords all over England, helps to explain the steady amounts the nuns' collectors and bailiffs were able to turn over to them.

With these monies, the priory's superiors were able to run their houses, even if on a very tight budget. The surviving household accounts of Elizabeth Stephenson, the prioress of Bungay from 1490 to sometime before 1526, for example, show a rising income with expenses which followed suit: in 1490 her income was £35 5s and her expenses were £35 3s; in 1513 her income had risen to £83 17s 10d and her expenses followed to £81 16s; three years later, she received £100 5s in revenues and paid out £100 6s.[117] She kept a narrow but positive margin between her income and expenses, and never began her accounts with the hefty arrears which often kept houses in a perpetual state of financial insecurity.

There is some evidence, in fact, which indicates that Bungay's superior saw an improvement in her annual income sometime in the mid-fifteenth century. From 1375 until 1433, the bailiff at Bungay was responsible for "foreign and household expenses," including raisins, fish, almonds, and saffron – fare which no doubt spruced up the nuns' diet and accented the meals served by the prioress's kitchen to the convents' many guests.[118] In the bailiff's account of 1433, however, John Kempner noted that these expenses would be found in the lady's book, that is, in the prioress's account;[119] they appear in Elizabeth

---

115 SRO, HD 1538/156/2, HD 1538/156/3, HD 1538/156/11.
116 SRO, HD 1538/156/15 (1495); HD 1538/156/16 (1497).
117 SRO, HD 1538/156/14, HD 1538/17, HD 1538/345–46.
118 Power, Medieval English Nunneries, pp. 140–41 notes that this type of food was purchased to enliven the nuns' regular meals. Tillotson, Marrick Priory, p. 16 remarks on similar luxury foods purchased by the monks of Selby Priory, but not by the nuns at Marrick. The thirteenth-century cellarer at Campsey Ash Priory paid for similar goods: SRO, HD 1538/174. See also: VCH, London, vol. 1, p. 460 for similar spices purchased by the cellarer at St Helen's Bishopsgate.
119 SRO, HD 1538/156/8.

Stephenson's accounts of the late fifteenth and sixteenth centuries, indicating that at some point in the middle of the fifteenth century the prioresses here realized enough of an increase in their revenues to cover these costs.[120]

While the bailiff and prioress at Bungay operated in the black, the lone cellarer's account shows her office was at a loss of £3. Drawing any conclusions about the financial management of this office from this single document is impossible, but the solvency demonstrated by the other accounts, the absence of financial troubles deep enough to be cited in the bishops' visitations, and Bungay's positive balance at the time of its dissolution in 1536, strongly suggest that the nuns handled the priory's finances well.[121]

While Bungay seems to have run smoothly, Marham Abbey navigated some troubled tides. The nine extant abbesses' accounts show them operating successfully within the limits of their revenues in four years, with information about two years missing. Joanna Narburgh exceeded her budget by £42 in 1446/47; and Joan Heyham overspent her income by £23 in 1492/93, and by £4 in the last surviving account, 1497/98.[122] Their problems were aggravated by the numerous debtors whose names were appended to the end of the accounts, owing the abbess money.[123] Some of these debts were long-standing, but each account shows the abbess steadily chipping away at them, collecting some of the money owed, and thereby ever decreasing her burden of debt.[124]

Surprisingly, in 1446 and 1497 – two of the three years when abbesses overspent their incomes – they did not start out with the often sizeable arrears with which they began the rest of their fiscal years. As with the debts slowly paid off at the end of the abbesses' accounts, however, these arrears also declined over the course of the fifteenth century, from over £44 in 1405 to £13 in 1497.[125]

John Nichols' careful analysis of the abbey's household and manorial accounts, and court rolls indicates that despite the abbesses' debts, the abbey was solvent throughout this its later history.[126] The abbey's manors always operated

[120] SRO, HD 1538/156/14 (1490); SRO, HD 1538/156/17 (1512); and SRO, HD 1538/345–46 (c.1530).

[121] For lack of debt at the Dissolution, see: PRO, SP 5/3 series where the Crown chronicled the debts owed by monasteries c.1536. For the episcopal visitation records: Jessopp, *Visitations*, pp. 39–40, 189, 260–61, 318.

[122] NRO, Hare 2205 194x5; NRO, Hare 2211 194x5; and NRO, Hare 2212 194x5 respectively.

[123] At the foot of most of the abbesses' accounts are names of people who were in debt to the abbey for various things. See, for example: NRO, Hare 2205 194x5, and NRO, Hare 2207 194x5. See also Chapter 4 of this book.

[124] Paxton, "The Nunneries of London," pp. 257–58 shows the prioress of St Helen's reducing her house's debt steadily over time as well.

[125] NRO, Hare 2201 194x5 for the £44 arrears in 1405; Hare 2204–09 194x5 for 1426, when arrears were £38; in 1455 they were £21; in 1456 they increased to £43; in 1468 they were down to £33; in 1470 they had dropped to £24; and by 1492 they were £13. By 1497 they were nil.

[126] Nichols, "The History and Cartulary," pp. 130–78, esp. pp. 168–78, where he analyses

within their incomes, and maintained a surplus at the end of each account which ranged from £12 to £57. Like their counterparts at Bungay, the nuns began to lease out their holdings late in the fourteenth century and the rents they thus collected remained steady and constituted a major portion of the abbey's revenues.[127] It is likely that some of this money was allowed for the abbesses' and their obedientiaries' use when their expenses exceeded their incomes, thus mitigating the potentially drastic effects of the abbesses' debts. The abbey was not in debt at the time of its dissolution, which supports John Nichols' suggestion that in the area of financial management the nuns were successful.

The financial stability of many of the diocese's other female houses is less easy to determine. Carrow Priory, substantially wealthier than Marham, weathered some rough times as well: in 1442, the bishop entrusted its finances to Thomas Wetherby, a prominent Norfolk man who lived at the priory until 1445.[128] In the same year, Alice Waryn, who had been elected prioress in 1430, was removed from her office and sent to Bungay for a time where she received an annual stipend from Carrow of 33s 4d.[129] These events surely indicate improper administration at Carrow. Two later prioresses, however, administered their incomes well enough to collect receipts greater than their expenses: Margaret Pygot collected £133 and spent £127; her successor Isabel Wygon took in £98 and paid out £81, with arrears under £4.[130] The cellarers at Carrow, on the other hand, overspent two out of three times, by £6 in 1484 and by £8 in 1520; this office was also burdened with small but nagging debts carried over from the previous years.[131] These fluctuations make a generalization difficult but the absence of financial problems in the sixteenth-century episcopal visitation records, combined with the lack of debt at the time of the priory's suppression, indicates that despite some intermittent trouble, the nuns at Carrow also ably governed their resources.

Inconclusive evidence exists for Campsey Ash Priory, the wealthiest of all of the female houses in the diocese. Though obviously no guide to the convent's economic stability, the single – and probably final – extant prioress's account shows Ela Buttery spending more than she took in by over £120.[132] As with

the manorial accounts discussed here in conjunction with court rolls and lists of the abbey's stocks of livestock and grain.

127 Ibid., p. 166.
128 Rye, *Carrow Abbey*, p. 7.
129 Ibid. Rye is quoting Norris here, but gives no reference for Waryn's removal from office; these are the only details we have about this incident. There is an entry in the Bungay Priory's bailiff's account of 1436/37, SRO HD 1538/ 156/9, which refers to the expenses of the Prioress Waryn's stay "of one day and one night." See above Chapter 1, p. 36, but this was nine years before her removal from office.
130 NRO, NRS 266882 42 E8 (1455), NRS 26884 42 E8 (1529).
131 NRO, NRS 26883 42 E8 (1484); NRO, Hare 5955 227x1 (1520); arrears equalled £3 in 1484, £12 in 1503, and £9 in 1520; NRO, Hare 5954 227x1 (1503).
132 PRO, SC6/H8/3401, dated 1536.

Carrow, however, Campsey Ash was neither in debt at the time of its suppression, nor mentioned in the bishops' records for any problems of debt or financial mismanagement.[133]

Two other houses apparently did have financial problems that were not easy to overcome. The prioress of Blackborough started her accounts with arrears of more than £19 in 1461, and over £23 in the following years, but she always took in more than she spent.[134] Her cellarer was not so fortunate. In the late fifteenth century this important office was running a deficit of £22 in both years for which accounts survive, and in 1471, the bailiff, Richard Call, served as the priory's cellarer, an indication that there was trouble here.[135]

Why Call took over this office and how long he kept it can only be surmised but remarks made thirty-five years later to Bishop Nykke indicate that Blackborough was still floundering. In 1514, Dame Agnes Grey complained that the house was in debt, and Dame Margaret Gigges said that the prioress did not render written accounts so she could spare the expense of an auditor.[136] Though subsequent visitations make no mention of the nuns' financial difficulties, the convent owed £79 at the time of the Dissolution.[137]

Redlingfield Priory had a rocky time as well. We have already noted that in the 1420s, Isabel Hermyte, prioress there, was banished to another convent for several moral transgressions; she was also accused of allowing some of the cloister buildings to fall into disrepair and of neglecting to produce accounts. These problems could have been the result of mismanagement or a lack of income.[138] Twenty years later, Prioress Lampet overspent her annual income, but only by about £3.[139] Early sixteenth-century episcopal visitation records show the house still in rough shape – no accounts, no refectory or infirmary.[140] Though later visitations indicate that the priory was well run, Redlingfield was, like Blackborough, in debt at the Dissolution.[141]

Crabhouse Priory was also bothered by debt: in the mid-fifteenth century, the nuns there received a license allowing them to acquire land in free alms because their holdings could no longer support them.[142] This house was not in debt at the Dissolution, an indication that perhaps Crabhouse, like most of the others, endured times of financial hardship but was not entirely undone by them. So while Blackborough, Redlingfield, and possibly Thetford were

---

[133] Campsey Ash is not among the houses listed in the Book of Debts: PRO, SP 5/1 or SP 5/4 series. For the bishops' records, see: Jessopp, *Visitations*, pp. 35–6, 133–34, 219–20, 290–92.
[134] Reading, Mapledurham Archives, C3, nos. 39, 40.
[135] Reading, Mapledurham Archives, C3, nos. 41, 43 respectively.
[136] Jessopp, *Visitations*, p. 107, she gave oral ones instead.
[137] Ibid.; for debt at the Dissolution: PRO, SP 5/4/144 and PRO SP 5/1/154r.
[138] VCH, *Suffolk*, vol. 2, pp. 83–4.
[139] SRO, HD 1538/327.
[140] Jessopp, *Visitations*, pp. 138–40.
[141] PRO, SP 5/1/160r by £13.
[142] CPR, 1446–52, p. 4.

financially unstable and in debt in the 1530s, most of the other female houses – from the very poor Marham Abbey to the wealthier Carrow and Bungay priories – handled their limited finances reasonably well.[143]

Administrative Irregularities

Administrative irregularities, such as not producing annual or daily accounts of income and expenses, or not filling household offices, can be seen as symptoms of bad management. But while a few of the diocese's female houses had intermittent problems with accounts and obedientiaries, most did not. Some superiors and obedientiaries hired outside auditors to tally up yearly manorial and household accounts, as at Carrow, where the prioress and cellarer each paid an auditor and a "maker of accounts."[144] Elizabeth Stephenson, prioress of Bungay, spent 10d for paper and ink in 1490 for accounts and for the book of the guesthouse written by John Underwood.[145] Margaret Cotur, cellarer there in 1406, paid 14d for parchment and ink for account rolls drawn up for that year, and another 8d for a scribe to keep the book of the household.[146]

These accounts were year-end tallies of accounts or ledgers that superiors and obedientiaries kept as daily entries of income and expenses. All of the extant household accounts for the female houses in the diocese contain references to these – usually termed "the lady's book" or "the lady's journal" – indicating that these nuns could write.[147] Some form of these accounts was to be shown to the whole convent.

---

143 For similar assessments of other female houses, see: Gasquet, *English Monastic Life*, p. 175 for the nuns at Grace Dieu Priory; Morris, *Nunburnholme*, p. 154; Nichols, "The Organization," pp. 30, 37 for Cistercian female houses; Paxton, "The Nunneries of London," pp. 261–63 for St Mary Clerkenwell and St Helen's; Tillotson, *Marrick Priory*, pp. 10–17 where he finds that the nuns there also administered their slim resources successfully. See also: *VCH, Hertford*, vol. 4, pp. 430–31, 433 for the nuns at St Mary de Pres and those at St Giles, Flamstead respectively.

144 NRO, Hare 5954 227x1 and NRO, NRS 26882 42 E.

145 SRO, HD 1538/156/14.

146 SRO, HD 1538/156/7.

147 NRO, NRS 26883 42 E8, 1485 account of Margery Palmer, cellarer at Carrow, where she says the names of the year's boarders "appears more fully in the book of the nuns." For other examples: Reading, Mapledurham Archives, C3 nos. 39, 40, 41, 43 (Blackborough); SRO, HD 1538/156/7 (Bungay); NRO, Hare 2201–09 194x5 (Marham): SRO, HD 1538/327 (Redlingfield). For similar accounting procedures in other female houses, see: Robert Dunning, "The Muniments of Syon Abbey: their Administration and Migration in the Fifteenth and Sixteenth Centuries," *Bulletin of the Institute of Historical Research* 37:95 (1964), pp. 103–111 examines the highly organized record-keeping practices of Syon. At least one of Catesby Priory's prioresses kept a daily tally of income and expenses also: C. M. Woolgar, ed., *Household Accounts from Medieval England* (Records of Social and Economic History, n.s. xvii and xviii, Oxford, 1992), p. 58, n. 1. Mary Erler generously shared this reference with me.

A few prioresses, however, failed to produce these accounts. Prioress Margaret Fincham did not display written accounts at Blackborough in 1514, but to save on the expense of an auditor, gave oral ones instead.[148] Elizabeth Virly, prioress at Flixton in 1493, did not produce written accounts for the bishop; nor did either of her successors, Margaret Punder in 1514, and Elizabeth Wright in 1520.[149] Wright explained that she was unaccustomed to figures and so had not written down what she had spent.[150] Either she learned or employed the skills of another, because in later years she did show the bishop her accounts. One of the Redlingfield prioresses was also enjoined by Bishop Nykke to exhibit annual accounts.[151] Katherine Segrime, prioress of Carrow in 1492, also failed to provide an account for that year; she did do so later, though, as her account of 1503 demonstrates.[152]

While these nuns had problems with numbers or perhaps could not write at all, many others had the necessary skills. Dame Ellen Burgeye, kitchener at Blackborough in the mid-1460s, kept her own accounts which, she said, she compared with the those of the prioress.[153] And those nuns who copied psalters, inscribed their names in books, or signed the papers which closed their priories demonstrate that many – perhaps most? – nuns had the skills necessary to keep accounts.[154]

A lack of officeholders could also have been a sign of administrative problems, and while most of the diocese's female houses did have at least some of the necessary personnel, Crabhouse may not have. The only officer we know existed at this small and poor place for certain was a cellarer sometime before 1514, though a lack of obedientiaries here might reflect as much a paucity of sources as it does a lack of skilled nuns.[155] The same can be said for Bruisyard and Shouldham, about which we have almost no information regarding monastic officers.[156] In the same year at Blackborough two of the nuns complained that the priory had been without a subprioress for the preceding four years.[157] Table 10 shows that the priory had a kitchener, sacrists, cellarers, and at least one president through the late fifteenth century and into the sixteenth century, but more than these we cannot identify. Obedientiaries at Flixton and Marham are equally under-represented.

---

148 Above, p. 141; and Jessopp, Visitations, pp. 107–8.
149 Ibid., pp. 47–8, 142–43, 185.
150 Ibid., p. 190.
151 Ibid., pp. 139–40, in 1514.
152 Ibid., p. 16; NRO Hare 5954 227x1.
153 Reading, Mapledurham Archives, C3, no. 39.
154 See above Chapter 2, pp. 67, 69, 71–2; PRO, SP 5/3/131–33.
155 In Bishop Nykke's visitation of 1514, Dame Agnes Smith was identified as "lately cellarer": Jessopp, Visitations, p. 109.
156 At Bruisyard, a nun named Margaret Bylan was called "president" of the abbey in a will dated 1493: Fitch, Suffolk Monasteries, p. 147. There is no information about obedientiaries at the Gilbertine house at Shouldham.
157 Jessopp, Visitations, p. 108.

For some of these houses, the problem could have been caused by an insufficient number of nuns, though most of the convents had at least ten nuns, enough certainly for a basic household staff.[158] Blackborough, however, had ten nuns in 1532, two of whom were novices;[159] Flixton had only five nuns, including the prioress.[160] The same reason has been suggested for two superiors at Marham also acting in the capacities of cellarer and bursar.[161] Could this problem have indicated a lack of skilled nuns? Nuns at Carrow occasionally held two offices simultaneously, or two nuns held one office together; as Table 10 shows, the superiors there occasionally also acted as cellarer, and from 1350 to 1366 Sybill Fastolf and Margery Enges were cellarers.[162] Both Elizabeth Skathowe and Katherine Socker were bursars at Marham from 1419 to 1426; Christiane Benet and Katherine Berry shared this office later between 1456 and 1470 (Table 10). Carrow's proximity to the city of Norwich could have made it a convenient stop for lay visitors, thus requiring two nuns to perform the duties of the important office of cellarer. At Marham, the nuns' lean resources could have made it necessary for good managers to assume two offices from time to time.

Failure to produce yearly accounts and doubling up on monastic offices signified trouble; except in the case of Flixton, however, these infractions were not chronic. As we have seen, only three of the female houses, Blackborough, Redlingfield, and Thetford, were in debt at the time of the Dissolution, a problem which has been directly linked to nuns' alleged inabilities to organize and manage their households and financial affairs.[163] The lack of evidence, indirect though it may be in some cases, for gross mismanagement and the debt which often accompanied it suggests that for the most part these houses were well managed throughout the later Middle Ages.

These kinds of administrative problems were actually more common in the diocese's wealthy male houses. Superiors and obedientiaries at Sibton Abbey and the Cathedral Priory in Norwich were among those who also did not keep

---

[158] Power, *Medieval English Nunneries*, p. 132 also suggests that the doubling up of monastic offices was due to lack of numbers. For the average number of nuns at each of these eleven female houses in the diocese of Norwich, see Chapter 2 of this book.

[159] Jessopp, *Visitations*, p. 311.

[160] Ibid., p. 47.

[161] Margery Harsyk was both abbess and cellarer in 1426: NRO, Hare 2204 194x5; and Joanna Narburgh acted as both abbess and bursar in 1446: NRO, Hare 2205 194x5. Nichols, "The History and Cartulary," p. 91 suggests that the doubling up of abbess and cellarer, and abbess and bursar, was due to an insufficient number of nuns at Marham in the last fifty years of its existence which prohibited the full complement of obedientiaries from being filled by individual nuns.

[162] Catherine Segrime acted as both prioress and cellarer in 1503: NRO, Hare 5954 227x1; Isabel Wygon was both prioress and cellarer in 1520: NRO, Hare 5955 227x1, as she was in 1529: NRO, NRS 26884 42 E8.

[163] See Power, *Medieval English Nunneries*, pp. 203–36 for the equation of debt and bad management.

or show annual written accounts.[164] The same problem existed at both Thetford St Stephens and Butley priories.[165] Also at the Cathedral Priory, Father Dionisius held several monastic offices, and the abbot of St Benedict at Holme held the offices of cellarer, sacrist, and almoner simultaneously.[166] A similar situation existed at Creake Abbey, and at Ixworth Priory laymen acted as obedientiaries.[167] Prior Snoryng of Walsingham was twice removed by the King for severe financial mismanagement.[168] And chronic debt plagued the diocese's male monasteries both rich and poor.[169]

Abuses in the Common Life?

The relatively efficient running of the majority of the female houses ensured that abuses in the common life – the proliferation of independent households, for example – did not occur.[170] We have already noted the existence of superiors' private rooms within the cloister, but there is no evidence of more flagrant flouting of the common life at any of these convents. Individual nuns in the diocese did not have separate chambers or eating quarters, as did some nuns in other parts of England.[171] In fact in 1514, Isabell Allen, precentor at

---

164 Denny, *Sibton Abbey Estates*, p. 33; Cheney, "Norwich Cathedral Priory," pp. 97–9; Jessopp, *Visitations*, passim for others.

165 *VCH, Suffolk*, vol. 2, p. 110 (Thetford St Stephens); ibid., pp. 97–8 (Butley).

166 Jessopp, *Visitations*, pp. 3–5 for the Cathedral Priory; ibid., p. 126 for St Benet at Holme.

167 Carthew, "A Cellarer's Account Roll of Creake Abbey," p. 358; *VCH, Suffolk*, vol. 2, p. 105.

168 Jessopp, *Visitations*, pp. 395–96.

169 For the debts of the male houses in the diocese, see: A. L. Bedingfield, ed., *A Cartulary of Creake Abbey* (Norfolk Record Society Publications, vol. 35, 1966), pp. xxi–xxiii; Cheney, "Norwich Cathedral Priory," p. 97; F. C. Elliston-Erwood, "The Premonstratensian Abbey of Langley," *NA* 21 (1920–22), p. 182; Howlett, "Account Rolls of Certain Obedientiaries," p. 532 where he illustrates how the cellarer was in constant debt to the abbey of St Benedict at Holme; and see: *VCH, Norfolk*, vol. 2, p. 337 for Wymondham Priory; ibid., p. 372 for Creake Abbey; ibid., p. 95 for Bromholm Priory; Rye, "Norfolk Monasteries," pp. 450–51 for Horsham St Faith Priory which was in debt at the Dissolution by £35 4s 8d; ibid., pp. 452–53 for the debt at Langley Abbey which equaled £120 16s 8d; ibid., pp. 454–55 for the debt at the priory of Thetford, St Sepulchre which came to £7 19d; ibid., pp. 454–55 for Pentney and Wormgay Priories, whose debts together totaled £16; ibid., pp. 456–57 for Coxford Priory whose debt equaled £26 13s 4d; ibid., pp. 458–59 for Wendling Abbey which owed £66 17s 11d; and ibid., pp. 460–61 for the £20 debt owed by the priory of Beeston.

170 See: Coulton, *Five Centuries*, vol. 4, p. 121 where he states that late medieval nuns had become like paying guests because their houses were so poorly endowed and managed. See also: Power, *Medieval English Nunneries*, pp. 315–23.

171 Power, *Medieval English Nunneries*, pp. 315–23 uses female monastic inventories and episcopal visitation records for convents in the diocese of Lincoln as evidence of many sleeping chambers and eating quarters. These same sources exist for most of the female houses in the diocese of Norwich: they do not indicate that such private chambers

Redlingfield between 1526 and 1532, complained to Bishop Nykke that there were no curtains in the nuns' dormitory to separate their beds.[172] Nor did any of the nuns hold lands privately, as did some of their counterparts elsewhere.[173]

While individual nuns did not own personal property, they did receive annual allowances or pittances of money or food and clothing, a widespread practice which, though clearly counter to the Rule of St Benedict, was nevertheless condoned by both the episcopal authorities and the legislative body of the Benedictine Order.[174] It is likely that the nuns at Bruisyard utilized the prebend system as it worked at Denney Abbey, one of the other houses of Poor Clares in England, where individual nuns received the profits from specifically designated pieces of the abbey's fenland for "their maintenance."[175]

At most of the diocese's other houses nuns were allotted specific amounts of money. At Flixton Priory, for example, each nun was given 5s annually for clothing from the profits of the manor of Flixton, by custom of the founders.[176] At Campsey Ash, the prioress received 10s, the sacrist 8s, the chamberer £8, the almoner 40s, the cellarer 13s 4d, and the infirmarer 6s 8d.[177] It is possible

existed, nor did Power use them in her discussion of this problem. See: PRO, SP 5/4/142 for the inventory of rooms and goods at Blackborough; Francis Haslewood, "Inventories of Monasteries Suppressed in 1536," *PSIA* 8 (1894), pp. 321–23 (Bruisyard); PRO, SP 5/1/130 (Campsey Ash); PRO, SP 5/1/110; and J. J. Coleman, "On the Excavation of the Site of Carrow Abbey, Norwich," *British Archaeological Association Journal* 38 (1882): pp. 168–69 for a map of the building plan (Carrow); PRO, SP 5/1/119 (Flixton); Nichols, "The History and Cartulary," p. 391 for his reconstruction of Marham Abbey's buildings and rooms; PRO, SP 5/1/131, and PRO, SP 5/3/133 (Redlingfield). For female houses in other dioceses, see: Clark, *English Register of Godstow Nunnery*, pp. lxxxiv, lxxxvii for the 1432 injunctions against private eating messes and households. Liveing, *The Records of Romsey Abbey*, p. 223 where the nuns there were admonished by the bishop to all eat together in the frater; Luce, "Injunctions," pp. 34, 38 for the 1387 episcopal injunctions against private eating messes and the acquisition of private property; Peacock, "Injunctions," pp. 51–2 to the Godstow Abbey nuns again; R. B. Pugh, "Fragment of an Account of Isabel of Lancaster, Nun of Amesbury, 1333–4," in *Festschrift zur Feier des zweihundejayrigen Bestandes des Haus- Hof- und Staatsarchivs*, 1 Bd. ed. Leo Santifaller (Vienna, 1949), pp. 487–98 where the nun details the expenses of her own personal household. R. M. Serjeantson, *A History of Delapre Abbey* (Northampton, 1909), pp. 16–18 for bishop's injunctions of 1435 that nuns were to eat together in the refectory at least four times a week.

172 Jessopp, *Visitations*, p. 139.
173 For nuns who held lands and rents privately, see: Morris, *Nunburnholme*, pp. 155–56 and Pugh, "Fragment of the Account of Isabel of Lancaster," p. 489.
174 Power, *Medieval English Nunneries*, pp. 323–34 for this practice in other female houses; and Knowles, *The Religious Orders*, vol. 2, pp. 240–43 for pittancers and their duties. According to Knowles, a system of wages developed in many of the male monasteries whereby instead of receiving clothes from the monastery, they were given money. See also: Harvey, *Living and Dying*, pp. 10, 43–4 and passim for food pittances for the monks at Westminster Abbey.
175 Bourdillon, *The Minoresses*, pp. 36–9; *VCH, Cambridge*, vol. 2, pp. 298–99.
176 SRO, HA 12/E1/15/1(c).
177 Taylor, *Index Monasticus*, p. 99 for these payments out of the foundation endowment. These payments are noted in Ela Buttery's account: PRO, SC6/H8/3401, dated 1536.

that, at least in the case of the chamberer, some of this yearly allowance went toward supplies which she needed to fulfill her household duties. These varying amounts might also reflect the hierarchy of officeholders at this house: £6 13s 4d was distributed annually among the rest of the nuns there.[178] The prioress at Campsey Ash gave another 5 marks annually to the nuns specifically for clothes.[179] Each nun at Crabhouse also received an annual pittance for clothes derived from the profits of the church of St Peter, Wiggenhale, rendered twice a year.[180] At Blackborough, £4 12s 5½d was earmarked for distribution to the nuns for their clothes.[181] And finally, only 20d was given each year to the nuns at Marham.[182]

These amounts reflect the relative wealth of the monasteries, with the nuns at Campsey Ash drawing more money annually than their sisters at Flixton, Blackborough, Crabhouse, or Marham. A similar pattern existed at female houses in other dioceses. The vicar of the church of St Clements, one of the appropriated properties of St Radegund's, annually gave 66s 8d for the nuns' clothing there.[183] At the wealthier St Mary de Pre, £21 6s 8d was distributed to the nuns for clothes.[184] By contrast, the nuns at Swaffham Bulbeck, a poor Benedictine priory in Cambridge, shared only 6s 8d annually.[185]

The nuns also received gifts of goods or money from testators. In 1504, for example, Thomas Beaufeld, citizen and alderman of Norwich, left 20d to each nun at Carrow Priory.[186] Each nun at Carrow also received 6s 8d from Baldwin Cratyng, the chaplain of Eye, in 1446; he bequeathed 3s 4d to the nuns at Flixton in the same will.[187] Bequests like these are common in wills from all four of the diocese's probate courts, as well as in wills enrolled in the Prerogative Court of Canterbury, and most gifts accompanied requests for intercessory prayers. Such gifts were given to female and male monastics because of their wider function in medieval society as charitable institutions and centers of spirituality whose existence in this temporal world helped in the greater effort of eternal salvation for all.

While pittances and bequests might have been permitted by ecclesiastical authorities, individual purses could threaten the communal life by encouraging

178 Taylor, *Index Monasticus*, pp. 99–100; and VE, vol. 3, p. 416.
179 CPR, 1370–74, p. 6; this money came from lands given to the priory in mortmain in 1370 by William Hoo, John de Hoo, William de Hoo, and Emma de Hoo, and was given to the nuns on the anniversary of William the elder.
180 Bateson, "The Register," p. 37.
181 Dugdale, *Monasticon*, vol. 4, p. 205.
182 Nichols, "The History and Cartulary," p. 90.
183 Gray, *The Priory of St Radegund*, pp. 142, 163 for this payment which was noted in both extant prioresses' accounts of 1449 and 1450.
184 Dugdale, *Monasticon*, vol. 3, p. 359.
185 William Palmer, "The Benedictine Nunnery of Swaffham Bulbeck," *Proceedings of the Cambridge Antiquarian Society* 31 (1929), p. 32. See: VCH, *Hertford*, vol. 4, p. 433 for the nuns at St Giles, Flamstead who each received 2s a year for clothing and ½d a week for food in the 1350s.
186 NRO, NCC 491–492 Popy.
187 NRO, NCC 126 Wilby.

the acquisition of luxury items and non-essential material goods.[188] The monks at St Benedict at Holme, for example, wore linen and boots instead of the wool and sandals which characterized their habits.[189] And at Elstow, the nuns were warned against wearing secular clothes instead of their traditional garb.[190] Similarly, one of the nuns at Carrow complained to the bishop that some of the young nuns wore silk waist bands.[191] Other than this complaint, the distribution of pittances and nuns' receipt of testamentary bequests did not contribute to a breakdown of the common life, or to a wild pursuit of worldly goods among the nuns in the diocese of Norwich. Indeed, the material lifestyles of these nuns seem to have been far from extravagant.[192]

A Prosopography of Superiors and Obedientiaries

How did the nuns acquire the administrative talent which enabled them to successfully manage their households on shoe-string budgets and in accordance with the communal structure of monastic rules? Obviously such talents required more than the prescribed qualities of industry and truth. Historians have suggested that female monastic superiors and obedientiaries were drawn exclusively from families of the upper echelons of late medieval society, who endowed their daughters with the skills necessary for household management to ensure favorable marriages.[193] While Joan Wiggenhall, the prioress of Crabhouse who planned and executed formidable building projects at this small priory, was related to people who could help finance her works, not all the diocese's superiors were so well-connected.

In fact, the prosopographical analysis used earlier to identify the social status of the nuns in the diocese as a whole indicates that only a small minority of officeholders came from wealthy families. Of the 203 identifiable officeholders in the diocese between 1350 and 1540 – 105 of whose social rank can be known for certain – none were from the aristocracy, and only 16 percent were from the upper gentry. In fact, as both the fixed and adjusted figures in Table 11 make clear, the majority of nuns who held monastic office in the late medieval diocese of Norwich – 65 percent – came from the middle ranks of late medieval society.

Five prioresses – Barbara Mason, Cecily Fastolf, Grace Sampson, Elizabeth

---

188 Like the luxury commodities shipped on a barge to Margaret Ratcliff, prioress of Swaffham Bulbeck, for her own use as they appear in her account of 1481: VCH, Cambridge, vol. 2, p. 227.

189 Jessopp, Visitations, p. 279.

190 Peacock, "Injunctions of John Langland," p. 53.

191 Jessopp, Visitations, p. 274.

192 Tillotson, Marrick Priory, pp. 13, 16–17 for a similar assessment of the lifestyle of the nuns at Marrick.

193 Jessopp, "The Ups and Downs," p. 49; Power, Medieval English Nunneries, pp. 4, 13, 42–3; Shahar, The Fourth Estate, pp. 39–40.

Table 11. *Social Rank of all Officeholders in the Female Monasteries
in the Diocese of Norwich, 1350–1540*

Social Rank	Officeholders in Known Social Rank (No.)	%	Adjusted Number of Officeholders in Social Rank (No.)	%
Titled Aristocracy	(0)	0	(0)	0
Upper Gentry	(33)	31	(33)	16
Parish Gentry	(56)	53	(132)	65
Urban	(13)	12	(32)	16
Yeoman	(3)	2	(6)	3
Total Known	(105)			
Total Adjusted	(98)		(203)	100

Note: As in Table 9, the first column lists the number of obedientiaries whose social rank can be known for certain. The second column of numbers is the total number of identifiable officeholders assigned to social groups based on the percentages of obedientiaries of known social rank. This adjustment balances the source bias discussed in Chapter 2, pp. 57–8. See Appendix 3 for further explanation of adjusted figures.

Dawney, and Ela Buttery – were from this middling group; their wills and their fates after the dissolution of their houses attest to their social rank of parish gentry.[194] The last prioress of Crabhouse, Elizabeth Studefield, can also be identified with a parish gentry family.[195] And these nuns were not anomalies: of the sixty-five abbesses and prioresses whose social status can be determined with some accuracy, none were from the aristocracy, twenty-four were from the upper gentry, while thirty-seven were from lesser gentry families. Only four superiors were from the urban bourgeoisie.[196]

The social status of most of the obedientiaries can be ascertained as well. Katherine Groome, precentor at Campsey Ash in 1532, was from a yeoman farmer family. Her mother's will indicates the family's rank; she had little more than a few pewter dishes and one cow to bequeath to her kin.[197] Katherine Symond, refecter and then second prioress at Campsey Ash, was from a parish gentry family.[198] So was Cecily Ryall, who served first as sacrist and later as subprioress at Carrow Priory in the late fifteenth century.[199] None of the obedientiaries in the diocese came from aristocratic families; nine were from

---

194 See Chapter 2 of this book, pp. 58–9.
195 PRO, SP 5/3/29.
196 A total of 115 superiors can be identified by name; we know the social rank of 65, approximately 57 percent of these women.
197 SRO, ASF IC/AA2/9, fol. 22.
198 See: Jessopp, *Visitations*, pp. 134, 219, 290. Her father's will is: SRO, ASF IC/AA2/9, fols. 51–52.
199 Rye, *Carrow Priory*, p. 40; Jessopp, *Visitations*, p. 17. Her father's will, by which I identify the family as parish gentry, is: NRO, NCC 103 Cobald.

the upper gentry, and nine were from the urban class. Like their superiors, the majority of obedientiaries in these eleven female houses – nineteen of them – were from lesser gentry families; three were from the rank of yeoman farmer.[200]

Not surprisingly, this distribution of monastic officials according to social rank reflects the overall social composition of these female monasteries – as the comparison of officeholders to the rest of the nuns in Table 12 demonstrates – with some slight variations. Most obedientiaries from wealthy urban families were found at Carrow Priory which does reflect the total population of nuns there. Upper gentry officeholders, on the other hand, made an equally strong showing at Bruisyard, Bungay and Campsey Ash: five upper gentry officers at each house. In the total population of nuns, a clear majority of this social rank were at Bruisyard.

The social status of these obedientiaries stands in stark contrast to what historians have previously believed about them in this later medieval period. These findings recall the issue of the criteria upon which election and appointment to these monastic offices were based. For if superiors and obedientiaries were not chosen because of their social standing in late medieval society, what factors did influence a nun's election or appointment to one of these monastic offices?

The careers of obedientiaries in the female houses in the diocese indicate that appointment to a monastic office was based not on social status, but rather on a nun's ability to carry out the duties of a particular office. We have already seen that Katherine Symond, a nun identified as from the rank of parish gentry, was first refectorer and then second prioress of Campsey Ash in the sixteenth century.[201] Bridget Cocket, also a lower gentry nun at Campsey Ash, started out as a novice in 1514, became second chamberer within twelve years, and then rose to become refectorer six years later.[202] Anne Martin, also from a parish gentry family, entered Carrow Priory as a novice in 1492, was cellarer by 1514, and within fifteen years was the infirmarer.[203] Following a similar course, Katherine Jerveys entered Carrow in 1492, was fourth prioress and precentrix by 1514, and then rose to third prioress by 1532.[204]

These examples could be given many times over. And unlike those obedientiaries who held office for only a short time – such as Mary White, who was a cellarer at Carrow for a brief tenure – nuns like Bridget Cocket, Anne Martin, and others who followed this career pattern of holding successively higher offices, must have shown administrative talent to continue to be appointed to various monastic offices, ascending from lesser ones, such as second chamberer,

---

200 Eighty-eight obedientiaries are known by name; of those we know for certain the social rank of 40, or 45 per cent.
201 See Jessopp, *Visitations*, pp. 134, 219, 290 for Katherine's career in officeholding.
202 Ibid., pp. 134, 219, 291.
203 Ibid.
204 Ibid., pp. 17, 145, 209, 273.

Table 12.   Social Rank of Nuns Compared to the Social Rank
of all Monastic Officeholders of the Female Monasteries
in the Diocese of Norwich, 1350–1540

Social Rank	All Nuns (No.)	%	All Officeholders (No.)	%
Aristocracy	(7)	1	(0)	0
Upper Gentry	(55)	10	(33)	16
Parish Gentry	(354)	64	(132)	65
Urban	(108)	20	(32)	16
Yeoman	(29)	5	(6)	3
Total Known	(170)		(105)	
Total Adjusted	(383)	100	(98)	100

Note: For explanations of adjusted figures see Tables 9 and 11, and Appendix 3.

to those with more responsibility and prestige, such as infirmarer and cellarer.[205] This career pattern can be discerned, in fact, in other female houses.[206]
    The career ladder of officeholding is most clearly visible in the rise of the
diocese's superiors: they were almost always elected to this highest monastic
office after holding a succession of lower ones, where they could hone and
demonstrate their managerial talents to their communities. At Carrow, for
instance, Margery Palmer served as cellarer for forty-four years before becoming
prioress in 1485.[207] Katherine Segrime was elected prioress in 1491, having
been refectorer and then cellarer for several years.[208] Joannna Narburgh was
bursar at Marham Abbey for twenty-one years before she held the position of
abbess for the following twenty years.[209] And Elizabeth Jenny was president
and then third prioress before she was elected to be prioress at Thetford in
1390.[210]
    These monastic offices entailed substantial administrative skills. We have
already seen the kinds of talents required of these women in the superiors' and

---

[205] Rye, Carrow Abbey, p. 42 where he says that Mary held this office sometime between
      1474 and 1480. She no longer held this or any other office in 1492; Jessopp, Visitations,
      p. 17.
[206] Liveing, The Records of Romsey, pp. 236–37: Elizabeth Rowthall was subsexter in 1502;
      by 1506 she was frater; in 1523 Agnes Harvey was chanter; three years later she was
      subprioress; ibid., for Clemence Maring who in 1523 was sexter, and in 1526 was also
      subprioress.
[207] Rye, Carrow Abbey, p. 42; NRO, NRS 26883 42 E8; and VCH, Norfolk, vol. 2, p. 354.
[208] Rye, Carrow Abbey, p. 42; NRO, Hare 5954 227x1.
[209] NRO, Hare 2201 194x5; NRO, Hare 2203 194x5; NRO, Hare 2204 194x5.
[210] Jenny was a nun at Thetford in 1381: PRO, E 179/45/5b; and became president and
      then third prioress between then and 1390 when she was elected prioress: Blomefield,
      An Essay, vol. 2, p. 92.

cellarers' accounts discussed earlier. Prioress Alice Lampet of Redlingfield, for example, was responsible for managing a considerable income from rents and from weekly payments from the priory's many boarders. She also made final decisions about a vast range of rental and agricultural activities; some properties were farmed out, as the situation demanded, or held in her own hands.[211] All of these monastic officers had income to collect and discharge in limited but numerous ways, and doing so successfully took considerable administrative and financial know-how.

Such knowledge and skill took time to acquire. Novices or young nuns, regardless of their social status, were not ready to take on the demanding tasks involved in running a monastery: operating its estates, counseling and negotiating relations among other nuns, and managing the monastic household, which included a static population of servants and boarders as well as the many itinerant visitors whose short-term stays temporarily increased a house's numbers. It is not surprising, then, that nuns were not supposed to be appointed to monastic offices until they had been professed for at least seven years.

In fact, most of the prioresses and abbesses of these late medieval convents were well into middle age when they acceded to this highest office. Like Alice Lampet, Bridget Cocket, and Anne Martin, nuns who proved themselves capable in their capacities as officeholders were re-appointed or elected to higher positions. Those who were unable to perform held their offices for only a short time. If social status had been the criteria upon which election or appointment to a monastic office was based then surely the social ranks of this cohort of officeholders would not so accurately reflect the distribution of social groups in the female monastic population as a whole. In other words, if officeholding in these female monasteries had been a function of elevated social status, then relative to the general population of these houses, many more aristocratic and upper gentry nuns would have been officers. Ability and merit, then, played a more significant part in acquiring and retaining monastic offices.

By contrast, the criteria for appointment to office used in many male houses – specifically in the Benedictine cathedral priories – appears to have had little to do with a monk's past experience, or with any previously proven administrative abilities. In fact, as Joan Greatrex put it, ". . . the guiding principle seems to have been constant change, thus resembling a rota, though without any predetermined order of succession."[212] Only at the Cathedral Priory in Canterbury were electors of priors concerned that the next one elected have demonstrated abilities to be an effective administrator. Otherwise, it seems that obedience was the overriding concern in these large male houses when their superiors chose monks to fill monastic offices.[213]

The nuns' household management extended beyond just feeding and clothing the nuns and maintaining the buildings of the cloister; it also included provisioning their staffs of servants as well as many guests. Both superiors and their obedientiaries collected a range of revenues which enabled the operation of their convents. Sharing a wide range of responsibilites among them – in the case of Marham Abbey, establishing an executive board of nuns who collected and dispersed the funds necessary to individual offices – the nuns were usually able to keep their houses operating without incurring the chronic debt which so often crippled the diocese's male houses. Except for Blackborough, Redling-field, and Thetford, these female monasteries appear to have weathered times of financial insecurity by adopting some of the same measures their secular counterparts did in this period of decline and dislocation.

This absence of debt was in large part a result of the administrative talents most of the convents' officeholders appear to have held. Despite a few instances of administrative irregularities, these mostly parish gentry obedientiaries were skilled managers who were rewarded by being assigned to higher household offices. The existence of a monastic career ladder must have been crucial to the proper functioning of these small and poor houses, most of which have been traditionally seen as bankrupt and moribund. Their achievements as administrators are further demonstrated by their abilities to maintain a suffi-cient number of household servants and staff, as well as numerous permanent and temporary visitors, all of whom contributed to the ever-changing popula-tions of these female houses.

4

The Monastic Community:
Clerical and Lay Residents

Female monastic communities, like their male counterparts, housed an ever shifting population. In addition to novices and nuns, a semi-permanent support staff of male clerics – priests, chaplains, and confessors – and household servants and agricultural laborers, or hinds, provided services essential to the spiritual and physical welfare of the professed residents and to the operation of their communities. In exchange for their work, staff members received wages and sometimes room and board. Another group who contributed to the population of a monastery were the recipients of monastic charity and hospitality. These included permanent tenants – almsfolk, pensioners, and corrodians – who were supported with money or with food, clothes and rooms at a priory's expense. Other residents were long- and short-term boarders who also enjoyed the nuns' hospitality, but paid for their accommodation. Also associated with these fluid communities were those who rented rooms or small cottages within the precincts.

By accommodating these people, the nuns fulfilled three of St Benedict's commands: to refresh the needy, clothe and care for the poor, and extend hospitality to guests and patrons.[1] Although the presence of lay people in the monasteries and the performance of charitable acts and hospitality appears antithetical to a cloistered life, such activities were as integral to a monastic vocation as the singing of the Divine Office.[2] Acts of hospitality and charity comprised the active part of a nun's religious vocation, in contrast to the contemplative quality of her life as defined by the daily recitation of the Divine Office, private meditation, and reading. Some monasteries, like Butley and

---

1 Gasquet, *The Rule of St Benedict*, Chap. 4 for care of the needy and poor; ibid., Chap. 53 for hospitality to guests and patrons.
2 Jean Leclercq, "Hospitality and Monastic Prayer," pp. 3–10 where he discusses the importance of monastic hospitality to both the recipients and monks, and the efforts to reconcile the seeming contradiction between providing for the lay visitors while protecting the cloister of the male religious. See also: Tillotson, "Visitation and Reform," pp. 14–15 for the normal part of monastic life boarders and recipients of nuns' charity and hospitality were.

Leiston abbeys in Suffolk, in fact, were founded specifically to provide food or shelter to anyone who wanted it.[3]

Despite the intention of Benedict's Rule, the presence of lay people in and around the monastic precincts, and the provision of charity and hospitality, could easily disrupt the nuns' insular world. Indeed, the regulation of any interactions between them and their servants and guests was a continuing concern of episcopal authorities throughout the later Middle Ages.[4] But what impact did the non-professed population have on the nuns in the diocese of Norwich? Was the presence of lay people so distracting that the nuns were unable to fulfill the myriad facets of their religious vocation, observe their daily rounds of prayer and carry out their missions of charity and hospitality without being spiritually or financially compromised?

Any attempt to answer these and other questions about the impact on the cloister of this population of servants and guests must start by identifying who these people were and then calculating, where possible, their numbers within each of the diocese's eleven female houses. The ratio of clerics, servants, and lay residents to nuns can indicate what burden, if any, the non-cloistered population presented to the nuns and their religious houses.

Support Staff

Among the most important residents of the female monasteries were the chaplains and priests, like the ones who traveled with Madame Eglyntyne and her companion in Chaucer's *Canterbury Tales*, who executed various sacerdotal functions the nuns could not perform for themselves.[5] Most female houses, like Swaffham Bulbeck in Cambridge, maintained at least two permanent chaplains, though Marham had one, and Redlingfield supported three.[6] Itinerant preachers, like the Dominican friar who stayed for a few nights at Blackborough Priory in 1532 while he heard the confessions of the nuns and some of their servants, also contributed to a priory's clerical population.[7] The household accounts of Carrow note annual payments to visiting preachers,

3   Mortimer, *Leiston Abbey Cartulary and Butley Abbey Charters*, p. 2.
4   Tillotson, "Visitation and Reform," passim.
5   Fisher, *The Complete Poetry and Prose of Geoffrey Chaucer*, p. 12, lines 162–63: "Another nonne with hir hadde she,/ That was her chapeleyn, and preestes thre." Ibid., pp. 297–307 for the tale the nun's priest tells. See also: Thompson, "Double Monasteries and the Male Element in Nunneries," pp. 145–65.
6   For female houses in general, see: Power, *Medieval English Nunneries*, p. 144. For Swaffham, see: Palmer, "The Benedictine Nunnery," p. 34. For the Norwich diocesan houses especially, see: PRO, SP 5/4/140 (Blackborough); SRO, HD 1538/156/17 (Bungay); *Carrow Abbey*, p. 16 (Carrow); SRO, HA/12/B2/18/14 (Flixton). For Marham, see: Nichols, "The History and Cartulary," p. 96; for Redlingfield, see: VCH, *Suffolk*, vol. 2, p. 84.
7   Jessopp, *Visitations*, p. 311.

confessors, and chaplains in addition to the permanent priests the priory maintained.[8]

Resident priests and chaplains received an annual stipend from the nuns which varied from house to house.[9] The standard annual wage for the resident chaplain at Carrow was £2 13s 4d; the cellarer at Bungay paid the priory's chaplain £3; the priest at Marham received £4 annually.[10] The higher wage paid to the priest at Marham may have reflected his double position as both convent and parish priest; the abbey's chapel also served as the parish church.[11] Most of the resident clerics received board in addition to their annual stipend, but at some priories, Bungay for example, the chaplains paid for their meals: Adam Cole, chaplain for the nuns there in 1406, paid the cellarer 52s for his food for the whole year.[12]

These clerics were as important to the convents' servants and guests as they were to the nuns. At Bungay the chaplain administered the sacraments to the nuns, their servants, and their permanent and temporary boarders.[13] The absence of a priest could therefore be a problem for the religious communities. At Flixton Priory, in 1493, one of their chaplains was away and the other priest's arm was broken; the nuns and their extended household were thus obliged to go elsewhere for services.[14]

In addition to resident priests like these, Campsey Ash Priory maintained a secular chantry of a warden and four chaplains. This foundation was unique: its location was inside the convent's precincts, where the nuns built the priests "a suitable house with chambers and a common room within the close near to the chapel, and [paid] the master thirteen marks yearly, and the four chaplains ten marks annually."[15] The chantry was continually supported by the Crown, who issued licenses to the nuns to acquire land in mortmain to support the five resident chaplains.[16] They were still at Campsey Ash in 1535 as they appear in the convent's *Valor* as a warden and four chaplains who lived at the house and received annual stipends from the priory.[17]

Though other female houses in medieval England maintained affiliated chantries – as did the nuns at Bruisyard[18] – siting a secular chantry actually

---

8   For example, see: NRO, Hare 5954 227x1, where the prioress paid 6s 8d to the convent's confessor.
9   Power, *Medieval English Nunneries*, pp. 114, 152 for the stipends at other female houses.
10 NRO, NRS 26883 42 E8 and NRO, NRS 26884 423 E8 (Carrow); SRO, HD 1538/156/7 (Bungay); and NRO, Hare 2206 194x5 and NRO, Hare 2207 194x5 (Marham).
11 For a discussion of convents' chapels as parish churches, see Chapter 5 below, pp. 147–56.
12 SRO, HD 1538/156/7; for this procedure at other female houses, see, Power, *Medieval English Nunneries*, pp. 144–45.
13 *Papal Letters*, vol. 5, p. 596.
14 Jessopp, *Visitations*, p. 47.
15 VCH, *Suffolk*, vol. 2, p. 113.
16 CPR, *1381–85*, p. 295 for permission in 1382; and CPR, *1388–92*, pp. 230–31 for another license issued in 1390.
17 VE, vol. 3, p. 417.
18 When Maud of Oxford petitioned the Crown to move from Campsey Ash to Bruisyard in 1356, she requested that her chantry foundation be allowed to move with her; it was,

within the precincts of a female monastery was highly unusual, and few other examples of this are known.[19] Though the original foundation at Campsey Ash was Maud's, the chantry's continued existence there after her departure to Bruisyard signifies the priory's wealth and reputation as a holy house.[20] That the chantries at both Campsey Ash and Bruisyard were founded at times when such foundations in monasteries were declining also reflects the spiritual promise of these two houses.[21]

Although chantry chaplains were rare, resident priests, and itinerant con-fessors and preachers were common to all female monasteries, and there is no evidence of the kinds of scandal between resident priests and nuns in the diocese that appear in bishops' visitations of female houses elsewhere in England.[22] The positive relations between the nuns in the diocese and the priests and chaplains who served them can be seen in their wills. Both John Colby, a chaplain at Bungay Priory who died in 1373, and one of his successors, Reginald Cakebrech, whose will is dated 1444, for example, made bequests to the nuns there and asked to be buried in their church.[23] Several of the chantry priests at Campsey Ash did the same, among them William Worsted, who requested burial "where the prioress and convent themselves are placed"; Robert Goselyne left the decision about where he was to be buried to the nuns.[24] Numerous priests and chaplains of Carrow also remembered the nuns with money and goods, and made similar burial requests.[25]

Male clerics were essential to the nuns' religious lives, but their household servants comprised a larger part of their staffs. Five maids and seven hinds served the nine nuns at Blackborough in the sixteenth century.[26] In her

to one of Bruisyard's manors, Rockhall Manor: CPR, 1354–58, pp. 484–86. See also VCH, Suffolk, vol. 2, p. 131.

19 Joel Rosenthal, The Purchase of Paradise: Gift Giving and the Aristocracy, 1307–1485 (London, 1972), p. 36. The other two female houses which had the advowsons of chantries were Cannington Priory, a Benedictine house in Somerset, and a Cistercian house, Greenfield Abbey in Lincoln. But these chantries were not established inside these convents' walls. Paxton, "London Nunneries," pp. 122–23 for chantry foundations in precincts of the Minories and St Helen's Bishopsgate.

20 Rosenthal, Purchase of Paradise, p. 40 where he discusses how chantry foundations both signaled and enhanced a house's prestige.

21 Ibid., p. 33 for the drop in monastic chantry foundations from the mid-fourteenth through the fifteenth centuries.

22 Power, Medieval English Nunneries, pp. 399–403.

23 NRO, NCC 35 Heydon (John Colby); NRO, NCC 18 Wylbey for the will of Reginald Cakebrech.

24 NRO, NCC 40 Hyrnyng for Worsted, whose will was dated 1414; NRO, NCC 46 Hyrnyng for Goselyne who was buried a year later.

25 William Baxtere wanted to be buried in the chapel of St John the Evangelist, on the south side of the church of the nuns of Carrow: NRO, NCC 86 Doke (1438); William Walsingham asked to be placed "in the church of the nuns at Carrow, before the door of the chapel of St Ann": NRO, NCC 115 Gelour (1474) also cited in Rye, Carrow Abbey, p. xviii. For bequests, see: NRO, NCC 51 Hyrnyng (1419); NRO, NCC 108 Brosyard (1458); and NRO, NCC 195 Gelour (1478).

26 PRO, SP 5/4/140.

account, the cellarer of Bungay paid her own staff of servants – two women, Alice and Johanna, launderers, a cook, a baker, and a maltster – as well as the prioress's.[27] At least four maids, a baker and her helper, a cook, a porter, a cowherd, two shop-workers, two threshers, a swineherd, a woodhauler, and six hinds lived at Flixton Priory in the fifteenth century.[28] At the Suppression, four household servants and seventeen hinds lived in the precincts of Redlingfield Priory.[29] Numerous maids, butlers, cooks, and hinds were also employed by the nuns of Carrow and Marham.[30]

Seasonal laborers, who helped with sowing, reaping, shearing, and slaughtering, also added to monastic household size at times prescribed by the agricultural calendar. Along with daily wages, these hired hands also received room and board. The prioress of Carrow, for example, made payments to reapers, who bound, gathered, and carted hay, oats, and rye, and to other seasonal laborers, most of whom lived in the precincts while they worked on the priory's home farm.[31] Seasonal laborers also boarded at Marham Abbey while working for the nuns there.[32]

These servants would have been more likely than resident priests to bring the outside secular world into the nuns' cloistered one. In 1364 at Marham, one of the abbey's servants, Katherine Martyn, was raped inside the close by an intruder.[33] Another member of the abbey's household, Roger Mendham, was killed in 1376 by Robert Malkynesson who was indicted for breaking and entering the abbey's close.[34] While there is little evidence for this kind of disruption at the diocese's female houses, these crimes must have been rude reminders of the world the nuns thought they had left behind.

---

[27] SRO, HD 1538/156/7.

[28] SRO, HA/12/B2/18/14. This document, an undated list of all of the people who lived within the Flixton Priory precinct, can be dated to 1414 because Elizabeth More is named as the last prioress, and her tenure ended with her death in 1414. Katherine Pilly was elected in 1414, but Elizabeth must have still been alive when the list was drawn up because she is listed as receiving a corrody. For Elizabeth's death and Katherine's election, see: *VCH, Suffolk*, vol. 2, p. 117.

[29] *VCH, Suffolk*, vol. 2, p. 84.

[30] For Carrow: the maids and launderers listed in NRO, Hare 5957 227x1; for Marham: NRO, Hare 2211 194x5.

[31] NRO, NRS 26882 42 E8, the prioress's account of 1455/56; and NRO, NRS 26883 42 E8, her account for 1484/85.

[32] See for example: NRO, Hare 2207 194x5 (1456/57) for the prebend of Richard Hawkyn, thresher; and NRO, Hare 2208 194x5 (1468/69) for the board of John Dobbes, John Mason and John Swanton, threshers.

[33] *CPR, 1361–64*, p. 435. The rapist, Alan de Ileye, was pardoned by the Crown.

[34] We know this crime occurred because a reference is made to it in *CPR, 1388–92*, p. 494 when Malkynesson's goods and chattels, which had been forfeit because of his crime, were sold for 5 marks to Thomas Upton.

Lay Boarders

The clerics and workers who earned wages and board were essential components of these religious communities. Equally important to the nuns' lives were those who benefitted from their charity, corrodians and pensioners. A corrodian was someone who obtained a grant of room, board, fuel, and clothes from a monastery, often in exchange for a piece of property, the rents from land, a single payment of cash, or services rendered.[35] And the quality and quantity of the food and board offered to these people varied according to their social rank.[36] Thomas Foster, a corrodian at the female house in Thetford, for example, had a private servant who had the same rights to room and board as one of the monastic household servants.[37] Such servants, as well as corrodians of lesser status, like Randulfus and Cecilia at Coxford Priory, drew "food and drink of a free servant."[38]

Corrodians often included ex-superiors like Katherine Pilly, prioress of Flixton. She resigned in 1432 after eighteen years of service to her community with a corrody which included rooms for herself and a maid. From the priory's kitchen, they received daily two white loaves of bread, eight whole loaves, and eight gallons of ale, with a dish for both. The convent also provided Pilly and her servant annually with 200 faggots and 100 logs for fuel and eight pounds of candles.[39]

While similar provisions were extended to all ex-superiors – even ones removed in disgrace, like Abbot John of Wymondham Priory, who among other transgressions "allowed his monks to buy and sell like merchants"[40] – more commonly in these female houses lay people entered into private agreements with the nuns for corrodies.[41] In 1414, at least fifteen corrodians had

---

[35] Sometimes corrodies are called liveries, as they are in: Denny, *Sibton Abbey Estates*, p. 26. See also: Richard Harper, "A Note on Corrodies in the Fourteenth Century," *Albion* 15 (1983), pp. 95–102; Ian Keil, "Corrodies of Glastonbury Abbey in the Later Middle Ages," *Somerset Archaeological and Natural History Society Proceedings* 108 (1964), pp. 113–31; John Tillotson, "Pensions, Corrodies and Religious Houses: An Aspect of the Relations of Crown and Church in Early Fourteenth-Century England," *Journal of Religious History* 8 (1974–75), pp. 127–43. But see: Joel Rosenthal, "Retirement and the Life Cycle in Fifteenth-Century England," in *Aging and the Aged in Medieval Europe*, ed. Michael Sheehan (Toronto, 1990), p. 175 who suggests that historians have exaggerated the popularity and frequency of corrodians.

[36] For the distinction between corrodies based on the social rank of the recipient, see: Keil, "Corrodies of Glastonbury," pp. 113–14 where he discerns six grades of corrodies at this male house in 1332/33; and Power, *Medieval English Nunneries*, p. 197.

[37] Jessopp, *Visitations*, pp. 303–4.

[38] Saunders, "A History of Coxford Priory," p. 318.

[39] VCH, *Suffolk*, vol. 2, p. 116.

[40] Jessop, *Visitations*, pp. 20, 21–3.

[41] For corrodies procured through private agreement with inmates of religious communities, see: Knowles, *The Religious Orders*, vol. 3, p. 266; Power, *Medieval English Nunneries*, pp. 190–97; Snape, *English Finances*, pp. 139–42; and Tillotson, "Pensions, Corrodies and Religious Houses," p. 131.

negotiated for their maintenance with the nuns at Flixton Priory. The house supported additionally twelve nuns, two chaplains, and twenty hinds and household servants.[42] The corrodians here included two brothers, their wives and two maids, three sisters, their maid and chaplain, Roger Hord and his wife Pamela, and a man named Blynd and his wife. All we know about these people is that they had two corrodies each from the priory; what these entailed is unknown. The document notes only that Blynd and his wife had bread, an unspecified amount of food, wood, and candles. Another corrodian there, Margaret Broton, was likewise provisioned.

Corrodians at the other female houses in the diocese included Nicholas Gernoun, Knight, at Bruisyard in the late fourteenth century.[43] He first appears in 1369 when he petitioned the Crown for permission to stay at the abbey so that he could be close to the King's kinswoman, Maud, Countess of Oxford.[44] He later received royal permission to hold his lands, keep his yearly rents, and live permanently there.[45] Thomas Foster was at Thetford with his wife, their three children, and a maid in the sixteenth century; John Bixley, butcher, of Thetford was also a corrodian there.[46] Two married couples obtained corrodies from the nuns at Crabhouse in the mid-fourteenth century, and Marham supported three corrodians in 1468, but only one in 1470.[47]

Corrodians differed from pensioners, like those at the male house of Sibton Abbey in Suffolk who lived within the abbey's precinct, but received yearly grants of money for their livelihood instead of food and clothes.[48] Sir Hugh Burre, a clerk from Lynton, was a pensioner at Blackborough in the late fourteenth century. Prioress Maud and her convent granted him a yearly pension of £20 which was to be collected from their holdings in nearby parishes.[49]

By far the most numerous lay members of all of the female houses were long-term boarders – referred to as prehendaries (*prehendarii*) – who paid for the food and board they received at the nuns' hands. The beleaguered lovers Richard Call, sometime bailiff and cellarer at Blackborough, and Margery Paston stayed for a while at this house until the Pastons came to terms with this unwelcome match.[50] No less than 250 boarders are known to have been at Carrow from the late fourteenth through the mid-fifteenth centuries.[51] These people included single women, like Alice de Cheselden, as well as

42 SRO, HA/12/B2/18/14.
43 Bourdillon, *The Minoresses*, p. 25; VCH, *Suffolk*, vol. 2, p. 132.
44 CPR, 1367–70, p. 219.
45 CPR, 1381–85, p. 161.
46 Jessopp, *Visitations*, pp. 303–4 for these corrodians at Thetford.
47 Bateson, "The Register," pp. 42–3; NRO, Hare 2208 194x5 (1468); and NRO, Hare 2209 194x5 (1470).
48 Denny, *The Sibton Abbey Estates*, p. 117.
49 CCR, 1389–92, p. 77.
50 Norman Davis, ed., *Paston Letters and Papers of the Fifteenth Century* (Oxford, 1971), vol. 1, p. 549. Above, Chapter 3, p. 98.
51 Rye, *Carrow Abbey*, pp. 48–52.

married ones like Joan Drake and her daughter, and Lady Margaret Kerdeston, her servant, and her daughter.[52]

Boarders often stayed for extended periods of time. The Countess of Suffolk's daughter, Phillipa, and her maid lodged at Bungay Priory for a total of sixty weeks between 1416 and 1417, as did her half-sister, Elizabeth.[53] Elizabeth and her servant, in fact, divided their time between Bruisyard and Bungay where "a brother there called 'le president'" taught her during her twenty-week stay.[54] The Countess's god-daughter, Katherine, also spent some time at Bruisyard with her mother.[55] And the nuns at Campsey Ash hosted Edward III's granddaughter, Phillipa, in the mid-fourteenth century.[56] Lengthy retreats like these were not unusual and appear to have been fairly common at female houses in other dioceses.[57]

Bungay Priory also drew an array of lodgers who stayed for various lengths of time: Thomas Wolsy, for example, paid 16s 3d for his nine-month stay there in 1490, and Margaret Alman paid 23s 4d for her year-long sojourn there in 1512.[58] The same mix can be seen at Marham Abbey where, for example, the daughter of the knight, Edmund Berry, boarded during the six-month stay of one Leonard Cotton.[59] The nuns at Redlingfield received £22 2s from Lady Katherine Boteler and others in 1447, as well as 100s 8d from Alice Charles and unspecified others of lesser social standing.[60]

While these houses accommodated both female and male boarders, the majority of the lay population of guests at these convents were women. Of the 250 people who boarded at Carrow throughout the fifteenth century, for example, at least 182 were women, including married women and their servants, as well as the daughters of local citizens, like the two unnamed daughters of Sir John White who boarded there.[61] The prioress's account from that house in 1503/04 names five boarders from whom the nuns received money; only two of them were male.[62] Likewise, of the sixteen boarders listed

---

[52] Ibid., p. 49 for Alice de Cheselden and the Drakes, and ibid., p. 50 for the Kerdestons.
[53] BL, Egerton 8776: Elizabeth sojourned at Bungay for 22 weeks, and again for 19 weeks.
[54] Ibid.
[55] Ibid.
[56] The length of her stay is not recorded, but we know she was going to spend some time at the priory because in 1356 the King appointed "Raymond Perpont to take carpenters, masons, and other workmen for the repair of the houses of the priory of Campsey", where Edward's son Lionel's daughter "was to dwell for a certain time": CPR, 1354–58, p. 352.
[57] No systematic study of boarders at female or male houses has been undertaken, but see: Palmer, "The Benedictine Nunnery," p. 32.
[58] SRO, HD 1538/156/14 for Wolsy; SRO, HD 1538/156/17 for Alman.
[59] NRO, Hare 2205 194x5 (1446/47).
[60] SRO, HD 1538/327. Katherine Boteler was the wife of Sir Andrew Boteler, Kt, and she was at Redlingfield in 1460 when she made her will: NRO, NCC 6–8 Betyns.
[61] Rye, Carrow Abbey, p. 52.
[62] NRO, Hare 5954 227x1.

in the cartulary of Marham, eleven were women.[63] Most of the *prehendarii* noted in the Marham abbesses' accounts are also female.[64]

Other boarders included children sent to the monasteries to be educated, and while the majority of the children educated at the houses in the diocese of Norwich were female, male children were not uncommon.[65] The nuns at Carrow received 21s from Thomas Elys for the room and food for his daughters who stayed at the priory for thirty-six weeks.[66] The nuns there also boarded the son of Sir John White and the son of Richard Dade.[67] Master Loveday paid the prioress of Bungay 68s 4d for his own food and board, and for the board and education of his two daughters, who stayed on after his departure.[68] The executors of Robert Brandon paid the abbess of Marham £7 13s 4d for boarding his two daughters.[69] William Gilbert paid the abbey 10s 7d for similar provisions the nuns there provided for his son Robert.[70] The nuns at Redlingfield also boarded young boys.[71]

Children were boarded at female monasteries all over medieval England. The suppression commissioners noted in their list of the inmates of the Benedictine nunnery, St Mary's, Winchester, no less than twenty-six children who were long-term residents there to be educated by the nuns.[72] At least twelve convents in the diocese of York boarded local children.[73] While we do not know for certain what kind of education the nuns provided, it most likely included basic English, reading and writing, and maybe some French.[74]

Shorter-term visitors also swelled a monastery's population, and their status

---

[63] NRO, Hare 1 232x.

[64] For example: NRO, Hare 2204 194x5 (1426/27), Anna Irmynglond and other sisters, and Agnes Copyldyk, with her lady, paid for their stays there; so did the daughters of Edmund Berry, Robert Eliston, sen., and William Copyldyk.

[65] For residence in female and male monasteries for the purpose of education, see: William Courtenay, *Schools and Scholars in Fourteenth-Century England* (New Jersey, 1987), p. 13 for female houses, and ibid., pp. 56, 77 for male ones; Moran, *The Growth of English Schooling*, passim; Nicholas Orme, *English Schools in the Middle Ages* (London, 1973), pp. 51, 243 for children in male houses, and ibid., pp. 53–5 for children in female convents. See also his: *Education and Society in Medieval and Renaissance England* (London, 1989), pp. 166, 170.

[66] NRO, NRS 26882 42 E8.

[67] Rye, *Carrow Abbey*, p. 52 for White's son; NRO, Hare 5955 227x1 (1520/21) for Julian Dade. See also: NRO, NRS 26882 42 E8 where John Ilberd and his four sons were at the priory; and Power, *Medieval English Nunneries*, p. 267.

[68] SRO, HD 1538/156/14.

[69] NRO, Hare 2207 194x5.

[70] NRO, Hare 2207 194x5.

[71] Jessopp, *Visitations*, pp. 138–40.

[72] Dugdale, *Monasticon*, vol. 2, p. 221.

[73] Moran, *The Growth of English Schooling*, p. 100 and Tillotson, "Visitation and Reform," p. 14 for girls at female houses in Yorkshire. VCH, *Lincoln*, vol. 2, p. 156 for children also at Gokewell; ibid., p. 152 for Nun Cotham; ibid., pp. 149–50 Heynings.

[74] Moran, *The Growth of English Schooling*, pp. 69, 115–16 for nuns teaching children to read English and some French; Power, *Medieval English Nunneries*, pp. 262, 276–78 says that children were taught to read English, but probably not to write it.

affected the quality of room and board they received. Bishops or their agents, whose visitation of a house may have included an overnight stay or at least a meal, papal emissaries, visiting religious from other houses, and royal commissioners would be shown the best a house had to offer. The royal commissioners who visited Marham Abbey in 1535, for example, dined with the abbess on the abbey's finest food and were bedded in the utmost comfort.[75] The traveling minstrels and strolling players who stayed for a few days at a time to entertain the canons and their guests at the Cluniac house in Thetford in 1498, and those who visited the monks at the Cathedral Priory in Norwich year-round, also contributed to a monastery's population.[76] The passing strangers for whom the prioresses of Crabhouse maintained a special reserve of cash belonged to this category of temporary guests as well.[77]

Renters

In addition to the employees, corrodians, pensioners, and long- and short-term boarders who lived in the nuns' guesthouses or working lofts, others lived within the priories' grounds as paying tenants under various lease and rental agreements. A mortuary list of Marham Abbey names sixteen women and men who had rented rooms and buildings within its close between 1401 and 1453.[78] Rents collected from tenants for cottages or rooms within the priory's precinct listed in the household accounts of Carrow indicate that this priory too sustained an active renter population. Thomas Wetherby, the man who oversaw the priory's finances for a time, lived "in a dwelling within the priory of Carrow," with his wife Margery, their two daughters and maids.[79] So did Elizabeth Yaxley, who in her will requested that her servants be allowed to continue to reside in her rooms there for a year after her death.[80] Helena Melton paid the nuns at Carrow 16s a year rent for one tenement situated next to the priory's granary.[81] And Joanna Pulham paid 10s for rent of one of the small houses within the convent's gates.[82]

Such paying tenants lived in the precincts of Bromholm, St Benedict at Holme, and Sibton Abbey, three of the diocese's male houses, as well.[83] And

[75] PRO, SP 5/2/246–48.
[76] John Hervey, "The Last Years of Thetford Cluniac Priory," NA 27 (1941), p. 3; John Wasson, "Visiting Entertainers at the Cluniac Priory, Thetford 1497–1540," Albion 9:2 (1977), pp. 128–34. Saunders, An Introduction, pp. 182–83 for the Cathedral Priory.
[77] Bateson, "The Register," p. 42.
[78] NRO, Hare 1 232x1.
[79] CPR, 1441–46, p. 366.
[80] Rye, Carrow Abbey, p. 52. Elizabeth's will is: NRO, NCC 104–108 Platfoote, and is dated 1530.
[81] NRO, Hare 5945 227x1.
[82] NRO, NRS 26882 42 E8.
[83] Redstone, "The Cellarer's Account," p. 50 for Bromholm; Rye, "Laymen Lodging," p. 9 for St Benet at Holme; and Denny, Sibton Abbey Estates, p. 26.

while it might seem that a renter market would have been more common in urban houses like Carrow, whose locations ensured a larger population in need of housing, a tenant population existed in both urban and rural monasteries, like Marham and Sibton abbeys, and the priories of Bromholm and St Benedict at Holme.

Social Rank of Personnel and Lay Boarders

These female houses accommodated a predominantly female lay population throughout the later Middle Ages, members of which came from diverse social backgrounds. Household servants were usually local people of minor if any social standing,[84] as were the identifiable corrodians and guests at Crabhouse and Flixton. The absence of local gentry visitors at these two houses, though, may be a result of the scarcity of sources for them. The boarders of unknown social status at Flixton and Crabhouse might also reflect the relative poverty of these two houses; Flixton was the poorest of the diocese's female houses and Crabhouse ran a close second.[85] Perhaps people from society's more elite groups sought to sojourn at wealthier houses which could more readily meet their needs.

The more abundant documents for Bungay, Carrow, Marham, Redlingfield, and Thetford, however, reveal a socially diverse group of lay boarders and other visitors, suggesting that finances did not necessarily determine the social standing of visitors to these convents. As we have seen, Bungay Priory managed relatively slim resources, but it nevertheless attracted the daughters of the Countess of Suffolk as well as persons of lower social rank. Similarly, Carrow, Marham, Redlingfield, and Thetford accommodated local notables like Lady Boteler, who stayed at Redlingfield, and George Sefoule, who was at Marham.[86] As none of these monasteries were very wealthy, their local reputation must have attracted these guests. Carrow Priory's mixture of local Norwich society must also have reflected its urban location.[87]

Bruisyard Abbey and Campsey Ash Priory were the only two female houses in the diocese whose clientele appear to have been strictly from the upper ranks of late medieval society. Lady Willoughby and her retinue were at Campsey

---

[84] Nichols, "The History and Cartulary," pp. 94–6 where he identifies Marham Abbey's hired household and seasonal help "peasant wage-earners."

[85] See above, Tables 2 and 7. Though we have seen that the *Valor* greatly under-estimated most monasteries' wealth, these figures are the only ones available to determine the wealth of these two houses.

[86] Lady Boteler can be identified as at least minor gentry from her will cited above: p. 118, note 58. George Sefoule was an esquire of Waterden: Roger Virgoe, personal conversation.

[87] For the social standing of Carrow's permanent lay population, see: Rye, *Carrow Abbey*, pp. 48–52; and Rye, "Laymen Lodging," p. 10.

Ash when the house was suppressed in 1537.[88] And perhaps like attracted like: certainly Maud, Countess of Oxford, drew people to Bruisyard by her presence there. Although one of the diocese's poorer convents, Bruisyard's exclusive status as a house of Poor Clares probably attracted socially prominent guests.[89] The abbey's exclusivity is further illustrated by the process by which one gained access to the abbey. Because it was a house of Poor Clares, one had to petition the pope to retreat there.[90] Eleanor, Duchess of Norfolk, for example, received papal permission to enter Bruisyard, "with four honest matrons," four times a year, providing that the abbess and her sisters consented. The duchess and her retinue could eat and drink at the abbey, but could stay overnight only "when urgent necessity arises."[91] Obtaining papal license to enter the abbey would certainly have been an obstacle to those of lesser social standing who could not afford this procedure.[92]

Papal permission to enter Bruisyard not only helped to screen the long-term boarders there, but must also have controlled their numbers. One of the reasons why Maud of Oxford wanted to leave Campsey Ash was because "of the great number of nobles who attend there," implying that fewer people – or fewer numbers of nobles – stayed at Bruisyard.[93] So while we can identify only one of the individuals who stayed at Campsey Ash while Maud was there, the King's granddaughter Phillipa, Maud's statement suggests that many nobles visited this house on a regular basis. Undoubtedly Campsey Ash's greater wealth – and possibly the existence of the chantry there – contributed to its ability to draw numerous guests from society's elite.

The social ranks of the lay population of these female houses mirrored the social composition of the nuns who lived in them. While most of the houses primarily supported guests, lodgers, and nuns from the middle ranks of society, Bruisyard maintained a greater percentage of upper gentry nuns and lay guests, indicating again that the wealth of a house did not necessarily affect its social composition. The financial status of Bungay and Carrow did not determine the social status of the boarders at these priories either. A monastery's reputation then must have influenced a person's decision about where to board one's children, or where to spend some time away from worldly concerns.

Convents in other dioceses also lodged a socially mixed populace of primarily female guests, indicating the female houses in Norfolk and Suffolk were representative of convents elsewhere in England.[94] Most of the Neville family women stayed at Grace Dieu, in the county of Leicester, at the same time as

---

88   PRO, SP 1/145/107.
89   VE, vol. 3, p. 443 gave the abbey a value of £56 12s, ranking the house sixth in wealth.
90   Bourdillon, The Minoresses, p. 62.
91   Papal Letters, vol. 9, p. 122.
92   Tillotson, "Visitation and Reform," p. 7 for an example of a woman of the local aristocracy who had to obtain a license from the archbishop of York to stay at Nunappleton.
93   Papal Letters, vol. 4, p. 37.
94   Tillotson, "Visitation and Reform," p. 7 for the convents in Yorkshire.

did others less well-known, including Joan Villian, and the daughter of Giles Jordan.[95] Similarly, Lady Beaumont boarded one of her daughters at this house for a year during the stay of two of the convent's neighbors, the daughters of Thomas Hunte who were there to be schooled by the nuns.[96] At Swaffham Bulbeck ten guests of varied social standing were resident at any one time in the history of this small house.[97] Catherine Paxton found the same mix of social groups among the lay residents of the London female houses, describing those at the Minories as "a veritable community of lay women residents in the precinct."[98]

By contrast, male monasteries seem to have catered to predominantly male boarders and guests of high social status. Male houses, for example, boarded exclusively male children, like those at Coxford, Old Buckenham, and Pentney.[99] In addition, it was not uncommon for abbots and priors to take in the sons of county gentry and the local aristocracy as grooms, as secular lords did, training the youths in the arts and manners befitting their status as future ecclesiastical and lay lords.[100] At least thirty-five of the fifty-one members of the household of Prior Hoo at the Cathedral Priory in Norwich were sons of the local aristocracy who were fed and clothed at his expense.[101]

The prevalence of male boarders at male monasteries might have been an acknowledgement of Chapter 61 of St Benedict's Rule which directed monks to accommodate only itinerant priests and brothers visiting from other houses.[102] Both the episcopal injunctions and the acts of the provincial chapters attest to this part of the Rule by stating it repeatedly.[103] Such admonitions undoubtedly signal that male houses were accommodating female lodgers, but the problem was not that little girls were boarding and being educated by monks and canons, nor was it one of women seeking spiritual retreat in a male monastery. Rather, the issue for ecclesiastical authorities was that priors and monks were entertaining women of "doubtful character," like the monks at Wymondham who entertained too many women with whom they drank too much.[104] So while male houses were continually cautioned to accept only male boarders and guests, similar restrictions about the sex of boarders and visitors at the female religious houses did not exist.

Clearly, though, women legitimately stayed at male monasteries, as the

---

95 Gasquet, *English Monastic Life*, p. 163.
96 Ibid., p. 162.
97 Palmer, "The Benedictine Nunnery," p. 32.
98 Paxton, "The Nunneries of London," pp. 168–71.
99 Jessopp, "The Norfolk Monasteries," p. 456 (Coxford); ibid., p. 452 (Old Buckenham); and ibid., p. 454 (Pentney).
100 Dobson, *Durham Priory*, pp. 122–23; Saunders, *An Introduction*, p. 162.
101 Ibid., p. 163.
102 Gasquet, *The Rule of St Benedict*, Chap. 61.
103 Jessopp, *Visitations*, pp. 3, 204; Pantin, *Documents*, pp. 189, 190, 205–6.
104 Jessopp, *Visitations*, pp. 6, 76 for this recurring problem at the Cathedral Priory; ibid., p. 96 for the problem at Wymondham.

Duchess of Norfolk did when she stayed at the male Cluniac house in Thetford.[105] And her social status was indicative of the type of people who did board at the male houses in the diocese. Consider, for example, the guests at Butley Priory. In 1516, Mary Tudor visited the priory; in 1526 Thomas, the third Duke of Norfolk was there with William Lord Willoughby and forty others who were at Butley to hunt; the Duke was there again in 1529 with the Earl of Surrey and his twenty-three servants; in 1530 the Countess of Suffolk dined sumptuously in the priory's garden.[106]

Butley was not the only male house to host medieval society's most elite members. Henry VII stayed at the Cluniac house in Thetford.[107] Henry VI and his entire entourage were at the White Friars in Ipswich for a time in 1452; the King also paid a long visit to Bury St Edmunds – from Christmas 1433 until April 1434.[108] Sir Oliver Kirbyte took a long retreat at St Benedict at Holme in 1454.[109] Even the corrodians at the Norwich Cathedral Priory were exclusively royal nominees.[110]

It is true that socially elite visitors like these were more likely to be noted in a priory's household accounts than were local parishioners or poor corrodians, and that male houses never refused entry to poorer laypeople who needed to rest for the night. But the difference between the status of long- and short-term residents at the male houses and those who boarded at the female ones is striking. And this contrast suggests a correlation between the generally wealthier and more prestigious male houses and the higher social rank of their guests. The greater prestige which monks and canons enjoyed as sacerdotal functionaries might also come into play here; perhaps too priors, monks, and canons actively fostered connections with people of elevated social status to further extend their monasteries' temporal spheres of influence. In any case, there seem to have been stronger ties between medieval English society's elite and male monasteries than there were between the aristocracy and female houses.

[105]   Harvey, "The Last Years of Thetford," p. 6.
[106]   Knowles, *The Religious Orders*, vol. 3, pp. 128–29. Knowles lists all of these guests and then says that this type of occurrence was rare!
[107]   Harvey, "The Last Years of Thetford," p. 18.
[108]   Zimmerman, "The White Friars," p. 198 for the King at the friary in Ipswich; VCH, *Suffolk*, vol. 2, p. 65 for the King at Bury St Edmunds.
[109]   Rye, "Laymen Lodging," p. 10.
[110]   Saunders, An *Introduction*, p. 162 says that the eight corrodians known to have been at the priory were ex-royal servants. They are noted in CCR, *1364–68*, pp. 391–92; CCR, *1392–96*, pp. 110–11, 240; CCR, *1399–1402*, pp. 71, 99, 382; and in CPR, *Edward III*, vol. 5, p. 11; CPR, *1461–67*, p. 110.

Numbers of Non-Professed Residents to Nuns

Ratio of Clerics and Servants to Nuns

The presence of servants and guests in female monastic communities, especially in small poor houses, is usually described as disruptive.[111] Unnecessary staff members, numerous corrodians, and guests – frequently relatives of superiors – have long been thought to have grossly outnumbered the nuns.[112] How many people lived and worked in the small female houses in the diocese of Norwich?

Table 13 shows the number of staff members – a group which includes male clerics, agricultural laborers and household servants – and the number of nuns at ten of the diocese's houses. As the figures in this Table make clear, information on each house varies widely: a great deal of detail covers many years for a few houses; significantly less information survives for others. But taken together, the figures reveal that, with some slight variation, the ratio of household help to religious inmates in these female houses averaged 1:1. At Bungay in 1406 the ratio was less, 5:8 – 10 staff members (clerics and servants) to 16 nuns.[113] The ratios at Blackborough, Crabhouse, and Marham also averaged out to about a 1:1 ratio.[114] Slightly higher ratios of servants to nuns can be discerned at Carrow where in 1530 a staff of 26 to 8 nuns inflates the average ratio to 13:4, and at Redlingfield, which maintained a higher ratio of 2.6:1, with 24 staff members to 9 nuns.[115]

Most of these communities then were not encumbered by a large, potentially costly number of servants or maids. The relatively large staff at Carrow reflects its larger population of guests; the number of servants at Redlingfield is more difficult to explain. The prioress's account of 1447/48 lists several boarders at this small house; if this lone account can be considered representative of the situation at Redlingfield – a dangerous proposition at best – perhaps a consistently sizeable staff here at the Dissolution also meant a large number of boarders. If the priory's staff indicated numerous boarders, their numbers might explain the financial problems the priory had in the 1420s

---

[111] Coulton, "The Truth," pp. 89–90; Power, *Medieval English Nunneries*, pp. 206–10, 225–26, 412–14; Snape, *English Monastic Finances*, pp. 139–45.

[112] Coulton, "The Truth," p. 51; Snape, *English Monastic Finances*, pp. 14–19. See also: Knowles, *The Religious Orders*, vol. 3, pp. 260–62.

[113] SRO, HD 1538 156/7.

[114] At Blackborough, the figures were: 13 servants to 9 nuns. See: PRO, SP 5/4/140. At Marham lived 14 servants and 9 nuns: PRO, E 117/14/22. Crabhouse numbers were: 6 helpers to 4 nuns: *Letters and Papers*, XII, p. 116, and Rye, "Norfolk Monasteries," p. 456. Note, though, that the Suppression Papers for Crabhouse say that there were 10 servants, 4 women and 6 hinds: PRO, SP 5/3/35. I think that the commissioners miscounted because both the *Letters and Papers* and the chantry certificates which Rye reproduces agree on 6 servants. I rely, therefore, on this figure.

[115] For Carrow, see: Rye, "Norfolk Monasteries," p. 452; for Redlingfield: PRO, SP 5/3/117.

Table 13. Ratios of Permanent and Temporary Residents to Nuns
in the Convents of the Diocese of Norwich, 1350–1540

(x = unknown numbers)

Convent	Clerics	Staff Servants	Corrodians	Boarders	Nuns	Number of Staff to Each Nun	Number of All Res. to Each Nun
Blackborough[a]							
1536	1	12			9	1.4	
Bruisyard[b]							
1369	2	x	1		12	0.16	0.25
1416	x	x		3	22		x
Bungay[c]							
1406	2	7		3	16	0.6	0.8
1416	x	x		4	12		
1490	2	9		7	10	1.1	1.8
1512	2	15		22	10	1.7	4.0
1530	2	12		30	10	1.4	4.4
Campsey Ash[d]							
1356	7	x		1	19	x	x
Carrow[e]							
1455	2	16		28	12	1.5	4.0
1484	2	16		14	13	1.4	2.0
1503	2	18		6	12	1.6	2.0
1520	2	19		24	12	1.7	3.8
1529	2	24		5	13	2.0	2.0
1536	2	15			8	2.0	2.0

a   PRO, SP 5/4/140.
b   Bourdillon, The Minoresses, p. 62 for the chaplains; PRO, E 179/45/5b for the nuns (1369); BL, Egerton 8776 for boarders; Papal Letters, vol. 6, p. 468 for nuns (1416).
c   SRO, HD 1538/156/7 for clerics, servants, boarders; PRO, E 179/45/5b for nuns (1406); BL, Egerton 8776 for boarders; see Appendix 3 for nuns (1416); SRO, HD 1538/156/14 for clerics, servants, boarders; Jessopp, Visitations, p. 39 for nuns (1490); SRO, HD 1538/156/17 for clerics, servants, boarders; Jessopp, Visitations, p. 318 for nuns (1512); SRO, HD 1538/345 for clerics, servants, boarders; Jessopp, Visitations, p. 318 for nuns (1530).
d   CPR, 1354–58, pp. 484–86 for clerics; ibid., p. 352 for boarder and nuns.
e   NRO, NRS 26882 42 E8 for clerics, servants, and boarders; see Appendix 3 for nuns (1455); NRO, NRS 26883 42 E8 for clerics, servants, and boarders; Jessopp, Visitations, p. 17 for nuns (1484); NRO, Hare 5954 227x1 for clerics servants, and boarders; Jessopp, Visitations, p. 17 for nuns (1503); NRO, Hare 5955 227x1 for clerics, servants, and boarders; Jessopp, Visitations, pp. 208–10 for nuns (1520); NRO, NRS 26884 42 E8 for clerics, servants, and boarders; Jessopp, Visitations, p. 273 for nuns. The number of servants is estimated from the wages paid to them. The prioress paid £21 6d in wages this year, but paid only £15 12s in the previous account (1529); Jessopp, "The Norfolk Monasteries," p. 452 (1536).

Convent	Staff					Number of Staff to Each Nun	Number of All Res. to Each Nun
	Clerics	Servants	Corrodians	Boarders	Nuns		
Crabhouse							
1536[f]	1	6			8	0.9	0.9
Flixton							
1414[g]	2	12	18		12	1.2	2.6
Marham[h]							
1426	1	6		5	11	0.6	1.1
1445	1	11		6	11	1.0	1.6
1455	7			11	10	0.7	1.8
1468	1	12	3	8	10	1.3	2.4
1470	1	11	1	7	10	1.2	2.0
1492	1	11		8	10	1.2	2.0
1497	1	11		6	9	1.3	2.0
1536	1	11			9	1.3	1.3
Redlingfield[i]							
1536	3	21			9	2.6	2.6
Thetford[j]							
1532	x	x	8		8	x	x
1536	2	8			5	1	1

f   Jessopp, "The Norfolk Monasteries," p. 456.
g   SRO, HA/12/B2/18/14.
h   NRO, Hare 2204 194x5 (1426); NRO, Hare 2205 194x5 (1445); NRO, Hare 2206 194x5 (1455);
    NRO, Hare 2208 194x5 (1468); NRO, Hare 2209 194x5 (1470); NRO, Hare 2211 194x5 (1492);
    NRO, Hare 2212 194x5 (1497); Jessopp, "The Norfolk Monasteries," p. 456 (1536).
i   VCH, Suffolk, vol. 2, p. 84.
j   Jessopp, Visitations, pp. 303–4 (1532); Jessopp, "The Norfolk Monasteries," p. 454 (1536).

under Prioress Isabel Hermyte, and perhaps those noticed later by Bishop Nykke in 1514.[116]

While figures for most of the houses are limited to one or two years – making it difficult to generalize about the size of their domestic and agricultural help – changes in the ratio of household help to nuns over time can be seen at Bungay, Carrow and Marham. For over seventy years the average number of staff members to nuns at Carrow and Marham was approximately the same: the average number of staff to nuns at Carrow was about 1.7:1, and the average ratio at Marham for the later Middle Ages was less than 1:1.[117] This stability

116   For these problems at Redlingfield, see: Chapter 3, p. 98 of this book.
117   The figures for Carrow are: 16 servants in 1455, see: NRO, Hare 2205 194x5; and
      Redstone, "Three Account Rolls," pp. 65–6; 16 again in 1484: NRO, NRS 26883, and
      Redstone, ibid., p. 66; 19 in 1503: NRO, Hare 5954 227x1; 19 in 1520: NRO, Hare
      5955 227x1. There were 19 again in 1529: NRO, NRS 26884; and Redstone, ibid., pp.

in numbers over time underlines the general soundness of household organization and administration of these two houses.[118] The ratio at Bungay rises from less than 1:1 in 1406, to slightly higher in the sixteenth century: 17 servants and clerics to 10 nuns in 1512, and then a staff of 14 to 10 nuns in 1530. Because the number of nuns is so constant at this house throughout the period, the increase in numbers of household staff must reflect, as it did at Carrow, an increased number of temporary guests.

Most of the female houses in the diocese then were not unduly burdened by chaplains, servants, and hinds. Because no similar study of the numbers of servants to nuns over time has been undertaken for other female monasteries, we cannot know if these houses were representative of others in England. But both St Radegund's and Swaffham Bulbeck in Cambridge were comparable to Carrow and Marham in size and show similar ratios of staff members to nuns.[119] By contrast, the much wealthier Romsey Abbey, in Hampshire, carried a seemingly excessive number of servants from time to time, which was the cause of some of its debt.[120]

While comparisons with female houses in other dioceses suggest similar ratios, the average 1:1 ratio of servants to nuns in most of the female houses in the diocese of Norwich contrasts strikingly to the ratios in many of the male houses in the diocese. The average ratio of household help to male religious in 1535 was at least 11:1, with as many as 16 servants to one canon at St Sepulchre, Thetford (16:1); 83 staff members to 9 monks at Pentney (9:1); and a staff of 65 to the 4 religious at Coxford (16:1).[121] The Cathedral Priory

---

66–7. We can be certain of these numbers because, though names are not specified in later accounts, the amounts of money the prioress paid to the priory's chaplains and servants are given; the amounts are the same in each account. For Marham the figures are: 6 servants in 1426 (NRO, Hare 2204 194x5); 11 in 1446 (NRO, Hare 2205 194x5); 7 in 1455 (NRO, Hare 2206 194x5); 12 in 1468 (NRO, Hare 2208 194x5); 11 in 1470 (NRO, Hare 2209 194x5); 11 in 1492 (NRO, Hare 2211 194x5); and 11 in 1497 (NRO, Hare 2212 194x5).

118 See above, Chapter 3, pp. 96–7; Nichols, "The History and Cartulary," p. 96 for similar conclusions.

119 Gray, The Priory of St Radegund, pp. 158, 163; and Palmer, "The Benedictine Nunnery," p. 31.

120 Peacock, "Injunctions Made," p. 57 where Bishop Langland told the nuns at Romsey that they must reduce the number of servants because they were part of the reason for the abbey's great debt. Romsey's value at the Dissolution, however, was £528.

121 VCH, Norfolk, vol. 2, p. 393 for St Sepulchre, Thetford; ibid., p. 390 for Pentney; ibid., p. 348 for Coxford. The ratio of servants to male religious can be calculated for nine other male houses: Sibton: 44 servants to 11 monks; Butley: 71 servants to 12 canons; at the Cluniac house in Thetford, 16 servants to 6 canons; VCH, Suffolk, vol. 2, pp. 90, 98, 110. In Norfolk, Horsham St Faith had 18 helpers to 7 monks; Beeston supported 13 servants for 3 canons; at Hempton, there were 15 helpers to 3 monks; at Weybourne, 3 servants to 2 monks; 21 servants for 6 monks at Langley; and 12 helpers for the 5 monks at Wendling. For these numbers, see: VCH, Norfolk, vol. 2, pp. 348, 382, 390, 393.

maintained 146 servants to an average of 40 monks (4:1), and the 12 canons at Butley supported over 100 servants and hinds (8:1).[122]

It might be argued that the greater wealth of the male houses could comfortably support an excessive number of servants regardless of how many religious inmates there were, and that these large male houses functioned much more like aristocratic households which catered to a sizeable and high status clientele. Although wealthier than the female convents in the diocese, not all of these male monasteries were very rich. St Sepulchre, Thetford, for example, was valued at only £39, Pentney at £170, and Coxford at £121.[123] Many of these houses, moreover, were hamstrung by debt, like the Cathedral Priory in Norwich.[124] Regardless of whatever financial distress their staffs may have imposed, the male houses' greater number of socially elite boarders probably required the kind of elaborate care and hospitality which only a large number of servants could provide.

Ratio of Staff and Lay Boarders to Nuns

Clerics and servants comprised only part of the non-cloistered population of these monasteries. The ratio of all lay residents to cloistered inmates must therefore also be computed to fully appreciate the impact these people had on these religious communities. Such figures can·be calculated for Bungay, Carrow, Flixton, Marham and Thetford.

The figures in Table 13 show that though Bungay, Carrow and Flixton were at times crowded with boarders, since the average ratio of household help and long-term lodgers to nuns at each of these female houses was 2:1. At Bungay, an average of 28 staff members and lodgers to 12 nuns equalled about a 2:1 ratio, a figure which includes the increased number of boarders in the 1500s.[125]

---

[122] Saunders, *An Introduction*, p. 163 for the average number of household servants and agricultural helpers at the Cathedral Priory. Note that this number excludes the staff of 51 attached to the prior's household. *VCH, Suffolk*, vol. 2, p. 98 for Butley. For the large household staffs of other male houses in the diocese, see: Jessopp, "The Norfolk Monasteries," p. 454 for the 9 canons at Pentney and their staff of 30; ibid., p. 456 for the 47 hinds and waiting servants at Coxford and the 4 canons who also lived there.

[123] See above, Chapter 1, Table 2 for these values and those of the other male houses for which these ratios can be determined. The Norwich diocesan male houses did not, furthermore, fit the 1:1 ratio which Knowles in *Religious Orders in England*, vol. 3, pp. 261–63 identifies for the male houses; Knowles further suggests that male monastic household staffs decreased in size throughout the later Middle Ages. Apparently such was not the case for the male houses in the diocese of Norwich. See also: Savine, *English Monasteries on the Eve of the Reformation*, pp. 218–19.

[124] Rye, "Norfolk Monasteries," pp. 454–56 for St Sepulchre, Thetford, Pentney, and Coxford; Cheney, "Norwich Cathedral Priory," p. 97 citing Saunders here.

[125] SRO, HD 1538/156/7. In 1406, for example, there were only three boarders. In 1490 the number had risen to 7 (SRO, HD 1538/156/14). The account of 1512, reveals 21 guests, and the last one, drawn up in 1530, lists thirty guests: SRO, HD 1538/156/17 for the prioress's account of 1512, and SRO, HD 1538/345 for her account of 1530.

The ratio of long-term guests to nuns at Carrow fluctuated between a high of 4:1 in 1455, and a low of 2:1, which was the priory's average in the sixteenth century.[126] Flixton Priory in the early fifteenth century housed 32 clerics, servants and corrodians to its 12 nuns, giving a ratio of 3:1.[127] By contrast, the numbers of staff members and long- and short-term boarders at Marham remained relatively stable throughout this later period.[128] The ratio of guests and household help to nuns there averaged just over 1:1 with 13 servants and guests to 11 nuns throughout the fifteenth century.[129]

Thus long- and short-term residents did occasionally out-number the nuns at Bungay, Carrow, and Flixton, but did not do so at Marham. Flixton was fairly crowded in 1414, but a lack of evidence makes it difficult to determine whether the priory always supported so many people. Conclusions, then, about the financial imposition or disruptive influences of the lay populace at this priory are untenable. The number of boarders at Bungay increased in proportion to nuns over time, and the monastic and household accounts extant for the priory show that it was financially healthy and did not suffer the chronic arrears which plagued a few of the other female monasteries.

The fluctuations at Carrow and the stability in numbers at Marham can be explained by circumstances particular to each house. Carrow's peak numbers in the mid-fifteenth century might reflect the presence in the priory's anchor-hold of Julian of Norwich, whose *Revelations of Divine Love* is well known;[130] the later surge in numbers could have been caused by another holy anchoress – who has disappeared from the records – or by the kind of sudden increase in visitors common to any urban center.[131] Marham Abbey's consistent 1:1 ratio of lay populace to nuns throughout the later Middle Ages perhaps was a result of its more remote setting in the western fens.[132]

The size of the non-professed population to nuns seems miniscule compared to those maintained at the Cathedral Priory in Norwich, whose household help

Throughout this time the number of nuns remained fairly stable, ranging closely from 12 in 1406, to 10 in 1490, to 9 in 1512, back up to 12 in 1530.

126 NRO, NRS 26882 42 E8 (1455) shows forty-six non-professed residents to twelve nuns; NRO, Hare 5954 227x1 (1503) reveals 26 staff members and boarders to twelve nuns.

127 The number of servants was eighteen, and the number of corrodians and long-term guests equaled fifteen: SRO, HA/12/B2/18/14.

128 In 1426, for example, the abbey accommodated five boarders; in 1446, six; in 1455, eleven; in 1468, eight guests and three corrodians; in 1470, seven guests and one corrodian; in 1492, eight guests; and in 1497, six.

129 Nichols, "The History and Cartulary," p. 97.

130 Rye, *Carrow Abbey*, pp. xiv–xxix for the numerous references in wills from the Norwich Consistory Court to Julian, which date from 1433 to 1478. She was at Carrow from at least 1433 until her death sometime before 1483.

131 Carrow's anchorhold was continually occupied: see: Gilchrist and Oliva, *Religious Women*, pp. 75, 98; and Rye, *Carrow Abbey*, Appendix IX, passim. Redstone, "Three Account Rolls," pp. 57–8 suggests that the nuns decreased their population of lay boarders while simultaneously increasing their sheep herd to better augment their income, but the swell in 1520/21 makes this suggestion difficult to justify.

132 Nichols, "The History and Cartulary," p. 97.

and lodgers numbered around 416 in the sixteenth century, to a religious population of 55 monks, making the ratio 7.5:1.[133] Counts of all non-professed temporary and permanent lodgers to monks, canons, and friars in other male houses in the diocese taken in 1535 show the male religious to have been significantly outnumbered even at the relatively poor monasteries. The ratio of non-monks to monks at Coxford Priory, which was worth £121, for example, was 25:1 (74 servants and boarders to 3 monks); the ratio at Pentney, valued at £170, was 9:1 (83 servants and boarders to 9 monks); and that at Brome-holme was 8:1 (33 boarders and servants to 4 monks).[134] These figures are far beyond historians' estimates that the average ratio of non-professed lodgers to male religious was about 4:1.[135]

The Financial Impact of Staff and Boarders

The financial impact of staff members and long- and short-term guests on female monastic communities has long been assumed to have been negative.[136] Corrodians, for example, might not have been able to give a house enough money or land to cover the costs of their life-time maintenance; this was the case at Creake Abbey in the fourteenth century.[137] Eileen Power in particular stressed the unwise corrody agreements nuns made, suggesting further that they accepted corrodians for the sole purpose of raising quick cash.[138] But the nuns in the diocese of Norwich do not appear to have done so; in fact, they seem to have limited their domestic servants and agricultural laborers, and their guests, to numbers they could support, thus mitigating any financial burden their servants and guests might have presented.

The fees and wages of full-time chaplains, maids, butlers, grooms, and hinds, and also of the seasonal laborers hired at various times of the year, varied from house to house. At Redlingfield the wages comprised 18 percent of Prioress

---

133 Saunders, An Introduction, p. 163.
134 Jessopp, "The Norfolk Monasteries," p. 456 (Coxford); ibid., p. 454 (Pentney); ibid., p. 460 (Bromholm). The other available figures are: 18 servants and boarders to 4 monks at Horsham St Faith; 21 non-professed to 6 monks at Langley; 40 lay residents to 5 canons at Buckenham; 16 to 6 canons at Thetford Cluniac; 12 boarders and servants to 5 monks at Wendling; 14 lay residents to canons at Beeston; but only 3 to 2 monks at Weybourne, and 1 to 2 at Weybridge. For these figures, see: Jessopp, ibid., passim.
135 Knowles, The Religious Orders, vol. 3, pp. 260–64; Savine, English Monasteries on the Eve of the Reformation, pp. 218–26.
136 Power suggests that monasteries, especially the female ones, were financially overburdened with extra mouths to feed and bodies to clothe throughout the later Middle Ages, Medieval English Nunneries, pp. 197–99, 212. Knowles and Savine disagree but look mostly at the non-professed population in male houses: The Religious Order, vol. 3, pp. 264, 267; Savine, English Monasteries on the Eve of the Reformation, especially pp. 264–65.
137 Bedingfield, A Cartulary of Creake Abbey, p. xviii.
138 Power, Medieval English Nunneries, pp. 197, 206–8.

Alice Lampet's expenses in 1447.[139] Because these are the only figures available for this house, little can be said about the drain they may have been, though they may have contributed to Redlingfield's apparently chronic financial difficulties.

The impact of the staff members on the finances of Bungay, Carrow, and Marham is easier to discern. At Bungay staff wages remained fairly stable: around £13, equal to approximately 16 percent of Prioress Elizabeth Stephenson's expenses, in 1513; and £14 for chaplains and servants wages seventeen years later, about 14 percent of the prioress's annual charges.[140] With the decline in the labor force, Carrow's labor costs rose steadily throughout the period: those paid by the prioress in 1455/56 were £16 – 12 percent of her expenses – and £21 in 1529/30, or 26 percent of her total costs.[141] Approximately 16 percent of cellarer's expenses were wages in 1481, 20 percent in 1503, and 19 percent in 1520.[142] The same expenses at Marham show a steady decline throughout the fifteenth century, but as the abbess's total expenses decreased in this later period the percentage that labor costs represented of her total expenses increased.[143] Wages at both Carrow and Marham averaged roughly 18 percent of their annual expenses; neither had trouble covering these costs.[144] Female houses of similar size and wealth in other parts of England spent about the same.[145]

139 They totaled £14 6s 8d: SRO, HD 1538/327, and see above Chapter 3, pp. 80–1 for the figures of wages.

140 SRO, HD 1536/156/17 for the prioress's account of 1513; and SRO, HD 1536/327 for the prioresses' accounts of the 1530s. The earlier prioress's account of 1490 shows payments only to the convent's chaplains, 52s 9d, and none to other servants. Fifty-two shillings equals about 5 percent of her total expenses for that year, which were £35 3s 8d: SRO, HD 1538/156/14.

141 NRO, NRS 26882 42 E8 (1455/56): the costs of wages in 1455/56 was £16 2s 2d, and her expenses totaled £127 13s (12%); and in 1529/30, wages were £21 6d, and outlay was £81 13s 8d (26%), NRO, NRS 26884 42 E8.

142 NRO, NRS 26883 42 E8: £15 in wages, £95 10s 7d in total expenses; NRO, Hare 5954 227x1: £16 4s 8d in wages, £82 2s 1d in expenses; NRO, Hare 5955 227x1 £19 17s 7d in wages, £98 16s 9d.

143 NRO, Hare 2204 194x5 (1426/27) when the abbess paid £19 2s 5d in wages; NRO, Hare 2205 194x5 (1446/47), she paid £16 2s; NRO, Hare 2207 (1456/57) she paid £15 15s 10d; and in the years 1468/69, 1470/71, and 1497/98, she paid £12 2s 8d, £12 10s 6d, and £12 8s 4d: NRO, Hare 2208 194x5, NRO, Hare 2209 194x5, and NRO, Hare 2212 194x5 respectively. See also: Nichols, "The History and Cartulary," pp. 96, 176.

144 For Carrow, see above, note 141. For Marham, fees totaled £19 2s 5d, and expenses totalled £127 6s 11d (15%) in 1426/27 (NRO, Hare 2204 194x5); in 1446/47 wages were £16 2s, and outlay £109 17s 1d (14.6%) (NRO, Hare 2205 194x5); in 1456/57, wages were £15 15s 10d, and expenses were £62 10s 2d (24%) (NRO, Hare 2207 194x5); in 1468/69 wages equaled £12 2s 8d and expenses £72 4s 8d (16.6%) (NRO, Hare 2208 194x5); in 1470/71 wages were £12 10s 6d, and expenses £64 44s 6d (18.75%) (NRO, Hare 2209 194x5); and in 1497/98 wages were £12 8s 4d, and expenses were £62 2s 10d (19%) (NRO, Hare 2212 194x5).

145 Gasquet, English Monastic Life, p. 168 for Grace Dieu; and Gray, The Priory of St Radegund, pp. 159–60.

Costs incurred by maintaining corrodians and boarders are more difficult to assess. In most of the extant household accounts – where payments for hospitality were noted – money for food, linen, bedding, clothes, candles, and fuel for corrodians and boarders is not distinguished from what was spent for the whole convent. This information was probably recorded in the daily ledgers and books of superiors and cellarers mentioned earlier in this study, but now lost. There is no way of calculating the costs of hospitality for long- and short-term boarders.[146] None of the convents, however, were reprimanded by bishops for spending too much on hospitality, as the canons at Langley were, for example, where such expenses were bankrupting the abbey.[147]

The accounts of Marham, however, are more revealing and show that the annual amount spent on maintaining the guesthouse averaged between £11 and £12.[148] In a few years the abbess supplemented the revenues specially marked for these expenses with income from the mill and the abbey's wool fell, indicating that at times the guesthouse cost more than she could handle.[149]

Superiors at both Marham and Carrow, in fact, occasionally carried debts from year to year from some of their boarders, making it difficult sometimes for the nuns to absorb the costs of hospitality. Two abbesses at Marham were owed about £6 a year for three of the nine years covered by accounts by three patrons for the room and board of their children.[150] Similarly, in two of the five years for which pertinent household accounts survive for Carrow, the nuns were owed money, but less than £3, in both 1520 and 1529.[151] At both houses, the same people owed for debts which had been accruing for some time. Robert Eliston, Edmund Berry, and William Copuldyke owed the abbess of Marham for the board of their children for four years running.[152] William Sayer and Nicholas Dade, chaplain, made incremental payments in both years to Prioress Isabel Wygon of Carrow for their own room and board, and for the board of a relative, on debts sixteen and twelve years old.[153] All of these people made yearly payments of a few shillings to the nuns at both convents which enabled the debts – at least at Marham – to be paid off over time.[154]

---

146 See, for example, the prioresses' and cellarers' accounts for Carrow: NRO, NRS 26882 42 E8, NRO, Hare 5954 227x1; SRO, HD 1538/156/17 (Bungay); SRO, HD 1538/327 (Redlingfield).
147 Elliston-Erwood, "The Premonstratensian Abbey of Langley," p. 181.
148 Nichols, "The History and Cartulary," pp. 173–74.
149 The years were 1446/47, 1492/93, and 1497/98 for profits from the mill; Nichols, "The History and Cartulary," p. 135.
150 NRO, Hare 2204 194x5 (1426): the debt was £5 12s; NRO, Hare 2205 194x5 (1446): arrears equaled £5 10s; NRO, Hare 2207 194x5 (1456): the amount was £6; and 10s was owed in 1468: NRO, Hare 2208 194x5. See also Chapter 3 above for a discussion of these debts.
151 NRO, Hare 5955 227x1 (1520), prioress acting as cellarer's account dated 1520; NRO, NRS 26884 42 E8 (1529), prioress's account of 1529.
152 NRO, Hare 2205 194x5 (1446).
153 See for example: NRO, NRS 26883 42 E8 (1484).
154 Since the accounts from Carrow are the last ones to survive from each of the offices of

Though these partial payments must have made it tough at times for the nuns at these two houses to make ends meet, these debts do not appear to have been too damaging: only Carrow was in debt in only one of the years in question here. The nuns seem to have handled most of these arrears by the kind of financial juggling the abbess of Marham did; the nuns at Carrow may have offset these debts by increasing their sheep herd.[155]

For the most part, the income guests generated at all of the diocese's houses appears to have covered their expenses. Take those at Carrow: the prioress there collected £16 from boarders, which constituted 12 percent of her income in 1455: this amount corresponded with the largest number of boarders the house accommodated.[156] In later years the money generated by boarders at Carrow declined along with their numbers: to only £1 in 1503, and £2 in 1529; in 1520, the nuns collected £4 from their guests, which coincided with an increased number of guests.[157]

A similar pattern can be seen at Marham. The figures in Table 13 show that, except for 1455, the number of boarders remained fairly constant, between five and eight. The income they generated averaged £1 8s, fluctuating with their numbers from £3 and five guests in 1426, to 16s and six guests in 1446 when the abbess struggled with debts accrued from previous years, to £1 and six guests in 1497.[158] In two years, the abbess collected more money: £5 in 1455, when she hosted the largest number of guests, eleven; and £5 in 1470, when the number of boarders – seven – was consistent with most years.[159]

Numbers and amounts at Bungay varied considerably. In 1406, the nuns received £5 from three lodgers, and in 1490 £3 from seven; this figure skyrocketed in 1512 to £18, as did the number of boarders, to twenty-two.[160] Bungay's prioress and cellarer seem to have been able to cover the costs of hospitality with the revenues their visitors generated.

While able to pay for themselves, the income these guests contributed to

---

priores and cellarer, we cannot know if the long-standing debts at this house were fully paid up.

155 See above Chapter 3, p. 97; Redstone, "Three Account Rolls," pp. 57–8 where she notes that the nuns at Carrow increased their sheep herd to augment their yearly revenues.

156 NRO, NRS 26882 42 E8; total receipts were £133.

157 NRO, NRS 26883 42 E8, dated 1484 when the income from boarders equaled 5.3% (£7) of the total income (£133). In 1503 the percent was .9 (£1) of income totaling £103; in 1520, it was 4.4% (£4) of income (£91); and in 1529, it amounted to .2% (£2) of revenues equaling £98: NRO, Hare 5954 227x1, NRO, Hare 5955 227x1, and NRO, NRS 26884 42 E8 respectively.

158 NRO, Hare 2204 194x5: 1426, £3 (2.3%) of receipts totaling £127; NRO, Hare 2205 194x5, 1446, 16s (1.25%) of £64; NRO, Hare 2212 194x5: 1497, £1 (1.7%) of £58.

159 In 1455 income from lodgers was £5 (5%) of the £101 in total receipts: NRO, Hare 2206 194x5. Except for NRO, Hare 2209 194x5, 1470, £5 (.6%) of £92.

160 In 1406 they collected £5 from boarders out of total revenues of £71: SRO, HD 1538/156/7. In 1490, they received £3 from boarders comprising 8.6% of their £35 sum of receipts: SRO, HD 1538/156/14. In 1512, lodgers paid £18 or 21.6% of the £83 total revenues collected: SRO, HD 1538/156/17.

their hosts rarely constituted a significant percentage of their annual incomes. Visitors at Carrow contributed at most 12 percent of the prioress's annual income in 1455; but in most years, the money thus generated totaled less than 1 percent of her income.[161] For the abbess at Marham lodgers' fees comprised between .01 and .08 percent of her annual income, except on one occasion when the abbess received 5 percent of her revenues from long-term boarders.[162] At Bungay, though, boarders' payments constituted significantly more of the nuns' income: about 6.5 percent in the fifteenth century, and a significantly high 21 percent of their total receipts in 1512.[163] The lone account of Alice Lampet, prioress of Redlingfield, indicates that she derived a full 30 percent of her annual operating income from her guests; we do not know their numbers, but their financial impact on the nuns at this small house appears to have been significant.

While Lampet derived a lot of her income from boarders, the amounts the diocese's other superiors and cellarers received from this source were considerably less than those taken in by nuns elsewhere.[164] The nuns at St Radegund's received £8 14s 4d from boarders in 1449/50, and £8 16s 2d in 1450/51, which equaled about 10 percent of their annual income.[165] At least one female monastery, Swaffham Bulbeck, charged what appears to have been a standard fee for overnight guests: 6d a week for the board of both children and adults: a penny a day, Sundays having been free.[166] The nuns in the diocese of Norwich seem to have charged the same.

Given these figures, it does not seem unreasonable to suggest that, except for the prioress of Redlingfield, the nuns in the diocese did not simply take in boarders as a revenue-producing strategy.[167] Financially good years did not necessarily correspond to a large number of guests: in 1503 when there were five guests at Carrow, for example, the cellarer's income was £103; seventeen years later, when the guesthouse was relatively full, with twenty-four boarders, her income was £91.[168] The same pattern is discernible at Marham, though we know that here the expenses of the guesthouse were from time to time difficult for the abbess to meet on her income alone. In 1426, the year with the lowest number of boarders, the abbess's income was the highest that she received in any of the fifteenth-century accounts which survive from this office, £127; this

161 See above, note 156.
162 For example: NRO, Hare 2208 194x5: 1468, £2 (1.9%) of £106; NRO, Hare 2211 194x5: 1492, £2 (2.8%) of £71. Five percent was generated in 1455, £5 of a total annual income of £101: NRO, Hare 2206 194x5.
163 See above note 160.
164 For Marrick Priory in York: Tillotson, *Marrick Priory*, p. 17.
165 Gray, *The Priory of St Radegund*, p. 142 for 1449/50, and ibid., p. 152 for 1450/51. Total revenues for those years equaled £80 22d, and £77 14s 1d respectively.
166 Palmer, "The Benedictine Nunnery," p. 32.
167 This is Power's assertion: *Medieval English Nunneries*, p. 262; but see: Palmer, "The Benedictine Nunnery," p. 32 who comes to the same conclusion presented here in his study of Swaffham Bulbeck.
168 NRO, Hare 5954 227x1 (1503); NRO, Hare 5955 227x1 (1520).

year was not one in which she could not meet her expenses which totaled £102.[169]

Numbers of guests did not necessarily decline in financially lean years: again at Marham – the house for which this information is best – in the two years when there were eight guests, the abbess's income fluctuated from £92 in 1468 to £46 in 1492.[170] When the abbey accommodated six boarders, she took in only £67 in 1446, but £58 in 1497.[171] While the nuns took in amounts that were not insubstantial, and were obviously helpful to the nuns, especially in years when revenues were down, the money would never have made them or their convents rich, indicating that they accepted long- and short-term visitors for other than pecuniary reasons.[172]

Since the majority of the diocese's female houses were never in serious debt, they do not fit the generalization that inflated numbers of household servants and/or exorbitant costs of hospitality plunged female houses into unremittable debt. While two of the convents were owed money from boarders, overall, the numerical patterns and financial status of the non-professed residents in the female houses in the diocese of Norwich do not fit the model described by monastic historians who decry the disabling effect on female monasteries of vast numbers of residents and the financial burdens they imposed. Though a lack of sources may explain the benign impact these secular residents appear to have had on the convents, debt and distraction caused by lay boarders are the stuff of episcopal visitations: those for the female houses in the diocese of Norwich are relatively silent on these matters.

The Impact of Staff and Boarders on Religious Life

Disruptions of the nuns' monastic life by staff members and guests were relatively minor. The complaints at Carrow about young nuns wearing silk waist-bands and gossiping mentioned earlier could easily have resulted from the presence of lay boarders, whose numbers could be sizeable.[173] The nuns at Flixton had too many dogs at one time, another possible effect of secular influence on the nuns there.[174] But other possible negative practices involving the non-professed population, like the sale of corrodies and the practice of favoring relatives as guests, were not in evidence among the diocese's female convents.[175] The only known incidence of a superior's relative boarding at a

169 NRO, Hare 2204 194x5.
170 NRO, Hare 2208 194x5 (1468); NRO, Hare 2211 194x5 (1492).
171 NRO, Hare 2205 194x5 (1446); NRO, Hare 2212 194x5 (1497).
172 Tillotson, "Visitation and Reform," p. 7 where he suggests that the fees nuns in Yorkshire collected from boarders were welcome additions to the nuns' tight budgets.
173 Above, Chapter 2, p. 72 and Chapter 3, p. 105. Jessopp, Visitations, p. 274; Bishop Nykke did not address this complaint in his injunctions.
174 Ibid., pp. 190–91.
175 Coulton, Five Centuries of Religion, vol. 3, p. 551; Power, Medieval English Nunneries,

convent in the diocese was at Marham where Margaret Narburgh, sister of Joanna Narburgh, boarded at the abbey for a time during her sister's tenure as abbess.[176] There is no evidence that any of the superiors sold corrodies to obtain cash, though irregularities at Thetford were brought to Bishop Nykke's attention. In 1532, one of the nuns reported that John Bixley had sold his corrody to Thomas Foster, who was using it to support his wife, three children and maids.[177] Bixley denied this claim and stated that Foster had purchased his own. Whether or not this resale took place is unknown. Another incident at Thetford concerned John Jerves who had apparently placed his infant daughter with the nuns, but had not paid them for her maintenance.[178]

Hints of more serious disruptions can be detected at Campsey Ash where numerous noble visitors were sufficiently distracting to prompt Maud of Oxford to move to Bruisyard. And young boys who boarded at Redlingfield Priory slept in the nuns' dorter, a situation which was addressed by the bishop in 1514.[179]

With the exception of Campsey Ash, the lay presence in these female houses seems to have been less disquieting and intrusive than it was at female houses in other parts of England, or at many of the male houses in the diocese of Norwich. The prioress of Swaffham Bulbeck took in corrodians to help pay off the debts which her predecessor had accrued.[180] Bishop Wykeham admonished the nuns at Romsey about their noisy boarders and about selling corrodies.[181] And at Nun Cotham in Lincolnshire, Bishop Longland reprimanded the prioress for imposing her relatives on the convent, and warned the nuns against allowing lay women to sleep in their dorter.[182] Access to the nuns by secular visitors was regulated at some of the convents in Yorkshire in order to curtail problems there as well.[183]

Lay residents in the diocese's male houses were just as troublesome. Many male Benedictine houses sold corrodies despite repeated injunctions against doing so by the Order's general chapters.[184] In addition to this abuse, secular lodgers wreaked continual havoc in some of the male convents. Throughout the late fifteenth and early sixteenth centuries, for example, guests at St Benet at Holme caused a serious decline in morals and monastic life among the monks there.[185] At Bromehill in 1514, the prior was ordered to install stocks and chains to punish the canons there for fancy dress and drunkenness, problems

---

pp. 197, 206–10, 225–26; Snape, *English Monastic Finances*, pp. 139–45 for the sale of corrodies.

[176] NRO, Hare 2206 194x5 in 1455.
[177] Jessopp, *Visitations*, pp. 303–4.
[178] Ibid., p. 304.
[179] Ibid., p. 140.
[180] Palmer, "The Benedictine Nunnery," p. 32.
[181] Luce, "Injunctions Made," pp. 40–1; Liveing, *The Records of Romsey*, p. 163.
[182] Peacock, "Injunctions of John Langland," pp. 56, 58.
[183] Tillotson, "Visitation and Reform," pp. 12–15.
[184] Pantin, *Documents*, vol. 45, pp. 68, 80, 88, 279–81, 288, 304 for injunctions against this practice in 1363, 1443 and 1444.
[185] Jessopp, *Visitations*, pp. 60–3, 126–28, 174–75, 213–15, and 278–84.

caused by the priory's many secular visitors.[186] The prior of Weybourne in Norfolk had a sister who was a corrodian at his house.[187] Relatives of a monastic superior – especially socially elite ones, like those at Butley Priory in Suffolk – could be particularly overbearing by demanding the kinds of special attention their status dictated and to which they were no doubt accustomed.[188]

The majority of female houses in Norfolk and Suffolk, then, in contrast to their male counterparts, were neither overcrowded nor led to financial ruin by too many mouths to feed and bodies to clothe. With the exceptions of Flixton, with eighteen corrodians in the mid-fifteenth century, and Bungay and Carrow's occasionally large numbers of visitors, the numbers of guests and lay residents at these houses remained small. In fact, the nuns seem to have kept the number of staff members and guests to those they could afford. By limiting their numbers, the nuns deployed financial prudence while performing their duties of charity and hospitality. These aspects of their monastic vocation, and the presence of the great variety of people in these small houses, illuminate many of the other roles these religious houses played in the broader contexts of parish and county.

186 Ibid., pp. 154–58.
187 Jessopp, "Weybourne Priory," p. 275.
188 Jessopp, Visitations, p. 54 (1493).

5

The Convent and the Community: Services Rendered by the Female Monasteries

The administration of charity and hospitality illustrates some of the services nuns rendered to society, services which satisfied both monastic ideals and also some of the spiritual needs of local lay people and parishioners. These cariative activities of courtesy bound the nuns to their secular communities in ways which created a time-honored and mutually beneficial relationship: the monasteries provided certain services according to a monastic ideal in exchange for a payment or simply the privilege of being in close proximity to a group of pious and prayerful women. These activities ensured interactions between the monastic and secular worlds, making the nuns an integral part of the local social landscape.

While the provision of hospitality and charity were important to both the providers and the recipients, the ways in which nuns interacted with local lay people were numerous and varied. Margaret Eriswell and Katherine Boteler, maid and baker of the abbess of Marham, for example, profited from the employment which the abbey provided, as did the eighteen other servants and hinds who worked there.[1] Remote and isolated houses like Marham, in fact, often attracted a variety of people who established permanent settlements upon which the monasteries depended for necessary goods and services.[2] Local villagers also benefitted from the economic and legal framework which their monastic lords provided through the use of mills, participation in local fairs, markets, and courts. And some monasteries, like Carrow Priory, maintained liveried personnel – employees and other associates who wore tunics and shirts of specific colors and patterns, which signaled the wearer's affiliation with the monastery. Maids, grooms, and others associated with the prioress's household wore russet-colored tunics of cloth threshed, fulled, cropped and woven at her expense.[3] The priory's chaplains and their servants wore shirts made of black and white wool.[4] Public symbols like these conferred prestige on the liveried

---

1 NRO, Hare 2204 194x5: abbess's account (1426/27).
2 A settlement grew up around another female house, Malling Abbey in Kent: Dugdale, *Monasticon*, vol. 3, p. 381.
3 See, for example: NRO, NRS 26882 42 E8 for Margaret Pygot's account of 1455.
4 NRO, Hare 5954 227x1, 1503 account of Catherine Segrime, prioress acting as cellarer.

attendants and also promoted the priory's interests beyond the confines of its walls.

Nuns interacted with their local communities in several other ways, such as distributing alms, providing intercessory prayers, and burying people in their cemeteries and churches. This chapter examines the wide range of services that the female houses provided, revealing the nuns' participation in activities which have hitherto been attributed solely to monks and canons, and also compares the services both the female and male religious provided. For example, did the nuns distribute fewer alms because their houses had fewer resources and were poorer than their male counterparts? Did both nuns and monks accommodate local parishioners by sharing their conventual churches and chapels? Were all social groups affected by the services both female and male houses offered, or rather, did some benefit more than others? The answers to such questions will show how these activities fostered significant relationships between the nuns and members of their local communities.

Monastic Charity

Provisions for the poor and indigent included both daily and occasional alms. Daily alms comprised scraps of food left after meals which were to be given to the poor outside a monastery's gates and represented corporate giving, that is, alms dispensed by the convent as a whole.[5] Occasional alms included money and food doled out at specific times, both by individual nuns and by the whole community. The clothing and daily food rations of a deceased nun, for example, went to the poor for a month after her death.[6]

The impact these diurnal and sporadic alms may have had is not easy to determine. As Barbara Harvey points out, the amount of daily food doles fluctuated according to seasonal variations in the monastic diet – which was more spartan in Lent, for example – and also to individual practices specific to each house.[7] And as Knowles pointed out for the male houses, the informal nature of daily food scraps and discarded clothing rendered them invisible in both household accounts and the *Valor*.[8] These casual contributions to the poor and needy are therefore usually underestimated.

While these informal alms remain impossible to calculate, the nuns gave to the poor on more particular occasions as well, including the anniversary of a founder's death, and specific feast days, and to a certain extent their impact can more easily be assessed. The nuns at Flixton, for example, dispensed 56s

---

[5]   Knowles, *The Religious Orders*, vol. 3, p. 265; Power, *Medieval English Nunneries*, p. 122; Tillotson, *Monastery and Society*, p. 3.

[6]   Harvey, *Living and Dying*, p. 13 for monks; Knowles, *The Religious Orders*, vol. 3, p. 265; Aungier, *History of Syon*, p. 245.

[7]   Harvey, *Living and Dying*, pp. 11–13

[8]   Knowles, *The Religious Orders*, vol. 3, p. 265.

8d annually on the obit of the convent's founder, Margery Creyke.[9] At Bungay the nuns gave at least 2s to the poor on the anniversary of the death of their founder, Gundreda, while the prioress there donated the larger sum of 12s 8d on the same day.[10] On Maundy Thursday, another traditional day of alms-giving, the nuns at Campsey Ash doled out 5s; the prioress and convent of Carrow gave at least 3s in addition to the 1 quarter and 2 bushels of rye they used to bake bread for the poor.[11] At Marham, the abbess and nuns gave 13d annually on Maundy Thursday to thirteen poor people, and spent 6d in bread for each as well.[12]

Other donations of money, food, and clothes were particular to individual priories. At Bungay, the bailiff made donations to the poor in money and in meat on the feast of St Anthony, while the nuns at Campsey Ash spent 14s on wheat for bread and red herring four times a year, and distributed this food to the poor.[13] And during Lent and at Easter, the nuns at Redlingfield gave money, bread, beef, and herring to the indigent outside their gate.[14] In addition, the prioress there gave £34 in 1447 in alms to the poor, which constituted her single largest expense.[15]

The prioress of Carrow made extensive charitable donations on a number of occasions. In one year, for example, Isabel Wygon gave 4d in alms at Christmas, and 4d to her poor servants on the same feast, on the Purification of the Blessed Virgin, the feast of St James, and on the day of the dedication of the priory's church.[16] She also gave alms on the feast of St Anthony, and commissioned the repair and replacement of clothes and shoes for her poor servants.[17] Numerous others also profited from the priory's cellarer: Margery Palmer gave Petronilla Paternoster, a kitchen maid, shoes, hose, shirts, tunics, and other garments; the boy who cared for the priory's sheep, a woman named Margaret Hastyngs, and a man called Robert Pygge were also clothed by her.[18]

Direct dispensations of alms like these were not the only ones nuns offered the poor. As patrons of other ecclesiastical properties, the nuns provided for the needy and poor at many other sites. The poor of the parish church of Ash – one of Campsey Ash's advowsons – for example, received 3s 6d from the nuns on the obit of one of their benefactors, Dame Anne Waylond.[19] And the

9 VE, vol. 3, p. 446.
10 Ibid., p. 431 for the nuns' contributions; SRO, HD 1538/345 for the prioress's.
11 For Campsey, see: VE, vol. 3, p. 416. For Carrow see, for example: the prioress as cellarer's account of 1455, NRO, NRS 26882 42 8E.
12 NRO, Hare 2211 194x5, the abbess's account for 1492/93 which is representative of this yearly dole.
13 SRO, HD 1538/156/5, and HD 1538/156/13 (Bungay); VE, vol. 3, p. 416 (Campsey Ash).
14 Ibid., p. 478.
15 SRO, HD 1538/327.
16 NRO, NRS 26884 42 E8.
17 Ibid. She spent 4d, and another 1s 6d on the clothes for the poor servants.
18 NRO, NRS 26883 42 E8. She spent 3s 10½d on these items.
19 VE, vol. 3, p. 416.

indigent of each of the parish churches appropriated to Bruisyard received 2s a year from the nuns there.[20]

Charitable dispensations like these were common to all monastic communities. The abbess and convent of Delapré Abbey in the diocese of Lincoln, for example, gave 5d annually on the anniversary of their founder's death.[21] The nuns at Marrick Priory in Yorkshire distributed 16s 8d worth of bread and 15s to the poor on Maundy Thursday; they dispensed 11s 6d in money among the local friars on the obit of their founder, Roger de Aske; and gave annually £2 in alms to the bailiff and keeper of the woods.[22] At Syon, the nuns donated any surplus revenues to the poor on the feast of All Souls, while the monks at Sibton Abbey in Suffolk gave a small amount of money to the poor at Easter.[23] The almoner at Norwich Cathedral Priory arranged for the ritual washing and feeding of the poor on Maundy Thursday. He provided bread, herring, and drink to as many poor men as there were monks in the priory. Other monasteries sat and fed thirteen poor folk at the refectory table on this day.[24] The almoner at St Benet at Holme in Norfolk gave clothes and shoes to widows, orphans, and poor clergy each year at Christmas.[25]

These annual dispensations for the poor can be assessed by determing how much nuns, monks, and canons spent on them. Savine, for example, calculated that religious houses' donations in alms averaged about 3 percent of their yearly revenues; Snape suggested a slightly higher figure of 5 percent.[26]

These estimations are flawed, however, by relying on the *Valor* for amounts, because the audit only excused certain – usually customary – donations as tax exempt; most of a house's alms were thus not recorded in the *Valor*, supporting Knowles' observation about the more informal alms.[27] The *Valor* can be even more problematic for assessing charitable outlay because it occasionally omitted the alms of a house completely. While the auditors noted the amounts spent on alms by female houses in the county of Suffolk, for example, they neglected to enter these expenses in the audits of any of the convents in Norfolk.[28] In fact, for Carrow, whose distributions to the poor are entered in all of the

---

[20] Ibid., p. 443.

[21] Serjeantson, *A History of Delapre Abbey*, p. 25.

[22] Dugdale, *Monasticon*, vol. 4, p. 244.

[23] Aungier, *History of Syon*, p. 244 for Syon; Denny, *The Sibton Abbey Estates*, p. 30.

[24] For Norwich Cathedral Priory, see: VE, vol. 3, p. 287. For this practice at other houses, see: Gray, *The Priory of St Radegund*, p. 172 for the treasurer's account which details the Maundy Thursday expenses; and Howlett, "Account Rolls of Certain Obedientiaries," pp. 536–37 for St Benet at Holme.

[25] Ibid., p. 537.

[26] Savine, *English Monasteries on the Eve of the Reformation*, pp. 228–29, 238; and Snape, *English Monastic Finances*, pp. 110–18.

[27] Savine, *English Monastic Finances on the Eve of the Reformation*, p. 235 where he acknowledges the limitations of the audit.

[28] For the female houses in Norfolk, see: VE, vol. 3, passim. Note also that Savine extracts the amounts which monasteries spent in alms: Savine, *English Monastic Finances on the Eve of the Reformation*, pp. 235–36, and while he notes those for the Suffolk female houses,

surviving household accounts, the royal assessors simply recorded that "alms to the poor have been deducted from the accounts"; none of these expenses are given.[29]

Any effort to calculate these amounts also suffers from discrepancies in the sources we do have.[30] We have already seen, for example, that the prioress of Redlingfield spent £34 in alms; the *Valor* entry for this priory is only £11.[31] Similarly, the bailiff, the prioress, and the cellarer at Bungay gave alms which totaled nearly £2; the audit notes that only 2s was spent annually on the poor.[32] Whether these discrepancies reflected individual almsgiving habits, as reflected for example in Prioress Lampet of Redlingfield's sole surviving account, or represented the convents' corporate gifts to the poor is possible but difficult to determine.

Finally, a tally of amounts spent on alms is skewed by the overall paucity of sources. We have already noted that both the prioresses and the cellarers of Bungay and Carrow gave alms. But religious houses extended charity through their superiors, almoners, and several other obedientiaries as well.[33] At the Cathedral Priory in Norwich, for example, at least five officers theoretically administered doles: the cellarer, almoner, chamberer, sacrist, and prior's cellarer. Each department contributed to the Maundy Thursday ritual, and to the daily feeding of the poor men who dined in the priory, as well as giving alms to the prisoners in the castle and to local anchorites and hermits.[34] The limited survival of household accounts from the female houses in the diocese of Norwich and the omissions in the *Valor*, then, show only part of the picture.

Calculating the amounts we do have shows that the cost of alms varied considerably from house to house. The abbesses of Marham spent an average of 11s a year on alms to the poor throughout the fifteenth century.[35] Mid-century and later, one of the prioresses of Carrow made similar payments averaging between 5s and 10s.[36] More concrete comparisons can be made in the amounts in alms spent according to the *Valor* by the nuns at Blackborough,

---

he omits the amount which the auditors allowed the nuns at Campsey Ash, which is noted in the *Valor* for that house. See: VE, vol. 3, p. 416.

[29] Ibid., vol. 3, p. 305.

[30] Tillotson, *Marrick Priory*, p. 22 notes that the *Valor* for this house says that the annual alms were given by ancient custom, prompting him to wonder if such moneys were still being given in 1535. He points out, though, that the household accounts for Marrick show alms-giving in amounts less than those that the *Valor* deducts. He assumes that this discrepancy is due both to the paucity of sources, i.e., a lack of all obedientiaries' accounts, and to the nature of the documents: the *Valor* being a tax audit, and the extant household accounts only partial records of the priory's expenses.

[31] See above, p. 141: VE, vol. 3, p. 475.

[32] See above, p. 141; VE, vol. 3, p. 431.

[33] Knowles, *The Religious Orders*, vol. 3, p. 265; Power, *Medieval English Nunneries*, p. 132.

[34] Saunders, *An Introduction*, p. 170.

[35] For example: NRO, Hare 2204 194x5, the abbess's account for the year 1426/27.

[36] NRO, NRS 26882 42 E8 where she spent 6s (1455); NRO, NRS 26883 42 E8 also acting as cellarer she spent 10s 3d (1484); and NRO, NRS 26884 42 E8 where she spent 5s (1529).

Bruisyard, Bungay, Campsey Ash, and Flixton in the sixteenth century. The Blackborough nuns gave £3 a year; at Bruisyard they contributed more than 50s in money and food.[37] The nuns at Bungay and Campsey Ash paid annually at least £22 and 22s respectively, and at Flixton, they spent just over 56s annually.[38]

As these charges varied, so too did the percentages they represented of the convents' total revenues. The money spent on alms comprised about 1 percent of the abbess of Marham's income, and 1 percent of the revenues of the prioresses of Bungay, Campsey Ash, and Carrow.[39] The percentages were much higher for Blackborough, Redlingfield, and Bruisyard: 7 percent for Blackborough, 13 percent for Redlingfield, and a full 17 percent for Bruisyard.[40]

Though these figures are only a portion of what the nuns gave, these estimates suggest that they bore no relation to a convent's overall value. The wealthiest house, Campsey Ash, spent less on alms – 22s – than did the poorest house, Flixton Priory, which gave over 56s. The diocese's other poorer houses, Blackborough and Bruisyard, also contributed significantly more to the poor than the diocese's wealthier ones.

Female monasteries in other parts of England show the same incongruities. While some donated less than 1 percent of their total income, a few convents contributed much more; and, as at the female houses in the diocese of Norwich, the amounts nuns elsewhere contributed in alms did not necessarily reflect their corporate wealth. Handale, a small and poor Cistercian house in York, for example, spent over £4 – at least 30 percent of its revenues – in alms, while the great pre-Conquest foundation, Shaftesbury Abbey, one of the wealthiest female monasteries, spent £13, only 1 percent of its yearly revenues.[41] Likewise, at Marrick Priory, whose annual income totaled £65, the nuns spent £9 on alms, or 14 percent of its revenues.[42]

---

[37] VE, vol. 3, p. 396 (Blackborough); ibid., p. 443 (Bruisyard).

[38] Ibid., p. 431 and SRO, HD 1538/345 for Bungay (1516); ibid., p. 416 (Campsey Ash); for Flixton, ibid., p. 446.

[39] The abbess of Marham's average income was £77; NRO, Hare 2205 194x5 (1446/47); NRO, Hare 2208 194x5 (1468/49) for example. The prioress of Bungay spent 14s in alms of an income of £61 11s 9d: VE, vol. 3, p. 431; and SRO, HD 1538/345 for her contribution in the 1530s of 12s 8d For Campsey Ash, see: VE, vol. 3, p. 416 where the prioress gave 5s out of £182. For Carrow: see HRO, NRS 26882 42 E8 for the prioress's donation of 6s out of £133 in income; NRO, HRS 26883 for her donation of 10s 3d out of an income totaling £87, and NRO, NRS 26884 42 E8 for her 5s in alms out of £91 in revenues.

[40] Blackborough's wealth was £42: VE, vol. 3, p. 396; ibid., p. 478 for Redlingfield's alms of £11 and wealth valued at £67, and SRO, HD 1538/327 for the prioress's contribution of £34 out of an income equaling £72. For Bruisyard see: VE, vol. 4, p. 443 for the abbey's alms of 50s and their yearly income of £56.

[41] Savine, *English Monasteries on the Eve of the Reformation*, p. 237 for Handale's doles (£4 19s 8d); ibid., p. 235 for those of Shaftesbury (£13 1s 11d). Handale was valued at £13 a year, and Shaftesbury at £1166 a year: Knowles, *Medieval Religious Houses*, p. 223 for Handale; ibid., p. 218 for Shaftesbury.

[42] Tillotson, *Marrick Priory*, p. 21.

Corporate wealth did not necessarily determine almsgiving at the male houses in the diocese of Norwich either. According to the *Valor*, from which the value of several of the female houses' contributions to alms are also derived, the canons at Ixworth gave more than £20 in alms – roughly 25 percent of their revenues; the wealthier monks at St Benet at Holme spent £5 – less than 5 percent of their annual income.[43]

Although monastic almsgiving has yet to be analyzed in terms of geographic location, this factor might in part explain the apparent disparity in almsgiving among female and male houses.[44] The relatively minor sums spent by Carrow's prioresses and cellarers may reflect the nuns' proximity to other institutions which also provided for the poor. That the nuns there made specific entries in their accounts suggests that these duties may have been more formalized because of their suburban location – which guaranteed a steady population of poor, drawn to the city of Norwich for possible employment as well as for its greater number of almsgiving institutions – than they were for the prioress of Bungay, whose location in a small market town may have rendered such highly regularized donations unnecessary. Specific references to money and goods do not appear in her accounts. The considerable amounts Redlingfield and Bruisyard spent, on the other hand, are more difficult to explain. Neither house was located close to other almsgiving institutions which suggests perhaps that responsibility for the poor fell more heavily on the nuns at these two places, which thus spent more than the convents founded in more populated areas.[45] And perhaps the substantial percentage of revenues which Bruisyard gave in alms reflects also its identification as a house of Poor Clares, an order dedicated to ministering to society's most vulnerable.

Geographic location might also explain the disparities between the alms given by Handale, on the northern Yorkshire coast, far from any other priory, and Shaftesbury, which was close to other female and male houses. Such proximity perhaps lessened the need for doles around this large Benedictine convent.[46] Similarly, Ixworth's remoteness from other charitable institutions may have made such doles more incumbent on the canons there than they were on the monks at St Benet at Holme, who were relatively close to both Hickling priory and the hospital of Horning.[47]

Amounts spent in alms were only one aspect of monastic charity, and they were meaningless if the money and the less formal dispensations of food and

43 Savine, *English Monasteries on the Eve of the Reformation*, p. 237 for Ixworth (£20 15s); for St Benet at Holme, ibid., p. 236 (£5 18s 8d). Ixworth was valued at £82; St Benet at Holme at £583: VCH, *Norfolk*, vol. 2, p. 331.

44 Scarisbrick, *The Reformation*, p. 52 alludes to this possibility but does not develop the idea.

45 See map, p. xiii.

46 Power, *Medieval English Nunneries*, p. 725 gives a map of all of the female houses in England.

47 For the locations of Ixworth and St Benet at Holme, see: VCH, *Suffolk*, vol. 2, p. 51 for the location of Ixworth; and VCH, *Norfolk*, vol. 2, pp. 314–15 for the site of St Benet at Holme.

clothing failed to reach those for whom they were intended. Abuses in almsgiving constituted one of the biggest problems for monasteries in late medieval England. The problem was serious enough to compel Henry V to address it in his proclamation for monastic reform in 1414.[48] His chief concern was the diversion of funds meant for alms by male monastic superiors who, Henry advised, should keep their hands out of their houses' coffers so that they could properly carry out their charitable duties. Likewise, the provincial chapters of the Benedictine monks legislated against the defrauding of alms throughout the fourteenth and fifteenth centuries.[49]

The concerns of the Crown and the provincial chapters, and their efforts to stem the abuses, seem to have had little effect on the practices of many of the male houses. Bishop Nykke continually rebuked the monks at St Benet at Holme for feeding daily food scraps to their dogs instead of to the poor who gathered outside their gates.[50] And most of the almoner's revenues went not to provisions for the poor but rather to wine for the brothers.[51] The monks at the Cathedral Priory in Norwich not only fed their dogs the scraps of food, but also gave much of their leftovers to those "non-indigent."[52] In fact, distributions to the poor dwindled substantially among all of the priory's obedientiaries who were supposed to make such contributions.[53] The bishop noted a similar across-the-board decline among the monks of Walsingham, while at Creake Abbey, instead of donating the copes of Abbot Brandon to the poor after his death, the monks sold them.[54]

Lapses in the distribution of both formal and informal alms have been attributed to a number of factors – including the decline in male Benedictine monasteries' resources, and a simplification and regularization of the distributions to maintain the intergrity of the cloister.[55] But these considerations could just as easily be applied to the female houses as well and, in general, these abuses were considerably more prominent in the male houses than they were in the female convents. Bishop Wyckham admonished the nuns at Romsey to give out alms according to order and custom, and the nuns at both Arden and Esholt, both small houses in Yorkshire, were instructed in the early fourteenth century to get rid of their alms-consuming dogs.[56] There is no evidence, however, to indicate that the nuns in the diocese of Norwich defrauded the alms which were meant for the poor.

[48] For Henry V's proclamations, see: A. R. Myers, ed., *English Historical Documents, 1327–1485* (New York, 1969), pp. 787–88.

[49] Pantin, *Documents*, vol. 45, pp. 47, 87 (1363); ibid., pp. 128, 280 (1444).

[50] Jessopp, *Visitations*, p. 215 for the visit of 1526; ibid., p. 279 for 1532.

[51] Howlett, "Account Rolls of Certain Obedientiaries," p. 537.

[52] Jessopp, *Visitations*, p. 203 (1526); ibid., p. 264 (1532).

[53] Cheney, "Norwich Cathedral Priory," p. 112 for Bishop Bateman's injunction in 1346 to give alms properly; and Saunders, *An Introduction*, pp. 169–70.

[54] Jessopp, *Visitations*, p. 251 (Walsingham); Carthew, "North Creake Abbey," p. 158.

[55] Harvey, *Living and Dying*, pp. 15, 21–2.

[56] Luce, "Injunctions Made and Issued," p. 36 for Romsey; and Tillotson, "Visitation and Reform," p. 15 for the Yorkshire houses.

Though no apparent correspondence between the wealth of a house and the amount of alms it bestowed seems to have existed, the considerably wealthier male houses would potentially have had a great deal more to give than the nuns. Yet the male monasteries were the biggest perpetrators of alms-fraud. The monks at Bury St Edmunds, it is true, gave a considerable amount of money in alms to the poor, and executed their charitable duties effectively.[57] But that so many of the other male houses in the diocese did divert funds, food, and clothing meant for alms while the poorer female houses did not, suggests perhaps that as women – traditionally seen as carers and nurturers – the nuns took these charitable responsibilities more seriously than did their male counterparts.[58] Medieval society and culture assessed women's contribution to society solely by their roles as wives and mothers. Religious women incorporated these criteria into their vocation which, if anything, stressed their roles as carers and nurturers, as prescribed by St Benedict's injunctions to care for the poor and needy.

The nuns' more consistent charitable activities might also mirror the growing sense of social responsibility which some have identified in later medieval testators' bequests. Mary Erler, for example, noticed such an emphasis among the bequests of late medieval vowesses to civic charitable institutions and services, suggesting perhaps a specifically female ethic.[59] Care for the poor may have also been more important to the nuns because they were less involved than monks and canons in wider affairs of the realm, and might therefore have been less distracted from such local concerns. It is possible then that the nuns carried out these duties more effectively because they were not thus diverted, and in the end serviced more people because of their local perspective, regardless of the reduced amounts at their disposal to give.

Religious Services

Daily and occasional alms were only part of what monasteries had to offer lay society; local communities also partook in many of the convents' religious services. All of a monastery's residents heard mass and received other sacraments from the nuns' chaplains and priests. The numerous maids, butlers and grooms of Bungay, for example, probably heard mass and received communion

---

57 VCH, *Suffolk*, vol. 2, p. 68.
58 Bynum, "Religious Women in the Later Middle Ages," pp. 130, 135; Janet Finch and Dulcre Groves, eds., *Labour of Love: Women, Work, and Caring* (London, 1983), is a series of articles whose central point is the culturally determined role of women as care-takers; Leclercq, "Monasticism for Men and Monasticism for Women," p. 330; Magli, "Il Problema," p. 637; and Sherry Ortner, "Is Female to Male as Nature is to Culture," in *Women, Culture, and Society*, ed. M. Z. Rosaldo and Louise Lamphere (California, 1974), passim. In this article Ortner describes how women behave according to societal conditions, not facts of nature.
59 Erler, "English Vowed Women," pp. 170–71.

on a more regular basis than did many others who had to deal with the vacancies and absenteeism that characterized parish life in the later Middle Ages.[60]

Such formal religious services could go well beyond mass and communion. Bruisyard Abbey's affiliation with the Friars Minor, for example, ensured that everyone associated with the abbey – bailiffs, reeves, and household servants and hinds – was granted the same indulgences as those enjoyed by people who visited certain basilicas and churches in Rome. Additionally, anyone connected to Bruisyard could choose their own confessor, who would absolve them of all of their sins and grant plenary remission at their hour of death.[61]

Parishioners farther flung than the immediate lay residents of a monastic community also participated in a house's religious services. Many conventual chapels and churches also functioned as parish churches where, as at St Radegund's in Cambridge, a screen divided parishioners from the nuns, allowing them to maintain the integrity of their cloister.[62] The nuns at Easebourne Priory in Sussex made similar structural modifications to accommodate themselves and the parishioners who also worshipped in their church.[63]

While parishioners' use of conventual churches as parish churches can be seen at female houses in other dioceses, the use of a conventual chapel by parishioners was significantly more prominent among the female houses in the diocese of Norwich than among their male counterparts. The conventual churches of Marham and Redlingfield were divided to serve local parishioners and the nuns;[64] so was the conventual church of Crabhouse.[65] Parishioners who worshipped in the nuns' churches would have been keenly aware of their presence behind the dividing screens; and proximity to these holy women

---

[60] For the state of parochial care in the later Middle Ages, see: T. E. Carson, "The Problem of Irregularities in the Late Medieval Church: An Example from Norwich," *Catholic Historical Review* 72:2 (1986), pp. 185–200; May McKisack, *The Fourteenth Century, 1307–1399* (Oxford, 1959), pp. 289–91; and A. R. Myers, *England in the Fourteenth Century* (New York, 1979), pp. 80–1; W. A. Pantin, "The Fourteenth Century," in *The English Church and the Papacy in the Middle Ages*, ed. C. H. Lawrence (London, 1965), pp. 183–85, 190; Snape, *English Monastic Finances*, pp. 77–83; and Wood-Legh, *Church Life in England*, pp. 139–40.

[61] *Papal Letters*, vol. 13:2, pp. 646–47. This indult was issued in 1476 but it was a reiteration of earlier papal decrees.

[62] Gray, *Priory of St Radegund*, p. 55. See also: Leclercq, "Hospitality and Monastic Prayer," pp. 5–9 for other examples of the division of monastic churches and chapels to accommodate the laity.

[63] W. H. St John Hope, *Cowdray and Easebourne Priory in the County of Sussex* (London, 1919), p. 98; Coldicott, *Hampshire Nunneries*, p. 61 for nuns' churches serving local parishioners as well. See also K. J. P. Lowe, "Patronage and Territorality in Early Sixteenth-Century Florence," *Renaissance Studies* 7:3 (1993), p. 270 for use of female and male conventual churches for public services.

[64] For Marham, see: Blomefield, *An Essay*, vol. 7, p. 386. For Redlingfield, see: VCH, *Suffolk*, vol. 2, p. 83.

[65] Bateman, "The Register," pp. 10–11.

heightened the power and enhanced the significance of the parishioners' prayers.[66]

By contrast, there is only one instance of a male house sharing its church with local lay people: at Binham Priory. And the priory had so neglected its parochial responsibilities that the parishioners intercepted the bishop on his way to the house for a visitation, and aired their grievances to him. The mortified prior and monks refused to greet the bishop as was their custom, but they later settled their differences with the disgruntled villagers.[67]

These parish churches, like all in medieval England, were the focal points of village life, ordering people's time, and their daily and seasonal routines.[68] The bells at Redlingfield, for example, signaled the time of day, and sounded both joyous and sorrowful tidings.[69] In the porch of the church at Marham one was baptized; in its cemetery one was buried.[70] The marriage banns of Thomas Hunston and Margaret Keroyle were read from the pulpit of the church at Crabhouse; their dower and dowry were announced at the church doors where the ceremony took place.[71] Between these milestones, moreover, parish churches maintained the cohesion of local society by serving as central meeting places and through church-ales and celebratory feast day processions.[72] Such occasions added color, meaning, and relief to the lives of those who toiled and lived close by.[73] And the nuns' facilitation of these activities, indirect as it may have been, was not lost on the villagers who relied on these churches for these and other services.

Local people also profited from more intangible, but nonetheless highly significant, services which the female houses provided: activities associated with death and life thereafter. Death was an ever-present concern for all who

---

66 See: Johnson, "*Mulier et Monialis*," p. 245 for the public opinion of nuns' prayers; and Leclercq, "Hospitality and Monastic Prayer," p. 9 where he points out that "the Order of St Benedict invited lay people to come and share its life of prayer," and so most convents made appropriate accommodations. Cf. Paxton, "London Nunneries," pp. 144–46 for shared conventual churches among the houses there.

67 Burstall, "A Monastic Agreement of the Fourteenth Century," pp. 211–13.

68 Eamon Duffy, *The Stripping of the Altars* (New Haven, 1992), esp. pp. 37–52 for the importance of the parish church and the ways in which it defined parish life in the later Middle Ages.

69 The sale of the bells at Redlingfield by the Crown brought £12: PRO, SP 5/3/132.

70 For the importance of burial, and the centrality of the parish cemetery, to people in the Middle Ages, see: Lorraine Attreed, "Preparation for Death in Sixteenth-Century Northern England," *The Sixteenth-Century Journal* 13:3 (1982), p. 37.

71 Bateman, "The Register," p. 11.

72 Lawrence Blair, *English Church Ales* (Michigan, 1940), pp. 1–3; and Gasquet, *Parish Life*, pp. 164–86, 233–52.

73 For the importance of parish celebrations, see: Imogen Luxton, "The Reformation and Popular Culture," in *Church and Society in England: Henry VIII to James I*, ed. Felicity Heal and Rosemary O'Day (London, 1977), pp. 60–1. See also: Charles Phythian-Adams, "Ceremony and the Citizen: The Communal Year at Coventry, 1450–1550," in *Crisis and Order in English Towns, 1500–1700*, ed. Peter Clark and Paul Slack (Toronto, 1972), pp. 57–85.

lived in this period of recurring plagues and epidemics; people were therefore concerned with arranging the disposition of their property before they died, planning a proper burial, and requesting the prayers necessary for the repose of their souls.

Wills embodied a testator's spiritual and temporal concerns: they expressed last wishes with regard to one's soul, and settled land and goods, transferring and securing family patrimony and lineage from one generation to the next. Improper handling or execution of wills not only imperiled one's soul, but also could put one's heirs at risk.[74] The recording, registering, and execution of wills were, therefore, highly significant acts undertaken by respected and responsible people. As we have seen, both the abbess of Marham and the prioress of Carrow had the canonical right to prove wills.[75] They also acted as witnesses and executrices who were specifically responsible for carrying out death-bed requests, thus permitting a soul to rest in peace.[76] The cartulary of Marham, for example, includes a list of people whose wills were proved at the abbey, several of whom requested that the abbess be their executrix.[77]

Just as the male religious were frequently named as executors or witnesses to wills, so too were numerous nuns: both superiors and rank and file nuns were appointed to implement testators' final requests – many of which were in Latin, again indicating at least a partially literate female monastic population.[78] The prioress of Thetford, for example, was named executrix of John Chippley's will dated 1374.[79] Isabel Long of Flixton made Margaret Punder, prioress of Flixton, one of her executors.[80] Margaret Dunne, a nun at Blackborough, not only executed her sister Alice's will, she also was executrix for Nicholas Goldborne.[81] Likewise, Lawrence Draper of Cromer named his sister Alice, a nun at Thetford Priory, to be an executrix of his will.[82] These examples are just a few, but they indicate that, like their male counterparts, nuns were considered responsible agents.

In addition to appointing nuns as executrices of wills, testators often requested burial in a convent's church or cemetery. The Countess of Oxford was buried at Bruisyard, as was Friar Simon Tunsted, the twenty-third Provin-

---

74 For the importance of making and executing wills in medieval England, see: Lorraine Attreed, "Preparation for Death," pp. 37–8; and Rowena Archer and B. E. Ferme, "Testamentary Procedure with Special Reference to the Executrix," *Reading Medieval Studies* 15 (1989), p. 6.
75 See above Chapter 1, p. 27.
76 Archer and Ferme, "Testamentary Procedure," p. 5.
77 NRO, Hare 1 232x.
78 Rye, *Carrow Abbey*, Appendix ix for numerous references to Carrow nuns who were charged with these duties. For these activities as signs of literacy: Moran, Literacy and Education," passim; but see also: K. B. MacFarlane, *Lancastrian Kings and Lollard Knights* (Oxford, 1972), p. 207 who does not agree.
79 NRO, NCC Heydon.
80 SRO, IC/AA2/6A, 9, 1517.
81 NRO, ANW 41 Bakon, dated 1521.
82 NRO, NCC 199 Heydon, 1382.

cial of the Order of Friars Minor.[83] Edmund of Ufford, brother of Robert, Earl of Suffolk, was buried next to his wife at Campsey Ash in 1375; nearly a hundred years later Isabel Ufford, Countess of Suffolk, was buried there next to her husband.[84] Among those interred at Carrow were a man named John Downe and the local dignitaries William Aslack, Robert Blickling, and Sir John Howard.[85] The nuns at Crabhouse and Marham also had the right to bury parishioners in their cemeteries.[86]

Indeed, the wills of both parish and county residents who wanted interment in a monastery display a marked preference for the female houses in the diocese. Of the 837 wills surveyed in the registers of the archdeaconry court of Suffolk between 1481 and 1518, for example, eight people requested burial at the female houses, but none wanted to be buried in male monastic cemeteries.[87] Of 1,628 wills analyzed in the registers of the Norwich Consistory Court and enrolled between 1370 and 1536, fifteen people specified burial at the female convents, but only eleven wanted to be interred in the grounds of the male religious houses (exclusively friars).[88]

While both sexes requested burial in the female houses, more men did so than women, reflecting the will-making population as a whole.[89] Only three of the eight people who requested burial in the female houses and whose wills were probated in the Suffolk Archdeaconry Court were women; and in the Norwich Consistory Court sample, all but one of the testators who wanted to be buried at one of the female houses were male. In the Marham cartulary, on the other hand, sixteen people requested interment in the abbey's graveyard: five were men, eleven were women.[90]

While some socially prominent people asked to be buried in the nuns'

83 For Maud: *Testamenta Vetusta*, p. 182; and also Bourdillon, *The Minoresses*, pp. 48 and 58.
84 For Edmund, see: NRO, NCC 93 Heydon; for Isabel, see: *Testamenta Vetusta*, pp. 193–94.
85 Blomefield, *An Essay*, vol. 4, pp. 525–26.
86 For Crabhouse, see: Bateman, "The Register," pp. 58–9.
87 Three people wanted to be buried at Campsey Ash (1481–98); one wanted burial at Bruisyard, one at Redlingfield (1501–06); one person requested burial at Campsey Ash in 1508; and two people desired to be interred at Bungay between 1513 and 1518. See Appendix 4 for more about the registers on the Suffolk Archdeaconry Court, the wills and their analysis.
88 Most of the people who desired burial in the female houses were those whose wills were proved between 1370 and 1426. Two people wanted burial at Campsey Ash; and two at Bungay (1370–83); one wanted to be buried at Bruisyard 1385; one requested interment at Blackborough and five wanted burial at Campsey Ash (1416–26). These requests decline and hereafter only one person requested burial at Bungay in 1445; another one requested the same in 1480; and one more wanted to be buried at Bungay in 1536. The requests for burial in the friaries were one in each of the following time periods: 1370–83; 1383–1408, 1416–26, 1473–91, and 1524–26; but three in 1436–44, and two in 1514–16. See Appendix 4.
89 Coppel, "Wills and the Community," p. 71; Harrod, "Extracts from Early Norfolk Wills," p. 111; Tanner, *The Church in Late Medieval Norwich*, p. 115 where he says that male testators out-numbered women by 3 to 1.
90 NRO, Hare 1 232x fol. 8v.

churches and cemeteries, a wide spectrum of social groups were represented in these requests.[91] Likewise, the cartulary of Marham records that Cecilia Narburgh, a member of an important local gentry family, was buried there, as were Matilda of Marham and Isabella Coupere, women of lesser social rank.[92] Those interred at Bungay, Campsey Ash, and Carrow follow the same pattern: while Isabel Countess of Suffolk was buried at Campsey Ash, local chaplains, such as Robert Gosselynne, requested burial in the sepulcher of Campsey Ash, next to the tomb of one Angus Phelipp;[93] and Alice Weene of Bungay wanted to be buried in the churchyard of Bungay:[94] all these people were of lesser social rank than esquires and knights.[95] The names of most of those buried in the cemetery of Crabhouse are lost to us now, but the nuns there surely honored the burial requests of people from diverse social ranks, as the nuns' church served as the parish church as well.[96]

By contrast, the male houses received requests for burial primarily from people of elevated social status, most of whom were men.[97] Sir Thomas Howard, Earl of Surrey and Duke of Norfolk, along with several of his relatives, was buried at Thetford Priory; Henry Fitzroy, Duke of Somerset, with the monks at Wymondham.[98] And the monks of Bromholm buried Sir John Paston and Sir William Calthorpe, both important citizens of the region.[99] The White Friars in Ipswich interred Sir John and Sir Thomas de Loudham, and Gilbert Denham, esq.[100]

Country-wide, this connection between the larger and wealthier male houses and the high social standing of those they buried is consistent with the pattern identified earlier in this study, the association of socially prominent people and the wealthy male monasteries.[101] The alliance between these two social powers reinforced the prestige of the monasteries and also conferred a certain amount of honor on those they feted, boarded, and buried. But while

---

91   Harrod, "Extract from Early Wills," p. 111 where he describes the social ranks of the people whose wills were generally proved in the archdeaconry courts. See also: Tanner, *The Church in Late Medieval Norwich*, p. 115 for a similar description of the range of social groups represented in the will registers he used.

92   NRO, Hare 1 232x, fol. 8.

93   NRO, NCC 16, 17 Hyrnyng (1416); Erler, "English Vowesses," p. 175.

94   NRO, NCC 72, 73 Underwood (1535).

95   For Carrow, see: Rye, *Carrow Abbey*, Appendix ix, passim.

96   Among those buried at Crabhouse about whom we do know are members of the local parish gentry: Edmund Perys, parson of Wattlington, William Trussbutt, rector of Wattlington, and Prioress Joan Wiggenhall's aunt and uncle, Margaret and John Wiggenhall, all buried there between 1429 and 1450: Bateman, "The Register," pp. 58–60.

97   Saunders, "A History of Coxford," p. 284 notes that many of the wealthy county gentry men were buried at this house in Norfolk.

98   George Edward Cockayne, *The Complete Peerage*, ed. H. A. Doubleday and Lord Howard de Walden, vol. 9 (London, 1936), pp. 610–20.

99   Ibid., p. 361 for Paston; ibid., pp. 371–72 for Calthorpe.

100   Zimmerman, "The White Friars," p. 204. Note too that Redstone, "The Carmelites," p. 194 states that many wealthy burgesses were buried here.

101   Harris, "A New Look at the Reformation," p. 99 found the same connection in the burial requests of aristocratic women.

society's most elite groups were more frequently drawn to the male houses, all social groups valued the power of the nuns' prayers, as their provision of intercessory activities and prayers demonstrates.

Intercessory prayers were the best way to lessen one's time in the fiery way-station of purgatory and enter into eternal bliss beyond.[102] And people of all social ranks requested or purchased as many of the nuns' prayers as they could afford, to be said not only on the day of death, but often also every year on the anniversary of their death. Obits like these are common in wills and in all of the extant household accounts, as are specific reminders to pray for someone's soul: at Bungay Priory, the prioress received 40s from Dame Hobert for singing for the souls of "Doward and others."[103] People also utilized the nuns' churches by maintaining lights, forming parish guilds or lay fraternities, and founding chantries.[104]

These services could be inexpensive or very pricey. Among the less expensive purchases of prayers was paying for candles to burn in front of a patron saint or before an altar.[105] At Blackborough, for example, a man named Le Sayre gave a rent in East Wynch to fund a lamp in the nuns' chapel before the image of St John the Evangelist for his soul and the souls of his heirs.[106] Similarly, Robert Ashfield and others paid the nuns at Campsey Ash 50 marks for three tapers to burn daily before the high altar there.[107]

A slightly more involved and costly way to shorten one's time in purgatory was to become a member of a parish or craft guild, and at least two of the diocese's female houses accommodated these religious, civic, and labor-related associations. The guild of the Holy Trinity maintained an altar in the convent church of Crabhouse.[108] The saddlers and spurriers of the city of Norwich instituted their guild in the conventual church at Carrow.[109] Guilds performed good works for their members both in this world and in the next by holding annual masses, feasts and processions, and burying members and ensuring that prayers were said on their behalf.[110] Lay fraternities hired their own chaplain

---

102 Alan Kreider, *English Chantries: The Road to Dissolution* (Cambridge, 1979), pp. 4–5; Rosenthal, *The Purchase of Paradise*, pp. 11–12.

103 SRO, HD 1538/156/17.

104 Kreider, *English Chantries*, p. 5.

105 Scarisbrick, *The Reformation*, pp. 4, 8.

106 Blomefield, *An Essay*, vol. 8, p. 33.

107 VCH, *Suffolk*, vol. 2, p. 114.

108 Bateman, "The Register," p. 59.

109 Rye and Tillet, "Carrow Abbey," pp. 465–66; and Lujo Brentano and Lucy Toulmin-Smith, eds., *English Gilds* (London: EETS, o.s., vol. 40, 1870), pp. 42–4 for the ordinances.

110 See: H. F. Westlake, *The Parish Gilds of Medieval England* (London, 1919). See also: Scarisbrick, *The Reformation*, pp. 19–39 for the importance of parish guilds in the later Middle Ages; and see: Toulmin-Smith, *English Gilds*, pp. lxxxi–xcii for a discussion of religious guilds. Craft or trade guilds accomplished similar goals though they were not fundamentally religious corporations. See Brentano's discussion of the history and development of craft guilds in Smith, *English Gilds*, pp. cxiv–clxiv.

if the members could afford one, or maintained an altar in a nearby chapel or church if their membership was poorer.[111]

Like Carrow and Crabhouse priories, female and male houses elsewhere also accommodated parishioners by housing guilds. At Romsey Abbey in Hampshire, the brotherhood of St George kept lights and an altar in the conventual church.[112] The Confraternity of St George maintained a chantry priest in the cathedral of Norwich, and the peltiers' guild held their annual high mass there too; the guild of Our Lady's Nativity was founded at Wymondham Priory, also in Norfolk.[113] And just as these fraternities provided their members with essential religious and social services, so too did they maintain a certain amount of social cohesion. Guild membership was not restricted by social status; this social integration was reinforced and nurtured by saints' feast day celebrations and an annual guild feast in which all members participated. By facilitating and supporting these guilds and fraternities, the nuns demonstrated some of the diverse ways they interacted with secular society – ways which made them an integral part of the local scene.[114]

Fraternities were open to all parishioners, but founding a chantry, as Countess Maud did at Campsey Ash and Bruisyard, was the single most important way people of the upper ranks of medieval society purchased prayers for the deceased.[115] Founders hired priests to say prayers for the repose of the souls of the founder, deceased family members, and others. Most large chantries further guaranteed swift passage through purgatory by providing alms to the poor, pastoral care of local parishioners, and often education for local children. In so doing, chantries, like the less exclusive parish and crafts guilds, were a major part of life in late medieval England. Chantries' affiliations with the nuns in the diocese, and the ties these intercessory foundations established between them and the lay people who erected altars, installed chaplains, and funded

---

[111] Barbara Hanawalt, "Keepers of the Lights: Late Medieval Parish Gilds," *Journal of Medieval and Renaissance Studies* 14 (1984), pp. 21–37; Kreider, *English Chantries*, p. 6; Scarisbrick, *The Reformation*, p. 20 describes lay fraternities as "poor men's chantries."

[112] Liveing, *The Records of Romsey Abbey*, pp. 182–83. The weavers' guild in Northampton maintained lights and established themselves in the conventual church of Delapre Abbey, a Cluniac female house as well: Serjeantson, *A History of Delapre Abbey*, p. 19.

[113] Toulmin-Smith, *English Gilds*, pp. 1, 29, 17–18 (Norwich Cathedral Priory); Catherine Firth, "Village Gilds of Norfolk in the Fifteenth Century," *NA* 18 (1914), p. 166 (Wymondham).

[114] Firth, "Village Gilds of Norfolk," pp. 175–79; F. W. Warren, "A Pre-Reformation Gild," *PSIA* 11 (1903), pp. 135–36 for the spectrum of activities of several parish guilds in Norfolk and Suffolk, and the range of social groups who participated in them. See also: Ben McRee, "Religious Gilds and Regulations of Behavior in Late Medieval English Towns," in *People, Politics and Community in the Later Middle Ages*, ed. Joel Rosenthal and Colin Richmond (Gloucester, 1987), pp. 108–22.

[115] Kreider, *English Chantries*; but see also: Kathleen Wood-Legh, *Perpetual Chantries in England* (Cambridge, 1965); Rosenthal, *The Purchase of Paradise*, pp. 31–52 also deals extensively with chantry foundations.

lights, signal the nuns' integrity and holiness which thus encouraged the establishment of intercessory institutions in their conventual chapels.[116]

The prayers of anchorites were also highly valued and enlisted by many to help the souls of both the living and the dead. And monasteries' support of these recluses constituted another way religious houses facilitated the intercessory prayers from which lay society profited.[117] Central to religious life in the Middle Ages, these renunciates symbolized the essential Christian life. Devoting their lives to prayer, anchorites were enclosed for life in small private cells attached to a church – those of female recluses were attached to the north side of a chapel – with narrow openings through which they could watch the celebration of the mass and receive food and offerings. These people were held in the highest esteem and though their prayers were said primarily for their own personal salvation, all of society benefitted from them.

The nuns at Crabhouse supported female anchorites from the twelfth through the fifteenth century.[118] The nuns at Carrow maintained both female and male anchorites: a recluse named Roger lived in the anchorite's cell there in the fifteenth century.[119] But probably the most famous medieval recluse was Julian of Norwich, whose anchorhold was in the churchyard of St Julian's, which was adjacent to, and one of, the properties of Carrow Priory.[120]

Julian's *Revelations of Divine Love* are among the few writings of late medieval English female holy women, and her fame – then as now – was widespread.[121] While she was important in her own right, her affiliation with Carrow undoubtedly contributed to Carrow's reputation as a holy house for those seeking temporary refuge from worldly concerns. Appreciation by those who sought Julian's own intercessory powers is evident in the numerous visitors she attracted – such as Margery Kempe – and the bequests local testators made to

116 Paxton, "London Nunneries," pp. 122, 128 for nuns' successful fulfillment of their roles as intercessors and executors of obits, and the public recognition of the nuns as such.

117 For anchorites in medieval England, see: Ann Warren, *Anchorites and Their Patrons in Medieval England* (Berkeley, 1985).

118 Gilchrist and Oliva, *Religious Women*, pp. 77, 99. NRO, DCN 44/76/94; I am grateful to Rachel Farmer and Frank Meeres for passing on this reference to an anchoress at Crabhouse in the late fifteenth century.

119 Tanner, *The Church in Late Medieval Norwich*, p. 59.

120 Blomefield, *An Essay*, vol. 4, p. 525; Rye, *Carrow Abbey*, pp. 7–8; *VCH, Norfolk*, vol. 2, p. 552.

121 The body of work on Julian and her writings is extensive. See, for instance: P. F. Chambers, *Juliana of Norwich. An Introductory Appreciation and Interpretive Anthology* (New York, 1955); R. H. Flood, *A Description of St Julian's Church, Norwich, and an Account of Dame Julian's Connection with It* (Norwich, 1936); Jennifer Heimmel, "God Our Mother"; *Julian of Norwich and the Medieval Image of Christian Feminine Divinity* (Salzburg, 1982); W. R. Inge, "*The Ancren Riwle* and Julian of Norwich," in *Studies of English Mystics* (New York, 1969), pp. 38–79; Robert Llewelyn, *All Shall Be Well: The Spirituality of Julian of Norwich for Today* (New York, 1982); E. I. Watkin, "Dame Julian of Norwich (1342–1413)," in *The English Way*, ed. Maisie Ward (New York, 1933), pp. 128–58.

her and also to the anchoresses enclosed in the cell after her death.[122] Some of Carrow Priory's other advowsons also supported female anchorites as did female houses in other dioceses and two friaries in Norwich.[123]

On a national level, most *reclusaria* for women were attached to parish churches or chapels, but it is interesting to note that in the diocese of Norwich and elsewhere, both female monasteries and mendicant houses were more popular sites for female anchorholds than were male monastic houses.[124] Financial support for these women was a primary concern for the recluses themselves, as well as for the episcopal authorities who sanctioned their enclosure, and so the location of the recluses' holds was an important consideration.[125] That more friaries and female monasteries accommodated female anchorites than the usually wealthier houses of monks and canons suggests that despite the relative poverty of female and mendicant houses, they were nevertheless deemed worthy places for these holy women to lead their lives in solitude and prayer.

The Impact of the Services Nuns Provided

The female houses in Norfolk and Suffolk, then, offered a wide range of spiritual services to the lay communities around them. All of these activities had profound consequences and carried tremendous significance for the populace who utilized them. Is it possible to determine how wide an impact these services might have had? How many poor and aged, for example, might have relied on the pensions and corrodies discussed earlier, and how many relied on the alms described above?

Medieval contemporaries believed that the number of poor increased, and although historians disagree about the extent to which this perception was based on actual numbers of poor, scholars do admit that the impact of the poor on society was aggravated by the social displacement which accompanied the demographic and economic changes of this later medieval period.[126] While it

---

122   Rye, *Carrow Abbey*, Appendix ix; Tanner, *The Church in Late Medieval Norwich*, pp. 130–31, 168–69.

123   Gilchrist and Oliva, *Religious Women*, pp. 75, 89–91; Tanner, *The Church in Late Medieval Norwich*, pp. 60, 176 for anchorites at other Carrow properties; and ibid., p. 59 for anchorites at the Carmelite Friary in the city, and one at the Franciscan house. Warren, *Anchorites and Their Patrons*, pp. 178–79, 197 for anchorites at two other female houses.

124   For example, of the 41 anchoress holds identified in the diocese of Norwich between 1100 and 1540, 31 were attached to parish churches, 4 to friaries, 5 to female monastic communities or their properties, and only one to a male monastic house: Gilchrist and Oliva, *Religious Women*, pp. 89–91. Though Warren in *Anchorites and Their Patrons* does not quantify anchoress cells specifically by site, this same pattern can be identified in her study as well.

125   Warren, *Anchorites and Their Patrons*, pp. 39, 90, and passim.

126   J. L. Bolton, *The English Medieval Economy, 1150–1500* (London, 1980), pp. 183–84,

is impossible to determine the precise number of poor people – especially in Norfolk and Suffolk, where flourishing cloth industries somewhat mitigated the effects of the depressions of the later Middle Ages – who relied on these houses for corrodies, pensions, and daily and occasional alms, it is nevertheless true that the female houses in the diocese contributed to the well-being of local and itinerant poor and indigent.

The significance of the monasteries' social and spiritual activities and their impact on society in late medieval England will likely be long debated. Some scholars suggest that monastic charity has been greatly exaggerated; others credit monasteries for the social services they dispensed, but maintain that after the Dissolution they were taken up by the new owners.[127] Still other historians believe that the monasteries' value to society, with their distribution of charity and hospitality and their facilitation of religious and social services, has been underestimated.[128] But the nuns' execution of these services – dispensing alms and hospitality, executing and granting probate of wills, facilitating intercessory prayers, and accommodating local parishioners in their chapels and cemeteries – had a long tradition. And the relationship between the convents and their local communities that these activities established and nurtured was an accepted part of the psychology of late medieval society. While it would be instructive to know exactly how many people benefitted from the nuns' services, not knowing does not detract from the fact that they intimately bound generations of people to the convents around which they lived.

The impact of these services can perhaps be better appreciated when considering what their disappearance must have meant to those who partook of them. Contemporary observers of the effects of the Dissolution complained that one of the biggest contributions female monasteries made to society was the education of children.[129] This complaint perhaps will resonate more soundly now that scholars have identified an increase in the level of literacy in this later medieval period, especially among medieval society's middling

190–91; W. K. Jordan, *Philanthropy in England, 1480–1660* (New York, 1959), pp. 54–76. Michel Mollat, *Les Pauvres au Moyen Age* (Paris, 1978); Miri Rubin, *Charity and Community in Medieval Cambridge* (Cambridge, 1986), passim; John A. Thompson, "Piety and Charity in Late Medieval London," *Journal of Ecclesiastical History* 16 (1965), pp. 182–85.

127 Coulton, "The Truth about the Monasteries," pp. 714–15; Rosenthal, "Retirement and the Life Cycle," p. 175; and Savine, *English Monasteries on the Eve of the Reformation*, pp. 263–64 for those who maintain that monastic charity and hospitality have been greatly exaggerated; Baskerville, *English Monks and the Suppression*, pp. 278–79 acknowledges the benefits to society of these activities in the male houses, but maintains that they were taken up by their subsequent owners.

128 Gasquet, *Henry VIII and the English Monasteries*, pp. 462–64, 467–71 discusses the negative impact of the Dissolution on society because these doles and acts of hospitality were eliminated; Jordan, *The Charities of Rural England*, pp. 191–213, 402–11; Scarisbrick, *The Reformation*, pp. 51–4, 71, 78.

129 Francis Gasquet, "Overlooked Testimonies to the Character of the English Monasteries on the Eve of the Suppression," *Dublin Review* 114 (1894), pp. 245–77; and Simon, *Education and Society*, pp. 180–82.

social groups, those groups who most clearly interacted with the nuns and their convents. In other words, if the literacy rate was rising in the fourteenth and fifteenth centuries, it is very likely that the nuns' part in this trend toward greater literacy was higher than has been suspected in the past.

Public provisions for corrodians and pensioners also declined with the suppression of the monasteries, in many places the only providers of these kinds of relief. Later historians, like Francis Blomefield for example, described the great loss to Norfolk society caused by the suppression of Carrow, not only because it educated and boarded children, but also because of the hospitality the priory showed to strangers.[130] Though opposition to the suppression of the religious houses in the diocese never reached the magnitude of the Pilgrimage of Grace, many prominent Norfolk men sympathized with the rebels in the north, and indeed some acts of resistance occurred in Norfolk itself.[131]

In many cases the responsibilities for the poor and indigent, and often for the education of both boys and girls, fell to the surviving parish churches and chantries.[132] But both priests and parishioners complained of these added burdens, and most of the chantries fell under the sword of royal reform in the 1550s.[133] The lack of these services then had an inestimable effect on society. And, as many historians have pointed out, though many monastic houses were far from perfect, they were nevertheless an essential part of late medieval society.[134] Though most historians focus on the negative aspects of the female (and male) houses at the Dissolution, the female monasteries' accommodation of lay people in the ways described above made the convents a crucial element of the social and cultural landscape, and their numerous contributions to society were not replaced.

All of the activities and services which integrated the female monasteries into the lay societies of Norfolk and Suffolk, though common to all monastic

---

130 Blomefield, An Essay, vol. 4, p. 528.
131 For the Pilgrimage of Grace, see: G. R. Elton, Policy and Police: The Enforcement of the Reformation in the Age of Cromwell (Cambridge, 1972), pp. 199–204; and his Reform and Reformation, England, 1509–1558 (Cambridge, 1977), pp. 260–72; Gasquet, Henry VIII and the English Monasteries, pp. 220–40; Knowles, The Religious Orders, vol. 3, pp. 325–35. Scarisbrick, The Reformation, p. 26 notes that though the Duke of Norfolk marshaled troops in the King's name to quell the rebellion, his men sympathized with the rebels. See also: T. H. Swales, "Opposition to the Suppression of the Norfolk Monasteries; Expressions of Discontent, the Walsingham Conspiracy," NA 33:3 (1964), pp. 254–65 where he describes opposition in Norfolk as "spasmodic and not sufficiently strong" largely because of a lack of strong leadership.
132 Jordan, Philanthropy in England, p. 80 and passim; Scarisbrick, The Reformation, pp. 92, 111–13 and passim.
133 Jordan, Philanthropy in England, p. 80 and passim; Kreider, The Road to Dissolution, passim.
134 Elton, Policy and Police, pp. 84–170 discusses the rebellions against the suppression which occurred in several places for the reasons cited above. See also: D. M. Palliser, "Popular Reactions to the Reformation during the Years of Uncertainty 1530–79," in Church and Society in England: Henry VIII to James I, ed. Felicity Heal and Rosemary O'Day (London, 1977), pp. 40–4.

houses, tended to have a greater impact on local people than on the county gentry or aristocracy. While male monasteries also fed and clothed the local poor and indigent – though perhaps to a lesser degree than did the nuns – monks and canons also serviced, in some essential ways, members of medieval England's higher social groups. The relationships which these interactions thus established and perpetuated between local people and the nuns and between society's elites and the monks and canons were reflected in the patronage all social groups showed to the female and male monasteries. Such public recognition of the female and male religious can nowhere be better seen than in the patronage which these activities garnered for them.

6

Patronage of the Female Monasteries

Acts of charity and hospitality and the provision of religious services and prayers promoted patronage of the female monasteries by a wide range of social groups. From queens to yeoman farmers, people publicly acknowledged the prayers and charitable services the nuns provided by granting religious houses certain privileges, land, money, and goods. Scholarly discussion of the patronage of medieval religious houses of women has focused, however, on the continuing ties between the heirs of founding families and their particular foundations. Both Anne Bourdillon and Janet Burton, for example, stress how such sustained patronage lent economic stability to a religious community.[1] Their views rely on original foundation grants and those made fifty or more years later by founders' heirs, an emphasis due to the number of twelfth- and thirteenth-century cartularies which survive, wherein such deeds were recorded.[2] Indeed, much of what we know about the patrons of male monasteries in the diocese of Norwich derives from records like these.[3]

Continuing patronage by later generations of a founder's family was by the later Middle Ages, however, increasingly rare.[4] In the diocese of Norwich, late medieval patronage by founding families of the female houses is evident only in a few cases. The Earls of Warwick were the primary patrons of Shouldham Priory from its foundation until the reign of Henry VII when it came into the

---

[1] Bourdillon, The Minoresses, p. 50; Burton, "Yorkshire Nunneries," pp. 18, 20–1, 26.

[2] For example: Constance B. Bouchard, Sword, Miter, and Cloister: Nobility and the Church in Burgandy, 980–1198 (Ithaca, 1987); Burton, "Yorkshire Nunneries," passim; Emma Mason, "The Donors of Westminster Abbey Charters: c. 1066–1240," Medieval Prosopography 8:2 (1987), pp. 23–39; Marc Meyer, "Patronage of the West Saxon Royal Nunneries in Late Anglo-Saxon England," Revue Benedictine 91 (1981), pp. 332–58; Susan Wood, English Monasteries and their Patrons in the Thirteenth Century (Oxford, 1955).

[3] Barbara Dodwell, ed., The Charters of Norwich Cathedral Priory (London: Pipe Roll Society, vols. 78, 84, 1974); Gransden, The Customary of the Benedictine Abbey of Bury St Edmunds, passim; Harper-Bill, Blythburgh Priory Cartulary, passim; Christopher Harper-Bill and R. Mortimer, eds., Stoke by Clare Cartulary, BL Cotton Appx. xxi (Woodbridge, 1982); Mortimer, Leiston Abbey Cartulary and Butley Priory Charters, passim; West, St Benet of Holme, 1020–1210, passim.

[4] Knowles, The Religious Orders, vol. 2, pp. 283–87.

hands of the Crown.[5] Two generations of the Countess of Oxford's family continued to bestow gifts on Campsey Ash, and later on Bruisyard, and their ties to the house were manifested in the ceramic tiles which bear the family's coat of arms found among the convent's remains.[6] But with the death of the Countess's daughter Maud the family's interests waned.[7] And only through the fourteenth century did the heirs of Muriel and Roger de Scales, founders of Blackborough, continue to champion this small fenland house.[8]

The infrequency of sustained familial patronage is true for female houses elsewhere in England as well: Amesbury Abbey, a royal foundation of Benedictine nuns, for example, had minimal contact with the Crown in this later period.[9] Among the male houses in the diocese of Norwich the exception proves the rule: William Calthorpe was buried at Creake Abbey where several of his ancestors had previously been interred. He also left £74 for reconstruction of the abbey's many buildings, and requested that his son Gurney contribute to the rebuilding of the choir and the presbytery, and finance other needed repairs.[10] Familial patronage of Aldeby Priory in Norfolk ran from its foundation c.1100 by Hubert and Agnes de Rye until 1466 and the death of their descendent Lady Isabel Morley. Here, however, the correlation between sustained family interest and economic security did not hold: Aldeby was ever on the brink of financial collapse and was valued in 1535 at only £25.[11]

If generations of founders' heirs did not continue to promote their families' monastic foundations, others did. Recall the Pope's grant of major indulgences, choice of confessor, and full remission of sins to all associated with Bruisyard Abbey.[12] The Countess of Suffolk patronized both Bruisyard and Bungay by boarding her daughters at each of these houses.[13] And the bequest of 40s by John Harleston, vicar of St Peter, Stowmarket, to his sister Marieta, a nun at Flixton, and the 6s 8d he left to be divided equally among all of the nuns there, is an example of patronage of a female convent by someone from lower on the social scale.[14] Indeed, a wide range of people, from Isabel Countess of Suffolk and her husband, to members of the leading families of the city of Norwich, to the parishioners of the remote and poor parish of Marham, requested burial in

---

[5] VCH, Norfolk, vol. 2, p. 413; Warren, Anchorites and their Patrons, pp. 201–6.
[6] Gilchrist and Oliva, Religious Women, pp. 90–1.
[7] Bourdillon, The Minoresses, p. 48 notes that the last of Maud's heirs to leave anything to Bruisyard, the family's last foundation, was Maud's daughter Maud, wife of Thomas de Vere, Earl of Oxford. She was buried at Bruisyard and bequeathed the manor of Wrabness to the nuns there.
[8] VCH, Norfolk, vol. 2, p. 350.
[9] VCH, Wiltshire, vol. 3, p. 255.
[10] VCH, Norfolk, vol. 2, p. 372.
[11] Ibid., p. 328.
[12] Above, Chapter 5, p. 148; Papal Letters, vol. 13:2, pp. 646–47.
[13] Chapter 4 above, p. 118; BL, Egerton 8776.
[14] NRO, NCC 26 Doke.

the diocese's female houses, a highly significant act of patronage in the Middle Ages.[15]

These and other examples suggest a correlation between certain monasteries and the level of medieval society which patronized them. The only instance of royal patronage seen thus far has been to Campsey Ash, the wealthiest female house in the diocese.[16] Flixton Priory, on the other hand, appears to have traded on the goodwill of people solely from the middling and lower social ranks of parish gentry and yeoman farmers. Was this correlation between wealth and the social standing of benefactors hard and fast? Not always. An analysis of wills and other sources indicates that while popes, members of royalty, peers of the realm, and the higher county gentry all supported the diocese's female houses, these socially elite groups tended to patronize the male monasteries in more substantial ways. Bishops, on the other hand, seemed to show more personal interest in the female monasteries than in their male counterparts.

Patronage of the female monasteries by people from the parish gentry and yeoman farmer groups, however, was significantly more substantial than it was for houses of monks and canons. Continuing patronage of the female convents by these lower social groups reflects the convents' local perspectives and goes a long way to explain how most of the nuns managed to operate their monasteries without falling into serious debt. While the favors and gifts granted to the nuns by these two social groups form the crux of this chapter, examining the patronage of the diocese's female houses by social groups high and low illustrates the ways patronage was influenced by class, gender, and geography.

Papal and Episcopal Patronage

Among patrons of medieval monasteries the most prestigious – and the ones whose gifts and grants of privilege were for the most part beyond dispute – were the popes. Until the Dissolution of the monasteries, Anglo-papal relations throughout the later Middle Ages affected the way both popes and royalty patronized religious houses.[17] And the potential for strained relations between

---

15 Chapter 5 above, pp. 151–2 for examples. For place of burial as an act of patronage, see: Brian Golding, "Burials and Benefactions: An Aspect of Monastic Patronage in Thirteenth Century England," in *England in the Thirteenth Century. Proceedings of the 1984 Harlaxton Symposium*, ed. M. W. Ormrod (Woodbridge, 1986), pp. 64–75; and Knowles, *The Religious Orders*, vol. 2, p. 286.

16 Edward III sent masons and builders to Campsey Ash to make ready the convent for the arrival of his granddaughter: *CPR, 1354–58*, p. 352. See above Chapter 4, p. 118.

17 A great deal has been written about this relationship: Timothy Cooper, "The Papacy and the Diocese of Coventry and Lichfield, 1360–1385," *Archivum Historiae Pontificae* 25 (1987), pp. 73–103; F. H. R. Du Boulay, "The Fifteenth Century," in *The English Church and the Papacy in the Middle Ages*, ed. C. H. Lawrence (London, 1965), pp. 192–242; Denis Hay, "The Church of England in the Later Middle Ages," *History* 53 (1986), pp. 35–50; Pantin, *The English Church in the Fourteenth Century*, pp. 81–6, 87–94;

these two powers was enormous, especially when jurisdictional disputes between them arose. Papal rights over the English clergy included the right to
tax all ecclesiastical personnel – nuns, monks, and canons included – to fill
vacant ecclesiastical offices, and to arbitrate in disputed spiritual cases, as well
as other matters concerning both the regular and secular clergy. But the Crown
could challenge any of these claims of papal authority in the interests of the
realm. Because these kinds of issues were more likely to involve the more
landed, wealthier, and more politically involved male monasteries, papal
patronage of them tended to be different from the favors popes showed to nuns.

Papal patronage of the diocese's female houses was limited to four types of
grants: plenary remission of sin and the extension of convents' chaplains'
sacerdotal duties to include all people associated with a particular house, as was
granted to Bruisyard, and to a lesser extent to those affiliated with Bungay;[18]
and appropriation of spiritual properties, like the Pope's grant of the church of
Sitton in 1414 to the nuns at Bruisyard.[19] Pope Urban V's relaxation of 140
days of penance to those who visited Bruisyard and gave alms for the nuns'
sustenance and for the repair of their collegiate church was a third way popes
patronized the diocese's female houses.[20] Boniface IX granted similar indulgences to Carrow and Thetford priories.[21] And Carrow enjoyed exemption
from episcopal jurisdiction in the installation of a prioress, the only other type
of favor granted to these houses by popes in this later medieval period.[22]

Papal grants to these monasteries conferred on them a certain amount of
prestige.[23] The exemption of Carrow from episcopal control in the election of
its superiors was especially significant as it set the convent beyond other
ecclesiastical authorities.[24] But why some popes recognized some houses and
not others is difficult to explain. No doubt Bruisyard curried more papal favors
than other female houses in the diocese because of its affiliation with the order
of Poor Clares, which placed the abbey under the Pope's special protection.
But the grants to Carrow, Thetford, and Bungay, houses without any obvious

R. N. Swanson, *Church and Society in Late Medieval England* (Oxford, 1989), esp. pp.
11–16; Michael Wilks, "Royal Patronage and Anti-Papalism from Ockham to Wyclif,"
in *From Ockham to Wyclif*, ed. Anne Hudson and Michael Wilks (Oxford, 1987), pp.
135–63; and Wood-Legh, *Church Life in England*, pp. 127–35, 144–49.

[18] *Papal Letters*, vol. 5, p. 596; and see Chapter 5, pp. 147–8 of this book (Bungay).

[19] *Papal Letters*, vol. 6, pp. 468–69, 489.

[20] Ibid., vol. 4, p. 49 in 1364. By virtue of its affiliation with the Friars Minor, Bruisyard
also received dispensations from paying all papal taxes (1296), and any and all secular
and other ecclesiastical taxes as well (1317): Bourdillon, *The Minoresses*, p. 64.

[21] *Papal Letters*, vol. 4, pp. 373 for Carrow (1391); ibid., pp. 374, 442 for Thetford (1391
and again in 1392).

[22] Blomefield, *An Essay*, vol. 4, p. 525; and above Chapter 1, p. 32.

[23] Dobson, *Durham Priory*, p. 209.

[24] Alfred Sweet, "The Apostolic See and the Heads of Religious Houses," *Speculum* 28
(1953), pp. 468–69 where Sweet discusses the great significance this exemption bestowed on the superiors of male houses.

connections with Rome, suggest that other factors – perhaps other patrons who interceded for these small houses – brought them to the attention of papal legates.

Popes' gifts to these female monasteries seem to have been representative of the types of favors granted to other female convents in England.[25] Boniface IX relaxed penances to almsgivers of Wilberfoss and St Clements priories in Yorkshire, and gave permission to the nuns of Heyning Priory in Lincoln to mortgage their properties to alleviate their poverty.[26] He also allowed the nuns' chaplains at Barking to say mass and perform other services in their oratory because of the number of people who flocked to the abbey to see the special cross which the nuns possessed.[27] Other convents received papal permission to acquire lands in mortmain.[28]

Several popes granted similar favors to many of the male houses in the diocese of Norwich. Papal confirmations of appropriated churches, for example, were granted to St Benet of Holme, Wymondham, Beeston, Bromehill, Ingham, and West Dereham.[29] Indulgences to penitents who gave alms for repairs were also given to the Norfolk houses of Castle Acre, Bromholm, Mountjoy, and Wendling.[30] Bromholm and Wendling no doubt secured these grants by virtue of the relics in their custody.[31] Exemption from episcopal or provincial jurisdiction was granted to Bury St Edmunds and to the Cluniac house of canons at Thetford.[32]

In general, however, papal patronage of the male houses encompassed a wider range of grants and privileges than those granted to the nuns, thus exhibiting a stronger connection between this highest ecclesiastical power and the wealthier and more politically active male houses. The abbots of both Bury St Edmunds and St Benet at Holme, for example, received the coveted right to *pontificalia*: permission to wear the sandals, dalmatic robes and tunics, gloves and ring, and carry the miter and staff, potent symbols of papal privilege which lent the superiors heightened prestige and gave them absolute authority over

---

25 Except for those granted to Syon, the largest, wealthiest, and latest foundation for women. For the lavish grants of privilege Martin V bestowed on the abbey, see: Aungier, *History of Syon*, pp. 36–8.

26 VCH, *Yorkshire*, vol. 2, pp. 126, 130 for Wilberfosse and St Clements; VCH, *Lincolnshire*, vol. 3, p. 149 for Heynings.

27 VCH, *Essex*, vol. 2, p. 118.

28 See for example: VCH, *Yorkshire*, vol. 2, p. 70 for this grant to the nuns at Kirklees Priory.

29 VCH, *Norfolk*, vol. 2, p. 334 (St Benet at Holme 1401); ibid., p. 337 (Wymondham, 1399); ibid., p. 373 (Beeston, 1401); ibid., p. 374 (Bromehill, 1395); ibid., p. 410 (Ingham, 1401); and ibid., p. 415 (West Dereham, 1399).

30 VCH, *Norfolk*, vol. 2, p. 357 (Castle Acre in 1401): ibid., p. 361 (Bromholm, 1401): ibid., p. 387 (Mountjoy, 1365); and ibid., p. 422 (Wendling, 1411).

31 Both houses claimed to have pieces of the Cross and Wendling had in addition a foot of St Lucy's and other sacred objects: VCH, *Norfolk*, vol. 2, pp. 361 and 422.

32 VCH, *Suffolk*, vol. 2, p. 65 for Bury St Edmunds in 1398; VCH, *Norfolk*, vol. 2, p. 367 for Thetford, 1399.

all in their jurisdictions.[33] Extensions of power and authority like these were not among the favors popes granted to abbesses and prioresses. Nor were confirmations of contested rights and holdings. In 1472, for example, Pope Sixtus IV confirmed Snape Priory's privileges and possessions in response to a dispute between the King, the bishop, and the prior over the priory's dependence on Colchester Abbey.[34]

Without extensive property holdings and complicated issues of dependence on monasteries of higher rank, the female houses in the diocese never had cause to call on Rome for such leverage. The differences in the size and wealth of the female and male monasteries in terms of worldly power, and the popes' patronage of each, suggest that their grants and favors were influenced by gender.

By contrast, the diocese's bishops often showed special attention to the female convents and not to houses of male religious. Bishop Brouns, for example, made testamentary bequests to more female houses in the diocese than houses of male religious.[35] To the prioress of Redlingfield he left 13s 4d, to each nun there 3s 4d, and another 15 marks to the entire convent to pay for a new grail. Brouns made similar monetary bequests to the superiors and nuns of Carrow and Flixton. He further requested that his executors distribute 40 marks equally among the poor religious in the diocese "both nuns and others holding property where the greatest need is pressing."[36] His bequests and grants to the diocese's male houses, on the other hand, were limited to the 40 marks he left to the monks of Eye in Suffolk for the reconstruction of their chapel, and his permission to the canons of Chipley to annex the collegiate church of Stoke-by-Clare because their house was in such a ruinous state.[37]

Other examples of bishops who especially favored houses of nuns in the diocese included Bishop Lyhert for Carrow, Flixton, and Redlingfield in 1472, and Bishop Bateman for Marham Abbey in 1349.[38] Bateman's brother Bartholomew was buried at Flixton, no doubt establishing a relationship between the nuns and the bishop which likely included patronage of some sort.[39] Bateman's niece boarded at Carrow in 1345, forging a connection between the priory and the bishop.[40] And finally, the nuns of Bungay Priory benefitted from the goodwill of Bishop Alnwick in 1431 when he gave them

---

[33] Sweet, "The Apostolic See," pp. 477–79.
[34] VCH, Suffolk, vol. 2, p. 79.
[35] His will is printed in: Ernst Jacob, "Two Documents Relating to Thomas Brouns, Bishop of Norwich," NA 33:4 (1965), pp. 433–48.
[36] Ibid., p. 436.
[37] Ibid., p. 434; VCH, Suffolk, vol. 2, p. 72 (Eye Priory); VCH, Norfolk, vol. 2, p. 99 (Chipley).
[38] Taylor, Index Monasticus, p. 11 (Carrow); ibid., p. 100 (Flixton); ibid., p. 88 (Redlingfield); ibid., p. 14 (Marham).
[39] Ibid., p. 100 notes that Batholomew was buried at Flixton but does not say that his brother the bishop patronized the priory in any way.
[40] Rye, Carrow Abbey, p. 48.

the advowson of a portion of the parish church of Mettingham, whose vicar was then to pray daily for their souls.[41]

While episcopal patronage of the male houses included more than just Bishop Brouns' advocacy of Eye and Chipley priories, mentioned above, it was relatively minimal. In 1475, for example, the monks of Great Massingham received episcopal permission to merge with West Acre Priory because they were so poor.[42] Poverty also motivated the bishop of Ely, acting as suffragan of the diocese of Norwich, to grant the poor monks of Mullicourt permission to collect money from anyone who came to their aid in exchange for a forty-day indulgence.[43]

The lack of episcopal grants like those mentioned above to the male houses in the diocese might reflect the laconic nature of the surviving bishops' registers where acts of episcopal patronage were routinely noted. Lack of more substantial support of the male houses might also have been due to the close connections between the bishops and the Cathedral Priory in Norwich, the diocesan seat. In general, relations between these two ecclesiastical powers were good, and bishops may not have wanted to jeopardize the situation by showing favor to rivals, like Bury St Edmunds or Walsingham, both of which wielded considerable local control.[44]

The more personal interest in the female houses on the part of the bishops is one area where gender differences between female and male monasteries proved to be positive for the nuns. Episcopal patronage was perhaps stronger for the female convents in the diocese because of their relative poverty which may have made them seem more deserving. Bishops' bequests to nuns might also signal their status and value as effective providers of welfare and religious services to local parishioners, and thus stand as a reward for their local concerns.

Female houses in other dioceses enjoyed a great deal more from bishops than did those in the diocese of Norwich. Bishops Grey and Arundel, prelates of the diocese of Ely, for example, granted the nuns of St Radegund's throughout the fourteenth and fifteenth centuries indulgences of forty days to people who contributed to the priory's various building projects, which were made necessary by storms and poverty.[45] The Archbishop of Canterbury also granted the nuns there indulgences.[46] Bishop Edyngton of Winchester exempted the nuns of Romsey and of St Mary's from paying tithes.[47] Edyngton also bequeathed to Isabella de Camoys, abbess of Romsey, a ruby ring and £20 for prayers for his soul; he left another £20 to be distributed among the nuns there to perform

41 BL, Add. Ch. 37427.
42 VCH, Norfolk, vol. 2, p. 386.
43 Ibid.
44 Cheney, "Norwich Cathedral Priory," p. 95; and Tanner, The Church and Late Medieval Norwich, pp. 159–62 for the relations between the bishops and the Cathedral Priory.
45 Gray, The Priory of St Radegund, pp. 37–8, 74–144.
46 Ibid., p. 79.
47 Liveing, The Records of Romsey Abbey, pp. 146–48.

works of charity in his name.[48] Throughout the fifteenth century other bishops of Winchester supported the nuns of Wintney Priory, a small Cistercian house in Hampshire, in their pleas to be excused from paying taxes.[49] The bishops of Lincoln granted similar favors to numerous female monasteries in their diocese.[50] Perhaps the bishops of Lincoln appear to have been more involved with the female houses there because there were more of them – at least 33 female houses in the diocese of Lincoln compared to the 11 in the diocese of Norwich – and several of them were poorer than those in the counties of Norfolk and Suffolk. Poverty might also explain the bishops of Winchester's support of Wintney Priory; as neither Romsey nor St Mary's were particularly poor, bishops' patronage of these two houses might have been due to their status as pre-Conquest foundations or simply personal preference.

Royal, Aristocratic, and Upper Gentry Patronage

Patronage of the diocese's female monasteries by secular society's most elite groups was, like that of popes and bishops, fairly limited and determined by gender. Royal patronage of the female houses was prescribed by the *Regularis Concordia*, the tenth-century agreement between English monasteries and the Crown which named the Queen as special protector of all the female houses and patron of all nuns.[51] Despite this position, the only queen to bestow any favors on the female monasteries in the diocese was Queen Anne, wife of Richard II, who granted the nuns of Redlingfield a yearly payment of 20 marks which was to be collected from some of her tenants and from the profits of her mills.[52] Her gifts to the nuns there likely reflected Anne's territorial interests, as a portion of her dower lands were located nearby in Suffolk.[53] In the same year as she made this grant, however, she also visited the abbey at Bury St Edmunds and it is possible that this small house of nuns came to her attention then.[54] These circumstances perhaps explain why this small priory of Benedictine nuns drew royal interest rather than the more prestigious houses, Campsey Ash and Bruisyard, both of which garnered a great deal of patronage from other members of royalty, and were also close to the Queen's dower lands. Whatever

---

[48] Ibid., p. 163.
[49] Coldicott, *Hampshire Nunneries*, pp. 122–23. Bishops intervened for the nuns of Wintney in 1398, 1401, 1422; between 1469 and 1484 Bishop Waynflete wrote to the Exchequer four times on behalf of the poor houses in his diocese; Wintney was included on each occasion.
[50] VCH, *Lincolnshire*, vol. 3, passim.
[51] Thomas Seymore, "Looking Back on the *Regularis Concordia*," *Downside Review* 78 (1960), pp. 286–92.
[52] CPR, 1381–85, p. 263.
[53] She held the nearby castle, town, manor, and honor of Eye in Suffolk, as well as all of the Earl of Suffolk's properties, who had died without an heir: CPR, 1381–85, pp. 125–27.
[54] VCH, *Suffolk*, vol. 2, p. 65.

the cause, this act of patronage on the part of the English nuns' special patron was the only time the female houses in the diocese benefitted from a queen in this later medieval period.[55]

More frequently royal patronage was demonstrated when the Crown granted the nuns licenses to acquire more property, either temporal or spiritual, in free alms: that is, to acquire properties which would no longer be subject to royal taxation or control. Edward III granted the nuns of Thetford the advowson of the church of Sts Peter and Paul in Livermere, rents totaling £10, and license to acquire lands in Suffolk.[56] Henry VI devised land in free alms to the nuns of Crabhouse.[57] And Richard II twice issued similar patents to Marham Abbey for land in the counties of Norfolk and Lincoln; he also granted the nuns of Redlingfield permission to secure land or rents to the value of £10.[58]

Occasionally monasteries acquired land in free alms without obtaining royal permission. For such infractions convents' superiors were either fined or pardoned.[59] In 1510, Margaret Punder, prioress of Flixton, received such a pardon for herself and her successors who might make the same mistake in the future; so did the prioress of Bungay.[60]

Exemptions from taxes and confirmations of all previously granted rights and privileges were other ways the Crown showed favor to the monasteries. Despite its greater wealth, Campsey Ash was excused from paying its tenths in 1352 and for the two years following; Flixton received a similar grant in 1348; and Thetford was pardoned from paying taxes by Henry VI.[61] Shouldham Priory, also a wealthy house, received exemptions like these more frequently, in 1380, 1444 and 1445, and in 1451; "all quarrels, impeachments, demands, and arrears" against the priory were also cleared.[62] Edward III confirmed all of

---

55 Meyers, "Patronage of the West Saxon Royal Nunneries," p. 357 states that royal patronage of female houses was less frequent and less generous in the later Middle Ages than it had been before the Conquest. And as Joel Rosenthal points out in "Kings, Continuity and Ecclesiastical Benefaction in Fifteenth-Century England," in *People, Politics, and Continuity in the Later Middle Ages*, ed. Joel Rosenthal and Colin Richmond (Gloucester, 1987), p. 168, fifteenth-century queens gave primarily to Queens' College and St John's College, both in Cambridge, and gave nothing to the female houses over which they were special patrons. The only other monasteries to which Anne gave lands were the Cathedral Priory of Wells and the Suffolk male house of Eye: *CPR, 1381–85*, pp. 117–18 for Wells; ibid., p. 491 for Eye.
56 *CPR, 1374–81*, p. 534.
57 *CPR, 1446–52*, p. 4; Chapter 3 above, p. 147.
58 Blomefield, *An Essay*, vol. 7, pp. 388, 390; Dugdale, *Monasticon*, vol. 5, p. 743 (Marham Abbey); *CPR, 1377–81*, p. 591 for Redlingfield. This license was originally granted by Edward III in 1344; it took nearly forty years for the sum to be attained.
59 Wood-Legh, *Church Life Under Edward III*, p. 66.
60 BL, Stowe Ch. 355 (Flixton); SRO, HD 12/B1/1/3 (Bungay).
61 *CPR, 1350–54*, p. 295 (Campsey Ash); *CPR, 1348–50*, pp. 13, 38 (Flixton); and Blomefield, *An Essay*, vol. 2, p. 91 (Thetford).
62 *CPR, 1377–80*, p. 534; *CPR, 1441–46*, pp. 315, 332; *CPR, 1446–52*, p. 499.

Carrow's rights and privileges in 1378; and Bungay twice received such grants, once in 1448 and again in 1466.[63]

Royal foundations of and contributions to the chantries, colleges, and large wealthy institutions like Westminster, Syon, and the Charterhouse in London are the most often cited examples of fifteenth-century royal patronage of religious institutions.[64] But confirmations of privileges, tax exemptions, and licenses to acquire land were granted, albeit less fervently and on a much smaller scale, not only to the female houses in the diocese of Norwich, but to smaller female houses elsewhere in England, like St Radegund's and Swaffham Bulbeck in Cambridgeshire, as well as to the nuns at Romsey Abbey in Hampshire.[65] Such favor was also shown at different times to other female houses, including Shaftesbury and Tarrant Kaines in Dorset, Lacock in Wiltshire, and Barking in Essex.[66]

By contrast, the Crown's gifts to male monasteries in the diocese of Norwich were substantially larger than any of those given to the female houses anywhere in England. While charting all the favors kings made to male monasteries would be beyond the scope of this study, a few examples will suffice to demonstrate differences between royal patronage of female and male houses. Richard II granted Creake Abbey in Norfolk £40 13s 4d out of his revenues in nearby Fakenham towards the reconstruction of some of its buildings which had been "perilously burnt."[67] The canons of Bromehill received licenses from Edward III to purchase extensive holdings in both Norfolk and Suffolk.[68] Similarly, the monks of Walsingham obtained royal permission on two occasions to acquire sizeable estates, once in 1385 and again in 1465 "in relief of their poor possessions."[69] And Henry IV relieved the canons of Butley Priory of their responsibility for a hospital because its operating costs were too much for them.[70] Two other male houses, Ixworth and West Acre, were given permission to hold fairs and markets.[71]

Other acts of royal favor towards the diocese's male houses included Henry VI's intercession on Creake Abbey's behalf against the Pope in the abbey's

63 CPR, 1377–81, p. 22 (Carrow, 1378); CPR, 1461–67, p. 494 and CPR 1446–52, p. 179 for Bungay.
64 Joel Rosenthal, "Kings, Continuity and Ecclesiastical Benefaction," pp. 161–71.
65 Gray, The Priory of St Radegund, pp. 74–144; VCH, Cambridge and the Isle of Ely, vol. 2, p. 227 for Swaffham Bulbeck; Liveing, The Records of Romsey Abbey, pp. 170 and 224.
66 VCH, Dorset, vol. 2, pp. 75, 89 for Shaftesbury and Tarrant Kaines; VCH, Wiltshire, vol. 3, p. 207 for Lacock; and VCH, Essex, vol. 2, p. 117 for Barking.
67 VCH, Norfolk, vol. 2, p. 371.
68 Ibid., p. 374. Edward twice granted a great deal of property, once in 1371 and again in 1374.
69 Ibid., pp. 394–95.
70 VCH, Suffolk, vol. 2, p. 96.
71 Ixworth was granted a market and two fairs by Richard II in 1384: VCH, Suffolk, vol. 2, p. 105. Edward IV licensed the canons of West Acre to hold a fair on the Translation of St Thomas the Martyr: VCH, Norfolk, vol. 2, p. 402.

attempt to annex Peterstone Priory.[72] The Crown's support of male monasteries was also expressed through denizenation, whereby the Crown extended its own authority over a monastery dependent on a foreign – usually French – order or power.[73] Though it might seem inappropriate to categorize denizenation as an act of patronage, many of these alien cells were suppressed; those that were saved and brought under control of the Crown were thus ensured a continued existence. Castle Acre and Thetford Priory, both alien cells of Cluny, were naturalized by Edward III.[74] The priory of Eye, a Benedictine house still dependent on the French foundation of Bernay, was granted denizenation through the efforts of Queen Anne; Wangford, another Cluniac house, was given national status by Richard II.[75]

Acts of patronage like these were significantly different from those made to the female monasteries. While Walsingham and Butley secured grants of land through pleas of poverty – though neither house was particularly poor – none of the male monasteries were exempted from paying tenths or fifteenths, one of the ways the Crown favored some of the female houses in the diocese.[76] These male houses could also well afford to pay for the requisite licenses to acquire new land and, as houses wherein masses and other sacraments could be performed in exchange for such gifts, perhaps fifteenth-century kings – especially those with questionable claims to the throne – saw more profit in bestowing extensive lands on the larger wealthier male houses than by simply exempting them from taxes.[77] No doubt the male monasteries' already substantial holdings also meant more to the royal coffers than the nuns' smaller and often less productive properties. Exempting the monks and canons from taxes then also would have decreased the flow of money into the royal treasury.

Similarly, by arbitrating disputes between rival authorities, as Henry VI did for Creake Abbey against the Pope, and nationalizing some of the houses still dependent on foreign foundations, the Crown gained greater visibility, more money, and heightened prestige, especially with regard to the French upon whom these houses were still dependent, and with whom intermittent warfare made such acts politically prudent. Though none of the female houses were cells of French monasteries, the nuns had neither the property nor the ability to perform the sacerdotal functions which enabled their male counterparts to garner more substantial and significant favors. The Crown therefore probably viewed the female houses as less important on a national political scale, suggesting that, like papal patronage, royal gifts and grants were weighted by gender.

---

[72] Bedingfield, "Cartulary of Creake Abbey," p. xxi.

[73] Knowles, *The Religious Orders*, vol. 2, pp. 159–66; M. M. Morgan, "The Suppression of Alien Priories," *History* 26:103 (1941), pp. 204–12.

[74] VCH, *Norfolk*, vol. 2, p. 356 (Castle Acre); ibid., p. 367 (Thetford).

[75] VCH, *Suffolk*, vol. 2, p. 74 (Eye); ibid., p. 88 (Wangford).

[76] The *Valor* lists Walsingham's revenues as £391 and Butley's as £318.

[77] Rosenthal, "Kings, Continuity," p. 171 suggests that this motive lay behind the foundation of chantries and other religious institutions by Yorkist and Lancastrian kings.

While members of the aristocracy were not particularly generous to mon-asteries of either sex in this later period, the pattern of giving by the counties' elites tracks the trend identified throughout this study: the highest social groups tended to support the large and wealthy male houses more frequently and generously than the female ones. The following discussion illustrates how the patronage of the counties' aristocracy and upper gentry was specific to a few of the diocese's female houses and was also limited to the late fourteenth century.

Grants of land from the local nobility indicate that they favored Bruisyard, Bungay, and Campsey Ash. The Countess of Oxford's chantry foundations at Bruisyard and Campsey Ash, as well as subsequent grants made by her heirs, and the Earl of Suffolk's placement of his daughters at Bruisyard and Bungay, are a few examples of aristocratic patronage of these particular houses. There are more: Margaret, Countess of Norfolk, granted Bruisyard the manor of Wilton in 1383.[78] The Countess of Oxford used her influence with the Crown to exact an exemption for the nuns at Campsey Ash from the tenth in 1358.[79] Robert, Earl of Suffolk, alienated to the nuns of Campsey Ash several manors and lands in the county and his executors devised to the nuns there the manor of Benges in 1368.[80] Edmund of Ufford, the Earl of Suffolk's brother, also granted considerable lands to Campsey Ash in 1353 and again in 1358.[81]

No doubt Maud, daughter of the Countess of Oxford whose family founded Campsey Ash, and the Uffords set an example for aristocratic patronage of both Bruisyard and Campsey Ash. The attention shown to Bruisyard may also have been due to its late foundation date which likely attracted grants of land from people eager to be seen as patrons of this new and unique abbey. Grants to Campsey Ash also reflected its status as the wealthiest of the female houses in the diocese. Bungay's attraction for the county's aristocracy might have been due to the priory's proximity to Bungay Castle, one of the Earl of Suffolk's estates. Affinity might account for the patronage shown to many of the diocese's houses by Anne, Lady Scrope of Harling, who was a lay sister at eight of the female convents, bequeathed books to some of the nuns who lived in them, and called herself kinswoman of three prioresses.[82]

Analysis of patronage of the female houses in the diocese by the region's upper gentry indicates that they too favored Bruisyard, Bungay, and Campsey Ash, suggesting that patronage of these convents by society's most elite invited the same from those of slighter lesser standing. Sir William Wychingham, Kt, and Sir Nicholas Gernoun gave gifts of land to Bruisyard.[83] Sir Roger de Boys

---

[78] Bourdillon, *The Minoresses*, p. 59 citing *CPR*, 1385–89, p. 527.

[79] *CPR*, 1358–61, p. 28: this pardon was in addition to the ones given by the King cited earlier.

[80] *CPR*, 1367–70, p. 88 for the Earl's grant; *CPR*, 1385–89, p. 154 for the manor of Benges.

[81] *CPR*, 1358–61, p. 28 (1353); ibid., p. 295 (1364).

[82] Chapter 2 above, p. 70.

[83] Taylor, *Index Monasticus*, p. 105.

donated land in mortmain to Bruisyard and to Campsey Ash, and made similar grants on two occasions to Flixton in the mid-fourteenth century.[84]

Other female monasteries benefitted from rather sporadic grants from local knights as well. Blackborough received land in mortmain from Edmund Keroyle, an important local figure, and also from Roger, Lord Scales.[85] Sir John Plaiz gave lands to both Marham and Thetford in 1385, and Shouldham profited from the largesse of Sir John Bardolf in the same decade.[86] Highly potent acts of patronage of Carrow by some of the city of Norwich's leading citizens are demonstrated by their requests for burial in the priory's church and cemetery.[87]

Carrow's appeal to the city's elite could have been its time-honored maintenance of and association with two anchorholds, one of which was inside the priory's precincts, the other just outside its walls attached to the church of St Julian, one of the priory's spiritual properties. As was mentioned earlier in this study, though Julian of Norwich was the most famous anchoress to reside there, anchoresses are known to have lived in both of the priory's holds from the twelfth century until past its dissolution.[88] The presence of anchoresses at Carrow no doubt enhanced its reputation as a holy house and perhaps the city's prestigious citizens viewed their support of it as double-edged: by giving to the convent, they were also benfitting from the prayers of the anchoresses which the nuns supported.

While aristocratic patronage of late medieval female houses in other parts of England was also minimal, the dukes of Norfolk and earls of Suffolk patronized many of the male houses in the diocese to a much greater degree. Dukes and duchesses of Norfolk, for example, were powerful patrons and frequent guests of the Cluniac canons at Thetford through the late fifteenth and sixteenth centuries.[89] Ducal families were also steady patrons of Walsingham and Letheringham.[90] The Earl and Countess of Suffolk granted lands to the priory of the Holy Sepulchre in Thetford, and also promoted the interests of Snape Priory.[91] Both Langley and Sibton abbeys enjoyed the support of noble families outside the diocese as well. In 1366 Sir James Audeley, Councillor of the Prince of Aquitaine and Wales, successfully petitioned the Pope for an indulgence for penitents who visited Langley, a priory of Premonstratensian canons, where many of his ancestors were buried.[92] And Ralph, the son of the

---

84 CPR, 1388–92, p. 332 (Bruisyard); CPR, 1358–61, p. 180 (Campsey Ash); CCR, 1374–77, pp. 354, 355, 356 for Flixton, dated 1376; and BL, Stowe Ch. 345 for a grant of lands to the nuns of Flixton dated 1356.

85 CPR, 1350–54, p. 183 for the grant from Edmund Keroyle; Taylor, Index Monasticus, p. 11 for that from Roger of Scales.

86 Ibid., p. 14 (Marham); ibid., p. 13 (Thetford); ibid., p. 32 (Shouldham).

87 Chapter 5 above, p. 151.

88 Ibid., pp. 155–6; Gilchrist and Oliva, Religious Women, pp. 74–7, 97–8.

89 Harvey, "The Last Years," p. 8; VCH, Norfolk, vol. 2, p. 368.

90 Ibid., pp. 396–97 (Walsingham); VCH, Suffolk, vol. 2, p. 108 (Letheringham).

91 VCH, Norfolk, vol. 2, p. 392 (Holy Sepulchre); VCH, Suffolk, vol. 2, p. 79 (Snape).

92 VCH, Norfolk, vol. 2, p. 420.

Earl of Stafford, obtained a license for the monks of Sibton to acquire lands in mortmain in 1385.[93]

The differences between how members of these high ranking groups patronized the diocese's female and male monasteries can only partly be explained by the shifting philanthropic tastes of these social groups which, by the early fifteenth century, ran more towards funding chantries, secular colleges, and local parish churches.[94] Aristocratic and upper gentry patronage was influenced by the same social and political concerns displayed by popes and kings: association with the larger and wealthier houses of monks and canons tended to confer more prestige, in part because of their sacramental functions. But while the aristocracy and upper gentry may have been more interested in the more publically prominent male houses, bequests in the wills of both the parish gentry and yeoman farmers clearly indicate that they patronized all of the female houses in the diocese to a significantly greater degree than they did their male counterparts.

Patronage by the Parish Gentry and Yeoman Farmers

The gift-giving pattern of Norfolk and Suffolk county residents can be seen in the wills enrolled in the Norwich Consistory Court and in the four archdeaconry courts: Norwich, Norfolk, Sudbury, and Suffolk.[95] Over 3,000 wills from these courts' probate registers were examined to discover how many and what kind of bequests people of these two lower social groups made to the female houses in the diocese. These wills span the 190-year period covered in this study. Appendix 4 describes the courts, the registers, their dates, and the numbers of wills examined in each. Because this analysis shows regional variations among testators' gift-giving patterns, separate figures will be given for each of the archdeaconries in the following discussion. Some general comments about this cohort of will-makers, their wills, and their bequests are

---

93 VCH, *Suffolk*, vol. 2, p. 90.

94 Gibson, *Theater of Devotion*, pp. 20–1 discusses the lack of patronage shown to East Anglian religious houses by the aristocracy and upper gentry and suggests that travels to London made people of these ranks aware of the larger, wealthier foundations there, which attracted their donations of money and lands. See also: Harris, "A New Look at the Reformation," pp. 99, 109, who notes that the aristocratic group she studied were not very active patrons of monastic houses. See also: Rosenthal, "Kings, Continuity," pp. 161, 168–69, who notes that the fifteenth century continued to see a decline in aristocratic patronage of ecclesiastical institutions which had begun in the last two decades of the fourteenth century.

95 While some historians caution against using wills to determine the piety of testators because their preoccupation with death might have been a stronger motive for making bequests to religious institutions than simple patronage, wills nevertheless indicate which religious groups testators preferred: see: Harris, "A New Look at the Reformation," p. 103 for her discussion of this issue.

necessary, however, to contextualize this analysis and the gift-giving pattern which emerges from it.

Most historians acknowledge that the social standing of medieval testators can be determined largely by the court in which their wills were registered.[96] People who held lands in more than one archdeaconry had probate of their wills granted in the Norwich Consistory Court and fall into the social category of parish gentry unless other evidence – a sizeable estate, for example – places them in another social group.[97] Testators whose wills were registered in one of the four archdeaconry courts tended to have less extensive holdings located in only one archdeaconry and so came from lower on the social scale.

This sample of parish gentry and yeoman farmer will-makers shared two characteristics (Table 14). First, like the majority of people who wished to be buried in convents' or friaries' cemeteries, the vast majority of testators were male, reflecting what historians have noticed about the will-making population as a whole in late medieval England.[98] Secondly, these testators showed a marked preference for friars.[99] Of the 1,537 parish gentry testators whose wills were examined for this study, 30 percent left money or goods to a monastic or mendicant house. Of that 30 percent, 65 percent were legacies to friaries, despite the fact that they comprised less than half the number of the diocese's male religious houses. All of the yeoman farmer testators in the archdeaconry of Norwich who made bequests to male religious made them to one or more of the mendicant houses. Similarly, in the archdeaconry of Suffolk, of the 155 people who left gifts to religious houses, 123 gave to the friaries.

While friars were the most popular recipients of testamentary gifts, the nuns in the diocese ranked second, as the figures in Table 14 show. Bequests to the female religious from the parish gentry and yeoman farmer groups whose wills have been sampled here significantly outnumbered those made to male monasteries, despite the fact that the population of monks and canons outnumbered the nuns by about 5 to 1, and that there were sixty-three male houses and only eleven female ones. In the wills of the parish gentry, houses of monks and canons trailed well behind the nuns.[100] Only 14 percent of these will-

---

96 J. S. W. Gibson, *Wills and Where to Find Them* (Chicester, 1974), pp. 93–5 for Norfolk wills; ibid., pp. 124–27 for Suffolk ones. See also: Harrod, "Extracts from Early Norfolk Wills," p. 111 where he discusses the social rank of the people whose wills were proved in the archdeaconry court of Norwich.

97 Tanner, *The Church in Late Medieval Norwich*, p. 115 where he notes that a significant minority of testators from his sample of wills from the Norwich Consistory Court were from lower down the social scale than historians have previously realized.

98 Coppel, "Wills and the Community," p. 71; Harrod, "Extracts from Early Norfolk Wills," p. 111; Tanner, *The Church in Late Medieval Norwich*, p. 115; and Chapter 5, p. 151 above.

99 Fleming, "Charity, Faith, and the Gentry of Kent," pp. 48–9; Peter Heath, "Urban Piety in the Later Middle Ages: The Evidence of Hull Wills," in *The Church, Politics, and Patronage in the Fifteenth Century*, ed. Barrie Dobson (Gloucester, 1984), p. 221; and Tanner, *The Church in Late Medieval Norwich*, p. 119.

100 Tanner, *The Church*, pp. 120–21 notes that of the Norwich city testators who made

Table 14. *Social Rank and Sex of Testators who Made Bequests to the Female Monasteries in the Diocese of Norwich 1350–1540*

Social Rank	Testators Male (No.) %	Female (No.) %	Total Bequests to Religious Houses[a] (No.)	Bequests to Friars (No.) %	Monks (No.) %	Nuns (No.) %
Parish Gentry	(81) 84	(15) 16	458	(299) 65	(63) 14	(96) 21
Yeoman Farmer	(40) 72	(15) 28	381	(308) 80	(15) 4	(58) 15
Total	(121) 80	(30) 20	839	(607) 72	(78) 9	(154) 18

Sources: Wills from the Norwich Consistory Court and the four archdeaconry courts: Norfolk, Norwich, Sudbury and Suffolk.

[a] Bequests outnumber testators because most testators gave to more than one religious house.

makers left gifts to monks or canons compared to the 21 percent who made bequests to nuns. Will-makers of yeoman farmer status show a similar pattern: 4 percent remembered male monastics, 15 percent made bequests to nuns.

The relative popularity of female houses compared to both mendicant and male monastic houses in the diocese raises some interesting points. The immense popularity of the friars in testators' religious bequests from every corner of medieval England demonstrates lay people's perceptions of the friars' holiness and their adherence to the life of Christ, especially in contrast to the monks and canons whose worldly ways were well known.[101] Despite the constant vilification of the friars in late medieval literature, the numerous bequests to them signal the high esteem in which they were held by the majority of the will-makers who considered their prayers and acts of charity more deserving of reward and more valuable than those of monks or canons.[102]

bequests to the Cathedral Priory, the majority remembered the church, not the priory, suggesting a similar disaffection among Tanner's sample of testators.

101 See for example, Fleming, "Charity, Faith, and the Gentry of Kent," pp. 48–9; Thomson, "Piety and Charity," p. 190.

102 Antifraternalism was not limited to Chaucer's satirically drawn friar, or to William Langland who closes the vision of Piers the Plowman with the Anti-Christ who appears in the form of a friar. Friar-bashing was also the stuff of theological and philosophical tracts. For Chaucer: Fisher, *The Complete Prose and Poetry of Geoffry Chaucer*, pp. 13–14, lines 208–270 for the Friar's portrait in the "Prologue" of the tales; ibid., pp. 134–43, lines 1665–2294 for "The Summoner's Tale" in which a friar is the butt of jokes. For William Langland, *The Vision of Piers the Plowman*, ed. A. V. C. Schmidt (New York, 1978), Passus XIX, and passim. See also: P. J. Croft, "The 'Friar of the Order Grey' and the Nun," *Review of English Studies* n.s. 32:125 (1981), pp. 1–16; Nicholas Havely, "Chaucer, Boccaccio, and the Friars," in *Chaucer and the Italian Trecento*, ed. Piero Boitani (Cambridge, 1983), pp. 249–68; Penn R. Szittya, *The Antifraternal Tradition in Medieval Literature* (New Jersey, 1986); and Arnold Williams, "Chaucer and the Friars," *Speculum* 28 (1953), pp. 499–513.

Testators appear to have felt as positively about the nuns and their monastic communities. Though the female houses received fewer bequests than did the friars – whose houses outnumbered the female convents by nearly three to one – the nuns were nevertheless patronized by a significant portion of the will-making population. Their bequests demonstrate that local people patronized the nuns to a significantly greater degree than the monks or canons whose houses were generally wealthier and curried more favor with popes, kings, and bishops.

Paradoxical as it seems, the nuns' favorable showing among testators is part of the broader pattern of the nuns' greater focus on local society. Though the male monasteries were larger and wealthier – and thus more often garnered the patronage of the rich and famous – the monks and canons were less locally inclined, as the alms-fraud and neglect of many of their spiritual properties indicate. It is not surprising then that the friars and nuns, with their acts of charity and accessibility to parishioners, were more highly regarded by local society. Testators' patronage might also reflect their increasing interest in social and civic welfare; did will-makers give more to friars and nuns because they cared more actively for the poor and indigent?[103]

The people who bequeathed gifts to the nuns had a third trait in common: their tendency to be from the same parish or town as the religious house they favored.[104] In the archdeaconry of Norwich, Alicia Bocher of Thetford left the prioress and nuns of the priory there 3s 4d and an acre of land; in the same archdeaconry Peter Payn, 'penter' of Norwich, gave 6d to Dame Anne Warner, a nun of Carrow; and Robert Serard, a worsted weaver from close by the city, left 1d to each of the nuns there.[105] A man who lived in the parish of Marham requested that 12d be given to each nun of the abbey there and 20d to the abbess.[106] And a man from Wormgay, the parish next to where Blackborough Priory was sited, remembered the nuns of that small house with his flock of twelve sheep.[107] The testators from the archdeaconry of Suffolk who made bequests to nuns were also usually local residents. Isabella Wellys from the parish of Hacheston, closest to Campsey Ash but not far from Bruisyard, left money to the nuns of both houses.[108] And a man named Robert Kyrspe of Laxfield gave his neighbors, the nuns of Bruisyard, 1s.[109] Proximity then played a large part in which of the diocese's female houses a testator of parish gentry or yeoman farmer status was likely to remember.

103 Chapter 5, p. 147 of this book.
104 Tanner, The Church, pp. 119–21 finds a similar proximity among the Norwich city testators.
105 NRO, ANW 96 Fuller, alias Roper for Bocher's will (1483); NRO, ANW 86 Cook for the 1509 will of Payn; NRO, ANW 79 Cook for Serard's will of 1506.
106 NRO, ANF 96 Batman, will (1516).
107 NRO, ANF 131–32 Grey (1464).
108 SRO, ASF 7 IC/AA2/3 in 1482: she left 6s 8d to the nuns at Campsey Ash and 3s 8d to those at Bruisyard.
109 SRO, ASF 68 IC/AA2/5 in 1506.

Table 15.   Number of Bequests Made by the Parish Gentry and Yeoman Farmer
Groups to the Female Monasteries in the Diocese of Norwich
between 1350 and 1540 in Four Intervals[a]

Social Rank	1350–1400 (No.) %	1401–50 (No.) %	1451–1500 (No.) %	1500–40 (No.) %	Total Bequests
Parish Gentry	(34) 35	(35) 36	(11) 11	(16) 16	96
Yeoman Farmer		(9) 16	(15) 26	(34) 59	58

Sources: Parish gentry figures derive from the wills registered in the Norwich Consistory Court.
Yeoman farmer bequests can be found in the wills registered in the four archdeaconry courts:
Norfolk, Norwich, Sudbury and Suffolk. No yeoman farmer bequests are listed for the period
1350–1400 because the archdeaconry registers begin in the mid-fifteenth century.

[a]   Percentages are those of total bequests per social group.

The number of bequests which the nuns received differed among the
testators of these two social groups and changed over time. While an overall
average of 21 percent of the parish gentry made bequests to female houses in
the 190 years covered in this study, as the figures in Table 15 show, between
1350 and 1450 up to 36 percent of this group left something to the nuns. This
percentage declined, however, to 11 percent between 1450 and 1500, but
slightly increased in the sixteenth century to 16 percent.[110] Yeoman farmers'
bequests to the female houses did just the reverse and increased from only 16
percent between 1400 and 1450 to 59 percent in the first half of the sixteenth
century.

While yeoman farmers made fewer donations to the diocese's female religious, these averages disguise some very distinct geographical variations. Of the
wills sampled here, 19 percent of the substantial farmer group in the archdeaconry of Norfolk, for example, left bequests to the convents; only 4 percent of
those in the archdeaconry of Norwich did (Table 16). Among testators in the
archdeaconry of Sudbury, 12 percent remembered nuns in their wills. Those
from the archdeaconry of Suffolk, on the other hand, were considerably more
generous in their patronage of the female houses. Of the 155 people who left
gifts to religious houses, 38 – 25 percent – included bequests to nuns and this
percentage remained constant over time.

The disparities in these percentages among will-makers from the diocese's
four archdeaconries perhaps reflected the economics and settlement patterns
of the areas as well as the geographic locations of the convents. Most of the

[110]   This percentage is slightly higher than that which Tanner found in his sample of
Norwich city testators of whom about 18 percent made bequests to the female religious,
mostly to the nuns at Carrow: Tanner, *The Church*, pp. 122–23; but see ibid., p. 119
where he notes a decline in bequests to both mendicant and monastic houses by his
sample of will-makers beginning around 1517.

Table 16. Number of Yeoman Farmer Testators who Made Bequests
to the Female Monasteries According to Archdeaconry

Archdeaconry	Number of Wills Examined	Number of Bequests to Religious Houses		Number of Bequests to Nuns	
		(No.)	%a	(No.)	%b
Norfolk	306	(48)	16	(9)	19
Norwich	300	(81)	27	(3)	4
Sudbury	177	(69)	39	(8)	12
Suffolk	837	(155)	19	(38)	25
TOTALS	1620	(353)	22	(58)	16

a   Percentages of bequests to religious houses are percentages of number of wills examined.
b   Percentages of bequests to nuns are percentages of bequests to religious houses.

convents in the county of Norfolk were clustered in the archdeaconry of
Norfolk, which, despite the region's poorer and more sparsely populated
settlements, likely explains the greater number of bequests to nuns from this
region as compared to the number of bequests for nuns in the archdeaconry of
Norwich.[111] While the archdeaconry of Norwich included the city of Norwich
and its prosperous environs, only one female house was located here, Carrow
Priory, hence the relatively poor showing of female houses in wills registered
in this archdeaconry's court.

The number of legacies to female houses from people in the archdeaconries
of Sudbury and Suffolk shows a similar pattern. The few bequests among
testators from Sudbury can in part be explained by the fact that there were
only two female houses here: Thetford and Redlingfield. By contrast, the
archdeaconry of Suffolk was not only the site of the majority of female houses
in the county, it was also more densely settled with a wealthier population,
guaranteeing more – and more valuable – bequests.[112]

Certain convents were consistently more popular among members of the
parish gentry (Table 17). Carrow Priory was named in fifty of the wills which
included gifts to female monasteries, constituting 52 percent of these bequests
and reflecting its location in the city of Norwich. The next most popular
convents were Flixton and Thetford: each received thirty-three bequests – 34
percent of all bequests to the convents. Bruisyard and Bungay garnered 30

111   Above Chapter 1, pp. 22–3.
112   Ibid., p. 23. Nesta Evans, "Inheritance, Women, Religion and Education in Early
      Modern Society as Revealed by Wills," in Probate Records and the Local Community, pp.
      53–70 notes that the same social and economic factors affected the testamentary
      bequests she analyzed from a population of will-makers which includes the parishes of
      Bungay and Flixton, parishes where two of the county's houses were located.

Table 17. The Female Monasteries in the Diocese of Norwich
Ranked According to Popularity
among Parish Gentry Testators in Four Periods

Monastery	1350–1400	1401–1450	1451–1500	1501–1540	Total Number of Wills w/Bequests to Convents (No.)	%[a]
Carrow	10	13	15	12	50	52
Flixton	9	10	11	3	33	34
Thetford	11	11	9	2	33	34
Bruisyard	4	8	14	3	29	30
Bungay	10	5	6	8	29	30
Campsey Ash	7	10	8	3	28	29
Redlingfield	5	6	11	3	25	26
Crabhouse	2	8	10	3	23	24
Shouldham	4	4	9	4	21	22
Blackborough	2	6	8	4	20	21
Marham	3	3	4	3	13	14

Sources: NRO, NCC will registers Heydon, Harsyk, Hyrnyng, Doke, Wylbey, Hubert, Cage, Spyrlyng, Grundisburgh, Alpe, Hyll, and Underwood. See Appendix 3 for analysis of the wills in these registers.

[a]   Percentages are based the on the total number of parish gentry wills which included bequests to nuns, 96.

percent of these donations; the rest of the diocese's female houses trailed considerably behind.

Lower on the social ladder, testators favored Thetford and Campsey Ash. People from Norwich and Norfolk archdeaconries clearly preferred Thetford over any of the other convents. Four yeomen from the archdeaconry of Norfolk remembered this small priory; Blackborough, Bungay, Carrow, Crabhouse, and Marham were beneficiaries in one will each.[113] Testators from the archdeaconry of Suffolk made more bequests (12) to Campsey Ash than to any other convent in the area. Bruisyard, the next most popular among people of this social level, was remembered in ten wills. Of the female houses in the diocese, only these two attracted the patronage of all levels of medieval society: local yeoman farmers, the county aristocracy, and the Crown.

113   Thetford was left money in: NRO, ANF 99 and 110 Grey (1466 and 1462), and in NRO, ANF 25 Bemond (1504) and NRO, ANF 93 Batman (1516). See: NRO, ANF 131–32 Grey (1464) for Blackborough; NRO, ANF 159–60 for Bungay and Flixton (1471); NRO, ANF 171 Grey (1466) for Carrow; NRO, ANF 96 Batman (1516) for Marham.

Lower status testators usually left the nuns bequests of money in amounts which were sometimes more, sometimes less than what the male religious received. For example, parish gentry bequests in wills enrolled in a late fourteenth-century register show that the nuns received £40 compared to the £110 the friars collected.[114] Members of the same group, whose wills were dated slightly later, however, made bequests to the nuns totalling £125, while those to the male religious – including monks, canons, and friars – amounted to only £74.[115] By contrast, testators of lesser social rank usually gave the friars more. Adam Onge of Berningham left 10s to the friars of Babwell, 3s 4d each to the Friars Preachers and to the Austin friars of Thetford. He bequeathed four bushels of corn to the nuns of the same place.[116]

Although a few people left money exclusively to female houses, wills most often included bequests to both female and mendicant houses. And in these cases, the parish gentry usually left more money to the male religious: Roger Lyng of Norwich, for example, left 8d to the friars of Babwell, 34s 4d to the friars of Clare, and 20s to the nuns of Thetford.[117] Among the substantial farmers and cloth workers in the archdeaconry of Suffolk who made bequests to both female and male houses, the nuns usually received more money, but the significance of the greater sum was mitigated somewhat by the fact that the testators remembered several male houses with lesser amounts of money while leaving only a single female house a larger bequest. William Trapett of Hepworth is a good example of this pattern of bequests: he gave 6s 8d to the nuns of Thetford, but left 3s 4d to each of the following: the Austin friars, the new (Carmelite) friars, and the friars of Babwell.[118]

Only occasionally did people devise goods to the religious houses, and the convents were much less likely to receive non-monetary gifts than were friars, monks or canons. Twelve people of parish gentry rank assigned specific goods to friaries; nine members of this group did so to the nuns.[119] Among the yeoman farmer group and others of lesser social status, nearly as many left particular items to the nuns as to the friars.[120]

People from all social ranks willed money and goods to individual nuns, but such legacies were less frequent than the corporate donations. Most often the recipient was a relative of the testator, like Marieta Harleston, a nun at Flixton,

---

114 The Norwich Consistory Court register is Heydon and it is dated 1370–83.
115 This later register, Harsyk, is dated 1383–1408.
116 SRO, ASD 86 Baldwyne (1439).
117 NRO, NCC 29 Heydon (1371).
118 SRO, ASD 38 Herveye (1474).
119 For goods to female houses see: NRO, NCC 55, 56, 57, 58, 63 Heydon; NRO, NCC 45 Harsyk; NRO, NCC 46 and 19 Hyrnyng; NRO, NCC 74 Hubert. For goods left to the friars see: NRO, NCC 8, 16 Hyrnyng; NRO, NCC 61 Doke; NRO, NCC 13 Hubert; NRO, NCC 17 Cage; NRO, NCC 48 Grundisburgh; NRO, NCC 9, 52, 67, 96 Spyrlyng; and NRO, NCC 24 and 57 Alpe.
120 For example, in SRO, ASF IC/AA2/3 where one person left goods to a friary, three people left things to female houses. But in SRO, ASF IC/AA2/1 and SRO, ASF IC/AA2/5 testators left goods to mendicant houses but not to female ones.

who was left a small sum of money by her brother John.[121] Similarly, a nun at Campsey Ash, Dame Margaret Harman, received 3s 4d from her brother Matthew Harman of Blaxhale.[122] John Purdy of Heigham bequeathed to his daughter Katherine, professed at Thetford, 1 quarter of barley.[123] The nature and infrequency of these personal gifts neither encouraged luxury nor spoiled the austerity of the nuns' monastic lifestyle.[124]

Because no systematic analysis of legacies to nuns compared to those made to the male religious has yet been undertaken, it is difficult to know if the type and number of bequests to the nuns in Norwich was representative of what nuns in other dioceses received from the local populace. But Claire Cross found a similar pattern of local gift-giving to female convents among testators in late medieval Yorkshire, and John Tillotson discovered local support for the nuns of Marrick Priory; he also similarly concluded that individual bequests did not spoil the nuns at this small house.[125] The nuns at Haliwell, a convent in London, were also favored by local people in this way, as were the nuns in the county of Hampshire, and those at Chester Priory in Cheshire.[126]

The examples of favors, privileges, grants of land, money, and goods illustrate several important aspects of the patronage shown to the female monasteries in the diocese of Norwich in the later Middle Ages. First, people from different social groups contributed to the welfare of these small and generally poor houses in a variety of ways. While popes sanctioned the acquisition of properties, the Crown lent further financial aid by pardoning taxes, and the local nobility made a few gestures of patronage to three of the diocese's female houses. However, patronage of the female houses by elite groups was generally less substantial than the privileges, favors, and gifts bestowed by these groups on the male religious. With larger holdings and greater wealth, the male houses were more frequently engaged in the kinds of disputes and litigation that only popes and kings could arbitrate, and such power plays ensured a certain degree of patronage by either authority. Members of the aristocracy benefitted from their patronage of male houses by the prestige that affiliations with these wealthy institutions could offer. While the favors and privileges awarded by society's elite to the female houses, though less frequent and less generous than those bestowed on monks, canons, and friars, lent credibility to the female convents and thus enhanced their reputations, the power and prestige which ensured more gifts to the male houses suggest that patronage, at least by these elevated social groups, was influenced by gender.

---

121   Above, p. 162.
122   SRO, ASF 44 IC/AA2/12 (1534).
123   NRO, ANF 110 Grey (1462).
124   As Power maintained in *English Medieval Nunneries*, pp. 325–30.
125   Cross, "Monasticism and Society," pp. 142–44; Tillotson, *Marrick Priory*, p. 13.
126   *VCH, Middlesex*, vol. 1, p. 176. (Haliwell); Coldicott, *Hampshire Nunneries*, pp. 107–08 where she notes that local clerics especially left money to all of the county's convents except for Romsey Abbey; and *VCH, Cheshire*, vol. 3, p. 149 where the editor notes that the nuns here were left bequests by local people in preference to the local friars.

Second, the patronage of the nuns by the parish gentry and yeoman farmers was, by contrast, much stronger. These two lower social groups overwhelmingly favored the nuns over monks and canons, and, considering the relative number of friaries to female convents, showed a significant preference for the nuns. While all members of the local gentry and yeoman farmers displayed this predilection, their choice of beneficiaries tended to be the nuns and convents located close by. This geographic pattern of patronage is in keeping with other patterns identified earlier in this study, such as the local origins of most of the convents' nuns, for example. Third, the consistent support of these houses by a significant portion of parish gentry testators reflects the convents' commitments to local people who in turn publicly acknowledged the nuns' concerns by bequeathing them money. And finally, this sustained patronage demonstrates better than any other measure medieval people's perception of the high quality of the nuns' religious vocation, expressed through their charitable activities and faithful execution of daily rounds of prayers, and thus the convents' wider significance to the lay communities up to the eve of the Reformation.

7

The Dissolution of the Female Monasteries

When Henry VIII pursued his divorce from Catherine of Aragon and severed ties with Rome, he initiated a chain of events which, among other things, closed all the monasteries and then transferred all of their land and goods to the Crown. The first parliamentary act which gave Henry the legal veneer permitting him to dissolve the monasteries in 1535/36 specified that houses whose annual revenues were less than £200 be dismantled – ostensibly because they were poor and their numbers minimal, that is, less than twelve. A second act, passed in 1539, ensured the closure of the monasteries which had survived the first round of suppressions.

Because most of the diocese's female convents were worth less than £200, they were closed in the first wave of suppressions in 1536/37; only Bruisyard and Shouldham survived until 1539.[1] Despite Bruisyard's valuation at £56 Abbess Mary Page successfully petitioned the Crown, paying £60 to ensure her abbey's continued existence.[2] Assuring Cromwell that neither she nor any of her nuns had alienated lands or goods, "or listened to indiscreet counsel," she begged him to intercede for them to the King so that they may "continue as his beloved bedeswomen."[3] Perhaps the nuns' good behaviour counted for something, but undoubtedly Bruisyard's affiliation with the Poor Clares also helped Page's cause. It is also likely that her success in keeping the abbey operating reflected its patronage by the noble families of Suffolk.

Shouldham Priory, also worth less than £200 – £138 – but considerably wealthier than Bruisyard, stayed open as well. Like other Gilbertine priories, Shouldham was permitted to continue because it was a house for both nuns and canons; it also provided the Crown with a place for ex-religious of either sex who wished to remain in religious life after their own houses were dissolved.[4]

While most of the convents then were considered too poor to continue,

---

[1] PRO, E 314/54.
[2] VCH, Suffolk, vol. 2, p. 132; above Chapter 3, p. 72.
[3] Letters and Papers, vol. ix, p. 376 no. 1094.
[4] Woodward, The Dissolution of the Monasteries, p. 68 suggests that the order was spared in the first round of closures because its master was Robert Holgate, a close friend of Thomas Cromwell's. See also: Joyce Youings, The Dissolution of the Monasteries (London, 1971), p. 50.

they appear to have been at least financially solvent judging by the amount of debt they carried when closed down. According to Thomas Legh, Richard Leyton, and John Ap Rice – the King's commissioners who visited the monasteries, surveyed their goods and properties, and executed the closures – only Blackborough, Redlingfield, and Thetford were in debt at this time.[5] The rest of the convents were, though not rich, at least operational when their buildings and properties passed into the hands of others. The physical condition of the convents and their furnishings, which were either sold off or carted away to London, give a more concrete idea of the state of these houses and the material quality of the nuns' lives at the time their houses were suppressed.

Physical Conditions in the Monasteries in 1536

Inventories describing the nuns' monastic quarters and their contents when the convents were dissolved survive for all but Bungay, Crabhouse, and Shouldham priories.[6] The royal agents complained that "the nunneries also of . . . Shouldham and Crabhouse make away with all they can, and make such pennyworths, as they are not able to pay any part of their debts, so that all the goods will be dispersed."[7] It is unclear from this statement whether the nuns themselves were making away with goods, or that others were doing so, but perhaps this explains why inventories are not extant for these two houses.[8] While the events at Crabhouse indicate that the nuns dispersed the priory's goods, it seems unlikely that the nuns at Shouldham would have been selling off the household furnishings of their still functioning priory.

At Blackborough, Carrow, Marham, and Thetford brief descriptions give us only very general clues about the conditions in which the nuns lived, but indicate that the buildings at Blackborough and Marham were not in good repair.[9]

---

5   PRO, SP 5/4/144: £79 4s 8d (Blackborough); PRO, SP 5/1/160r: £13 4s 2d (Redlingfield); and Jessopp, "The Norfolk Monasteries at the Time of the Suppression," p. 455: £17 15s 10d for Thetford.

6   PRO, SP 5/1/119r for Crabhouse where there is a brief notice that "Henry Webb bought all of the goods and chattels in the inventory besides the plate." According to the county commissioners, this priory was in "requisite repair": Jessopp, "The Norfolk Monasteries," p. 457. Both the royal agents' reports and also those of the county commissioners who subsequently visited the monasteries are printed here.

7   Letters and Papers, vol. x, pp. 220–21 no. 563; they said the same thing about the nuns at Blackborough.

8   The nuns of Crabhouse were further accused by royal agents of selling lands unlawfully, that is, after the convent was earmarked for suppression, to a Mr. Conysbie; the commissioners ". . . sequestered and stayed the prioress from future alienation": Letters and Papers, vol. ix, p. 271 no. 808.

9   The record for Thetford is the least detailed of these, specifying only that "stuff in the dorter" was bought by Magister Fulmerston; the napery in the chapel was sold to a person called Butte who also purchased the "stuff in the priory": PRO, SP 5/1/119r. According to the county commissioners, the priory was in good repair: Jessopp, "The Norfolk Monasteries," p. 455.

A list of all the things Jacob Joskyn purchased from the King's agents as they closed Blackborough Priory, for example, included "stuff in the hall, the stuff in the parlor, and the stuff in the chamber over the parlor."[10] Blackborough's buildings were dilapidated, no doubt reflecting the priory's poverty and debt.[11] At Marham only the high altar, dorter, guest chamber or two, kitchen, and brewhouse remained.[12] The small abbey was also in very bad physical condition at this time; church vestments and plate found in the dormitory suggest disarray, but whether this ruinous state was due to mismanagement or poverty is difficult to say.[13] Christopher Jenny, a King's serjeant-at-law, pillaged the abbey of its ornaments, furnishings, and building materials, and "left the house uncovered and bare," encouraging others to do the same.[14]

The items sold off at Carrow indicate that this priory might also have been run down, though the county commissioners reported that the house was in very good repair.[15] Of all of the priory's household and church furnishings only a few items remained: six vestments and certain old pieces tied thereto; a fire fork; a pewter basin; six candlesticks and a chafing dish; a bell and its chain in the frater; a little old table in the choir; an old lectern; an old cupboard in the vestry; a hanging in St Edmund's chamber; a table in the misericord; three broken chests; a broken cupboard; and a hanging in the blue chamber.[16]

A broader range of material comfort and physical conditions existed at Bruisyard, Campsey Ash, Flixton, and Redlingfield, with furnishings at the richest house, Campsey Ash, of a higher quality than the simpler but adequate ones at Flixton, the diocese's poorest house. Even at Redlingfield and Bruisyard, which fell between Campsey Ash and Flixton in estimated wealth, the nuns did not live in the dire physical conditions often suggested as their fate, but possessed simple domestic fittings and appear to have invested in highly decorated priests' vestments, altar cloths and ornaments.

Three mattresses, four feather beds, bolsters, and pillows, in conditions "goode and badde," comprise part of the inventory in the rooms at Flixton. Ten pairs of sheets, cushions, table coverings and linen towels and napkins were also listed, indicating that there was sufficient bedding for the eight nuns who lived there at this time.[17] The buttery, kitchen, and frater seem to have been adequately if not extravagantly supplied as well.[18]

10 PRO, SP 5/4/141–42r. Non-itemized goods from various other rooms are listed here as well.
11 Jessopp, "The Norfolk Monasteries," p. 452.
12 PRO, SP 5/1/120r.
13 Jessopp, "The Norfolk Monasteries," p. 453; VCH, Norfolk, vol. 2, p. 370.
14 Letters and Papers, vol. x, pp. 220–21 no. 563.
15 Jessopp, "The Norfolk Monasteries," p. 453.
16 PRO, SP 5/1/111.
17 VCH, Suffolk, vol. 2, p. 117 where the editor remarks that the "chambers were well supplied with bedding." In total these were valued at 34s 9d. There were seven nuns and the prioress Elizabeth Wright living at the priory in 1532, the date of the last episcopal visitation.
18 Francis Haselwood, "Inventories of Monasteries Suppressed in 1536," PSIA 8 (1894), p. 89.

The choir chest at the priory contained several copes and suits of vestments of purple, red, and white silk and worsted cotton, notable among which were an old vestment of red and green silk with swans of gold, a red silk vestment decorated with white cranes, and "Seynt Kateryns cote of clothe of gold," a vestment fitting for a house founded in this saint's honor.[19] Various other satin and linen altar cloths and hangings were also found here; so were "diverse Bokes . . . and a payer of Candelstykes of Coper."[20] These items were worth 54s 11d; these and the church plate, which was valued at £5 15s 4d, were the most valuable of the recorded possessions of this small house.

At the slightly richer Bruisyard and Redlingfield, the nuns' church and the more numerous domestic furnishings were in better condition. Priests' vestments, altar cloths and hangings were made of a variety of colorful materials including red and blue bawdkyn, white, red, blue and yellow silk, crimson, blue, and black velvet at both houses, as well as suits of russet damask and black at Redlingfield.[21] Silver chalices and paxes were used in the churches of both houses – though these eucharistic utensils were more numerous at Bruisyard – and both houses had alabaster tables, candlesticks, mass books, and a pair each of little organs: in the church at Bruisyard, and by the high altar and in the choir at Redlingfield.[22] Hangings and cruets in the Lady Chapel at Redlingfield also counted among the priory's possessions.[23]

Domestic furnishings included trestle tables, hangings, cupboards, and chairs in the parlor rooms at both Bruisyard and Redlingfield.[24] Each house also had five separate rooms which contained at least one set of beds, bolsters, testers, bankers, blankets, sheets and pillows, as well as decorated hangings of saye or of painted cloth. The numerous blankets and bed coverings which fill the list of contents of what were clearly bedrooms at these two small houses suggest a higher level of comfort for the nuns at Bruisyard and Redlingfield than was indicated for those at Flixton. Chairs and cushions were also among the bedroom furnishings of both houses. This accommodation was more than sufficient for the number of nuns who lived at Bruisyard, but may have been slightly less than enough for those at Redlingfield.[25] Only five beds were noted at this priory, and these would not have been enough for the eight nuns who

---

[19] Ibid., p. 88.

[20] Ibid., p. 89.

[21] The inventory of Bruisyard has been printed in: Francis Haselwood, "Monastery at Bruisyard," PSIA 7 (1889/91), pp. 320–23; the inventory for Redlingfield in Haselwood, "Inventories," pp. 95–8.

[22] The plate at Bruisyard was valued at 63s 4d: Haselwood, "Monastery," pp. 321–23; at Redlingfield these goods were worth £4 4s: Haselwood, "Inventories," pp. 95–6.

[23] Ibid.

[24] Haselwood, "Monastery," p. 322 for Bruisyard; Haselwood, Inventories," p. 97 for Redlingfield.

[25] The number of nuns at Bruisyard can only be pieced together; evidence from wills suggests that there were probably about 10 at the most in 1539 which is, coincidentally, the number of beds counted in the inventory.

were resident there in 1536. But at least two of them purchased some of the furniture when their monastery was suppressed, and so it is possible that Redlingfield also had enough bedding and linen to accommodate all of the nuns there.[26]

In general, Redlingfield appears to have been better equipped than Bruisyard, reflecting the priory's slightly better economic status, and perhaps its easier accessibility to guests and boarders.[27] Redlingfield had a pantry, while Bruisyard did not, and the priory's kitchen, buttery, bakehouse, and brewery had not only a greater number of but also more expensive utensils and linen. And while the contents of these rooms at Bruisyard were not assigned values, the abbey's kitchen and buttery utensils and napery were worth only a little more than 10s 6d.[28] By contrast, the same utensils inventoried at Redlingfield were worth 27s 4d.[29] There were fewer contents in the bakehouse and brewhouse at Bruisyard, but they were not given monetary values at either house.

Estimations of monetary worth were not assigned to the contents of the bakehouse and brewhouse at Campsey Ash either, but the priory's greater wealth was reflected in the church ornaments, plate, and domestic furnishings which far surpassed in quality and quantity those found at any of the other houses. Alabaster tables, silver and latten candlesticks, crucifixes, sensors, bells and paxes were more numerous in the church and Lady Chapel here, hangings and altar clothes more elaborately decorated and made of finer material.[30] Vestments included "vi olde cotidiane" ones as well as ones of crimson and green velvet, and a cope of blue with angels and ten stars.[31]

Contents of some of the rooms included at least twelve featherbeds and mattresses each with a pair of blankets, bolsters, and sheets or coverlets, and several of the seven bedrooms also had tables and chairs with cushions.[32] The priory also had steward's and auditor's chambers, rooms appropriate for this better-endowed and wealthier priory. Its parlor was fully furnished with cupboards and tables, and a little carpet for the windows; the buttery, pantry, and kitchen were stocked with table cloths, linen towels and napkins, kettles, platters, and dishes numerous enough to have served the priory's many guests and relatively large number of nuns.[33] Campsey Ash's household supplies from

---

26 The suppression papers for Redlingfield list 7 nuns and the prioress Grace Sampson; only 5 beds are noted in the priory's inventory. For the number of nuns see: PRO, SP 5/3/116r.

27 See above Chapter 4, pp. 125–7.

28 Haselwood, "Monastery," pp. 321, 323 where not all items are assigned values: 6 platters and 12 dishes in the kitchen, for example. The values which were given were 5s 16d for what was in the kitchen; 17d for the contents of the buttery; and 2s 20d for napkins, sheets, and cloths.

29 Haselwood, "Inventories," p. 97: the contents of the kitchen were valued at 13s 1d; the buttery and pantry 20d; and the napery was worth 13s 8d.

30 Haselwood, "Inventories," pp. 113–14.

31 Ibid., p. 113.

32 Ibid., pp. 114–15.

33 Ibid., p. 115. Because neither other contemporary suppression documents nor later pension lists survive for Campsey Ash, we do not know how many nuns were at the

these rooms were valued at over 30s, and its plate, vestments, and church furnishings were worth more than £24.

Though far from complete descriptions of rooms and their furnishings, these inventories at least provide some indication of the physical conditions of the nuns' lives at the time of the Dissolution. Not lavishly provisioned or decorated, the rooms and their contents seem to have been at least simple and utilitarian, as at Flixton, and at best more abundant, of higher quality, and very comfortable, as at Campsey Ash.

The royal agents not only inventoried the convents' possessions, they also reported on the nuns: their numbers and ages, the quality of their religious lives, and whether or not they wished to remain professed and be transferred to another house, or dispensed from their vows. All of these issues had direct bearing on how the Dissolution affected these women and how they survived after it.

The Status of the Nuns at the Time of the Dissolution

The numbers of nuns at most of the houses – Blackborough, Carrow, Crabhouse, Marham, Redlingfield, Shouldham, and Thetford – are known for certain. For the other female priories in the diocese figures must be based on how many nuns were resident in a particular house at the time of the last episcopal visitation, as was done above for Flixton. The fluctuations of this monastic population, discussed earlier in this study, showed a rebound from post-plague declines throughout the fifteenth and early sixteenth centuries; by the time of the Dissolution I estimate that about 133 nuns lived in the diocese.[34]

Most of the diocese's female monastic population were fairly young when their monasteries were dissolved, about 32 years of age.[35] Several superiors, for example, lived for at least thirty years after the suppressions: Cecily Fastolf, last prioress of Bungay, died in 1568; the last prioress of Carrow, Cecily Suffield, died in 1565.[36] Both Grace Sampson, ex-prioress of Redlingfield, and Elizabeth

---

house in 1536. At the last episcopal visitation in 1532, however, there were 17 nuns and the prioress Ela Buttery.

[34] Chapter 2, pp. 38–9 of this book.

[35] Ibid., p. 46. For example, the nuns at Campsey Ash were: Christine Abell, thirty-six in 1532, so forty in 1536 when the house was suppressed; Margaret Bacon was sixty-eight in 1523, so seventy-two in 1536; Dorothy Brampton was thirty-four in 1532, making her thirty-eight in 1536; Anne Butler was thirty in 1532, so thirty-four in 1536; Margaret Clarke was only twenty-eight in 1532, so thirty-two upon suppression; Margaret Harman was thirty-five at the last episcopal visitation, so thirty-nine in 1536; and Anne Winter was thirty-two in 1532, making her thirty-six when Campsey was suppressed in 1536. See: Jessopp, Visitations, pp. 291–92.

[36] For Cecily Suffield's date of death, see: NRO, ANW burial register of the parish of St Clements, fol. 4.

Fincham, ex-prioress of Shouldham, died in 1561.[37] And the last prioress of Blackborough, Elizabeth Dawney, died in 1555.[38]

Several rank and file nuns also lived well past the Dissolution. At least four of the Bruisyard nuns were still alive some twenty years later when they appeared in the 1557 will of Nicholas Hare.[39] Joan Plomstead, ex-nun of Shouldham Priory, was still alive in 1555, as were two of her fellow ex-nuns, Margaret Scorer and Faith Smyth.[40] Joan Dereham, another nun from Should-ham, was still living in 1568 in King's Lynn, the closest sizeable town to the priory.[41] Elizabeth Beaufeld, an ex-nun of Bungay, was buried close by the priory in Lowestoft in 1599.[42]

While most of the nuns in the diocese of Norwich were middle-aged in 1536/37, some were older. Elizabeth Hoth, last prioress of Thetford, for example, was still alive in 1553 when she reported to the royal commissioners that she was then a hundred years old, making her about eighty-eight when her house was suppressed in 1536.[43] Three other prioresses died within the first twelve years of their convents' closure, indicating that they too were older at the Dissolution. The last abbess of Marham, Barbara Mason, died in 1538; Elizabeth Wright of Flixton died in 1549; and Ela Buttery of Campsey Ash died in 1546.[44]

With a few exceptions, superiors at many female houses in other dioceses were also older than the rank and file nuns, averaging about 56 years of age in 1536.[45] These superiors' older ages coincide with findings presented earlier about the career ladder of monastic officeholding. Recall that the top rung of the ladder was occupied by superiors who were at least middle-aged by the time they acceded to this highest office after having successfully held a series of lesser ones.[46] Those superiors who, like Cecily Fastolf, Elizabeth Dawney, Elizabeth Fincham, and Cecily Suffield, lived well past 1536 do not necessarily discount

---

[37] G. Baskerville, "Married Clergy and Pensioned Religious in Norwich Diocese, 1555," *EHR* 48 (1933), p. 205. Grace Sampson's will is: NRO, NCC 235 Bircham.

[38] Baskerville, "Married Clergy," p. 205.

[39] PRO, PCC Prob 11/39/46.

[40] Baskerville, "Married Clergy," pp. 210, 214.

[41] PRO, E 178/3251.

[42] PRO, E 178/3251 for a special commission's report dated 1568/69 on the number of surviving ex-religious and their pensions.

[43] Baskerville, "Married Clergy," pp. 210–11. Hoth told the commissioners she was "of an hundreth years and more."

[44] Mason's will was proved in 1538: Tymms, *Wills and Inventories*, p. 133. For Elizabeth Wright, see: Baskerville, "Married Clergy," p. 205; Ela Buttery's will was proved in 1546: NRO, NCC 261 Hyll.

[45] Agnes Bradrigge, last prioress of Yedingham, was in her early forties at the Suppression: Clay, "Yorkshire Monasteries," p. 171 says forty-four; VCH, *Yorkshire*, vol. 3, p. 128 says forty-one. She was elected in 1525. The last superior of Arthington, Elizabeth Hall, was forty-five: Purvis, "A Selection of Monastic Rentals," p. 141; she had been elected in 1532.

[46] See Chapter 3 above, pp. 107–8.

the existence of a career ladder based on merit, however, as they had been elected to their positions not long before the suppressions.[47] This same pattern is evident elsewhere. Morpheta Kingswell, last prioress of Wherwell, lived for another thirty-four years, and Elizabeth Martyn, last superior of Wintney, another fifty, indicating that these women were also younger than average among their colleagues. Both of these prioresses had also been elected only a few years before their houses were dissolved.[48]

Many nuns elsewhere in England also survived the dissolution of their houses by many years. A calculation of the ages of 165 nuns and superiors from seventeen female houses shows that while a few women were over sixty – some well past this age – the average age of a nun at this time was about forty, older than the median age of the nuns in the diocese of Norwich.[49] The ages of twelve nuns of Thicket Priory in Yorkshire represent the range at convents in other dioceses: three nuns were in their twenties, three in their thirties, three in their forties, and two in their sixties.[50] The nuns at the Minories in London exhibit this same pattern: while two nuns were very old – Agnes Hunt was seventy-six and Joan Crosby ninety-five – most of the nuns of this abbey were in their early

---

[47] Election dates are uncertain for two of these superiors. Elizabeth Dawney was elected sometime between 1514 and 1532 and since Blackborough was suppressed in 1537, she was prioress there for between 5 and 22 years. Likewise, Cecily Suffield was elected prioress of Carrow between 1532 and 1535; Carrow was dissolved in 1536 making her tenure as superior between 1 and 4 years. For Cecily Fastolf, Grace Sampson, and Elizabeth Fincham, though, the evidence is clear that they had only held this high office for short periods of time, suggesting that they were in their late thirties or early forties when turned out of their monasteries. Cecily Fastolf was elected prioress of Bungay in 1526; the priory was suppressed in 1537 making her tenure as superior 11 years. Grace Sampson was elected in 1524; Redlingfield was closed down in 1537, so she was prioress for 13 years. Elizabeth Fincham was prioress of Shouldham for 8 years before its suppression. Jessopp, Visitations, passim; VCH, Norfolk, vol. 2, pp. 351, 354, 414; and VCH, Suffolk, vol. 2, pp. 82, 85.

[48] Coldicott, Hampshire Nunneries, pp. 143, 164, 166.

[49] Nuns' ages were sometimes noted by the royal commissioners. The convents for which this information is available are, in Yorkshire: Arthington, Baysdale, Esholt, Hampole, Handale, Swine, Nunkeeling, Thicket, Wilberfosse, Wykeham, and Yedingham; see: John Clay, ed., Yorkshire Monasteries: Suppression Papers (Yorkshire Archaeological Society Record Series 48, 1912); and J. S. Purvis, ed., A Selection of Monastic Rentals and Dissolution Papers, in Miscellanea III (Yorkshire Archaeological Society Record Series 80, 1931). Other houses include Aconbury in Hereford: F. C. and Penelope Morgan, "Some Nuns, Ex-religious and Former Chantry Priests Living in the Diocese of Hereford (c.1554)," Woolhope Naturalists Field Club Transactions 27 (1963), p. 139; Langley Priory: Letters and Papers, vol. x, p. 297; Pollesworth Priory in Warwick: ibid., vol. xiv, pp. 85–6. Catherine Paxton includes the ages of the nuns of the Minories and St Helen's, Bishopsgate, both in London, in her thesis, "The Nunneries of London," pp. 302–07. See also Joyce Youings, "A Rare Survival: Letters Patent Granting a Pension to a Lincolnshire Nun in 1539," Archives 7 (1966), p. 229 for the young age of an ex-nun of Heynings Priory.

[50] Purvis, "Small Yorkshire Priories," p. 161.

forties or younger.[51] Nationwide, of all of the nuns whose ages can be determined, approximately 28 percent were between the ages of twenty and thirty; 27 percent were between thirty and forty years of age; 15 percent were between forty and fifty; and 25 percent were over fifty years old.[52]

The nuns' relative youth meant that they had long and uncertain futures ahead of them in a temporal world from which they had been cloistered for many, many years. While the Crown provided a modicum of support, theoretically it was dependent on the royal commissioners' assessments of the quality of religious life within each convent. Any hint of scandal nullified the promise of financial support from the Crown, and the agents' reports indicated that religious life had been severely compromised at four of the diocese's eleven female houses.

Richard Leyton and Thomas Legh reported that nuns at Blackborough were suspected of "incontinen," and that two nuns at Shouldham and five at Marham were accused of having had children by both laymen and priests.[53] Marham's abbess, Barbara Mason, for example, was charged with having borne a child by the prior of Pentney Priory.[54] The prioress of Crabhouse had apparently given birth to a child; two other nuns there had children by single men, and another nun had two, one by a priest, one by a layman.[55]

The commissioners' reports did not, however, necessarily reflect the truth. The agents' questionable methods of obtaining information have cast serious doubt on the validity of their claims.[56] David Knowles pointed out that the countless accusations of sodomy and incontinence among the male religious were both exaggerated and unfounded.[57] There is no reason therefore to readily accept the commissioners' negative evaluations of the quality of the nuns' religious lives.[58] It is very likely, for example, that at least one of the accused

---

51 Paxton, "The Nunneries of London," p. 302.
52 There are numerous other nuns whose exact ages are unknown but who either lived well beyond the dates of their convents' suppressions, or about whom other evidence indicates that they were relatively young. Jane Wadham, late sexton of Romsey Abbey, for example, was young enough when her house was closed in 1539 to have borne children by 1543: Coldicott, *Hampshire Nunneries*, p. 146.
53 Jessopp, "The Norfolk Monasteries," p. 444 for Blackborough and Shouldham, ibid., p. 445 for Marham.
54 Ibid., p. 450.
55 *VCH, Norfolk*, vol. 2, p. 410.
56 *Letters and Papers*, vol. ix, p. 218 no. 651 for Thomas Legh's excuses for and denials of accusations against him regarding his behavior during the visitations. See also: Sybil Jack, "The Last Days of the Smaller Monasteries in England," *Journal of Ecclesiastical History* 21 (1970), p. 102 where she comments on the agents' willingness to seek out and exploit scandals; A. G. Dickens, *The English Reformation* (New York, 1964), pp. 141–42 offers an opposing view.
57 Knowles, *The Religious Orders*, vol. 3, pp. 270–79, 282–85, 289, 296–98 for the commissioners' personalities and their reports.
58 Gasquet, *English Monastic Life*, p. 159 where he similarly disregards the royal visitors' reports about the nuns at Grace Dieu Priory because of other contradictory evidence;

Crabhouse nuns was the one already punished for her offence by Bishop Nykke in 1514.[59] In addition, another round of visitations carried out at the King's command by members of the county gentry flatly contradicts the royal commissioners' claims.[60]

The county inspectors, Thomas Mildmay and Richard Southwell, reported that the Blackborough, Carrow, and Thetford nuns were "of good fame," or "of good conversation and living."[61] About Marham Abbey the county men said only that "five of the nuns were of scandalous report, whereof three require dispensations," and the rest would continue in their religious lives.[62] Similarly, the agents claimed that all of the nuns of Crabhouse lived respectable lives; three nuns wanted to be released from their vows while one wanted to remain a nun.[63] While it is unlikely that the county commissioners would defame the convents where some of their peers' female kin may have lived in the past, the fact that several of these accused nuns requested transfers to other houses rather than be dispensed from religious life suggests that they had not violated their vows. If the nuns had really done so, they would not have remained nuns and been transferred to – and accepted by – other convents.[64] Nor would they have been awarded pensions by the Crown, as were the nuns of Shouldham.[65] Rather, they would have been summarily dismissed by the commissioners, like the nuns who lived in other parts of England who were found to be incontinent, unruly, or otherwise not genuine in their vocations.[66]

Neither royal nor county commissioners' reports survive for the county of Suffolk, so an assessment of the quality of religious life at the convents there must be based on the final episcopal visitations and the treatment of the Suffolk nuns after the Dissolution. Bishop Nykke visited all of the Suffolk houses in 1532 and except for some complaints about the strictness of Ela Buttery,

and Knowles, *The Religious Orders*, vol. 3, p. 481 Appendix VIII where he demonstrates examples of such conflicting evidence in the cases of Grace Dieu and of Denney Abbey in Cambridgeshire.

59 Jessopp, *Visitations*, pp. 108–10, and see here Chapter 2, p. 72.
60 The county commissioners' visitations included only the monasteries in the county of Norfolk. Their itineraries are: PRO, SP 5 2/246–254; Jessopp, "Norfolk Monasteries," pp. 450–63 for their reports.
61 Ibid., pp. 452, 454, 456.
62 Ibid., p. 456 and see: PRO, SC 6/Henry VIII/2621 and PRO, E 117/14/22. The three dispensed nuns were Barbara Mason, Mary Te, and Dorothy Lovell. Those who remained nuns were Clare Sherbone, Elizabeth Lightfoot, and Elizabeth Plummer.
63 Jessopp, "The Norfolk Monasteries," p. 456 and PRO, SP 5/3/35.
64 Palmer, "The Benedictine Nunnery," pp. 34–5 argues a similar point for the nuns there. Despite the royal commissioners' reports of unchaste nuns at Swaffham, nuns from other houses who desired to remain in religious life were sent there after the suppression of their own houses.
65 See below, pp. 196, 198.
66 For examples of nuns elsewhere who did not receive pensions because of their transgressions: G. A. J. Hodgett, "The Unpensioned Ex-Religious in Tudor England," *Journal of Ecclesiastical History* 13 (1962), p. 201; Dugdale, *Monasticon*, vol. 4, p. 114 for the nuns at Pinley Priory in Worcester.

prioress of Campsey Ash, and about the quality of food and the time it was served, there were apparently no problems.[67] Moral lapses and ill conduct do not seem to have been part of religious life among the nuns of these houses.[68] In fact, some of the Bruisyard and Bungay nuns received life-time pensions which indicates that, like their counterparts in Norfolk and elsewhere, they had remained faithful to their monastic vows.

Unlike the majority of nuns in other dioceses whose houses were closed in this first wave of suppressions, only eight nuns in the diocese of Norwich wanted to remain in religious life and be transferred to other convents: four from Carrow, one from Crabhouse, and three from Marham.[69] The rest were released from their vows of poverty and obedience. But their unwillingness to remain habited and cloistered did not necessarily mean that their monastic vows or religious lives had lost any meaning. The lives of several ex-nuns indicate that, for all but a handful, personal poverty, communal living, and a strong identification as ex-nuns and good catholics continued to define their lives.

Pensions and Rewards

With the first suppressions, in which all but two of the diocese's female convents were closed, formal pensions were provided for superiors only.[70] The rest of the nuns, like their counterparts elsewhere, were given "rewards" at the time they were either excused from their vows or moved to another female monastery.[71] The amounts the diocese's superiors and rank and file nuns received as either one-time awards or annual pensions, their relation to a convent's wealth, and how they were administered were for the most part similar to how the system worked for nuns in the rest of the country.

All of the diocese's superiors whose houses fell in 1536/37 received both single payments at the time their convents were suppressed and life-time pensions from the Crown, except for the prioress of Bungay.[72] Of the two

---

[67] Jessopp, *Visitations*, pp. 290–92.

[68] Ibid., p. 318 (Bungay); ibid., pp. 318–19 (Flixton); ibid., p. 297 (Redlingfield).

[69] Jessopp, "The Norfolk Monasteries," p. 245 (Carrow); PRO, SP 5/3/35 (Crabhouse); PRO E117/14/22 (Marham). By contrast, Woodward, *The Dissolution of the Monasteries*, p. 74 calculated that 85 percent of the nuns remained in orders and were transferred to other houses.

[70] Youings, *The Dissolution of the Monasteries*, p. 44.

[71] Hodgett, "The Unpensioned Ex-Religious," p. 201 estimated that in the diocese of Lincoln only 28 nuns were pensioned, and that 221 were given this one time award. Hodgett estimated though that country-wide, 305 nuns were unpensioned, but 605 received annual life-time pensions.

[72] Elizabeth Wright, last prioress of Flixton, was allowed £6 13s 4d; her house was valued at £23; Barbara Mason, last abbess of Marham, received 66s 10d at the time her house was dissolved when its value was £42. These allowances are noted alongside the pension amounts awarded to each woman in PRO, E 314/54.

houses dissolved in 1539, only the prioress of Shouldham was awarded a life-time pension.[73] How the prioress of Bungay and the abbess of Bruisyard survived after their houses were closed is unknown.

Pension amounts for the nine superiors who received them were not fixed by any legislative body, but historians suggest that amounts were left to the discretion of the royal agents who often used the value of a house, as designated by the *Valor*, as a guide.[74] And to a certain extent, superiors' pensions do show a correlation between the wealth of a monastery and the amount awarded (Table 18).[75] The prioress of wealthy Campsey Ash obtained £23 6s 8d, more than any other superior in the diocese received.[76] Not only could this positive correlation have reflected the priory's greater wealth, but it could also have resulted from the royal and aristocratic patronage the priory attracted, perhaps enhancing Buttery's status among her colleagues. At the lowest end of the scale, the prioress of Crabhouse received the least amount of money.

Most of the others received similar small sums which reflected the relative poverty of their houses. But two examples suggest that a convent's estimated value was not the only deciding factor in the commissioners' assignments of life-time pensions.[77] After Ela Buttery's pension, the next largest was given to Grace Sampson, the last prioress of Redlingfield, who received £13 6s 8d. While not the poorest house in the diocese, it was far from wealthy, valued in 1535 at £67, and heavily in debt. Equally curious is the comparatively small amount assigned to Elizabeth Fincham, the last prioress of Shouldham; her house was the second wealthiest in the diocese and yet she obtained a pension of only £5.

Circumstances particular to each of these two priories might explain their superiors' pensions. Edmund and Grace Bedingfield, two of the priory's main benefactors, purchased Redlingfield Priory and allowed Grace Sampson to stay in her old lodgings after the suppression.[78] Perhaps the Bedingfields intervened on her behalf to procure a larger pension than the commissioners might have been considering. Shouldham Priory was a double house of nuns and canons, and despite the fact that the Gilbertine houses were originally founded for women, with the canons attached as adjuncts specifically to serve the nuns, the prior of Shouldham was pensioned with £20 a year while Elizabeth Fincham

[73] PRO, E 101/76/29, E 314/20, E 101/533/4, and E 178/3234.

[74] Knowles, *The Religious Orders*, vol. 3, p. 406; Woodward, *The Dissolution of the Monasteries*, pp. 143–44; and Youings, *The Dissolution of the Monasteries*, p. 52.

[75] Dickens, *The Reformation*, p. 172 for the amounts being greater than what was awarded to the rank and file nuns. Gasquet, *Henry VIII and the English Monasteries*, pp. 438, 440–42; Woodward, *The Dissolution of the Monasteries*, p. 144; and Youings, *The Dissolution of the Monasteries*, pp. 73–4 for those who see a correlation between a superior's pension and the wealth of her monastery.

[76] PRO, E 314/54.

[77] Catherine Paxton found similar disparities in the pensions given to superiors of the London monasteries: "The Nunneries of London," p. 297.

[78] NRO, NCC 235 Bircham, her will.

Table 18. *Pensions Received by the Monastic Superiors*
of the Female Monasteries in the Diocese of Norwich

| Name of Superior | Pension Received | | | Monastery | Value in 1535 |
	£	s	d		£
Ela Buttery	23	6	8	Campsey Ash	182
Grace Sampson	13	6	8	Redlingfield	67
Cecily Suffield	8			Carrow	64
Elizabeth Wright	6	13	4	Flixton	23
Elizabeth Dawney	6			Blackborough	42
Barbara Mason	5			Marham	42
Elizabeth Fincham	5			Shouldham	138
Elizabeth Hoth	5			Thetford	38
Elizabeth Studfield	4			Crabhouse	24

Sources: For pensions: PRO, E 314/54. The pension amounts for the prioress of Bungay and the abbess of Bruisyard are unknown. For values, *Valor Ecclesiasticus.*

received only £5.[79] Did the commissioners' assignment of these two pensions reflect the generally lower status of women in medieval society and the Church? If it did, the prior's significantly larger award is consistent with the pattern identified throughout this study of more generous favors shown to the male religious by contemporary authorities throughout the Middle Ages. As we shall see, the canons of Shouldham also received more money annually than the nuns there, further supporting the alliance between the male religious and both ecclesiastical and secular authorities.

Pensions of superiors in other dioceses more consistently corresponded to the economic status of their houses, and ranged from the £100 pension given to the abbess of Wilton, to the £26 13s 4d the prioress of Polesworth received for life.[80] While Wilton was worth more than £600, the abbess's pension may also have been due to her status as superior of one of England's oldest female foundations. The amount received by the prioress of Pollesworth mirrored her relatively poor convent, valued at less than £110. The prioress of Marrick, by comparison, received only £5 a year; her house was considerably poorer.[81]

Pension arrangements for rank and file nuns and monks were not made until after the suppression of Lewes Abbey at the end of 1537, and so support for the nuns turned out in 1536 was very limited. Most of them received only a single

[79] PRO, E 101/533/4.
[80] For Wilton, see: Dugdale, *Monasticon*, vol. 2, pp. 330–31; for Pollesworth: *Letters and Papers*, vol. xiv, pp. 85–6.
[81] See: VE, *passim* for the values cited here; and Dugdale, *Monasticon*, vol. 4, p. 246 for the prioress of Marrick's pension.

award of money at the time their convents were closed down. These one-off payments varied both among the residents of a single house and also from convent to convent. At Blackborough, for example, four nuns were awarded 26s 8d each; four others received 20s.[82] The three nuns of Crabhouse who wished to be released from their monastic life were each given 26s 8d; two of the nuns of Marham secured the same, while two others from the abbey drew 45s a piece.[83] Each of the Redlingfield nuns were paid 23s 4d.[84] These amounts average out to 47s, or £2 7s. While these awards undoubtedly cushioned the blow of dislocation, they could hardly have supported the women for more than a couple of years.

The few nuns in the diocese who were pensioned by the Crown always received less than their superiors procured. Four of the nuns of Shouldham, for example, each obtained annually 40s; one other nun had only 13s 4d a year.[85] Two ex-Bungay nuns also collected money from the King's agents, despite the assertion by Thomas, Duke of Norfolk, that by the time he arrived to claim the priory as his own, all of the nuns had disappeared, thus forfeiting their rights to any money.[86] Mary Loveday and Elizabeth Duke were awarded 60s and 40s in 1536; another Bungay nun, Katherine Hubbert, appears on a later pension list, dated 1569, as having had a pension of 40s per year.[87] The same document notes the names and dates of death of two more Bungay nuns, one of whom was Cecily Fastolf, last prioress of this house, but says only that the commissioners were unable to determine whether or not these two ex-religious had pensions.[88]

A few other nuns in the diocese procured life-time support but not from the Crown. Nicholas Hare purchased Bruisyard after its suppression, and in his will of 1557, he directed his wife Katherine to continue to support Margaret Loveday, Florence Rouse, Florence Scuteler, and Jane Wentworth, all ex-nuns of the abbey.[89] Katherine was to maintain annual payments of 53s to Loveday, Scuteler, and Wentworth, and 20s to Florence Rouse for as long as these ex-nuns lived. Hare appears to have been the only owner of any of the dissolved monasteries in the diocese who was responsible for the pensions of the previous tenants.[90]

Unlike the superiors' pensions, those awarded to rank and file nuns bore little relation to the wealth of their monasteries. The nuns of Shouldham,

---

82 PRO, SP 5/4/130–50.
83 PRO, SP 5/3/29 for Crabhouse; PRO, E 315/405 for Marham.
84 PRO, SP 5/3/116.
85 PRO, E 101/533/4.
86 *Letters and Papers of Henry VIII*, vol. x, p. 241 no. 599, and ibid., p. 514 no. 1236; Jack, "The Last Days of the Smaller Monasteries," p. 102.
87 PRO, E 101/533/4 (Loveday and Duke); PRO, E 178/3251 (Hubbert).
88 Ibid.; the other nun was Elizabeth Beaufeld.
89 PRO, PCC Prob 11/39/46.
90 Another Bruisyard nun, Margery Bacon, appears in the 1569 special commission's list. But the royal commissioners note only her date of death and that they cannot ascertain whether or not she ever had a pension: PRO, E 178/3251.

much wealthier than Bungay, were paid considerably less than the amount Mary Loveday, ex-nun of Bungay, secured. Disparities between the wealth of a convent and the pension amounts awarded to their inmates might in part be explained by the social rank of the recipients, or by their status in the convent, with senior nuns pensioned at a higher rate than those who had not been professed as long.

These annual pensions were distributed in biannual installments at either the town of Bury St Edmunds or the city of Norwich.[91] Not infrequently then the nuns had to travel to pick up their payments; Elizabeth Hoth, the aged last prioress of Thetford, for example, had settled in the city of Norwich, but was nevertheless obliged to send someone to Bury to pick up her pension.[92] Two ex-nuns of Shouldham who also lived in Norwich had to go to Bury twice a year for their payments as well.[93]

Amounts awarded to 824 rank and file nuns in other dioceses indicate that, like the pensions given to the nuns in the diocese of Norwich, nuns within a single house usually received different amounts of money. Three of the nuns at Marrick, for example, received annually 20s, three others 26s 8d; four nuns secured 40s; one received 53s 4d, and another 66s 8d.[94] At Neasham Priory in Durham, all of the nuns were given 26s 8d a year for the rest of their lives.[95] Such variations notwithstanding, these nuns' pensions show a more concrete correlation to their convents' values. Neither house was very wealthy, but Marrick was a little better off than Neasham, which was valued at only £20 17s 7d.[96] By contrast, the nuns of Polesworth, much wealthier than either Marrick or Neasham, were each pensioned with 40s a year.[97]

The pensions of all nuns averaged 33s 4d, less than the 47s average secured by the few nuns in the diocese of Norwich. This lesser amount might have been due to the larger number of very poor houses in other dioceses, like York, which decreased the overall average of pension amounts for all nuns. If this was the case, then the values of female houses in other parts of England show a stronger connection with pension amounts than did those for the diocese of Norwich.

Like their female counterparts, most of the monks and canons who were displaced by the early closures were not pensioned either. They were, however, provided with other ecclesiastical positions by the Dukes of Norfolk and Suffolk, who took possession of most of the smaller male houses.[98] In addition,

---

91 W. C. Richardson, A History of the Court of Augmentation (Baton Rouge, 1961), passim; Youings, The Dissolution of the Monasteries, pp. 52, 62, 77, 91–116.

92 Gasquet, Henry VIII and the English Monasteries, p. 444: the late abbess of Canonsleigh and seventeen ex-nuns from that house also sent an agent to pick up their pensions.

93 Baskerville, "Married Religious," p. 211.

94 Letters and Papers, vol. xv, p. 547; Clay, "Yorkshire Monasteries," pp. 134–35.

95 Dugdale, Monasticon, vol. 4, p. 548.

96 VE, vol. 5, p. 67 for Marrick; Dugdale, Monasticon, vol. 4, p. 548 for Neasham.

97 Letters and Papers, vol. xiv, pp. 85–6.

98 Baskerville, "The Married Clergy," pp. 202–03 for the actions of the Dukes of Norfolk and Suffolk. For the alternatives available to the ex-male religious, see: Baskerville,

the male religious who were pensioned were awarded substantially larger pensions than their female counterparts received: the prior of Shouldham received £20 while, as we have seen, the prioress there was awarded only £5.[99] The eight canons there were also pensioned at a higher rate than the nuns: each canon received 54s 4d; the nuns received between 40s and 13s 4d. The abbot of Bury St Edmunds procured an annual pension of 50 marks, and each of his monks obtained between £6 and £8.[100] The prior of Westacre was given £40 a year, and the monks at Walsingham secured pensions of at least £5 each.[101] Even monks from poor houses took in more money than did nuns from houses of comparable worth. The canons of Weybourne, for example, received £3 from the Crown.[102] The average pension a monk or canon received in the diocese was £6, slightly higher than £5 – the national average for the male religious – and more than three times what a nun secured.

The substantially larger amounts awarded to monks, canons, and their superiors surely reflected the higher standing of men in medieval society, but also the greater value placed upon the male religious by society's elite – especially the Crown. That many of the ex-male religious were offered other ecclesiastical offices also suggests that the Dissolution entailed a greater change in lifestyle for nuns than it did for their male counterparts, who could prosper even more by combining their pensions with the money derived from the many new benefices they were now able to hold.[103]

The inadequacy of the nuns' pensions was exacerbated by the fees and taxes attached to them.[104] Pensioners had to pay a statutory fee of 4d per £ on each instalment, and pay the agents who issued the money 11s in addition to whatever fees the scribes demanded.[105] The impact on the nuns' lives of these

English Monks and the Suppression of the Monasteries, pp. 182–86, 251–52; Gasquet, *Henry VIII and the English Monasteries*, pp. 447–51; Hodgett, "The Unpensioned Ex-religious," pp. 195–202; Knowles, *The Religious Orders*, vol. 3, pp. 389–92; Scarisbrick, "Henry VIII and the Dissolution of the Secular Colleges," pp. 51–66; S. Sheppard, "The Reformation and the Citizens of Norwich," *NA* 38 (1983), p. 47; and Woodward, *The Dissolution of the Monasteries*, pp. 147–49.

99 See above, pp. 196–7.
100 Baskerville, *English Monks and the Suppression of the Monasteries*, p. 189.
101 Baskerville, "Married Clergy," pp. 213–14, 211 for Westacre and Walsingham respectively.
102 Ibid., p. 212.
103 Margaret Bowker, "Henrician Reform and the Parish Clergy," in *The English Reformation Revised*, ed. Christopher Haigh (Cambridge, 1987), pp. 75–93: revenues thus earned were additional to the pensions received from the Crown, which were not forfeit when another position was taken.
104 G. A. J. Hodgett, *The State of the Ex-Religious and Former Chantry Priests of the Diocese of Lincoln, 1547–1572* (Lincoln Record Society, vol. 53, 1959), p. xvii.
105 Richardson, *A History of the Court of Augmentations*, pp. 178–79; Youings, "A Rare Survival," p. 227.

inadequate pensions was further exacerbated by the problem of arrears, and the cessation after 1552 of the pensioning of the ex-religious.[106] As we have seen, several nuns in the diocese who were pensioned lived past this date.

Post-Dissolution Life

Faced with little or no financial support the nuns had few options. While released from their vows of obedience and poverty, the women were still bound to their oath of chaste living until 1549.[107] Examples of ex-nuns who opted to marry despite their enduring vow of chastity are rare, and though some of the diocese's nuns may have married, there is no evidence to indicate when or to whom.[108]

Some of these displaced women could have counted on family support, as Claire Cross and Noreen Vickers have described for Yorkshire and Catherine Paxton has found in London.[109] But very few examples of this kind of support from friends or relatives exist for the nuns in the diocese of Norwich. Christopher Willoughby left 20s in 1498 to Dame Ann Eco of Bruisyard that "I promised her for term of her life now that she made her entry."[110] And Philip Calthorpe, Knight, bequeathed to Dorothy his daughter at the same abbey an annual rent of 40s for her life.[111] While some nuns, like Jane Drury, returned to families who could afford to support them for the rest of their lives, most of the ex-nuns were from families lower on the social scale for whom such a return was either not an option, or not an easily acceptable one.[112] Roger Gigges, for example, left his sister, Margaret, a nun at Blackborough, 20s "if she lives."[113]

---

[106] A. G. Dickens, "The Edwardian Arrears in Augmentation Payments and the Problems of the Ex-Religious," *EHR* 55 (1940), pp. 385, 388.

[107] The year the Statute of Six Articles was repealed under Edward VI.

[108] Name changes of course would make it difficult to track these women. For the rarity of these cases on a national level, see Dickens, "Edwardian Arrears," p. 407. For examples of those who did marry: Hodgett, *The State of the Ex-Religious*, pp. xix–xx for the diocese of Lincoln; Claire Cross and Noreen Vickers, *Monks, Friars, and Nuns in Sixteenth-Century Yorkshire* (The Yorkshire Archaeological Society, Record Series vol. 105, 1991 and 1992), pp. 540, 546, 561, 582, 593, 607; and Paxton, "The Nunneries of London," pp. 302–3.

[109] Cross and Vickers, *Monks, Friars, and Nuns*, pp. 539, 543–44, 545, 568, 570, 575, 581–82, 587, 590, 594, 597; and Paxton, "The Nunneries of London," pp. 305–06 but many of her examples are pre-1540.

[110] PRO, PCC Prob 11/11/35.

[111] NRO, NCC 197 Platfoote (1532).

[112] For Drury and nuns in other parts of England whose families could afford to provide to care for them, see above Chapter 2, pp. 55–60. See also: W. A. J. Archbold, *The Somerset Religious Houses* (Cambridge, 1892), p. 103 where he posits that since most nuns were "of good standing" they needed less help in their post-institutional lives than did monks.

[113] NRO, NCC 256–58 Attmere (1534).

His uncertainty about whether his sister was dead or alive indicates how removed the nuns could be from their natal families.

Without much financial support from the Crown and perhaps separated for too long from their families many of the diocese's nuns set up house on their own.[114] Some of the Flixton nuns purchased altar cloths and candlesticks; others bought featherbeds, coverletts, bolsters, and pillows; still another nun purchased "the stuff in the fraytor."[115] Grace Sampson bought all of the goods in Redlingfield's "new chamber" for 10s.[116]

Most of the diocese's ex-nuns had to find some means of support. Two ex-nuns from Campsey Ash, Isabella Norwich and Bridget Cocket, ran a school together in Dunwich.[117] Several other ex-nuns moved to towns, traditional magnets for the unemployed because of their greater economic opportunities.[118] In addition to Joan Dereham, ex-nun of Shouldham, who moved to the nearby town of King's Lynn, and Barbara Mason, last abbess of Marham, who lived out her remaining days in Bury St Edmunds, many ex-nuns moved to the city of Norwich, including the last prioress of Thetford, Elizabeth Hoth, and Ela Buttery, the last superior of Campsey Ash.[119]

Many of these women lived together in their new locations. At least three people whose wills were proved in the mid-1540s made bequests to ex-nuns of Carrow who were sharing quarters in the parish of St Peter Hungate: Cecily Suffield, last prioress of Carrow, Anne London, Joan Bond, and Agnes Swanton.[120] At least two of the ex-nuns of Shouldham, Joan Plomstead and Margaret Scorer, also continued to reside together in St Stephen's, Norwich.[121] Interestingly, these two parishes had been the sites of informal communities of religious women in the fifteenth century.[122] In addition, both Elizabeth Dawney and Ela Buttery left all of their belongings to fellow ex-nuns,

114 Paxton, "The Nunneries of London," pp. 304 and 309 for Sibyl Kirke, a nun of Kilburn Priory, who set up her own household, and for the goods of two former nuns, Margery Frauncys, a nun of Haliwell, and Elizabeth Rollesley, last prioress of St Helen's Bishopsgate, who bequeathed in their wills items they may have purchased from their priories when they were suppressed.

115 PRO, SP 5/1/110: the prioress Elizabeth Wright bought three altar cloths and three candlesticks; another nun bought a green silk vestment.

116 PRO, SP 5/3/133.

117 Thomas Roberts, mercer of Thetford, mentions in his will that these two ex-nuns rent a room from him there "where they keep school": NRO, NCC 520–521 Popy. I am grateful to Diarmaid MacCulloch for this reference.

118 Patten, "Patterns of Migration and Movement of Labour," passim.

119 PRO, E 178/3251 (Dereham); Baskerville, "Married Clergy," p. 210 (Hoth); ibid., p. 205 (Buttery and Mason); Tymms, Wills and Inventories, p. 133 (Mason also); and NRO, ANW burial registers for the parishes of St Clement, St Michael at Plea, and St Stephen's, passim.

120 These are: NRO, NCC 75 Wymer, the will of Thomas Waterman, priest (1546); NRO, NCC 75–77 Wymer, John Waterman, also a priest (1546); and NRO, NCC 169 Punting (1545), the will of Thomas Cappe. John Waterman bequeathed to Joan Bond his best feather bed, a pair of his best sheets, a fulson blanket, and three pillows.

121 Baskerville, "Married Clergy," p. 211.

122 Gilchrist and Oliva, Religious Women, pp. 71–2.

indicating that these women at least stayed in contact after the suppressions of their houses.[123]

Financial necessity certainly kept these and other nuns together and in contact after their houses had been closed, but a sense of community and identity with other women must also have influenced their continued existence together. Perhaps it was one of the only ways left to them to carry out any kind of religious life. The Reformation in England did not allow for any religious orders for women, thereby increasingly restricting them to the more isolated and secluded sphere of family.[124] Whether the ex-nuns of the diocese continued their daily monastic routine is not known, but their burial arrangements and testamentary requests – like bequests to high altars, and supplications for prayers for their souls and the souls of their friends – indicate that these women still adhered to the old doctrines of faith.[125]

Many of these ex-religious also maintained their singular status as nuns long after it would have meant anything. All but two of them refer to themselves as catholic or "late nun," or "sometime prioress" in their wills.[126] In 1553, Elizabeth Hoth referred to herself as "still a good catholic woman."[127] Two years later, Joan Plomstead, ex-nun of Shouldham, called herself the same with no other living than the 40s she received yearly from the Crown.[128] The number of bequests made to these ex-nuns by local testators in the 1540s indicates that their continued status as holy and religious women was recognized and publicly acknowledged by a wider audience.[129]

Ex-nuns in other parts of England evidenced a similar adherence to their monastic way of life, continuing to live together after their convents were shut down.[130] Both Elizabeth Shelly and Morpheta Kingsmill, ex-superiors of St

---

[123] Dawney's will is: NRO, NCC 47 Mayett (1539); Buttery's is: NRO, NCC 261 Hyll (1546).

[124] Harris, "A New Look at the Reformation," p. 90 touches on this aspect of the Reformation. Lyndal Roper, The Holy Household, Women and Morals, in Reformation Augsburg (Oxford, 1989) discusses this effect of the Reformation on women there. See also: Gerhild Williams, "The Woman/The Witch: Variations on a Sixteenth-Century Theme," in The Crannied Wall: Women, Religion and the Arts in Early Modern Europe, ed. Craig Monson (Ann Arbor, 1992), p. 2.

[125] Barbara Jermingham's will, printed in Fitch, Suffolk Monasteries, p. 235, is dated 1537; she was a nun at Campsey Ash. The will of Cecily Fastolf, last prioress of Bungay, is: NRO, NCC 131 Lyncolne; Grace Sampson's will is: NRO, NCC 235 Bircham, dated 1561; and the will of Barbara Mason, last abbess of Marham, is printed in: Tymms, Wills and Inventories, pp. 133–35. The will of Ela Buttery, last prioress of Campsey Ash, is: NRO, NCC 261 Hyll; and that of Jane Drury, who had been a nun at Bruisyard, is: NRO, NCC 93–94 Cooke. See Harris, "A New Look at the Reformation," p. 90 for aristocratic women's adherence to the traditional faith as well.

[126] The two who do not refer to themselves as ex-religious were Ela Buttery and Jane Drury.

[127] Baskerville, "Married Clergy," p. 211; and Blomefield, An Essay, vol. 2, p. 92.

[128] Ibid., vol. 7, p. 423.

[129] See for example in addition to those cited above: NRO, NCC 275–78 Mingay (1542); NRO, NCC 169 Punting (1545); NRO, NCC 51-2 Hyll (1537).

[130] Elizabeth Throckmorton, last abbess of Denny Abbey in Cambridge, returned to her

Mary's and Wherwell in Hampshire, were still residing in communities with several other ex-nuns from their houses.[131] And several more ex-religious remembered nuns from their communities in their wills.[132] Like their counterparts in the diocese of Norwich, these women demonstrated a lasting commitment to the beliefs and practices of catholicism and to their identities as nuns.[133]

The Devolution of Property

While the nuns slowly drop out of the written sources and so disappear from view, their monasteries' properties and buildings remained and were either temporarily leased or bought by members of the county or parish gentry.[134] The transfers to others of Bruisyard, Redlingfield, and Bungay have already been mentioned.[135] Though the lands and buildings of Marham Abbey were temporarily leased to Thomas Bukworth, Nicholas and Katherine Hare, who were responsible for pensioning the Bruisyard nuns, eventually bought both Bruisyard and Marham.[136] Anne, Lady Oxford, bid on Blackborough Priory, but the priory and its properties was leased to a local man for twenty-one years and then granted to the Bishop of Norwich.[137] Flixton Priory was leased in 1537 to Richard Warton, who had been the nuns' former steward; seven years later it went to John Tasburgh.[138] And the nuns' house at Thetford was leased for twenty-one years to Richard Fulsome before it was held by the Clere family.[139]

To a large degree, the status of these new owners mirrored the social ranks and local origins of the monasteries' original founders. Sir William Willoughby acquired Campsey Ash; Crabhouse went to Sir John Gage.[140] Carrow Priory

family's manor in Coughton with two of her fellow ex-nuns, where they continued to observe a religious lifestyle: VCH, *Cambridge*, vol. 2, pp. 301–2, and VCH, *Warwickshire*, vol. 3, p. 78. Cross and Vickers, *Monks, Friars, and Nuns*, pp. 527, 577, 592.

131 Coldicott, *Hampshire Nunneries*, pp. 143–44.

132 For other examples, see: Cross and Vickers, *Monks, Friars, and Nuns*, pp. 532–33, 535, 536, 537, 544, 560, 561, 584, 586, 588, 593, 595–96; Hodgett, "The State of the Ex-religious," passim; and Paxton, "The Nunneries of London," pp. 308–9.

133 Coldicott, *Hampshire Nunneries*, pp. 143–44; Cross, "Women in Sixteenth-Century Yorkshire," p. 309; Paxton, "The Nunneries of London," pp. 307–08.

134 For the status of some of these new owners, see: T. H. Swales, "The Redistribution of Monastic Lands in Norfolk at the Dissolution," NA 34 (1966), pp. 14–44.

135 See above, p. 195 for Bruisyard and Bungay; and VCH, *Suffolk*, vol. 2, p. 82 (Bungay); ibid., p. 84 (Redlingfield); and ibid., p. 307 (Flixton).

136 Nichols, "The History and Cartulary," pp. 216–17 and VCH, *Suffolk*, vol. 2, p. 132.

137 VCH, *Norfolk*, vol. 2, p. 351.

138 VCH, *Suffolk*, vol. 2, p. 117, and Diarmaid MacCulloch, *Suffolk and the Tudors*, pp. 66, 74.

139 Dugdale, *Monasticon*, vol. 4, p. 476.

140 Taylor, *Notitia Monastica*, p. 523 (Campsey Ash); Dugdale, *Monasticon*, vol. 6, p. 570 (Crabhouse).

was granted upon its suppression to John Shelton, esq., of Norfolk;[141] and Shouldham Priory stayed in the King's hands until 1553 when it was sold to Thomas Mildmay, one of the county commissioners who had visited and reported on the state of the diocese's monasteries in 1535.[142]

In addition to Bruisyard Abbey, two other sites became important recusant centers later in the sixteenth century. Edmund Bedingfield, who, as we have seen, bought Redlingfield, not only allowed Grace Sampson to continue to live in the priory, but his family also sheltered a number of other ex-nuns and monks in manors at Denham and Oxborough, the family's main seat.[143] And John Tasburgh, who acquired the lease of Flixton in 1544, supported a small community of ex-monks who lived in the nuns' priests' quarters.[144] Perhaps some of the nuns remained close by as well. Though these later incarnations reflected the new owners' religious views, and while other secular households also served as sanctuaries for recusants, that these three houses did so suggests a recognition factor for people who capitalized on the convents' established reputation as holy and catholic houses.

The Social Impact of the Dissolution

The closure of these houses seems to have met little resistance in the diocese. A plot to rebel against the closures failed to effect any changes or draw the type of attention that the Pilgrimage of Grace did in the north.[145] These smaller houses would have been more important to local people than to those of greater social and political prominence who perhaps could have been more effective in fighting for the monasteries' continued existence.[146] Indeed, it has recently been pointed out that because many of the smaller houses in the diocese lacked strong patrons who were willing to fight for them no resistance was offered at all.[147] In any case, those powerful enough to have led any opposition were the very ones who stood to gain from the acquisition of monastic property.[148]

---

141 VCH, Norfolk, vol. 2, p. 354; see also Swales, "The Redistribution of Monastic Lands," p. 24.
142 VCH, Norfolk, vol. 2, p. 414.
143 See above, p. 196 and also Diarmaid MacCulloch, "Catholic and Puritan in Elizabethan Suffolk," Archiv für Reformationsgeschichte 72 (1981), pp. 249, 252; the other ex-nun was Susan Silvarde, formerly of Barking Abbey in Essex, who died in 1568; see also MacCulloch, Suffolk and the Tudors, p. 174, n. 71, and PRO 178/3251.
144 J. W. Wilton, Monastic Life in Norfolk and Suffolk (Norfolk, 1980), p. 54.
145 T. H. Swales, "Opposition to the Suppression of the Norfolk Monasteries, Expressions of Discontent, The Walsingham Conspiracy," NA 33:3 (1964), pp. 254–65.
146 MacCulloch, Suffolk and the Tudors, p. 20 agrees.
147 Thompson, "Monasteries and their Patrons," pp. 119–22.
148 MacCulloch, Suffolk and the Tudors, passim; Swales, "The Redistribution of Monastic Lands," passim. For the situation elsewhere see: G. A. J. Hodgett, "The Dissolution of Religious Houses in Lincolnshire and the Changing Structures of Society," Lincolnshire Architecture and Archaeology, Society Reports and Papers 4 (1951), pp. 83–99.

The impact on local people who relied on the convents for the services the nuns provided can only be imagined. Workers' anxieties about unemployment and increased entry fines to leases with new landlords were very vocally expressed, especially in the more isolated rural places like Blackborough and Crabhouse.[149] Though most of those employed by the nuns did receive severance pay when the houses were closed, the suppressions caused many people to be at least temporarily out of work.[150] Tenants may have had similar fears.

The poor and indigent who had been cared for by the nuns were forced to seek alms of food and clothing elsewhere in the diocese; the children who had been educated by the nuns had to go elsewhere too. The loss of these services was an especially troubling issue for contemporaries throughout the country.[151] Though responsibility for these services fell on the surviving parish churches and chantries, priests and parishioners complained at these added burdens.[152]

The psychological effects on the parishioners who had worshipped in the convents' churches and marked their calendars by rituals facilitated by the nuns can never be quantified. Nor can the absence of one of the social mechanisms by which a yeoman farmer or parish gentry family could enhance their local reputation and status by having one of their daughters enter one of these convents as a nun.[153] But while these things cannot be clearly demonstrated, there is no doubt that these small houses were intricately linked with their local communities in ways which were crucial to the lives of those who partook in the various services and who relied on the nuns and the efficacy of their prayers. Though never as wealthy or politically prominent as many of their male counterparts, the female monasteries were nevertheless important features of the local landscape.

We should perhaps not be surprised that their passing did not create the kinds of events that reach down in history. Founded mostly by local people who endowed these religious houses with small and localized properties, the history of these convents is one of quiet houses of prayer where monastic

---

149 Swales, "Opposition to the Suppression," passim; and Blomefield, An Essay, vol. 9, p. 32 (Blackborough); ibid., p. 167 for Crabhouse; Jessopp, "The Norfolk Monasteries," passim for the servants and hinds with no other means of support.

150 PRO, SP 5/3/29; PRO, SP 5/3/116; PRO, SP 5/4/140; and PRO, E 101/631/26 for the one-time awards of money.

151 J. Ayer, ed., The Catechism of Thomas Becon (Cambridge, 1884), pp. 376–77; Blomefield, An Essay, vol. 4, p. 528; Francis Gasquet, "Overlooked Testimonies to the Character of the English Monasteries on the Eve of the Suppression," Dublin Review 114 (1894), pp. 245–77; and Simon, Education and Society, pp. 180–82.

152 Jordan, Philanthropy in England, p. 80 and passim; Kreider, English Chantries, passim; J. J. Scarisbrick, The Reformation and the English People (Oxford, 1984), pp. 92, 111–13, and passim.

153 Bynum, "Religious Women in the Later Middle Ages," p. 124 suggests that the members of the tertiary groups and beguinages in the thirteenth century came from sectors of society which were ascending the social scale. She suggests that perhaps the prestige of having religious daughters somewhat allayed their anxieties about their rising wealth and status by legitimizing their new positions.

personnel led the lives to which they were vowed. Their lower social and cultural profiles to a certain extent make them difficult to study, and make their houses the kinds of institutions which rarely attract the attention that the larger, wealthier, and more publicly visible male monasteries do. Nevertheless, the female monastics and their convents in the diocese of Norwich reveal a great deal about religious life for women in the later Middle Ages and the effects they had on those around them.

Conclusion

Most of the eleven female houses in the diocese of Norwich were small and relatively poor, founded by local people whose social status ranged from gentry and noble women and men, to a bishop and king. Regardless of their social status, however, founders tended to endow their foundations with a few local manors, except in the cases of Campsey Ash and Shouldham priories, whose more elite founders invested their monasteries with more extensive properties. The middling social status of most of the convents' founders and the local properties with which they were endowed firmly established these as local gentry foundations, with shared architectural features, such as moated precincts and courtyard layouts.

Four of the convents were sited in the poor and sparsely populated western fens of the county of Norfolk; three in the more populous and wealthier area of High Suffolk; two in small market towns, and two outside the town walls of the cities of Norwich and Thetford. These geographic locations were liminal, marginal spaces perfect for the establishment of a community of religious who, while ministering to the needs of others, spent most of their lives in daily rounds of communal prayer and private meditation and reading.

Though the convents did acquire other properties throughout their histories, their original endowments and geographical locations to a certain extent prescribed their revenues, keeping these houses relatively poor, isolated, and locally focused. And while poverty and isolation are usually seen as negative attributes of female religious life, theoretically at least, they were very much in keeping with the Rule of St Benedict and his monastic ideal. As such, it is very likely that these qualities were conscious considerations for founders, and actively pursued by the nuns who lived in these female religious houses.

The identification of many of the diocese's convents with local founders of lesser social status is further reflected in the social rank of most of the monasteries' nuns. Like several of their founders, the vast majority of the diocese's nuns were from parish gentry families, most of whom lived within a five to ten mile radius of the convent their family members chose to enter. Novices had to exhibit certain qualities to be accepted by a community – legitimacy of birth, and the ability to read or to learn to do so – and usually entered a convent with personal items like clothing, bedding, and eating utensils. While novices usually also were required to give the community a gift of money, the amounts were reasonable and affordable for the parish gentry women who entered, and at least two of the convents set aside funds to provide the dress, bedding, and other items for novices who could not afford them.

After a year's probation, which included learning the round of the Divine Office and the prayers and rituals particular to each house, novices could take their vows of poverty, chastity, and obedience. Their profession ceremony, presided over by the bishop, signaled their permanent retreat from the temporal world and acceptance into the cloistered one of their fellow sisters. Though their days focused on the daily offices of prayer, times were also set aside for private meditation and reading. The number of books owned by both the convents and individual nuns, and the existence of libraries in at least three of the houses indicate that many of these nuns could and did read.

Their lives were not, however, completely devoted to communal prayer and individual spiritual exercises. The convents' limited sources of income and their ever-changing populations of boarders and guests meant that the nuns had to be vigilant stewards of their finances, and skilled administrators of their monastic households. While a superior was ultimately responsible for the operation of her community, she was helped by any number of household officers, or obedientiaries, whose duties varied in complexity from procuring enough food and drink, as a cellarer did, to ensuring that bedding supplies were sufficient for all of the nuns and their many overnight guests, as a chamberer did, to caring for the priest's vestments and church furnishings, as the sacristan did. The daily tasks entailed in these offices gave the obedientiaries a certain flexibility in their daily routine of prayer, including the right to leave their precincts to negotiate business on their monastery's behalf.

A hierarchy of household offices appears to have existed in these convents whereby nuns could acquire and hone administrative talents, which were recognized and rewarded by assignments to higher status positions with more responsibilities and greater prestige. This career ladder indicates that access to monastic office was based on merit, not on social status.

In household administration the nuns were for the most part very successful, and there is little evidence of the kinds of administrative irregularities that often resulted from inept management. While at a few houses nuns occasionally had to double up on monastic offices, communal eating and sleeping quarters were maintained, yearly accounts were usually produced – in oral if not written form – and the officers' accounts which survive indicate that they kept journals or ledgers wherein weekly income and expenses were noted.

The nuns' success as household managers can best be seen in their houses' finances. Most of the convents, though not well-endowed from the start, were nevertheless able to operate without the crushing weight of chronic debt. Though Marham and Carrow had some tough times, only Blackborough, Redlingfield, and Thetford were in debt at the time of the Dissolution, and only Redlingfield appears to have suffered chronically; the other two, like most of the rest of the diocese's female monasteries, seem to have alternated between periods of solvency and debt. In times of economic stress the nuns adopted the same kinds of estate management strategies as did secular landholders who were faced with similar fluctuations in tenant population, rising wages, and falling grain prices.

While responsibility for their estates and household management rested solely with the nuns, they employed staffs of priests, household servants, and agricultural laborers who helped. All of these people were paid wages, but many also received food and board, like the priests who conducted religious services, and seasonal laborers who usually lived in the precincts during peak times of sowing and harvest. Though clearly separated from the nuns' cloistered world, these staff members were nevertheless part of the greater monastic household, and often participated in the masses and other services which were carried out in the nuns' churches and chapels.

These staff members not only helped with the nuns' housekeeping and agricultural tasks: servants and hinds also aided the nuns in their duties to others. In keeping with the Rule of St Benedict, which informed the spirit of all of these monastic communities, the nuns were to provide for the poor and needy, and extend hospitality to strangers and patrons alike. The nuns executed these duties in several ways: they gave daily and occasional alms to the poor, extended the use of their churches to local parishioners, witnessed and executed wills, buried people in conventual chapels and cemeteries, and said intercessory prayers for the repose of testators' souls. These activities intimately bound the nuns to their local communities, and such services also helped to attract the patronage of local people.

Though popes, kings, and some members of the counties' nobility and upper gentry granted exemptions from taxes and gave grants of land, patronage by members of these elite groups was limited to the fourteenth century. Patronage by parish gentry and yeoman farmers, however, was significantly greater, more frequent and more consistent. While testators overwhelmingly favored friars as beneficiaries of their bequests, local people gave significantly more to the nuns than they did to monks or canons. This sustained patronage by local testators – whose social status mirrored that of the vast majority of nuns, and many of the convents' founders – reflected the nuns' commitment to them, signaled a public acknowledgement of that commitment, and demonstrates that these small and generally poor houses were vital and active institutions right up to the Dissolution.

The quality of religious life at the female houses in the diocese appears to have been high, and suggests a population of nuns generally well-suited to their vocations. While the spiritual and emotional fulfillment of their lives can only be deduced, the episcopal visitations tell us about a few scandals: an unfit prioress and a few nuns who had children, women who found monastic life difficult or impossible. Other examples of distress include Katherine de Monte Acuto who fled Bungay Priory in the mid-fourteenth century, and was "vagabond in secular attire in diverse parts of the realm."[1] And Alice Tuddenham, born Wodehouse, fled an unhappy marriage and became a nun at Crabhouse sometime before 1429.[2] She was a nun there some forty-three years later "still

---

[1]   CPR, 1374–77, p. 490 for the King's order for her arrest and delivery to the prioress. This incident is also in: J. J. Raven, "The Ecclesiastical Remains of Bungay," PSIA 4 (1874), p. 70. Raven mistakenly refers to Monte Acuto as the prioress.

[2]   Alice married Thomas Tuddenham in 1418 and remained with him until 1425. She gave

doing penance."[3] Her adjustment to convent life may never have been a happy one, though a tenure of forty-three years is hard to dismiss as intolerable. These few instances of scandal and profligate nuns are the only ones known to have occurred in these eleven convents in the 190 years covered in this study.

In many significant ways, the female monasteries in the diocese of Norwich were representative of convents located elsewhere in England. Many were founded by women of middling social rank who endowed their houses in marginal areas with small local estates. Though variations existed, the monastic populations of several convents in other dioceses were local women of gentry status. And scholars have recently discovered that nuns elsewhere were also adept managers of their estates and households, who marshalled together their resources and gifts of money, land, and goods from patrons to operate their houses. Similarities such as isolated geographic locations, small endowments that helped to keep the convents relatively poor, and the inherent necessity to rely on the support of outsiders suggest the parameters of a specifically female monastic piety.

These characteristics of female monasteries stand in stark contrast to how male religious houses functioned, indicating that gender made a difference between female and male monastic life in the later Middle Ages. Male houses, for example, tended to be founded by people of significantly higher social status with extensive lands, making these foundations larger and wealthier than the convents of nuns. More numerous and larger estates helped to make the male religious and their houses more prestigious and more susceptible to the kinds of territorial disputes that often embroiled secular lords with similarly large holdings. These characteristics of male monastic foundations combined with the exclusive rights of the male religious to perform the sacraments to give monks and canons greater public visibility and higher prestige.

Their superior status, however, compromised the quality of life in many of the diocese's male religious communities and appealed significantly more to society's most elite groups than to the local parishioners with whom the nuns were more popular. Scandals involving superiors who stole from their priories' treasuries to outfit their mistresses, monks who squandered their houses' resources on drinking and gambling, and canons who neglected the needs of the poor and of local parishioners were considerably more common among the male religious in the diocese than among the houses of nuns.

To a certain extent, the monks' and canons' greater wealth allowed for these and other abuses which were addressed repeatedly by provincial chapters and bishops, and by Parliament and the Crown. With greater resources there was

birth to a daughter whose father was apparently not Thomas, but Alice's father's chamberlain. Sometime between 1425 and 1429 she made her profession at Crabhouse. For the details of her divorce case, see: Roger Virgoe, "The Divorce of Sir Thomas Tuddenham," NA 34:4 (1969), pp. 406–19.

3   See NRO, NCC 122–5 Gelour for the will of Thomas's sister, Margaret Bedingfield; she bequeathed Alice 10 marks in 1472. Power, Medieval English Nunneries, p. 30 recounts this story as well. See also: NRO, BL vi b (viii).

more to spend, more potentially to give to the poor, more theoretically to relieve the male religious of the burdens and distractions of poverty, more also to tempt and divert. Defrauding alms to the poor and frittering away revenues which precipitated heavy debt go a long way to explain why the monks and canons fared so badly with local testators whose perceptions of male monastic life were undoubtedly colored by these and other problems.

While these difficulties discouraged the patronage of local people, the male houses were nevertheless able to garner the goodwill and largesse of society's most prestigious groups. Their bias in favor of the monks and canons reflected the patriarchies of both medieval society and the Church which accorded men a higher status and greater authority than women. Members of royalty and the aristocracy would of course want to be associated with the male religious for the prestige such connections could bring, but also for their shared interests and concerns.

Just as in secular society, the generally lower status accorded women by both temporal and ecclesiastical powers had a definite impact on the female religious houses and the lives of nuns. But did they internalize this bias? Penelope Johnson has found in the writings of Hildegard of Bingen and Heloise of the Paraclete, as well as in ordinary administrative documents, that regardless of the Church's negative views of women, nuns in early medieval northern France were very conscious of their elevated status as holy women, particularly in comparison to the status of secular women.[4] Other historians have observed the same positivity: Merry Wiesner found, for example, that German nuns openly expressed their opinions on religious matters and thought of themselves as belonging to a special group.[5] And both Caroline Walker Bynum and Mary Perry have criticized the assumption that nuns internalized the misogyny of the Church, or were oppressed by the controlling patriarchal order.[6] Perry in particular emphasizes the ways religious women "empowered themselves through community, chastity, enclosure, and mystical experiences."[7] Finally, Yvonne Parry and John Tillotson have shown nuns' use of their own agency in embracing and determining the parameters of their own religious lives.[8]

It is also possible that nuns were held in higher esteem than monks, canons,

---

4 Penelope Johnson, "*Mulier et Monialis*: The Medieval Nun's Self-Image," *Thought* 64:254 (1989), pp. 242–53.

5 Merry Wiesner, "Nuns, Wives, and Mothers: Women and the Reformation in Germany," in *Women in Reformation and Counter Reformation Europe: Private and Public Worlds*, ed. Sherrin Marshall (Bloomington, 1989), p. 26.

6 Bynum, "Religious Women," p. 136 warns against assuming that nuns and other holy women internalized the misogyny of the Church. See also: Mary Elizabeth Perry, *Gender and Disorder in Early Modern Seville* (Princeton, 1990).

7 Ibid., p. 4.

8 Parry, " 'Devoted disciples of Christ'," passim for the nuns at Amesbury requesting and acquiring a translation of the Rule of St Benedict so they could more fully follow its precepts. Tillotson, "Visitation and Reform," esp. pp. 3, 20 for nuns' resistance to certain rules and injunctions, and how their resistance to enclosure affected bishops' enforcement of it.

or other male religious because the female monastics had greater obstacles to overcome in their pursuit of a religious life. That is, women were perceived by Church and society to have more carnal natures which thus rendered them more susceptible to evil and easier prey to lust than men, whose carnal desires were inherently less problematic. Having more to conquer – and doing so successfully – nuns may have been considered to be holier and more worthy of people's respect and patronage.

Though we do not have writings like those of Heloise or Hildegard, all of the ex-nuns in the diocese of Norwich whose wills survive, except for Cecily Fastolf, refer to themselves as ex-prioresses and ex-nuns, suggesting that their religious status was still strong and positive ten and twelve years after their identity as religious women ceased to signify anything to the society in which they lived.[9] Their burial requests, as well as the gifts they made to high altars, statues, and lights, confirm their positive identifications as remnants of and loyalists to a papist Church which was decidedly out of favor by the time they drew up their wills.

Other nuns in the diocese shared this very conscious adherence to their status as religious women despite the shifting winds of doctrine in sixteenth-century England. When submitting her pension request in 1553, Elizabeth Hoth, last prioress of Thetford, referred to herself as "still a good catholic woman."[10] Two years later in 1555, Joan Plomstead, an ex-nun of Shouldham, called herself "a good catholic woman," with no living other than the 40s she received yearly from the Crown.[11] If these nuns had not had positive and lasting self-images as nuns in the first place, it seems unlikely that they would have clung so tenaciously to them so many years after the fact. And though several of these women remained together after their houses were suppressed, mere institutionalization would not explain their persistent self-images.[12] Their singular status as nuns after the Dissolution was reinforced by the likes of Thomas Godsalve, the elder of Norwich who, in 1542, left 40s a year to Katherine Bloomfield, "sometime nun of Campsey . . . whom I esteem to be a woman of much virtue and honeste desiring her honestely to pray for me."[13]

As a Bride of Christ, a nun's special status began with her profession, after which a positive self-image was reinforced throughout her life as one whose prayers were sought for intercession and whose acts of charity were especially valued by society. A nun's special status encompassed more, however, than these personal and spiritual benefits. Her self-worth was further cultivated and nurtured by the administrative talents numerous nuns showed as officeholders in whose hands the financial welfare and smooth running of their convents rested.

---

[9] For their wills, see above pp. 59, 105–6.
[10] Baskerville, "Married Clergy," p. 211; and Blomefield, An Essay, vol. 2, p. 92.
[11] Ibid., vol. 7, p. 423.
[12] For the Dissolution and the fates of the nuns thereafter, see Chapter 7 of this book.
[13] NRO, NCC 275–78 Mingay.

Appendix 1: Sources and Methodology

This study of late medieval English nuns relies to a great extent on identifying individuals in the diocese of Norwich in the later Middle Ages. Knowing their names and then finding out as much about them as possible then allowed me to calculate their numbers, estimate their ages, and determine their social backgrounds. This prosopographical method of analysis relied on a variety of both published and unpublished material. While some of these sources are discussed in chapters in this book, it is worthwhile to discuss some of the problems with the sources, and how I compensated for them.

The most obvious place to look for nuns is in bishops' registers, which usually include profession lists and visitation records. Unfortunately, these were not included in registers of the bishops of Norwich, which are filled mostly with institution lists of male clerics. Records of episcopal visitations are extant, however, between 1492 and 1532, and they do include the names of nuns in most of the convents.

Because I wanted to identify the nuns between 1350 and the Dissolution, the visitation records are good only for the end of the period. Luckily, the Poll Tax lists of the early 1380s (PRO, E 179/45/5b) exist, which allowed me to identify most of the nuns in most of the convents between 1350 and 1400. For the years 1400–1450, I had to rely on a combination of papal letters (*Calendar of Entries in the Papal Registers Relating to England and Ireland: Papal Letters* (1904), vol. 6, p. 468); miscellaneous documents from the convents themselves, like SRO, HA/12/B2/18/14; the episcopal visitations of the Bishop of Lincoln (A. H. Thompson, ed., *The Visitations of the Religious Houses in the Diocese of Lincoln* (1927), pp. 413–17); and various charters, pedigrees, heraldic visitations, and wills. To identify the nuns who lived between 1450 and 1532, I utilized *Visitations of the Diocese of Norwich, 1492–1532*, ed. Augustus Jessopp (1888); PRO, E 101/76/29, and E 117/14/22; NRO, Hare 2209 194x5, 211 194x5, 2212 194x5; and SRO, ASF IC/AA2/5/29.

In addition to these, I also found many nuns listed in various royal documents, like the IPM, CCR, and CPR, and these were supplemented by both published and unpublished heraldic visitations and family pedigrees. These were potentially doubly helpful for the family ties pedigrees could establish, which would help me to identify family members and nuns' social backgrounds and geographic origins.[1]

---

[1] I consulted the following: Arthur Campling, *East Anglian Pedigrees*, pt. 1 (Norfolk Record Society, 13, 1940); Arthur Campling, *East Anglian Pedigrees*, pt. 2 (Harleian Society, vol. 97, 1945); A. W. Hughes Clarke and Arthur Campling, eds., *The Visitation of Norfolk Made A.D. 1664 by Sir Edmund Bysshe, Knt., Clarenceaux King of Arms*, vol. 1, A–L

Heraldic visitations and family pedigrees presented several problems: they focused on the later period, daughters were often not named, or sometimes not mentioned at all, and these records are good for members of prominent families, but not for those lower on the social scale. As I quickly discovered, most of the diocese's nuns were not from families with extensive pedigrees likely to be included in heraldic visitations so I had to look elsewhere for nuns and their families.

By far the most forthcoming sources for identifying nuns and establishing their social rank were wills, especially those registered in the Norwich Consistory Court. These wills, and those enrolled in the probate courts of the diocese's four archdeaconry courts in the counties of Norfolk and Suffolk, not only allowed me to know the names of nuns from lower social groups – who turned out to be the majority – because siblings and parents usually named their beneficiaries, but the wills also compensated for the date problem raised in the episcopal and heraldic visitations. The earliest NCC register includes wills primarily from parish gentry testators, dated from 1370 to 1383; these and those from all of the subsequent NCC registers allowed me to fill in the time gaps I encountered from the sources mentioned above.

The archdeaconry will registers start much later, but also helped to fill in some of the empty time periods. The wills registered in these courts dated from the 1430s onwards; not only did they help identify nuns in the fifteenth century, but they also represented a social group – the yeoman farmers – which has not previously been seen as one from which nuns came.

Wills also helped to redress the other problem I encountered with the sources, that some of the convents are better documented than others so that identities of the nuns who lived at Bruisyard, Marham, and Shouldham, for example, are much more difficult to ascertain. Among the diocese's female

(Norfolk Record Society, 4, 1934), pt. 2, M–Z (Norfolk Record Society, 5, 1934); G. H. Dashwood, *Viscomites Norfolciae or Sheriffs of Norfolk from the First Year of Henry II, to the Fourth Year of Queen Victoria, Inclusive* (Stow Bardolf, 1843); Hamon Le Strange, *Norfolk Official Lists from the Earliest Period to the Present Day* (Norwich, 1895); Alfred William Morant, *Pedigrees of Norfolk Families* (Norwich, 1870); Anthony Norris, compiler, *A Collection of Pedigrees of Norfolk Families, Digested in Alphabetical Order, and Compiled from the Most Authentic Public Evidences, Wills, Records, Title Deeds, and Monuments* (MSS, Coleman Library, Norfolk Central Library, n.d.); P. Palgrave-Moore and Michael Sawyer, *A Selection of Revised and Unpublished Norfolk Pedigrees* (Norfolk Genealogy, vols. 6, 8, 13, 17, 1974–85); Walter Rye, *Norfolk Families* (Norwich, 1911–13); Walter Rye, *The Visitation of Norfolk, Made and Taken by William Hervey, Clarenceaux King of Arms, Anno 1563* (Harleian Society, vol. 32, 1891). The Suffolk heraldic visitations include: Joan Corder, ed., *The Visitation of Suffolk, 1561* (Harleian Society, n.s. vols. 2–3, 1981); Joseph Jackson Howard, ed., *The Visitation of Suffolke, Made by William Hervey, Clarenceaux King of Arms, 1561, with Additions from Family Documents, Original Wills, Jermyn, Davy and Other Manuscripts*, 2 vols. (Lowestoft, 1866–1876); Walter Metcalf, *The Visitations of Suffolk Made by Hervey, Clarenceaux, 1561, Cook, Clarenceaux, 1577, and Raven Richmond Herald, 1612* (Exeter, 1882); Joseph Muskett, *Suffolk Manorial Families Being County Visitations and Other Pedigrees*, 3 vols. (Exeter, 1900).

houses, those in the county of Norfolk tend to be better referenced than those in the county of Suffolk. In large part this is due to the abundance of antiquarian works which were carried out in Norfolk, but household accounts are also extant for Blackborough, Carrow, and Marham, which add a great deal of information about these two houses in particular. For convents in Suffolk, a handful of accounts survive for Bungay, Campsey Ash, and Redlingfield, but information about the diocese's five other convents is scattered among charters and miscellaneous royal records.

While clearly not all of the diocese's nuns have been or can be identified, the combination of the above sources allowed me to retrieve the names of 553 who lived between 1350 and 1540. From these I was able to calculate the total female monastic population in the diocese, and determine the social backgrounds of most of the nuns.

Appendix 2: Calculating Numbers of Nuns

In addition to wanting to identify the nuns in the diocese, I wanted to estimate how many there were between 1350 and 1540, to see fluctuations in the number of nuns over time, to assess which convents were most popular with recruits, and, finally, to gage how representative my findings of social rank and geographic origins of individual nuns might have been for the greater female monastic population.

Because we do not have profession lists, which list the names of novices who entered a convent, we do not have the kind of ready information that would tell us how many nuns lived in the diocese. In order to calculate how many nuns there were, and how long they lived as nuns, I had to organize data collected from a variety of sources and extrapolate from that data.

For some nuns, calculating how long they had lived as such was easy because they had given this information to the bishop. For others, however, I had to rely on information culled from a variety of other documents. I created a database with all of the nuns' names and every time they appeared in a source; by sorting by date I could see over how many years a nun appeared in the sources and then make a conservative estimate of how many years she lived as a nun. I termed the number of years a woman lived as a nun 'nun years'. This quantification revealed 193 nuns – 35 percent of the 553 nuns known by name – whose monastic careers I could track over various lengths of time.

The average number of 'nun years' was calculated by adding up the tenures of the 193 nuns for whom this information is available, which equals 4,913, and then dividing that number by 193, which equals 25.4 years. The average length of time a woman was a nun between 1350 and 1540 was thus 25 years. The nuns' tenures can be broken down into three separate periods of time, thus allowing us to see changes over time. The tenures of 43 nuns are known for the fourteenth century, and their tenures total 1,205 years; divide that figure by 43 and the average 'nun years' for the fourteenth century comes to 28 years. Making the same calculations for the fifteenth and sixteenth centuries: 92 nuns' tenures in the fifteenth century total 2,738 years, which divided by 92 gives an average of 30 'nun years' in that century; totaling the years of the 58 nuns whose tenures are known in the sixteenth century comes to 970, which divided by 58 gives an average of 16.7 'nun years' in that century.

Estimating 'nun years' was only part of the solution to the problem of calculating the total population of nuns in the diocese. I also needed to know how many nuns were in each of the eleven convents. Sorting the database by name of convent made it possible for me to count the number of nuns who lived in each of the eleven convents at fifty-year intervals, 1350–1400, 1400–1450, 1450–1500, and 1500–1540. (See Table 3 in the text of this book.)

Table 19. Calculations for the Total Population of Nuns
in the Diocese of Norwich, 1350–1540

Monastery	Average Number of Nuns	x 190	÷ 25	Total Nun Population	Number Known (No.)	%
Blackborough	8.5	1615	64.6	64.6	(34)	54
Bruisyard	15.5	2945	117.8	117.8	(62)	53
Bungay	12.5	2375	95	95	(50)	53
Campsey Ash	20	3800	152	152	(81)	53
Carrow	21	3990	159.6	159.6	(85)	53
Crabhouse	8	1520	60.8	60.8	(32)	53
Flixton	11	2090	83.6	83.6	(44)	53
Marham	11	2090	83.6	83.6	(44)	53
Redlingfield	9.5	1805	74	74	(38)	51
Shouldham	10	1900	76	76	(41)	54
Thetford	10.5	1995	79.8	79.8	(42)	53
TOTAL				1046.8	(553)	53

By averaging the four numbers thus calculated for each house, I could estimate the number of nuns who lived in each of the houses at any one time during the 190 years covered in this study. So, for example, I estimated that the average number of nuns at Blackborough at any one time between 1350 and 1540 was 8.5.

Having calculated the average number of nuns per house for the 190-year period, and the average 'nun years' of a nun at 25, I could then figure the total population of nuns in the diocese. Table 19 shows these calculations. By multiplying the average monastic population for a house by 190 – the number of years covered in this study – and then dividing the sum by 25 – a nun's average 'nun years' – and then adding those eleven figures, I estimate that the total number of nuns in the diocese was at least 1,046. Of these I can identify 553 (53 percent) by name.

Appendix 3: Prosopographical Analysis

Prosopography is the study of a specific group of people. By accumulating and analyzing biographical data on the people involved in a particular institution or historical event, rather than focusing on the constitutional or legal frameworks within which the institutions existed or events occurred, historians can achieve a richer understanding of the institution to which the group belonged or the event in which they participated. Utilizing the extraordinary records which survive for the cathedral chapters of Durham and York, R. B. Dobson was able to present personal profiles of the monks and canons who populated these religious houses. The profiles included geographic and family backgrounds, social status, and the average amount of time any one of these men lived as a religious or prebendary throughout the later Middle Ages.[1] Such a study tells us a great deal about a priory's recruitment patterns and the social origins of its novices. A similar prosopographical analysis was carried out in the 1960s by G. A. J. Hodgett who compiled the names and careers of the male ex-religious from Elizabethan pension lists and found that male clerical careers continued – and in fact flourished – after the Dissolution of the monasteries. This knowledge added a useful corrective to previously held views of the effects of the Dissolution on the male clergy, which saw them as poor victims of government policy.[2]

Prosopographical analysis has advantages and limitations. Among its positive attributes is that it allows historians to discern specific patterns (in social status and geographic origins, for example) in a group of people whose association in a particular institution often disguises important differences among them. Identifying these differences often facilitates a better understanding of the institution to which the people belonged, for example, by exposing recruitment patterns. A prosopographical analysis can also provide insights into the nuanced distinctions among social groups, and into the mechanisms by which they attained recognition in society. Such a study also can reveal important changes over time.

Limitations to this type of inquiry, especially for the medieval period, concern the biased nature of extant sources, which are most plentiful for society's elites, the aristocracy and upper gentry. Groups of lesser social rank tend to be left out of these inquiries, giving a lop-sided view of a particular event or institution because the more visible elite people tend to be seen by historians who study them as the norm. Historians' insistence that all medieval

---

[1] Dobson, "University Graduates," passim.
[2] G. A. J. Hodgett, "The Unpensioned Ex-religious in Tudor England," *Journal of Ecclesiastical History* 13 (1962).

nuns were from the aristocracy is a case in point. By focusing exclusively on the wills of society's elite, for example, Power and those who followed her identified medieval nuns as solely from the upper ranks of society. When historians generalized from this small group of women to comment on the entire population of female religious in the later Middle Ages this identification became problematical as it distorted our notion of the social composition of the female monasteries. The elevated social group, though atypical from the start – because of their high visibility in the sources – then became the typical group who inhabited female convents.

These problems can be overcome by widening the source basis of the analysis to include a variety of sources, as has been done for this prosopograhical study of the nuns of the diocese of Norwich who lived between 1350 and 1540. Sources such as the wills of the lesser gentry and yeoman farmer groups have broadened this analysis and counteracted the lop-sided dependence on the more plentiful records of society's elite. The results of this examination reveal that, contrary to what historians have held about late medieval nuns, most of them were not from the ranks of the elite; rather a majority of them – 64 percent – came from families of the parish gentry, many of whom lived close to the convents they entered. This preponderance of nuns from the middling ranks of medieval Norfolk and Suffolk society goes far in explaining the convents' limited financial status as well as their lower visibility in the sources and in the history of their times. The prosopographical analysis also reveals that the recruits to medieval convents changed over time. Anglo-Saxon female houses as well as many of the Norman foundations for the female religious appear to have been populated exclusively by women from the upper social ranks.

Family Background and Social Rank

To place a nun in her familial context I constructed another database, using PC File+, entitled LOCFAMS. Using NORWNUNS sorted by names of nuns as a guide, several sources were searched to try to match a nun's surname with others who had the same last name and who therefore might be related to her. In constructing LOCFAMS the most useful sources were: PCC, NCC, ANF, ANW, ASD, ASF will registers, *Inquisitions Post Mortem*, heraldic visitations, pedigrees, and local genealogical works, Parliamentary registers, lists of county and parish officeholders, lay subsidy lists, muster rolls, surname studies, and *Calendar of Fine Rolls*.

In order to execute this analysis I adopted certain guidelines. For example, I restricted my searches of a nun's family to a fifty-year period around her appearance in the sources. For example, Katherine Clifton was a nun at Marham Abbey in 1367; when I searched through the Feudal Aids for anyone with the surname of Clifton, I looked between 1342 and 1392. A sample entry for the field "Information," for example, in the record of Sir Adam Clifton, would note that the *Inquisitions Post Mortem*, vol. 12 of Edward III, notes that he was a knight, Lord of Topcroft Manor and lands all over Norfolk, and that he names his daughter Katherine in his will.[3]

After having determined a nun's family background, I assigned her to a social rank and in so doing I kept to certain criteria. Social rank was assigned partially on the basis of where a nun's relative's will was probated. Probate law dictated that a Norfolk or Suffolk person with property in only one archdeaconry sought probate of her or his will in the local archdeaconry court. If a person held property in both Norfolk and Suffolk then the will went to the Consistory Court in Norwich. If someone owned property in more counties than Norfolk and Suffolk, their will was proved in the Prerogative Court of Canterbury.[4] Although historians generally follow this rule and assign social rank accordingly, there are some exceptions to it. For example, Robert Ufford, Duke of Suffolk, had lands in more than three counties but his will was proved in the Suffolk archdeaconry court.[5] So when deducing a nun's social status from information in a relative's will, I did not assume that a testator in the Consistory Court of Norwich was necessarily a member of the upper or even parish gentry. I relied instead on information about land holdings provided in the will or in auxiliary material to decide to which social group a testator belonged.

These assignments to social groups were made only when concrete evidence existed about a nun's family. I did not assume that a surname necessarily connoted social rank. For example, a woman named Cecily Fastolf was the last prioress of Bungay. The Fastolfs were an important merchant and landowning family in Norfolk and Suffolk, but a thorough search of all of their extant wills reveals no Cecily among their clan. The social rank of the nuns whose last names were Bedingfield, also a very prominent upper gentry family, was similarly revealed to be from a Bedingfield clan of minor gentry status. The Bedingfield families' wills yielded nothing to indicate that Bedingfield nuns were part of this important county family. This lack of information indicated to me that these women were from cadet branches of the family, not from the upper gentry main branch. The proliferation of lower status cadet branches of gentry families in the fifteenth and sixteenth centuries makes the assignment of a nun's social rank based solely on surname unreliable and misleading.[6]

In addition, my assignment of social rank to a nun whose male kin were titled "knight" or "esquire" changed over the centuries. If a nun's father or brother was called "knight" or "esquire" before 1400, for example, I assigned

---

3   IPM, Edward III, vol. 12, p. 105.
4   For a discussion of wills and their places of probate, see: J. S. W. Gibson, Wills and Where to Find Them (Chichester, 1974), pp. 93–5 for Norfolk, and pp. 124–27 for Suffolk. See also: Norman Tanner, The Church in Late Medieval Norwich, 1370–1532 (Toronto, 1984), p. 115.
5   Robert Ufford's will is transcribed in: W. S. Fitch, Suffolk Monasteries (n.p., n.d., MSS), vol. 3, p. 23.
6   For the proliferation of cadet families, see: K. B. McFarlane, The Nobility of Later Medieval England (Oxford, 1973), pp. 268–78; and G. E. Mingay, The Gentry (London, 1976), pp. 1–17.

her to the rank of upper gentry. After 1400 if a nun's male kin were identified as "knights" I still put her in the upper gentry, but if they were called "esquire," I relegated her to the rank of parish gentry. These assignments are in keeping with the changing nature of the gentry in the later Middle Ages.[7] When male kin were not titled but held extensive land holdings, I assigned the nun to upper gentry rank as well. Those with untitled male kin who held only local property I placed in parish gentry status.

The percentages of nuns in the five social ranks offered in Chapters 2 and 3 of this study are based on two sets of figures, known and adjusted. The sources allow us to be certain of the social status of approximately 170 of the 553 identifiable nuns – or 31 percent of them. But for several reasons I suggest that the status allocation of the remaining 383 nuns of the Norwich diocese can be adjusted to fairly reflect the social status of those nuns whose social rank is known for certain.

I justify the adjustment of nuns of unknown social rank into identifiable social groups because of the source bias discussed earlier. The identities of Norfolk and Suffolk's aristocracy and upper gentry families are known; their family members are easy to identify through wills, pedigrees and heraldic visitations. Less easy to identify because of their relative invisibility in the sources are those families from lower down the social scale, the parish gentry and the yeoman farmer groups. Wills, and sometimes pedigrees which show cadet branches of upper gentry families, reveal that a member of one of these lower social groups was a nun, but for the most part members of these social groups are less easy to identify. I would suggest then that since we can be fairly certain of who the upper status nuns were the rest must have come from families of lesser social status.

The adjusted figures of nuns in social ranks, discussed at length in Chapter 2 and delineated in Table 9, were computed in the following manner. First, I totaled the numbers for the urban, the parish gentry, and the yeoman farmer groups (24 + 78 + 6 = 108). Next, I calculated what percentage each of those figures is of 108: 22 percent, 72 percent, and 5.5 (6) percent respectively. I then applied these percentages to the number of nuns whose social status is unknown (383): 22 percent of 383 is 84; 72 percent of 383 is 275.6 (276); 5 percent of 383 is 22.9 (23). By adding these figures to the corresponding numbers of nuns whose social rank has been identified with some certainty, I arrived at the adjusted numbers and percentages. The adjusted totals are then: urban nuns 24 + 84 = 108; parish gentry 78 + 276 = 354; and the yeoman

---

7   Christopher Dyer, *Standards of Living in the Later Middle Ages* (Cambridge, 1989), pp. 10–26; P. W. Fleming, "Charity, Faith and the Gentry of Kent, 1422–1529," in *Property and Politics*, ed. A. J. Pollard (Gloucester, 1984), pp. 36–58; Nigel Saul, "The Religious Sympathies of the Gentry in Gloucester, 1200–1500," *Transactions of the Bristol and Gloucester Archaeological Society* 98 (1980), pp. 99–112; and G. M. A. Vale, *Piety, Charity and Literacy among the Yorkshire Gentry, 1370–1480* (York: Borthwick Papers no. 50, 1976). As a guide to manorial lords in Norfolk, I relied on W. J. Blake, "Norfolk Manorial Lords in 1316," *NA* 30 (1952), pp. 235–61, 263–86.

farmer group 6 + 23 = 29. I then readjusted the percentages to reflect this redistribution of numbers of nuns in social groups.

The same method was used to arrive at the social distribution of all officeholders, abbesses and prioresses, and obedientiaries.[8] Since the highest percentage of nuns and obedientiaries of known social status belonged to the parish gentry, it does not seem unreasonable to suggest, as the adjusted figures do, that the majority of all of the identifiable diocesan nuns and officers were also from this middle rank of society in Norfolk and Suffolk.

In conjunction with NORWNUNS, the database LOCFAMS facilitated the identification of a nun's geographic origin, and to this end again I adhered to certain criteria. I assigned geographic origins to those nuns whose parents' wills or Inquisition Post Mortems survive wherein they stated where they lived or gave the location of their main residence, or if such information was included in a pedigree. Robert Wingfield stated in his will, for example, that he was from Bungay.[9] He left his daughter Anne King, a nun at Bungay Priory, a small amount of money; I therefore assume that she also was from Bungay since that is where her father and mother lived. Similarly, both Rye and Dashwood identify in their pedigrees that Jane Dereham, a nun at Crabhouse in the sixteenth century, was the daughter of Thomas Dereham of Crimplesham, Norfolk, and his wife Isabel.[10] Jane, then, is one of the 106 nuns whose geographic origins can be positively identified.

Toponymics also helped locate a nun's geographical origins. Alice de Crow-mere, a nun at Thetford in the fourteenth century, was from the village of Cromer. We can be certain of this placement because her brother Lawrence Draper, of Cromer, chaplain of Eriswell left his sister a bequest in his will; he also named her an executor.[11] Assignments to geographical locations based on names are possible for nuns in the fourteenth century, but less so for later ones.

Table 20 provides the list of the twenty-two nuns and their female kin who can positively be identified as such, and the convents they entered. Table 21 shows those women who may have been related but for whom such positive identification has not yet been possible. These lists demonstrate that most women chose different convents from their relatives.

8   For officeholders and their social ranks, see Chapter 3, Tables 11 and 12.
9   NRO, NCC Albaster, 181–82.
10 Walter Rye, ed., The Visitation of Norfolk, Made and Taken by William Hervey, Clarenceaux King of Arms, Anno 1563 (Harleian Society, vol. 23), p. 105; G. H. Dashwood, ed., The Visitation of Norfolk in the Year 1563 Taken by William Hervey, Clarenceaux King of Arms (Norwich, 1878), p. 228.
11 NRO, NCC 199 Heydon (1382).

Table 20.   *Female Religious Relations of Nuns of the Diocese of Norwich,*
1350–1540

Below are listed the names, surnames first, of nuns and their kin for whom it can
be positively ascertained that they had female relatives in other houses.

Surname/Forename	Relationship	Convent	Date
Appleton[1]			
Anne		Unknown	1504
Unknown	maternal aunt	Bruisyard	1504
Beauchamp[2]			
Katherine		Shouldham	1369
Unknown	great aunt	Shouldham	1335
Blickling[3]			
Katherine		Bruisyard	1420
Joanne	sister	Denney	1420
Calthorpe[4]			
Dorothy		Bruisyard	1479
Margaret	paternal aunt	Bruisyard	1479
Clere[5]			
Alice		Bruisyard	1488
Elizabeth	sister	Bungay	1488, 1492/93

[1]   Muskett, *Suffolk Manorial Families*, p. 329.
[2]   Dugdale, *Baronage*, vol. 1, p. 226.
[3]   NRO, NCC 95 Hyrnyng (1420): Anne Blickling, widow of Roger, citizen of Norwich,
names these two nuns, her daughters, in her will. But note also that in the will of Robert
Blickling, NRO, NCC 130–32 Betyns (1452), he leaves bequests to Katherine and his
kinswoman Ellen Mortimer at Bruisyard, and to his niece Isabel Asgar at Denney.
Whether Anne and Roger were related is unnkown; Roger's relation to Katherine is also
unknown.
[4]   Rye, *Norfolk Visitation*, p. 64.
[5]   Norris, *Pedigrees*, p. 282, says that Alice was the daughter of Edmund Clere of Stokesby,
who died in 1488, and Elizabeth, daughter and co-heir of Thomas Charles. Norris says
that Alice's sister, Elizabeth, was a nun at Bungay. I think he was mistaken here because
an Elizabeth Clere was a nun at Bungay and appears in her mother's will, NRO, NCC
131–35 Woolman (1493). But Norris also says, op. cit., about Elizabeth Clere that her
sister Alice was at Bruisyard. Dashwood, *Visitation*, vol. 2, p. 271, says that Alice was a
nun at Bruisyard and her sister Elizabeth was at Bungay. Dashwood cites Edmund Clere's
will proved in 1488; NRO, NCC 15 Woolman (1488) is the will of Edmund Clere of
Stokesby. But this will says nothing about daughters as nuns, and in fact leaves £10 to
his daughter Anne for her marriage. Elizabeth Clere, *generosa*, of Takelweston cited
above, leaves 40s to Elizabeth Clere, a nun of Bungay, and to Anne. Dashwood, ibid.,
pp. 316–17, says that Anne was the testator's niece and that she was a nun at Denney.

Surname/Forename	Relationship	Convent	Date
Cobbe[6]			
Elizabeth		Blackborough	1493
Margery	paternal aunt	Blackborough	1493
Corbet[7]			
Phillipa		Campsey Ash	1433
Alice	paternal aunt	Campsey Ash	1433
Dereham[8]			
Jane		Crabhouse	1530
Elizabeth Fincham	niece	Shouldham	1527
Drury[9]			
Anne		Redlingfield	1450
Catherine	sister	Unknown	1450
Fitzralph[10]			
Alice		Thetford	1440, 1445
Matilda	paternal aunt	Bruisyard	1440, 1445
Hetherset[11]			
Agnes		Carrow	1354
Alice	aunt	Carrow	1327
Herveringham[12]			
Anne		Bruisyard	1473
Katherine	niece	Barking	1473
Hubberd[13]			
Katherine		Bungay	1568
Anne	sister	Denney	d.1549

6   PRO, PCC 11/10/4, the will of William Cobbe of Sandringham. Elizabeth is his daughter; Margery is his sister.
7   NRO, NCC 130 Surflete, the will of Guy Corbet, Esq. Phillipa is his daughter, and Alice is his sister.
8   Dashwood, *Visitation*, vol. 1, pp. 228, 231.
9   Muskett, *Suffolk Manorial Families*, p. 347.
10 NRO, NCC 125 Doke (1440) for the will of Alice's father and Matilda's brother, John, and NRO, NCC 75 Wylby (1445) for Julian Fitzralph, John's wife who also mentions both nuns.
11 Norris, *Pedigrees*, p. 605. Note also that Rye, *Carrow Abbey*, 44, lists a Matilda Hetherset as a nun at Carrow, and that Alice was cellaress in 1346, and prioress in 1349. He also notes a Julian Hetherset at Carrow who was cellaress throughout the 1330s. He notes that Matilda, Alice, and Julian were all still there in 1370. I cannot identify whether Matilda, Alice, Julian, and Agnes, whom he does not mention, were related.
12 PRO, PCC Prob 11/6/12, the will of Margaret de la Pole whose sister is Anne, and niece is Katherine.
13 PRO, E 178/3251: special commission to find ex-religious who were still receiving pension from the Crown. Katherine is listed as having lived in the archdeaconry of Norwich after the Dissolution; she died on May 28, 1550. An Anne Hubberd is listed as an ex-nun of Denney in this document. She also lived in the archdeaconry of Norwich and died on November 23, 1549. Because of their residences after the Dissolution, I think they were sisters.

Surname/Forename	Relationship	Convent	Date
Jerningham[14]			
Anne	sister	Bruisyard	1483
Thomasina	sister	Denney	1483
Barbara	sister	Campsey Ash	1483
Mortimer[15]			
Ellen		Bruisyard	1452
Isabel Asgar	niece of Ellen's kinsman	Denney	1452
Pygot[16]			
Margaret		Carrow	1444
Alice	sister	Carrow	1457
Segrime[17]			
Katherine		Carrow	1520
Joan	sister	Stratford at Bow	??
Studfield[18]			
Margaret		Crabhouse	1537
Elizabeth	niece	Denney	1520s
Todenham[19]			
Joan		Shouldham	1438
Margery	sister	Carrow	1438
Verly[20]			
Catherine		Carrow	1350–80
Mary	sister	Carrow	1350–80
White[21]			
Unknown		Bungay	1492
Unknown		Denney	1492
Unknown	unknown	Unknown	1492
Wiggenhale[22]			
Etheldreda		Crabhouse	1460
Unknown	sister or cousin	Campsey Ash	1460

[14] Norris, *Pedigrees*, p. 706; see also the 1498 will of Lady Anne Scrope of Harling, widow of Lord Scrope of Bolton, who named all three of these nuns as her kinswomen: *Testamenta Eboracensia*, pp. 149–54.

[15] NRO, NCC 130–32 Aleyn for the will of Robert Blickling. Ellen was his kinswoman; Isabel was his niece.

[16] Rye, *Carrow Abbey*, p. 39, says that Alice was prioress at Carrow when Margaret was there, and that they were both daughters of Ralph Pygot, spicer of Norwich.

[17] Paxton, "The Nunneries of London," p. 31, note 87.

[18] Norris, *Pedigrees*, p. 1125, says that Margaret was the daughter of Richard Studfield, and that Elizabeth was Margaret's brother Thomas's daughter.

[19] Norris, *Pedigrees*, p. 1125: both nuns were daughters of Sir Robert Todenham of Ereswell, Oxborough.

[20] Rye, *Carrow Abbey*, p. 46.

[21] NRO, NCC 131 Woolman for the will of Elizabeth Clere.

[22] NRO, NCC 10 Betyns for the will of John Wiggenhale of Sudbury. Etheldreda was his niece; he had another niece at Denney.

Table 21. Uncertified Relations of Nuns of the Diocese of Norwich, 1350–1540

The following are nuns who were probably related, but for whom no specific connecting evidence exists.

Surname/Forename	Convent	Date
Bardwell[1]		
Anne	Campsey Ash	1514, 1526
Eleanor	Thetford	1492
Mary	Thetford	1492
Bertram[2]		
Elizabeth	Carrow	1462
Isabel	Carrow	1447
Brakle[3]		
Agnes	Redlingfield	1437
Ellen	Redlingfield	1437
Brewse[4]		
Alice	Redlingfield	1479
Ursula	Denney	1479
Fastolf[5]		
Cecily	Bungay	1552
Dorothy	Bruisyard	1514
Sibill	Carrow	1354
Loveday[6]		
Mary	Bungay	1538
Margaret	Bruisyard	1538

[1] Jessopp, *Visitations*, pp. 134, 290 for Anne; ibid., p. 33 for Eleanor, a nun, and Mary a novice.

[2] Rye, *Carrow Abbey*, p. 43 says that Elizabeth was the daughter of John Bertram whose will was proved in 1462. He says also that there was a nun there named Isabel Bertram. He does not say that Isabel was in John's will or if or how these women were related.

[3] NRO, NCC 30–32 Doke for the will of John Hakon of 'Wyneton' who left 40s to each of these nuns but did not say that they were related.

[4] *Fragmenta Genealogica*, p. 57 says that Alice was the daughter of Sir Thomas Brewse of Topcroft and Mary, daughter of Sir John Calthorpe. He says that this branch is part of the Breweses of Little Wenham, a Suffolk pedigree of which there was an Irsula who was a nun at Denney.

[5] Norris, *Pedigrees*, p. 449 notes that Cecily died in 1552 and left bequests to two nieces, Elizabeth and Florence. Ibid., p. 445 he says that Dorothy was at Bruisyard in 1514 and was prioress there in 1529. She was the daughter of Thomas Fastolf of Pettaugh, Suffolk and Anne, daughter of Reginald Rouse, esq. Ibid., p. 449 he mentions Sibill who was the daughter of Alexander Fastolf. Norris speculates that all of these nuns were somehow part of the same family line.

[6] NRO, NCC 11–12 Underwood for the will of Elizabeth Loveday. She left a smock and other goods to her aunt Margaret. She also left a smock to Mary but did not say if or how she was related to her or to Margaret.

Surname/Forename	Convent	Date
Norwich[7]		
Isabel	Campsey Ash	1492
Margaret	Campsey Ash	1492
Shouldham[8]		
Katherine	Shouldham	1464
Margaret	Redlingfield	1464
Isabel	Barking	1464
Margaret	Barking	1464
Wetherby[9]		
Alice	Carrow	1444
Joan	Shouldham	1444
Willoughby[10]		
Elizabeth	Campsey Ash	1498
Jane	Bruisyard	1498

[7] Jessopp, *Visitations*, p. 36 says that both nuns were listed in episcopal visits, but does not say if or how they were related.

[8] NRO, NCC 329–30 for the will of Catherine, widow of William Goodrede of Middleton, Norfolk, who left 40s to each of these nuns, but did not say if or how they might be related.

[9] NRO, NCC 30–32 Wylby for the will of Thomas Wetherby, esq. at Carrow where he left money to his daughter Alice, and also left a bequest to a Joan Wetherby. Thomas did not specify the relationship between the two nuns.

[10] PRO, PCC Prob 11/11/35 for the will of Christopher Willoughby who left 5 marks to Elizabeth and 10 marks to Jane. The relation among all three is unclear.

Appendix 4: Analysis of Wills

In order to gage the perception and popularity of the female convents in the diocese of Norwich between 1350 and 1540, I analyzed the wills of over 3,000 testators from the five courts wherein probate was granted to most Norfolk and Suffolk residents: the Norwich Consistory Court (NCC) and the archdeaconry courts of Norfolk, Norwich, Sudbury and Suffolk (ANF, ANW, ASD and ASF respectively) (Table 22).

My analysis of these registers and the wills recorded in them was instructed by the following criteria. To best sample these wills, I sampled the extant wills by examining the first hundred which included bequests to any religious house, female or male, mendicant or monastic. For the wills in the NCC I looked at the earliest surviving register, Heydon, and then looked at registers whose incipit dates were ten years apart until 1536.

The same procedure was followed in the archdeaconry registers with a minor modification. Significantly fewer people whose wills were proved in ANF, ANW and ASD courts made bequests to the female religious. I therefore examined fewer registers from these archdeaconries because I judged that the sampling of the registers I had carried out was representative of what I would find in the remaining registers. For example, I analyzed the earliest register of the ANF, which includes wills proved between 1495 and 1478, and from 1483 to 1487, the ANF register whose wills begin ten years later, from 1501 to 1505, and the ANF register which includes wills from 1512 to 1513. I stopped sampling wills from other registers in this archdeaconry because I concluded that my sample of 243 wills examined was representative of what I would find in later registers. By contrast, I analyzed several of the ASF registers because the number of testators who left money or goods to the nuns was much greater.

I did not consult Prerogative Court of Canterbury (PCC) will registers for this study of gift-giving to the female religious in the Norwich diocese for two reasons. First, other studies of aristocratic and upper gentry patronage of monastic houses in the later Middle Ages have shown that these elite groups tended in their wills to patronize the big and relatively new foundations in London – Westminster, Syon and the Charterhouse, for example – friaries or chantries or secular colleges.[1] Second, because so few nuns came from families

---

[1] W. K. Jordan, *Philanthropy in England, 1480–1660* (London, 1961), passim; Gail M. Gibson, *Theater of Devotion: East Anglian Drama and Society in the Late Middle Ages* (Chicago, 1989), pp. 20–1; Joel Rosenthal, *The Purchase of Paradise: Gift Giving and the Aristocracy, 1307–1485* (London, 1972), passim; and John A. Thompson, "Piety and Charity in Late Medieval London," *Journal of Ecclesiastical History* 16 (1965), pp. 91–103.

whose members' wills would have been proved in this high court, I judged that my time would be better spent looking for patronage among the social groups from which the majority of nuns hailed.

Table 22. Names and Dates of Registers Sampled
with Numbers of Wills Read in Each

Register	Dates	Number of Wills in Register	Number of Wills Read	Percentage of Whole Register
Norwich Consistory Court:[1]				
Heydon	1370–1383	692	223	32
Harsyk	1383–1408	304	304	100
Hyrnyng	1416–1426	540	100	19
Doke	1436–1444	752	126	17
Wylbey	1444–1448	419	103	25
Hubert	1473–1491	273	119	44
Cage	1500	292	100	34
Spyrlyng	1524–1516	222	101	45
Grundisburgh	1524–1526	221	100	45
Alpe	1526–1532	138	100	72
Maryett	1528–1531	91	91	100
Hyll	1531–1546	237	100	42
Underwood	1536–1538	61	61	100
Total Number of Wills		4,242		
Total Number of Wills Read			1,628	
Percentage of Total				38
Norfolk Archdeaconry Court:[2]				
Grey	1475–1478, 1483–1487	148	100	68
Bemond	1501–1505	43	43	100
Batman	1512–1513	152	100	66
Total Number of Wills		343		
Number of Wills Read			243	
Percentage of Total				71

[1] There are fifty-seven registers in the NCC, forty-nine of which include the time period covered in this study. Roughly 17,000 wills are included in the forty-nine registers.

[2] For the archdeaconry court of Norfolk there are thirteen registers of wills which include the years in this study. Three of them, Liber 1, Shaw and Sparhawk, are so badly damaged that they are impossible to read. These registers include approximately 1,500 wills.

Register	Dates	Number of Wills in Register	Number of Wills Read	Percentage of Whole Register
Norwich Archdeaconry Court:[3]				
Fuller alias Roper	1469–1503	152	100	66
Randes	1519–1529	147	100	68
Cook	1530–1538	153	100	66
Total Number of Wills		452		
Number of Wills Read			300	
Percentage of Total				66
Sudbury Archdeaconry Court:[4]				
Baldwyne	1439–1461	171	100	58
Hervye	1473–1490	165	77	46
Total Number of Wills		336		
Total Number of Wills Read			177	
Percentage of Total				53
Suffolk Archdeaconry Court:[5]				
IC/AA2/1	1444–1452	172	100	58
IC/AA2/3	1481–1498	185	100	54
IC/AA2/5	1506–1513	173	100	59
IC/AA2/6A	1508–1540	58	58	100
IC/AA2/7	1513–1518	302	275	98
IC/AA2/9	1524–1527	102	102	100
IC/AA2/12	1534–1538	139	50	36
Total Number of Wills		1,131		
Total Number of Wills Read			785	
Percentage of Total				69

[3] There are seven registers of wills in the archdeaconry of Norfolk which include the 240 year period covered in this study. These registers comprise approximately 1,300 wills.
[4] Ten will registers from the archdeaconry of Sudbury survive include the years covered in this study; they comprise 1,658 wills.
[5] Fourteen will registers from the Suffolk archdeaconry court survive and include the period of this study; they comprise 2,590 wills.

Bibliography

Manuscript Sources

Cambridge, University Library

Add. Ms. 8335

London, British Library

Add. Ms. 5808, fol. 191b
Add. Ms. 19,144, fol. 356
Add. Ms. 29,692, fol. 138
Egerton Ms. 3137
Egerton Roll 8776
Sloane Ms. 2400
Stowe Ch. 343
Stowe Ch. 348

London, Public Record Office

E 101 (Exchequer Augmentation Office) 76/21, 76/29, 533/4,631/26
E 117 (Exchequer Kings' Remembrancer Church Goods) 14/22
E 178 (Exchequer Pension Lists) 3251, 178/3234
E 179 (Clerical Subsidies) 45/5b, 45/6b/ 45/7c, 45/9, 45/14, , 45/16
E 314 (Exchequer Records Receipts for Pensions) 20, 314/54
E 315 (Exchequer Records Miscellaneous Books) 245, 315/405

Prerogative Court of Canterbury Will Registers:
PCC Prob 11/6/12
PCC Prob 11/8/9
PCC Prob 11/10/4
PCC Prob 11/11/35
PCC Prob 11/19/5
PCC Prob 11/22/33
PCC Prob 11/39/46

State Papers, Henry VIII:
Suppression Papers: SP 5 1/130, 1/110, 1/119, 1/131, 1/147, 1/259
SP 5/2/246–48
SP 5/3/27, 3/29, 3/35, 3/116, 3/117, 3/126–27, 3/131, 3/133
SP 5/4/132, 4/138, 4/140, 4/144, 4/150

Miscellaneous Documents:
SC 6 (Minster's Accounts) H 8/2621

Ipswich, Suffolk County Record Office

Household and Manorial Accounts:
  Bungay
  HD 1538/156/1–156/17
  HD 1538/345

  Campsey Ash Priory
  HD 1538/174

  Redlingfield Priory
  HD 1538/327

Will Registers:
  ASD 1–100 IC 500/2/9 (Baldwyne)
  ASD 1–77 IC 500/2/11 (Herveye)
  ASD 188 Shaw

  ASF 1–100 IC/AA2/1
  ASF 1–100 IC/AA2/3
  ASF 1–100 IC/AA2/5
  ASF 1–58 IC/AA2/6A
  ASF 1–275 IC/AA2/7
  ASF 1–100 IC/AA2/9
  ASF 1–51 IC/AA2/12
  ASF 10, fols. 51–2

Miscellaneous Documents:
  HA 12/B2/9/29
  HA 12/B2/18/14
  HA 12/E1/15/1(c)

Norwich, Norfolk County Record Office

Dean and Chapter of Norwich Records:
  DCN 29/3
  DCN 88/9–88/15

Archdeaconry of Norwich Parish Registers:
  St Michael at Plea
  St Clements

Household and Manorial Accounts:
  Marham Abbey
  Hare 1 232x1
  Hare 2201 194x5–2212 194x5

  Carrow Priory
  Hare 5954 227x1
  Hare 5955 227x1
  Hare 5957 227x1

NRS 26882 42 E8–12884 42 E8
Phi 454/577x9

Will Registers:
  ANF 1–222 Grey
  ANF 1–40 Bemond
  ANF 1–100 Batman
  ANF 188 Shaw

  ANW 41 Bakon
  ANW 1–100 Fuller, alias Roper
  ANW 1–100 Cook
  ANW 1–100 Randes

  NCC 1–223 Heydon
  NCC 1–304 Harsyk
  NCC 1–100 Hyrning
  NCC 1–126 Doke
  NCC 1–96 Wylbey
  NCC 1–119 Hubert
  NCC 1–100 Cage
  NCC 1–101 Spyrlyng
  NCC 1–100 Grundisburgh
  NCC 1–100 Alpe
  NCC 1–100 Hyll
  NCC 1–73 Underwood
  NCC 1–46 Maryett
  NCC 181–82 Albaster
  NCC 57–8, 130, 188 Alyn
  NCC 317 Attmere
  NCC 235 Bircham
  NCC 58–9, 159, 206, 229–30, 250–51, 252 Brosyerd
  NCC 103, 104 Cobald
  NCC 91, 93–4 Cooke
  NCC 9, 196 Coraunt
  NCC 34–5 Gilberd
  NCC 5 Godsalve
  NCC 97–100 Gyles
  NCC 23–4, 74 Herbert
  NCC 199 Heydon
  NCC 51, 260–61, 280 Hyll
  NCC 131, 184 Lyncolne
  NCC 47 Mayett
  NCC 95, 275–78 Mingay
  NCC 90–1 Multon
  NCC 27, 216 Palgrave
  NCC 104–8, 197 Platfoote
  NCC 491–92, 520–21 Popy
  NCC 169 Punting
  NCC 130, 152–53 Surflete

NCC 126, 130–32 Wylbey
NCC 75, 75–7, 268 Wymer

Miscellaneous Documents:
 BL vi b (viii)
 Ms. 21484
 Microfilm Reel 124/7
 Phi/187/577x3
 Phi/451/557x8

Reading, Mapledurham Archives

C3 nos. 39–43

Printed Sources

Ayer, J., ed., *The Catechism of Thomas Bacon.* Parker Society, 1984.
Bateson, Mary, ed., "The Register of Crabhouse Nunnery." *Norfolk Archaeology* 11 (1892), 1–71.
Bedingfield, A. L., ed., *A Cartulary of Creake Abbey.* Norfolk Record Society 35, 1966.
Bliss, W. H. and J. A. Twemlow, eds., *Calendar of Entries in the Papal Registers relating to Great Britain and Ireland: Papal Letters.* London, 1893–19
Bloom, Harvey, ed., *Liber Elemosinarii: The Almoner's Book of the Priory of Worcester.* Worcester Historical Society, 1911.
Blunt, John Henry, ed., *Myroure of Oure Ladye.* EETS, extra series 19, 1873.
Calendar of Close Rolls. London, 1906–1939.
Calendar of Fine Rolls. London, 1908–1921.
Calendar of Patent Rolls. London, 1905–1916.
Caley, J. and Joseph Hunter, eds., *Valor Ecclesiasticus.* 7 vols. London, 1810–1834.
Canning, Raymond, trans., *The Rule of St Augustine: Masculine and Feminine Versions.* London, 1984.
Carthew, G. A. "A Cellarer's Account Roll of Creake Abbey, 5 and 6 Edward III." *NA* 6 (1864), 314–59.
Clark, Andrew, ed., *The English Register of Godstow Nunnery.* EETS, o.s. vols. 129–130, 142, 1905–1911.
Clarke, A. W. Hughes and Arthur Campling, eds., *The Visitation of Norfolk Made A.D. 1664 by Sir Edmund Bysshe, Knt., Clarenceaux King of Arms.* 2 vols. Norfolk Record Society, vols. 4 and 5, 1934.
Clay, John, ed., *Yorkshire Monasteries: Suppression Papers.* Yorkshire Archaeological Society Record Series 48, 1912.
Corder, Joan, ed., *The Visitation of Suffolk, 1561.* Harleian Society, n.s., vols. 2 and 3, 1981.
Cotton, Charles, ed., "St Austins's Abbey, Canterbury Treasurers' Accounts, 1468–9 and Others." *Archaeologia Cantiana* 51 (1940), 66–103.
Cozens-Hardy, Basil and Enest Kent, eds., *The Mayors of Norwich, 1403–1835.* Norwich, 1983.

Crittall, E., ed., "Fragment of an Account of the Cellaress of Wilton Abbey, 1299." *Wiltshire Record Society Publications* 12 (1956), 142–156.

Dashwood, G. H. *Vicscomites Norfolciae or Sheriffs of Norfolk from the First Year of Henry II, to the Fourth Year of Queen Victoria, Inclusive.* Stow Bardolf, 1843.

Dashwood, G. H., ed., *The Visitation of Norfolk in the Year 1563 taken by William Harvey, Clarenceaux King of Arms.* Norwich, 1878.

Davis, Norman, ed., *Paston Letters and Papers of the Fifteenth Century.* Oxford, 1971.

Denny, A. H., ed., *The Sibton Abbey Estates; Selected Documents, 1325–1509.* Suffolk Record Society Publications, vol. 2, 1960.

Director-General of the Ordinance Survey. *Map of Monastic Britain.* Southampton, 1954.

Dodwell, Barbara, ed., *The Charters of Norwich Cathedral Priory.* Pipe Roll Society, n.s. 78, 84, 1974–76.

Dugdale, William, ed., *Monasticon Anglicanum.* 8 vols. in 6. London, 1817–1840.

Evelyn-White, H. G. "An Unpublished Fourteenth-Century Rent Roll from Butley Priory." *East Anglian Notes and Queries* n.s. 11 (1905–06), 1–6, 28–30, 59–60, 72–3, 87–8.

Farrow, M. A. *Index of Wills Proved in the Consistory Court of Norwich, 1370–1550.* Norfolk Record Society, vol. 16, 1943–45.

Fegen, Ethel S., ed., *The Journal of Prior William More.* Worcester Historical Society, 1914.

Fernie, E. C. and A. B. Whittingham. *The Early Communar and Pitancer Rolls of Norwich Cathedral Priory with an Account of the Building of the Cloister.* Norfolk Record Society, vol. 41, 1972.

Feudal Aids. London, 1908–1921.

Fisher, John, ed., *The Complete Poetry and Prose of Geoffrey Chaucer.* New York, 1977.

Flower, C. T., "Obedientiars' Accounts of Glastonbury and Other Religious Houses." *Transactions of St Paul's Ecclesiological Society* 7 (1912), 50–62.

Fowler, Joseph, ed., *Extracts from the Account Rolls of the Abbey of Durham, 1303–1541.* Surtees Society, vols. 99, 100, 103, 1898–1901.

Fry, Timothy, ed., *The Benedictine Rule.* Collegville, 1981.

Gairdner, J. and R. H. Brodie, eds., *Letters and Papers, Foreign and Domestic, of the Reign of Henry VIII, 1509–1547.* London, 1862–1910.

Gasquet, Francis, ed., *The Rule of St Benedict.* New York, 1966.

Gransden, Antonia, ed., *The Customary of the Benedictine Abbey of Bury St Edmunds in Suffolk.* Henry Bradshaw Society, vol. 99, 1973.

Greatrex, Joan, ed., *Account Rolls of the Obedientiaries of Peterborough.* Northamptonshire Record Society Publications, 1984.

Harley, Marta Powell, ed., *A Revelation of Purgatory by an Unknown Fifteenth-Century Woman Visionary.* New York, 1985.

Harrod, Henry. "Extracts from Early Norfolk Wills." *NA* 4 (1849), 111–27.

Harper-Bill, Christopher, ed., *Blythburgh Priory Cartulary.* 2 vols. Woodbridge, 1980–1981.

Harper-Bill, Christopher and R. Mortimer, eds., *Stoke by Clare Cartulary, BL Cotton App.x.xxi.* Woodbridge, 1982.

Hassal, W. O., ed., *The Cartulary of St Mary Clerkenwell.* Camden Society, 3rd ser. lxxi, 1949.

Howard, Joseph Jackson, ed., *The Visitation of Suffolke, Made by Willaim Hervey,*

Clarenceaux King of Arms, 1561, with Additions from Family Documents, Original Wills, Jermyn, Davy, and Other Manuscripts. 2 vols. Lowestoft, 1866–1876.

Howlett, Richard, ed., "Account Rolls of Certain of the Obedientiaries of the Abbey of St Benedict at Holme, 19 Henry VI – 16–17 Henry VIII." *Norfolk Antiquarian Miscellany* 2 (1883), 530–49.

Hudson, William and John Tingey, eds., *The Records of the City of Norwich*. 2 vols. Norwich, 1906–1910.

Hunter, Joseph, ed., *A Catalogue of the Deeds of Surrender of Certain Abbeys: The Eighth Report of the Deputy Keeper of the Public Records*. London, 1874.

Inquisitions Post Mortem. London, 1913–1987.

Jacob, Ernst. "Two Documents Relating to Thomas Broun, Bishop of Norwich." *NA* 33:4 (1965), 427–49.

Jessopp, A. H., ed., *Visitations of the Diocese of Norwich, 1492–1532*. Camden Society, n.s. 43, 1888.

King, P. I., ed., *The Book of William Morton, Almoner of Peterborough Monastery, 1448–1467*. Northampton Record Society, xvi, 1954.

Kirk, R. E. G., ed., *Accounts of the Obedientiaries of Abingdon Abbey*. Camden Society, n.s. 51, 1892.

Kitchin, G. W., ed., *Compotus Rolls of the Obedientiaries of St Swithun's Priory, Winchester*. Hampshire Record Society, 1892.

Kock, Ernst A., ed., *Three Middle-English Versions of the Rule of St Benet and Two Contemporary Rituals for the Ordination of Nuns*. EETS, o.s. 120, 1902.

Langland, William. *The Vision of Piers Plowman*. Edited by A.V. C. Schmidt. New York, 1978.

Le Strange, Hamon. *Norfolk Official Lists from the Earliest Period to the Present Day*. Norwich, 1895.

Lunt, W. E., ed., *The Valuation of Norwich*. Oxford, 1926.

Maskell, William, ed., *Monumenta Ritualia Ecclesiae Anglicanae*. London, 1882.

Metcalf, Walter. *The Visitations of Suffolk Made by Hervey, Clarenceaux, 1561, Cook, Clarenceuax, 1577, and Raven Richmond Herald, 1612*. Exeter, 1882.

Mortimer, Richard, ed., *Leiston Abbey Cartulary and Butley Priory Charters*. Woodbridge, 1979.

Myers, A. R., ed., *English Historical Documents, 1327–1485*. New York, 1969.

Nicolas, Nicholas, ed., *Testamenta Vetusta: Being Illustrations from Wills of Manners, Customs, etc., as well as of the Descents and Possessions of Many Distinguished Families from the Reign of Henry II to the Accession of Queen Elizabeth*. 2 vols. London, 1826.

O'Mara, Veronica. *A Study and Edition of Selected Middle English Sermons*. Leeds Texts and Monographs, n.s. 13, 1994.

Palgrave-Moore, Patrick, ed., *Index of Wills Proved in the Norfolk Archdeaconry Court, 1453–1542*. Norfolk Genealogy, vol. 3, 1971.

Palgrave-Moore, P. and Michael Sawyer. *A Selection of Revised and Unpublished Norfolk Pedigrees*. Norfolk Genealogy, vols. 6, 8, 13, 17, 1974–1985.

Pantin, William, ed., *Documents Illustrating the Activities of the General and Provincial Chapters of the English Black Monks, 1215–1540*. 3 vols. London, 1931–1937.

Picard, J. M., trans., and Y. de Pontfarcy, ed., *Saint Patrick's Purgatory*. Dublin, 1985.

Pugh, R. B. "Fragment of an Account of Isabel of Lancaster, Nun of Amesbury, 1333–4." In *Festschrift zur Feier des zweihundejayrigen Bestandes des Haus-, Hof- und Staatsarchivs*, 1 bd. Edited by Leo Santifaller. Vienna, 1949.

Purvis, J. S., ed., "A Selection of Monastic Rentals and Dissolution Papers." In *Miscellanea III*. Yorkshire Archaeological Society Record Series 80, 1931.

Raine, James, ed., *The Durham Household Book; or the Accounts of the Bursar of the Monastery of Durham, 1530–34*. Surtees Society 18, 1844.

———, *Testamenta Eboracensia, a Selection of Wills from the Register at York*. 6 vols. Surtees Society, 1836–1902.

———, *Wills and Inventories from the Archdeaconry of Richmond, 1442–1578*. Surtees Society, vol. 26, 1853.

Redstone, L. J., ed., "Three Carrow Account Rolls." *NA* 29 (1946), 41–88.

———, "The Cellarer's Account for Bromholme Priory, Norfolk, 1415–16." *Norfolk Record Society* 17 (1944), 45–91.

Rye, Walter, ed., *The Visitation of Norfolk, Made and Taken by William Hervey, Clarenceaux King of Arms, Anno 1563*. Harleian Society, vol. 32, 1891.

Scarfe, Norman, ed., *Clare Priory: Seven Centuries of a Suffolk House*. Cambridge, 1962.

Serjeant, W. R. and K. R., eds., *Index of the Probate Records of the Court of the Archdeaconry of Sudbury, 1439–1700*. British Record Society, 2 vols., 1884.

Seton, W. W., ed., *Two Fifteenth-Century Franciscan Rules*. EETS, o.s. 148, 1914.

Sharpe, Reginald, ed., *Calendar of Wills Proved and Enrolled in the Court of Hustings, London (AD 1258–1688)*. 2 vols. London, 1889.

Stephenson, Carl and Frederick Marcham, eds., *Sources of English Constitutional History*, vol. 1. New York, 1972.

Stevenson, Joseph, ed., *Chronicon Monasterii de Abingdon*. London, 1858.

Swift, Eleanor, ed., *The Obedientiary Rolls of Battle Abbey*. Sussex Archaeological Collections 78, 1938.

Tanner, Norman, ed., *Heresy Trials in the Diocese of Norwich, 1428–31*. Camden Society, 4th ser., vol. 20, 1977.

Tanner, Thomas, ed., *Notitia Monastica*. London, 1744.

Taylor, R. C., ed., *Index Monasticus: or the Abbeys and Other Monasteries, Alien Priories, Friaries, etc., in the Diocese of Norwich*. London, 1821.

Thompson, A. H., ed., *Visitations of the Diocese of Lincoln, 1517–1531*. Lincoln Record Society Publications, vols. 33, 35, 37, 1940–1947.

———, *Visitations of Religious Houses in the Diocese of Lincoln*. Canterbury and York Society, vols. 17, 24, 33, 1915–1927.

Tolhurst, John, ed., *The Customary of Norwich*. Henry Bradshaw Society, vol. 82, 1984.

———, *The Ordinal and Customary of the Benedictine Nuns of Barking Abbey*. Henry Bradshaw Society, vols. 65 and 66, 1926–1927.

Toulmin-Smith, Lucy, ed., *English Gilds*. EETS, o.s. 40, 1870.

Twemlow, J. A., ed., *Calendar of Entries in the Papal Registers relating to Great Britain and Ireland: Papal Letters*. London, 1915

Tymms, Samuel, ed., *Wills and Inventories from the Registers of the Commissary of Bury St Edmunds and the Archdeaconry*. Camden Society 49, 1850.

Walcott-MacKenzie, E. C. "Inventories and Valuations of Religious Houses at the Time of the Dissolution." *Archaeologia* 43 (1871), 287–306.

West, J. R. *St Benet of Holme 1020–1210. The Eleventh- and Twelfth-Century Sections of Cott. Ms Galba Eii; The Register of the Abbey of St Benet of Holme*. Norfolk Record Society, vols. 2 and 3, 1932.

Wright, Thomas. *St Patrick's Purgatory; An Essay on the Legends of Purgatory, Hell, and Paradise Current During the Middle Ages.* London, 1844.

Secondary Sources

Adamson, J. W. "The Extent of Literacy in England in the Fifteenth and Sixteenth Centuries." *The Library* 4th ser. 10 (1910–1930), pp. 163–195.

Allison, K. J. "The Norfolk Worsted Industry in the Sixteenth and Seventeenth Centuries: 1. The Traditional History." *Yorkshire Bulletin of Economic and Social Research* 12 (1960), pp. 73–83.

Anson, P. F. "Papal Enclosure for Nuns." *Cistercian Studies* 3 (1968), pp. 109–23, 189–206.

Anstruther, O. P. *A Hundred Homeless Years.* London, 1958.

Archbold, W. A. J. *The Somerset Religious Houses.* Cambridge, 1892.

Archer, Rowena and B. E. Ferme. "Testamentary Procedure with Special Reference to the Executrix." *Reading Medieval Studies* 15 (1989), pp. 3–34.

Aston, Margaret. *Lollards and Reformers: Images and Literacy in Late Medieval Religion.* London, 1984.

Atkinson, Clarissa. *Mystic and Pilgrim: The Book and the World of Margery Kemp.* Ithaca, 1983.

Attreed, Lorraine. "Preparation for Death in Sixteenth-Century Northern England." *The Sixteenth Century Journal* 13:3 (1982), pp. 37–66.

Aungier, G. J. *The History of Syon Monastery.* London, 1840.

Baker, Alan. "Changes in the Later Middle Ages." In *A New Historical Geography of England before 1600,* ed. H. C. Darby. Cambridge, 1976, pp. 186–247.

Baker, George. *The History and Antiquities of the County of Northamptonshire,* 2 vols. London, 1822–30.

Barrett, Alexandra. "Introduction." In *Women's Writing in Middle English,* ed. Alexandra Barrett. New York, 1992, pp. 1–23.

———. "The Revelations of Saint Elizabeth of Hungary: Problems of Attribution." *The Library* 6th series 14 (1992), pp. 1–11.

Baskerville, G. "The Dispossessed Religious after the Suppression of the Monasteries." In *Essays Presented to Reginald Poole,* ed. Henry W. Davis. Oxford, 1927, pp. 436–65.

———. "Married Clergy and Pensioned Religious in Norwich Diocese, 1555." *EHR* 48 (1933), pp. 43–64, 199–228.

———. *English Monks and the Suppression of the Monasteries.* New Haven, 1937.

Bateson, Mary. "Archbishop Warham's Visitation of Monasteries." *EHR* 6 (1891), pp. 18–35.

Bazire, Joyce and Eric Colledge, eds., *The Chastising of God's Children and the Treatises of Perfection of the Sons of God.* Oxford, 1957.

Bell, David N. *What Nuns Read: Books and Libraries in Medieval English Nunneries.* Cistercian Studies series 158. Michigan, 1995.

Bell, H. E. "The Price of Books in Medieval England." *The Library* 4th ser. 17 (1937), pp. 312–32

Bell, Susan Groag. "Medieval Women Book Owners: Arbiters of Lay Piety and

Ambassadors of Culture." In *Women and Power in the Middle Ages*, ed. Mary Erler and Maryanne Kowaleski. Chicago, 1988, pp. 149–87.

Bennett, H. S. "The Production and Dissemination of Vernacular Manuscripts in the Fifteenth Century." *The Library* 5th ser. 1 (1947), pp. 167–78.

Bennett, Judith, et al. "Introduction." In *Sisters and Workers in the Middle Ages*, edited by Judith Bennett, et al. Chicago, 1989, pp. 1–10.

Beresford, Maurice and Finberg, H. P. R. *English Medieval Boroughs: A Handlist.* Devon, 1973.

Berman, Constance. "Women as Donors and Patrons to Southern French Monasteries in the Twelfth and Thirteenth Centuries." In *The Worlds of Medieval Women: Creativity, Influence, Imagination*, ed. Constance Berman, et al. Morgantown, 1985, pp. 53–68.

Bernard, G. W. *The Power of the Early Tudor Nobility: A Study of the Fourth and Fifth Earls of Shrewsbury.* New York, 1985.

Bitel, Lisa. "Women's Monastic Enclosures in Early Ireland: A Study of Female Spirituality and Male Monastic Mentalities." *Journal of Medieval History* 12:1 (1986), pp. 15–36.

———. *Isle of Saints: Monastic Settlement and Christian Community in Early Ireland.* Ithaca, 1990.

Blair, Lawrence. *English Church Ales.* Ann Arbor, 1940.

Blake, W. J. "Fuller's List of Norfolk Gentry." *NA* 32 (1961), pp. 261–91.

Blomefield, Francis. *An Essay Toward a Topographical History of the County of Norfolk.* 11 vols. London, 1805–1810.

Boase, Thomas. *English Art 1100–1216.* Oxford, 1953.

Boffey, Julia. "Women Authors and Women's Literacy in Fourteenth- and Fifteenth-Century England." In *Women and Literature in Britain, 1150–1500*, ed. Carol Meale. Cambridge, 1993, pp. 159–82.

Bolton, Brenda. "Mulieres Sanctae." In *Women in Medieval Society*, ed. Susan Mosher Stuard. Pennsylvania, 1976, pp. 141–58.

Bolton, J. L. *The English Medieval Economy, 1150–1500.* London, 1980.

Bouchard, Constance B. *Sword, Miter, and Cloister: Nobility and the Church in Burgandy, 980–1198.* Ithaca, 1987.

Bourdillon, Anne. *The Order of Minoresses in England.* Manchester, 1926.

Bowker, Margaret. "The Henrician Reformation and the Parish Clergy." In *The English Reformation Revised*, ed. Christopher Haigh. Cambridge, 1987, pp. 75–93.

Brundage, James A. and Elizabeth Makowski. "Enclosure of Nuns: the Decretal *Periculoso* and its Commentators." *Journal of Medieval History* 20 (1994), pp. 143–55.

Bullough, Vern. "Medieval Medical and Scientific Views of Women." *Viator* 4 (1973), pp. 487–93.

Burgess, Clive. " 'By Quick and By Dead': Wills and Pious Provisions in Late Medieval Bristol." *EHR* 102:405 (1987), pp. 837–58.

Burnet, Gilbert. *The History of the Reformation of the Church of England.* London, 1679–1753.

Burstall, Bryan. "A Monastic Agreement of the Fourteenth Century." *NA* 31 (1957), pp. 211–18.

Burton, Janet. *Monastic and Religious Orders in Britain, 1000–1300.* Cambridge, 1994.

————. *The Yorkshire Nunneries in the Twelfth and Thirteenth Centuries*. York: Borthwick Papers, no. 56, 1979.

Bush, Michael. *The English Aristocracy: A Comparative Synthesis*. Manchester, 1984.

Bynum, Caroline Walker. " '. . . And Woman His Humanity': Female Imagery in the Religious Writing of the Later Middle Ages." In *Gender and Religion: On the Complexity of Symbols*, ed. Stevan Harrell and Paula Richman. Boston, 1986, pp. 257–88.

————. "The Female Body and Religious Practice in the Later Middle Ages." In *Zone 3; Fragments for a History of the Human Body*, ed. Michel Feher with Ramona Naddaff and Nadia Tazi. New York, 1989, pp. 160–219.

————. *Holy Feast, Holy Fast: The Religious Significance of Food to Medieval Women*. Berkeley, 1987.

————. *Jesus as Mother: Studies in the Spirituality of the High Middle Ages*. Berkeley, 1982.

————. "Religious Women in the Later Middle Ages." In *Christian Spirituality: High Middle Ages and Reformation*, ed. Jill Rait, Bernard McGenn, and John Meyendorff. London, 1987, pp. 121–39.

Campling, Alfred. *East Anglian Pedigrees*. Pt. 1. Norfolk Record Society, 13, 1940.

————. *East Anglian Pedigrees*. Pt. 2. London: Harleian Society, vol. 97, 1945.

Carey, Hilary. "Devout and Literate Laypeople and the Pursuit of the Mixed Life in Later Medieval England." *Journal of Religious History* 14 (1987), pp. 361–81.

Cardman, Francine. "The Medieval Question of Women and Orders." *Thomist* 42 (1978), pp. 582–599.

Carpenter, Christine. "The Fifteenth-Century Gentry and their Estates." In *Gentry and Lesser Nobility in Late Medieval England*, ed. Michael Jones. Gloucester, 1986, pp. 36–60.

Carson, T. E. "The Problem of Irregularities in the Late Medieval Church: An Example from Norwich." *Catholic Historical Review* 72:2 (1986), pp. 185–200.

Carthew, G. A. "North Creake Abbey." *NA* 7 (1871), pp. 153–68.

Catto, J. "Religion and the English Nobility in the Later Fourteenth Century." In *History and Imagination: Essays in Honor of Trevor-Roper*, ed. H. Lloyd-Jones, V. Pearl, and B. Worden. New York, 1982, pp. 43–55.

Chambers, P. F. *Juliana of Norwich. An Introductory Appreciation and Interpretive Anthology*. New York, 1955.

Cheney, Christopher. "Norwich Cathedral Priory in the Fourteenth Century." *Bulletin of the John Rylands Library* 20 (1936), pp. 93–120.

Chettle, H. F. and Ernst Loftus. *A History of Barking Abbey*. Barking, 1954.

Clarke-Maxwell, W. G. "The Outfit for the Profession of an Austin Canoness at Lacock, Wiltshire in the Year 1395 and Other Memoranda." *Archaeological Journal* 69 (1912), pp. 117–24.

Clay, Rotha Mary. *The Medieval Hospitals of England*. London, 1909.

Cokayne, George Edward. *The Complete Peerage*, ed. H. A. Doubleday and Lord Howard de Walden, vol. 9. London, 1936, pp. 610–20.

Coldicott, Diana. *Hampshire Nunneries*. Ipswich, 1989.

Coleman, J. J. "On the Excavation of the Site of Carrow Abbey, Norwich." *British Archaeological Association Journal* 38 (1882), pp. 72–81.

Colvin, H. M. *The White Canons in England*. Oxford, 1951.

Constable, Giles. *Medieval Monasticism: A Select Bibliography*. Toronto, 1976.

————. *Monastic Tithes from their Origins to the Twelfth Century*. Cambridge, 1964.

Cook, A. H. "Five Account Rolls of Blackborough Priory." *NA* 22 (1926), pp. 83–5.

Cooper, J. P. "The Social Distribution of Land and Men, 1463–1700." *EHR* 20:3 (1976), pp. 419–40.

Cooper, Timothy. "The Papacy and the Diocese of Coventry and Lichfield, 1360–1385." *Archivum Historiae Pontificae* 25 (1987), pp. 73–103.

Copinger, Walter. *The County of Suffolk . . . Index nominum et locorum . . .* London, 1904–1905.

———. *The Manors of Suffolk: Notes on their History and Devolution.* 11 vols. London, 1905–1911.

Coppel, Stephen. "Wills and the Community: A Case Study of Tudor Grantham." In *Probate Records and the Local Community*, ed. Philip Riden. Gloucester, 1985, pp. 71–90.

Corbett, Maryanne. "An East Midland Revision of the 'Northern Homily Cycle'." *Manuscripta* 26 (1982), pp. 100–7.

Cornwall, J. "The Early Tudor Gentry." *EcHR* 2nd ser. 17 (1965), pp. 456–75.

Coulton, G. G. "The Truth about the Monasteries." In *Ten Medieval Studies*, ed. G. G. Coulton, 3rd edn. Cambridge, 1930, pp. 84–107.

———. *Five Centuries of Religion.* 4 vols. Cambridge, 1927–1950.

———. *Medieval Studies.* Oxford, 1915.

Councer, C. R. "The Dissolution of the Kentish Monasteries." *Archaeologia Cantiana* 47 (1935), pp. 126–143.

Courtenay, William. *Schools and Scholars in Fourteenth-Century England.* New Jersey, 1987.

Croft, P. J. "The 'Friar of the Order Gray' and the Nun." *Review of English Studies* n.s. 32:125 (1981), pp. 1–16.

Cross, Claire. "Monasticism and Society in the Diocese of York, 1520–1540." *TRHS* 5th ser. 38 (1988), pp. 131–145.

———. "The Religious Life of Women in Sixteenth-Century Yorkshire." In *Women in the Church*, ed. W. J. Sheils and Diana Wood. *Studies in Church History*, vol. 27. Oxford, 1990, pp. 307–24.

Cross, Claire and Noreen Vickers. *Monks, Friars, and Nuns in Sixteenth Century Yorkshire.* Yorkshire Archaeological Society, Record Series, vol. 105, 1995.

Daichman, Graciela. *Wayward Nuns in Medieval Literature.* New York, 1986.

Darby, H. C., ed., *A New Historical Geography of England before 1600.* Cambridge, 1973.

Davenport, F. G. *The Economic Development of a Norfolk Manor, 1086–1565.* New York, 1906.

Davis, R. H. C. *King Stephen.* New York, 1967.

Davis, Natalie Z. "Histories Two Bodies." *American Historical Review* 93:1 (1988), 1–30.

Deanesly, Margaret. *The Lollard Bible and Other Medieval Biblical Versions.* Cambridge, 1920.

———. "Vernacular Books in England in the Fourteenth and Fifteenth Centuries." *Modern Language Review* 15 (1920), pp. 349–58.

Denholm-Young, N. *The County Gentry in the Fourteenth Century.* Oxford, 1969.

Diamond, Arleyn. "Chaucer's Women and Women's Chaucer." In *The Authority of Experience: Essays in Feminist Criticism*, ed. Arleyn Diamond and Lee Edward. Amherst, 1977, pp. 60–83.

Dickens, A. G. "Robert Parkyn's Narrative of the Reformation." *EHR* 62 (1947), pp. 58–83.

———. "The Edwardian Arrears in Augmentation Payments and the Problems of the Ex-religious." *EHR* 60 (1940), pp. 384–418.

———. *The English Reformation.* New York, 1964.

Dickinson, J. C. *Monastic Life in Medieval England.* New York, 1961.

———. *The Later Middle Ages: from the Norman Conquest to the Eve of the Reformation.* London, 1979.

———. *The Origins of the Austin Canons and their Introduction into England.* London, 1950.

Diringer, David. *The Illuminated Book: Its History and Production.* London, 1958.

Dobson, R. B. "The Propsopography of Late Medieval Cathedral Canons." *Medieval Prosopography* 15:2 (1995), pp. 67–92.

———. "Recent Prosopographical Research in Late Medieval English History: University Graduates, Durham Monks, and York Canons." In *Medieval Lives and the Historian: Studies in Medieval Prosopography*, ed. Neithard Bulst and Jean-Philippe Genet. Michigan, 1986, pp. 181–200.

———. *Durham Priory, 1400–1450.* Cambridge, 1973.

Dobson, R. B. and Sara Donaghey. *The History of Clementhorpe Nunnery*, vol. 2 of *The Archaeology of York*, ed. P. V. Addyman. London, 1984.

Douglas, D. C. *The Social Structure of Medieval East Anglia.* Oxford, 1927.

Doyle, A. I. "Publication by Members of the Religious Orders." In *Book Production and Publishing in Britain 1375–1475*, ed. Jeremy Griffiths and Derek Pearsall. Cambridge, 1989, pp. 1–20.

Du Boulay, F. R. H. "The Fifteenth Century." In *The English Church and the Papacy in the Middle Ages*, ed. C. H. Lawrence. London, 1965, pp. 192–242.

———. *The Lordship of Canterbury: An Essay on Medieval Society.* London, 1966.

Duffy, Eamon. *The Stripping of the Altars.* New Haven, 1992.

Dugdale, William. *Baronage of England.* London, 1675.

Dunn, F. I. "Hermits, Anchorites and Recluses: A Study with Reference to Medieval Norwich." In *Julian and her Norwich: Commemorative Essays*, ed. F. D. Sayer. Norwich, 1973, pp. 18–26.

Dunning, Robert W. "The Muniments of Syon Abbey: their Administration and Migration in the Fifteenth and Sixteenth Centuries." *Bulletin of the Institute of Historical Research* 37:95 (1964), pp. 103–11.

———. "Patronage and Promotion in the Late Medieval Church." In *Patronage, the Crown, and the Provinces in Later Medieval England*, ed. Ralph A. Griffiths. Gloucester, 1981, pp. 167–80.

Dyer, Christopher. "The Social and Economic Background to the Rural Revolt of 1381." In *The English Rising of 1381*, ed. R. Hilton and T. H. Aston. Cambridge, 1984.

———. *Lords and Peasants in a Changing Society: The Estates of the Bishopric of Worcester.* Cambridge, 1980.

———. *The Standard of Living in the Later Middle Ages.* Cambridge, 1989.

Erler, Mary. "English Vowed Women at the End of the Middle Ages." *Medieval Studies* 57 (1995), pp. 155–203.

Eckenstein, Lena. *Women Under Monasticism: Chapters on Saint Lore and Convent Life between AD 500–1500.* Cambridge, 1896.

Elkins, Sharon. *Holy Women of Twelfth-Century England.* Chapel Hill, 1988.

Elliston-Erwood, F. C. "The Premonstratensian Abbey of Langley." *NA* 21 (1920–22), pp. 175–234.

Elton, G. R. *Policy and Police: The Enforcement of the Reformation in the Age of Cromwell.* Cambridge, 1972.

———. *Reform and Reformation. England, 1509–1558.* Cambridge, 1977.

Evans, Nesta. "Inheritance, Women, Religion and Education in Early Modern Society as Revealed by Wills." In *Probate Records and the Local Community*, ed. Philip Riden. Gloucester, 1985, pp. 53–70.

Evenett, H. O. "The Last Stages of Medieval Monasticism." *Studia Monastica* 2 (1960), pp. 387–419.

Finch, Janet and Dulcre Groves, eds., *Labour of Love: Women, Work, and Caring.* London, 1983.

Firth, Catherine. "Village Gilds of Norfolk in the Fifteenth Century." *NA* 18 (1914), pp. 161–203.

Fleming, P. W. "Charity, Faith, and the Gentry of Kent, 1422–1529." In *Property and Politics*, ed. A. J. Pollard. Gloucester, 1984, pp. 36–84.

Flood, R. H. *A Description of St Julian's Church, Norwich, and an Account of Dame Julian's Connection with It.* Norwich, 1936.

Foot, Mirjam. *Pictorial Bookbindings.* London, 1986.

Freedberg, David. "The Structure of Byzantine and European Iconoclasm." In *Iconoclasm: Papers given at the Ninth Spring Symposium of Byzantine Studies*, ed. Judith Herrin and Anthony Bryer. Birmingham, 1977, pp. 165–78.

Fuller, Thomas. *The History of the Worthies of England.* 3 vols. London, 1952.

Gambrier-Parry, Thomas Robert. "Lending Books in a Medieval Nunnery." *Bodleian Quarterly Record* 5:55 (1927), pp. 188–89.

Gasquet, F. A. *English Monastic Life.* London, 1905.

———. *The Eve of the Reformation.* London, 1919.

———. "Overlooked Testimonies to the Character of the English Monasteries on the Eve of the Suppression." *Dublin Review* 114 (1894), pp. 245–77.

———. *Parish Life in Medieval England.* London, 1909.

———. *Henry VIII and the English Monasteries.* London, 1925.

Gerould, G. H. *North-English Homily Collection.* Oxford, 1902.

Gibson, Gail McMurray. *Theater of Devotion: East Anglian Drama and Society in the Late Middle Ages.* Chicago, 1989.

Gibson, J. S. W. *Wills and Where to Find Them.* Chicester, 1974.

Gilchrist, Roberta. *Gender and Material Culture. The Archaeology of Religious Women.* London, 1993.

Gilchrist, Roberta and Marilyn Oliva. *Religious Women in Medieval East Anglia.* Norwich, 1993.

Gillespie, Vincent. "Vernacular Books of Religion." In *Book Production and Publishing in Britain, 1375–1475*, ed. Jeremy Griffiths and Derek Pearsall. Cambridge, 1989, pp. 317–44.

Goldberg, P. J. P. "Lay Book Ownership in Late Medieval York: The Evidence of Wills." *The Library* 6th ser. 16:3 (1994), pp. 181–89.

Golding, Brian. "Burials and Benefactions: An Aspect of Monastic Patronage in Thirteenth-Century England." In *England in the Thirteenth Century. Proceedings of the 1984 Harlaxton Symposium*, ed. W. M. Ormrod. Woodbridge, 1986, pp. 64–75.

Graham, Rose. *St Gilbert of Sempringham and the Gilbertines: A History of the Only English Monastic Order.* London, 1901.

Graves, Coburn V. "English Cistercian Nuns in Lincolnshire." *Speculum* 54 (1979), pp. 492–99.

Gray, Arthur. *The Priory of St Radegund*. Cambridge Antiquarian Society, vol. 31, 1898.

Greatrex, Joan. "On Ministering to 'Certayne Devoute and Religiouse Women': Bishop Fox and the Benedictine Nuns of Winchester Diocese." In *Women in the Church*, ed. W. J. Sheils and Diana Wood. *Studies in Church History*, vol. 27. Oxford, 1990, pp. 223–36.

———. "Prosopography of English Benedictine Cathedral Chapters: Some Monastic *Curricula Vitae*." *Medieval Prosopography* 16:1 (1995), pp. 1–26.

———. "Some Statistics of Religious Motivation." In *Religious Motivation: Biographical and Sociological Problems for the Church Historian*, ed. Derek Baker. *Studies in Church History*, vol. 15. Oxford, 1978, pp. 179–186.

Gundersheimer, Werner L. "Patronage in the Renaissance: An Exploratory Approach." In *Patronage in the Renaissance*, ed. Guy Lytle and Stephen Orgel. New Jersey, 1981, pp. 3–23.

Gunn, S. J. *Charles Brandon, Duke of Suffolk c.1483–1585*. Oxford, 1988.

Hackett, Rosalind. "Women in African Religions." In *Religion and Women*, ed. Arvind Sharma. New York, 1994, pp. 61–92.

Hamburger, Jeffrey F. "Art, Enclosure and the *Curia Monialium*: Prolegomena in the Guise of A Postscript." *Gesta* XXXI/2 (1992), pp. 108–34.

Hanawalt, Barbara. "Keepers of the Lights: Late Medieval Parish Gilds." *Journal of Medieval and Renaissance Studies* 14 (1984), pp. 21–34.

Harper, Richard. "A Note on Corrodies in the Fourteenth Century." *Albion* 15 (1983), pp. 95–102.

Harper-Bill, Christopher. "A Late Medieval Visitation: The Diocese of Norwich in 1499." *PSIA* 34 (1980), pp. 35–42.

Harris, Barbara J. "A New Look at the Reformation: Aristocratic Women and Nunneries, 1450–1540." *Journal of British Studies* 32 (1993), pp. 89–113.

Harvey, Barbara. *Living and Dying in England, 1100–1540, The Monastic Experience*. Oxford, 1993.

Haslewood, Francis. "Inventories of Monasteries Suppressed in 1536." *PSIA* 8 (1894), pp. 83–116.

———. "Monastery at Bruisyard." *PSIA* 7 (1889/91), pp. 320–23.

———. "Will of Sir Walter Quyntyn, of Ipswich." *PSIA* 7 (1887–1889), pp. 111–12.

Hasted, Edward. *History of Kent*. London, 1886.

Hatcher, John. "Mortality in the Fifteenth Century: Some New Evidence." *EHR* 2nd. ser. 39 (1986), pp. 19–38.

———. *Plague, Population and the English Economy*. London, 1977.

Havely, Nicolas. "Chaucer, Boccacio, and the Friars." In *Chaucer and the Italian Trecento*, ed. Piero Boitani. Cambridge, 1983, pp. 249–68.

Hawkins, Sherman. "Chaucer's Prioress and the Sacrifice of Praise." *Journal of English and German Philology* 63 (1964), pp. 599–624.

Hay, Denis. "The Church of England in the Later Middle Ages." *History* 53 (1986), pp. 35–50.

Heath, Peter. "Urban Piety in the Later Middle Ages: The Evidence of Hull Wills." In *The Church, Politics, and Patronage in the Fifteenth Century*, ed. Barrie Dobson. Gloucester, 1984, pp. 209–34.

Heffernan, Thomas. "The Rediscovery of the Bute Manuscript of the 'Northern Homily Cycle'." *Scriptorium* 36 (1982), pp. 118–29.

Heimmel, Jennifer. *"God Our Mother": Julian of Norwich and the Medieval Image of Christian Feminine Divinity*. Salzburgh, 1982.

Herlily, David and Christiane Klapisch-Zuber. *Tuscans and their Families*. New Haven, 1985.

Hervey, John. "The Last Years of Thetford Cluniac Priory." *NA* 27 (1941), pp. 1–28.

Hibbert, F. A. *The Dissolution of the Monasteries as Illustrated by the Suppression of the Religious Houses of Staffordshire*. London, 1910.

Hilpisch, Stephanus. *A History of Benedictine Nuns*. Collegeville, 1958.

Hinnebush, William. *The History of the Dominican Order: Origins and Growth to 1500*. 2 vols. New York, 1966.

Hodgett, G. A. J. "The Dissolution of Religious Houses in Lincolnshire and the Changing Structure of Society." *Lincolnshire Architectural and Archaeological Society, Reports and Papers*, 4th ser. pt. 1 (1951), pp. 83–99.

———. "The Unpensioned Ex-Religious in Tudor England." *Journal of Ecclesiastical History* 13 (1962), pp. 195–202.

———, ed., *The State of the Ex-Religious and Former Chantry Priests in the Diocese of Lincoln, 1547–1574*. Hereford: Lincoln Record Society 53 1959.

Hollingsworth, T. H. "A Demographic Study of the British Ducal Families." In *Population in History*, ed. D. V. Glass and D. E. C. Eversley. London, 1965, pp. 358–64.

Hood, Christobel, ed., *The Chorography of Norfolk*. Norwich, 1938.

Horrox, Rosemary. "Urban Patronage and Patrons in the Fifteenth Century." In *Patronage, the Crown, and the Provinces in Later Medieval England*, ed. Ralph A. Griffiths. Gloucester, 1981, pp. 145–66.

Hoskins, William G. "English Provincial Towns in the Early Sixteenth Century." *TRHS* 5th ser. 6 (1956), pp. 1–19.

Huber, Raphael. *A Documented History of the Franciscan Order, 1182–1517*. Milwaukee, 1944.

Hughes, P. *The Reformation in England*. New York, 1951.

Hull, Suzanne. *Chaste, Silent, and Obedient: English Books for Women, 1475–1640*. California, 1982.

Hunt, Noreen. "Notes on the History of Benedictine and Cistercian Nuns in Britain." *Cistercian Studies* 8:2 (1973), pp. 157–177.

Hutchins, J. *History and Antiquities of Dorset*, 3rd ed. London, 1861–73, vol. 3.

Inge, W. R. "*The Ancrene Riwle* and Julian of Norwich." In *Studies of English Mystics*. New York, 1969, pp. 38–79.

Jack, S. "The Last Days of the Smaller Monasteries in England." *Journal of Ecclesiastical History* 21 (1970), pp. 97–124.

James, M. R. *A Descriptive Catalogue of the Second Series of Fifty Manuscripts* (nos. 51–100) *in the Collection of Henry Yates Thompson*. Cambridge, 1902.

James, Mervin. *Family, Lineage and Civil Society: A Study of Society, Politics, and Mentaility in the Durham Region, 1500–1640*. Oxford, 1974.

Jessopp, Augustus. "The Norfolk Monasteries at the Time of the Suppression by Henry VIII." In *The Norfolk Antiquarian Miscellany*, ed. Walter Rye. Norwich, 1883, pp. 434–63.

————. "Ups and Downs of a Norfolk Nunnery." In *Frivola, Simon Ryan and Other Papers*, ed. Augustus Jessopp. London, 1896, pp. 28–67.

————. "Weyborne Priory." *NA* 10 (1888), pp. 271–76.

————. *Before the Great Pillage*. London, 1910.

Johnson, Penelope. "The Cloistering of Medieval Nuns: Release or Repression, Reality or Fantasy?" In *Gendered Domains: Rethinking Public and Private in Women's History*, ed. Dorothy O. Helly and Susan M. Reverby. Ithaca, 1992, pp. 27–39.

————. *Equal in Monastic Profession*. Chicago, 1991.

————. "*Mulier et Monialis*: The Medieval Nun's Self-Image." *Thought* 64:254 (1989), pp. 242–53.

Johnstone, Hilda. "The Nuns of Elstow." *Church Quarterly Review* 133:265 (1941), pp. 46–54.

Jordan, W. K. *Philanthropy in England, 1480–1660*. New York, 1959.

————. *The Charities of Rural England, 1480–1660*. London, 1961.

Jordon, William C. "The Cistercian Nunnery of La Cour Notre-Dame de Michery. A House that Failed." *Revue Benedictine* 95:3–4 (1985), pp. 311–20.

Keil, Ian. "Corrodies of Glastonbury Abbey in the Later Middle Ages." *Somerset Archaeological and Natural History Proceedings* 108 (1964), pp. 113–31.

Kelly, Edward. "By Mouth of Innocents: The Prioress Vindicated." *Papers on Language and Literature* 5 (1969), pp. 362–74.

Kent, F. W., Patricia Simons and J. C. Eade, eds., *Patronage, Art, and Society in Renaissance Italy*. Oxford, 1987.

Ker, N. R. *Medieval Libraries of Great Britain: A List of Surviving Books*, 2nd edn. London, 1964.

————. *Medieval Manuscripts in British Libraries; Supplement to the Second Edition*, ed. Andrew G. Watson. London, 1987.

Kerridge, Eric. *The Farmers of Old England*. London, 1973.

Kershaw, Ian. *Bolton Priory: The Economy of a Northern Monastery, 1268–1325*. Oxford, 1973.

King, Archdale A. *Liturgies of the Past*. Wisconsin, 1959.

Knowles, David. "English Monastic Life in the Later Middle Ages." *History* n.s. 39 (1954), pp. 26–38.

————. *Saints and Scholars*. Cambridge, 1962.

————. *The Monastic Order in England*. Cambridge, 1941.

————. *The Religious Orders in England*. 3 vols. Cambridge, 1948–1959.

Knowles, David and R. Neville Hadcock, eds., *Medieval Religious Houses in England and Wales*, 2nd edn. London, 1971.

————. "Additions and Corrections to Medieval Religious Houses." *EHR* 72 (1957), pp. 60–87.

Kreider, Alan. *English Chantries: The Road to Dissolution*. Cambridge, 1979.

Kriehen, A. "Studies in the Sources of the Social Revolt in 1381." *AHR* 6 (1901), pp. 480–84.

Le Goff, Jacques. *The Birth of Purgatory*, trans. Arthur Goldhammer. Chicago, 1984.

Leclercq, Jean. "Hospitality and Monastic Prayer." *Cistercian Studies* 8:1 (1973), pp. 3–24.

————. "Medieval Feminine Monasticism: Reality Versus Romantic Images." In *Studies in Honor of St Benedict of Nursia*, ed. Rozanne Elder. Kalamazoo, Studies in Medieval Cistercian History, iii, 1981, pp. 53–73.

————. "Monastic Life for Men and Monastic Life for Women." *Cistercian Studies* 6:4 (1971), pp. 327–33.

————. "Profession According to the Rule of St Benedict." *Cistercian Studies* 5 (1970), pp. 252–73.

————. "The Spirituality of Medieval Feminine Monasticism." In *The Continuing Quest for God: Monastic Spirituality in Tradition and Transition*, ed. William Skudlarek. Minnesota, 1982, pp. 114–26.

Legge, Dominica M. *Anglo-Norman in the Cloisters. The Influence of the Orders upon Anglo-Norman Literature.* Edinburgh, 1950.

Leis, Nancy. "Women in Groups: Ijaw Women's Associations." In *Women, Culture, and Society*, ed. Michelle Rosaldo and Louise Lamphere. California, 1981, pp. 223–42.

Lekai, L. J. *The Cistercians: Ideas and Reality.* Ohio, 1977.

Leotaud, A. "Monastic Officials in the Middle Ages." *Downside Review* 56 (1938), pp. 391–409.

Lepine, David, " 'My Beloved Sons in Christ': The Chapter of Lincoln Cathedral 1300–1541." *Medieval Prosopography* 16:1 (1995), pp. 89–113.

Levin, Carol. "Introduction." In *Ambiguous Realities: Women in the Middle Ages and the Renaissance*, ed. Carol Levin and Jeanie Watson. Detroit, 1987, pp. 14–21.

Liljegren, S. B. *The Fall of the Monasteries and Social Changes in England.* Lung, 1924.

Little, A. G. "Corrodies at the Carmelite Friary of Lynn." *Journal of Ecclesiastical History* 89 (1958–59), pp. 8–29.

Little, Bryan. *Abbeys and Priories in England and Wales.* London, 1979.

Liveing, H. G. D. *The Records of Romsey Abbey.* Winchester, 1906.

Llewelyn, Robert. *All Shall Be Well: The Spirituality of Julian of Norwich for Today.* New York, 1982.

Lochrie, Karma. *Margery Kempe and Translations of the Flesh.* Philadelphia, 1991.

Lowe, K. P. J. "Patronage and Territoriality in Early Sixteenth-Century Florence." *Renaissance Studies* 7:3 (1993), pp. 258–71.

Luce, R. "Injunctions Made and Issued to the Abbess and Convent of the Monastery of Romsey after his Visitation by William of Wykeham, A.D. 1387." *Hampshire Field Club and Archaeology Society, Proceedings* 17 pt. 1 (1949), pp. 31–44.

Luxton, Imogen. "The Reformation and Popular Culture." In *Church and Society in England: Henry VIII to James I*, ed. Felicity Heal and Rosemary O'Day. London, 1977, pp. 57–77.

Lytle, Guy Fitch. "Religion and the Lay Patron in Reformation England." In *Patronage in the Renaissance*, ed. G. F. Lytle and Stephen Orgel. Princeton, 1981, pp. 65–114.

MacCulloch, D. N. J., ed., *The Chorography of Suffolk.* Suffolk Record Society Publications, vol. 19, 1976.

————. "Catholic and Puritan in Elizabethan Suffolk." *Archiv für Reformationsgeschichte* 72 (1981), pp. 232–87.

————. *Suffolk and the Tudors: Politics and Religion in an English County, 1500–1600.* Oxford, 1986.

MacKenzie, Neil. "Boy into Bishop: A Festive Role Reversal." *History Today* 37:12 (1987), pp. 10–16.

MacLeish, Andrew, ed., *The Medieval Monastery.* Minnesota, 1988.

Magli, Ia. "Il Problema Antropologico-Culturale del Monachesimo Femminile." *Enciclopedia delle Religioni*, vol. 3, pp. 627–41.

Mann, Ethel. *Old Bungay*. London, 1934.

Mason, Emma. "The Donors of Westminster Abbey Charters: ca. 1066–1240." *Medieval Prosopography* 8:2 (1987), pp. 23–39.

Mate, Mavis. "Property Investment by Canterbury Cathedral Priory, 1250–1400." *Journal of British Studies* 23 (1984), pp. 1–21.

McClenaghan, B. *The Springs of Lavenham and the Suffolk Cloth Trade in the XV and XVI Centuries*. Ipswich, 1924.

McFarlane, K. B. *Lancastrians Kings and Lollard Kights*. Oxford, 1972.

——. *The Nobility of Later Medieval England*. Oxford, 1973.

McGerr, Rosemary, ed., *"The Pilgrimage of the Soul." A Critical Edition of the Middle English Dream Vision*. New York, 1990.

McKinley, Richard. *Norfolk and Suffolk Surnames in the Middle Ages*. London, 1975.

McKisack, May. *The Fourteenth Century, 1307–1399*. Oxford, 1959.

McLaughlin, Eleanor. "Equality of Souls, Inequality of Sexes: Women in Medieval Theology." In *Images of Women in the Jewish and Christian Traditions*, ed. Rosemary Ruether. New York, 1974, pp. 213–66.

McRee, Ben. "Religious Gilds and Regulations of Behavior in Late Medieval English Towns." In *People, Politics and Community in the Later Middle Ages*, ed. Joel Rosenthal and Colin Richmond. Gloucester, 1987, pp. 108–22.

Meale, Carol. "Patrons, Buyers, and Owners: Book Production and Social Status." In *Book Production and Publishing in Britain, 1375–1475*, ed. Jeremy Griffiths and Derek Pearsall. Cambridge, 1989, pp. 201–38.

Mertes, Kate. *The English Noble Household, 1250–1600: Good Governance and Political Rule*. New York, 1988.

Meyer, Marc. "Patronage of the West Saxon Royal Nunneries in Late Anglo-Saxon England." *Revue Benedictine* 91 (1981), pp. 332–58.

Mingay, G. E. *The Gentry: The Rise and Fall of a Ruling Class*. London, 1976.

Mitchell, J. B. "Suffolk Agriculture in the Middle Ages." *Report of the British Association*, 1938, p. 445.

Mollat, Michel. *Les Pauvres au Moyen Age*. Paris, 1978.

Monson, Craig, ed., *The Crannied Wall: Women, Religion and the Arts in Early Modern Europe*. Ann Arbor, 1992.

Moorman, J. R. *The Grey Friars in Cambridge, 1225–1538*. Cambridge, 1952.

Moran, Jo Ann Hoeppner. "Literacy and Education in Northern England, 1350–1550. A Methodological Inquiry." *Northern History* 17 (1981), pp. 1–23.

——. *The Growth of English Schooling, 1340–1548*. New Jersey, 1985.

Morant, Alfred William. *Pedigrees of Norfolk Families*. Norwich, 1870.

Morgan, F. C. and Penelope. "Some Nuns, Ex-Religious and Former Chantry Priests Living in the Diocese of Hereford (c.1554)." *Woolhope Naturalists Field Club Transactions* 27 (1963), pp. 135–48.

Morgan, M. "The Suppression of the Alien Priories." *History* 26:103 (1941), pp. 204–12.

Morgan, Nigel. *Early Gothic Manuscripts (II), 1250–85*. London, 1988.

——. "Texts and Images of Marian Devotion in Thirteenth-Century England." In *England in the Thirteenth Century: Proceedings of the 1989 Harlaxton Symposium*, ed. W. M. Ormrod. Woodbridge, 1991.

Morris, M. C. F. *Nunburnholme: Its History and Antiquities*. London, 1907.

Morris, Richard and Walter Skeat. *Specimens of Early English*. Oxford, 1872.

Mortimer, Richard. "Religious and Secular Motives for Some English Monastic Foundations." In *Religious Motivation: Biographical and Sociological Problems for the Church Historian*, ed. Derek Baker. Oxford, 1978, pp. 77–85.

Muskett, Joseph. *Suffolk Manorial Families Being County Visitations and Other Pedigrees*. 3 vols. Exeter, 1900.

Myers, A. R. *England in the Fourteenth Century*. New York, 1979.

———. *England in the Late Middle Ages*. London, 1979.

Myers, J. N. L. "Notes on the History of Butley Priory, Suffolk." In *Oxford Essays in Medieval History Presented to Herbert E. Salter*. Oxford, 1934, pp. 190–206.

Nicholls, J. W. *The Matter of Courtesy*. Cambridge, 1985.

Nichols, John. "The Internal Organization of English Cistercian Nunneries." *Citeaux* 30:1 (1979), pp. 23–40.

Nichols, John and Lilian Shank, eds., *Distant Echoes 1: Medieval Religious Women*. Cistercian Studies Series: no. 71. Kalamazoo, 1984.

———. *Medieval Religious Women: Peaceweavers*. Cistercian Studies Series: no. 72. Kalamazoo, 1987.

Nichols, J. G. *Annales and Antiquities of Lacock Abbey*. London, 1835.

O'Carroll, Maura. "The Educational Organisation of the Dominicans in England and Wales, 1221–1348: A Multidisciplinary Approach." *Archivum Fratrum Praedicatorum* 50 (1980), pp. 23–62.

O'Day, Rosemary. *Education and Society, 1500–1800*. London, 1982.

O'Faolain, Julia and Lauro Martines, eds., *Not In God's Image*. New York, 1973.

Oliva, Marilyn. "Aristocracy or Meritocracy? Office-holding Patterns in Late Medieval English Nunneries." In *Women in the Church*, ed. W. J. Sheils and Diana Wood, pp. 197–208. *Studies in Church History*, vol. 27. Oxford, 1990.

Orme, Nicholas. *Education and Society in Medieval and Renaissance England*. London, 1989.

———. *English Schools in the Middle Ages*. London, 1973.

Ortner, Sherry. "Is Female to Male as Nature is to Culture." In *Women, Culture, and Society*, ed. M. Z. Rosaldo and Louise Lamphere. California, 1974, pp. 67–88.

Owst, G. R. *Literature and Pulpit in Medieval England*. New York, 1961.

———. *Preaching in Medieval England*. New York, 1965.

Palliser, D. M. "Popular Reactions to the Reformation during the Years of Uncertainty 1530–70." In *Church and Society in England: Henry VIII to James I*, ed. Felicity Heal and Rosemary O'Day. London, 1977, pp. 35–55.

Palmer, William. "The Benedictine Nunnery of Swaffham Bulbeck." *Proceedings of the Cambridge Antiquarian Society* 31 (1929), pp. 30–65.

Pantin, W. A. "The Fourteenth Century." In *The English Church and the Papacy in the Middle Ages*, ed. C. H. Lawrence. London, 1965, pp. 157–94.

———. *The English Church in the Fourteenth Century*. Cambridge, 1955.

Parrey, Yvonne. " 'Devoted Disciples of Christ': Early Sixteenth-Century Religious Life in the Nunnery at Amesbury." *Bulletin of the Institute of Historical Research* 67 no. 164 (1994), pp. 240–48.

Patten, John. "Changing Occupational Structures in the East Anglian Countryside, 1500–1700." In *Change in the Countryside: Essays on Rural England, 1500–1900*, ed. H. S. A. Fox and R. A. Butlin. London, 1979, pp. 103–21.

———. "Patterns of Migration and Movement of Labour to Three Pre-Industrial

East Anglian Towns." In *Pre-Industrial England: Geographic Essays*, ed. John Patten. Folkstone, 1979, pp. 143–162.

———. "Population Distribution in Norfolk and Suffolk during the Sixteenth and Seventeenth Centuries." In *Pre-Industrial England: Geographic Essays*, ed. John Patten. Folkstone, 1979, pp. 71–92.

Peacock, Edward. "Injunctions of John Langland, Bishop of Lincoln, to Certain Monasteries in his Diocese." *Archaeologia* 48 (1882–3), pp. 49–64.

Pearsall, Derek. *Old and Middle English Poetry*. London, 1977.

Perceval, Charles Spencer. "Remarks on Some Early Charters and Documents Relating to the Prior of Austin Canons and the Abbey of Austin Canonesses at Canonsleigh, in the County of Devon." *Archaeologia* 60 (1866), pp. 417–50.

Phipson, R. M. "Notes on Carrow Priory, Norwich." *NA* 9 (1884), pp. 215–55.

Phythian-Adams, Charles. "Ceremony and the Citizen: The Communal Year at Coventry, 1450–1700." In *Crisis and Order in English Towns, 1500–1700*, ed. Peter Clark and Paul Slack. Toronto, 1972, pp. 57–85.

Platt, Colin. *The English Medieval Town*. London, 1979.

Pollock, Frederick and Frederick Maitland. *The History of English Law before the Time of Edward I*. Cambridge, 1898.

Postan, M. M. *The Medieval Economy and Society*. Berkeley, 1972.

Postan, M. M. and E. E. Rich, eds., *The Cambridge Economic History*. Cambridge, 1952.

Postles, David A. "Heads of Religious Houses as Administrators." In *England in the Thirteenth Century: Proceedings of the Harlaxton Symposium*, ed. W. M. Ormrod. Woodbridge, 1991, pp. 37–50.

Pound, John. *Tudor and Stuart Norwich*. Chichester, 1988.

Powell, Edgar. *The Rising in East Anglia in 1381*. Cambridge, 1896.

Power, Eileen. *Medieval English Nunneries*. Cambridge, 1922.

———. *Medieval Women*, ed. M. M. Postan. Cambridge, 1975.

Raven, J. J. "The Ecclesiastical Remains of Bungay." *PSAI* 4 (1874), pp. 65–76.

Raymo, Robert. "Works of Religious and Philosophical Instruction." In *A Manual of the Writings in Middle English*, vol. 7, ed. Albert E. Hartung. Connecticut, 1986, 2255–2368.

Redstone, V. B. "The Carmelites of Ipswich." *PSIA* 10 (1898–1900), pp. 189–96.

———. "Chapels, Chantries, and Gilds in Suffolk." *PSIA* 12 (1906), pp. 1–87.

Richardson, W. C. *A History of the Court of Augmentations*. Baton Rouge, 1961.

Richmond, Colin. *John Hopton. A Fifteenth-Century English Gentleman*. Cambridge, 1981.

———. "Religion and the Fifteenth-Century Gentleman." In *The Church, Politics and Patronage in the Fifteenth Century*, ed. R. B. Dobson. Gloucester, 1984, pp. 193–208.

Riddy, Felicity. " 'Women Talking about the Things of God': a Late Medieval Subculture." In *Women and Literature in Britain, 1150–1500*, ed. Carol Meale. Cambridge, 1993, pp. 104–27.

Rigaux, Dominique. "The Fransiscan Tertiaries at the Convent of Sant'Anna at Folign." *Gesta* XXX1/2 (1992), pp. 92–8.

Rogers, J. T. *A History of Agriculture and Prices in England*. 7 vols. Oxford, 1866–1902.

Roper, Lyndal. *The Holy Household, Women and Morals, in Reformation Augsburg*. Oxford, 1989.

Rosaldo, Michelle. "Women, Culture, and Society: A Theoretical Overview." In *Women, Culture, and Society*, ed. Michelle Rosaldo and Louise Lamphere. California, 1974.

Rosenthal, Joel. "Kings, Continuity and Ecclesiastical Benefaction in Fifteenth-Century England." In *People, Politics and Continuity in the Later Middle Ages*, ed. Joel Rosenthal and Colin Richmond. Gloucester, 1987, pp. 161–77.

——. "Retirement and the Life Cycle in Fifteenth-Century England." In *Aging and the Aged in Medieval Europe*, ed. Michael Sheehan. Toronto, 1990, pp. 173–88.

——. *The Purchase of Paradise: Gift Giving and the Aristocracy, 1307–1485.* London, 1972.

Rubin, Miri. *Charity and Community in Medieval Cambridge.* Cambridge, 1986.

Russell, J. C. "The Clerical Population of Medieval England." *Traditio* 2 (1944), pp. 177–212.

——. *British Medieval Population.* Alburquerque, 1948.

——. "How Many of the Population were Aged?" In *Aging and the Aged in Medieval Europe*, ed. Michael Sheehan. Toronto, 1990, pp. 119–27.

Rye, Walter and Edward Tillet. *An Account and Description of Carrow Abbey, Norwich, together with an Appendix of Charters.* Norwich, 1884.

Rye, Walter. "Laymen Lodging in Monasteries." *History Teacher's Miscellany* 1 (1923), pp. 9–10.

——. *Carrow Abbey, otherwise Carrow Priory; near Norwich, in the County of Norfolk; its Foundation, Buildings, Officers, and Inmates with Appendices.* Norwich, 1889.

——. *Norfolk Families.* Norwich, 1911–1913.

St John Hope, W. H. "Inventories of the Parish Church of St Peter Mancroft." *NA* 14 (1901), pp. 153–240.

——. *Cowdray and Easebourne Priory in the County of Sussex.* London, 1919.

Saul, Nigel. "The Religious Sympathies of the Gentry in Gloucestershire, 1200–1500." *Bristol and Gloucester Archaeological Society Transactions* 98 (1980), pp. 99–112.

Saunders, H. W. "A History of Coxford Priory." *NA* 17 (1910), pp. 284–370.

——. *Introduction to Obedientiary and Manor Rolls of Norwich Cathedral Priory.* Norwich, 1930.

Savine, A. *English Monasteries on the Eve of the Reformation.* Oxford Studies in Social and Legal History, vol. 1. Oxford, 1909.

Scarisbrick, J. J. "Henry VIII and the Dissolution of the Secular Colleges." In *Law and Government Under the Tudors*, ed. Claire Cross, David Loades, and J. J. Scarisbrick. Cambridge, 1988, pp. 51–66.

——. "The Pardon of the Clergy, 1531." *Cambridge Historical Journal* 12 (1956), pp. 22–39.

——. *The Reformation and the English People.* Oxford, 1984.

Schock, Richard. "Chaucer's Prioress: Mercy and Tender Heart." In *The Bridge: A Yearbook of Judeo-Christian Studies*, ed. John Oesterreicher. New York, 1956, pp. 239–55.

Schulenburg, Jane. "Strict Active Enclosure and Its Effects on the Female Monastic Experience (ca. 500–1100)." In *Distant Echoes: 1. Medieval Religious Women*, ed. John Nichols and Lilian Shank. Kalamazoo, 1984, pp. 51–68.

——. "Women's Monastic Communities, 500–1100: Patterns of Expansion and

Decline." In *Sisters and Workers in the Middle Ages*, ed. Judith Bennett, et al. Chicago, 1989, pp. 208–39.

Searle, Eleanor. *Lordship and Community: Battle Abbey and its Banlieu*. Toronto, 1974.

Serjeantson, R. M. *A History of Delapre Abbey*. Northampton, 1909.

Shahar, Shulamith. *The Fourth Estate: A History of Women in the Middle Ages*. London, 1983.

Sheail, J. "The Distribution of Taxable Population and Wealth in England during the Early Sixteenth Century." *Transactions and Papers, Institute of British Geography* 55 (1972), pp. 55–70.

Sheppard, Elaine. "The Reformation and the Citizens of Norwich." *NA* 38 (1981), 44–58.

Simon, Joan. *Education and Society in Tudor England*. Cambridge, 1966.

Sinclair, Karen. "Women and Religion." In *The Cross Cultural Study of Women. A Comprehensive Guide*, ed. Margot Duley and Mary Edwards. New York, 1986, pp. 107–24.

Skeat, Walter. *Specimens of Early English*. Oxford, 1872.

Small, John. *English Metrical Homilies from the Manuscripts of the Fourteenth Century*. Edinburgh, 1862.

Smith, R. A. L. "The Central Financial System of Christchurch, Canterbury, 1186–1512." *EHR* 55 (1940), pp. 353–369.

———. *Collected Papers*. London, 1947.

Snape, R. H. *English Monastic Finances in the Later Middle Ages*. New York, 1926.

Southern, Richard. *Western Society and the Church in the Middle Ages*. Middlesex, 1970.

Suckling, Alfred. *The History and Antiquities of the County of Suffolk*. 2 vols. N.P., 1846–1848.

Sugano, Douglas I. "Apologies for the Magdalene: Devotion, Iconoclasm, and the N-Town Plays." *Research Opportunities in Renaissance Drama* 33 (1994), pp. 165–76.

Swales, T. H. "Opposition to the Suppression of the Norfolk Monasteries: Expressions of Discontent, the Walsingham Conspiracy." *NA* 33:3 (1964), pp. 254–65.

———. "The Redistribution of the Monastic Lands in Norfolk at the Dissolution." *NA* 34 (1969), pp. 14–44.

Swanson, R. N. *Church and Society in Late Medieval England*. Oxford, 1989.

Sweet, Alfred. "The Apostolic See and the Heads of Religious Houses." *Speculum* 28 (1953), pp. 468–84.

Symons, Thomas. "Looking Back on the *Regularis Concordia*." *Downside Review* 78 (1960), pp. 286–92.

Szittya, Penn R. *The Antifraternal Tradition in Medieval Literature*. New Jersey, 1986.

Tack, Theodore. "Women in the Augustine Order." *Tagastan* 29 (1983), pp. 87–100.

Tanner, Norman. *The Church in Late Medieval Norwich*. Toronto, 1984.

Thirsk, Joan, ed., *The Agrarian History of England and Wales, 1500–1640*. Vol. 4 of *The Agrarian History of England and Wales*, ed. H. P. R. Finberg. Cambridge, 1967.

Thomas, Hugh M. *Vassals, Crusaders, and Thugs: The Gentry of Angevin Yorkshire, 1154–1216*. Philadelphia, 1993.

Thompson, Benjamin. "Monasteries and their Patrons at Foundation and Dissolution." *TRHS* 6th series vol. 4 (1994), pp. 103–26.

Thompson, A. H. "Double Monasteries and the Male Element in Nunneries." In *The Ministry of Women: A Report by a Committee appointed by His Grace the Lord Archbishop of Canterbury.* London, 1919.

———. *The English Clergy and their Organization in the Later Middle Ages.* Oxford, 1947.

———. "A Corrody from Leicester Abbey, A.D. 1393–4, with Some Notes on Corrodies." *Leicestershire Archaeological Society Transactions* 14 (1926), pp. 114–34.

Thompson, John A. "Piety and Charity in Late Medieval London." *Journal of Ecclesiastical History* 16 (1965), pp. 178–95.

Thompson, R. M. "Obedientiaries of St Edmund's Abbey." *PSIA* 35:2 (1982), pp. 91–103.

Thompson, Sally. "The Problem of the Cistercian Nuns in the Twelfth and Early Thirteenth Centuries." In *Women in the Church,* ed. Derek Baker. *Studies in Church History,* vol. 1, Oxford, 1978, pp. 227–252.

———. *Women Religious. The Founding of English Nunneries after the Norman Conquest.* Oxford, 1991.

Thomson, John A. F. " 'The Well of Grace': Englishmen and Rome in the Fifteenth Century." In *The Church, Politics and Patronage in the Fifteenth Century,* ed. Barrie Dobson. Gloucester, 1984, pp. 99–114.

Thrupp, Sylvia. *The Merchant Class of Medieval London.* Chicago, 1948.

Tillotson, John. "Pensions, Corrodies and Religious Houses: An Aspect of the Relations of Crown and Church in Early Fourteenth-Century England." *Journal of Religious History* 8 (1974–75), pp. 127–43.

———. *Marrick Priory: A Nunnery in Late Medieval Yorkshire.* York: Borthwick Papers no. 75, 1989.

———. *Monastery and Society in the Late Middle Ages: Selected Account Rolls from Selby Abbey, Yorkshire, 1398–1537.* Woodbridge, 1989.

———. "Visitation and Reform of the Yorkshire Monasteries in the Fifteenth Century." *Northern History* 30 (1994), pp. 1–21.

Trexler, Richard, ed., *Persons in Groups.* Binghamton, 1985.

Usilton, Larry. "The Kings' Women and their Corrodies." In *The Worlds of Medieval Women: Creativity, Influence, Imagination,* ed. Constance Berman, et al. Morgantown, 1985, pp. 69–86.

Vale, Malcolm G. A. *Piety, Charity and Literacy Among the Yorkshire Gentry, 1370–1480.* York: Borthwick Papers no. 50, 1976.

Verheijen, L. "La 'Regula Puellarum' et la 'Regula Sancti Augustini'." *Augustiniana* 4 (1954), pp. 258–268.

———. *La Regle de Saint Augustin.* Paris, 1967.

Victoria History of the County of Bedfordshire, 1, London, 1904.

Victoria History of the County of Cambridgeshire and the Isle of Ely, 2, London, 1948.

Victoria History of the County of Chester, 3, London, 1980.

Victoria History of the County of Dorset, 2, London, 1908.

Victoria History of the County of Essex, 2, London, 1907.

Victoria History of the County of Hertfordshire, 4, London, 1971.

Victoria History of the County of Kent, 2, London, 1926.

Victoria History of the County of Lincolnshire, 2, London, 1906.

Victoria History of London, London, 1909.
Victoria History of the County of Middlesex, 1, London, 1969.
Victoria History of the County of Norfolk, 2, London, 1906.
Victoria History of the County of Oxfordshire, 2, London, 1907.
Victoria History of the County of Somerset, 2, London, 1969.
Victoria History of the County of Suffolk, 2, London, 1911.
Victoria History of the County of Warwickshire, 3, London, 1945.
Victoria History of the County of Wiltshire, 3, London, 1956.
Victoria History of the County of Yorkshire, 3, London, 1974.
Virgoe, Roger and David Dymond. "The Reduced Population and Wealth of Early Fifteenth-Century Suffolk." *PSIA* 36:2 (1986), pp. 73–100.
Virgoe, Roger. "The Crown and Local Government: East Anglia under Richard II." In *The Reign of Richard II: Essays in Honor of May McKisack*, ed. F. R. H. Du Boulay and Caroline Baron. London, 1971, pp. 218–241.
———. "The Crown, Magnates, and Local Government in Fifteenth-Century East Anglia." In *The Crown and Local Community in England and France in the Fifteenth Century*, ed. J. R. L. Highfield and Robin Jeffs. Gloucester, 1981, pp. 72–87.
———. "The Divorce of Sir Thomas Tuddenham." *NA* 34:4 (1969), pp. 406–19.
Wake, Joan and W. A. Pantin. *Delapre Abbey, Northampton: Its History and Architecture*. Northampton Record Society, 1959.
Wakelin, M. F. "A New Vernacular Version of a Nun's Profession." *Notes and Queries* 229 (1984), pp. 459–61.
Warren, Ann. *Anchorites and their Patrons in Medieval England*. Berkeley, 1985.
Warren, F. W. "A Pre-Reformation Gild." *PSIA* 11 (1903), pp. 134–47.
Wasson, John. "Visiting Entertainers at the Cluniac Priory, Thetford 1497–1540." *Albion* 9:2 (1977), pp. 128–34.
Watkin, Alfred. "An English Mediaeval Instruction Book for Novices." *Downside Review* 57 (1939), pp. 477–88.
Watkin, E. I. "Dame Julian of Norwich (1342–1413)." In *The English Way*, ed. Maisie Ward. New York, 1933, pp. 128–58.
Wedgewood, J. C. *History of Parliament, 1439–1509, Register*. London, 1936–1938.
Westlake, H. F. *The Parish Gilds of Medieval England*. London, 1919.
Wilks, Michael. "Royal Patronage and Anti-Papalism from Ockham to Wyclif." In *From Ockham to Wyclif*, ed. Anne Hudson and Michael Wilks. Oxford, 1987, pp. 135–63.
Williams, Arnold. "Chaucer and the Friars." *Speculum* 28 (1953), pp. 499–513.
Williams, David. "Tudor Cistercian Life: Corrodians and Residential Servants." *Citeaux* 34:3–4 (1983), pp. 284–310.
Williams, Gerhild. "The Woman/The Witch: Variations on a Sixteenth-Century Theme." In *The Crannied Walls: Women, Religion, and the Arts in Early Modern Europe*, ed. Craig Monson. Ann Arbor, 1992.
Wilton, J. W. *Monastic Life in Norfolk and Suffolk*. Norfolk, 1980.
Winney, James, ed., *The Prioress' Prologue and Tale*. Cambridge, 1975.
Witte, Stephen P. "*Muscipula Diaboli* and Chaucer's Portrait of the Prioress." *Papers on Language and Literature* 13 (1977), pp. 227–37.
Wogan-Browne, Jocelyn. " 'Clerc u lais, miune u dame': Women and Anglo-Norman Hagiography in the Twelfth and Thirteenth Centuries." In *Women and Literature in Britain, 1150–1500*, ed. Carol Meale. Cambridge, 1993, pp. 61–86.

————. "Saints' Lives and the Female Reader." *Forum for Modern Language Studies* 27 (1991), pp. 314–32.

Wood, Susan. *English Monasteries and their Patrons in the Thirteenth Century.* Oxford, 1955.

Wood-Legh, K. L. *Studies in Church Life in England Under Edward III.* Cambridge, 1934.

————. *Perpetual Chantries in England.* Cambridge, 1965.

Woodward, G. W. O. "A Speculation in Monastic Lands." *EHR* 79 (1964), pp. 778–83.

————. *The Dissolution of the Monasteries.* New York, 1966.

————. "The Exemption from the Suppression of Certain Yorkshire Priories." *EHR* 76 (1961), pp. 385–401.

Woolgar, C. M., ed., *Household Accounts from Medieval England.* Records of Social and Economic History, n.s. xvii and xviii. Oxford, 1992.

Youings, Joyce. "A Rare Survival: Letters Patent Granting a Pension to a Lincolnshire Nun in 1539." *Archives* 7 (1966), pp. 226–29.

————. *The Dissolution of the Monasteries.* London, 1971.

————. "The City of Exeter and the Property of the Dissolved Monasteries." *Transactions of the Devonshire Association for the Advancement of Science, Literature and Art* 84 (1952), pp. 122–41.

Zimmerman, B. "The White Friars at Ipswich." *PSIA* 10 (1891–1900), pp. 196–204.

Unpublished Works

Bokenham, Joseph, compiler. *An Alphabetical List of the Arms and Crests of the Gentry of the Counties of Norfolk and Suffolk, as well as Ancient and Modern, in Two Parts, Collected by the Best Authors and Most Authentic Manuscrpits.* MSS, Coleman Library. Norfolk Central Library, 1765.

Byrne, Mary. "The Tradition of the Nun in Medieval England." Ph.D. diss., Catholic University, 1932.

Candon, Sister Mary Patrick. "The Doctrine of the Herte." Ph.D. diss., Fordham University, 1963.

Ellis, John Tracy. "Anti-Papal Legislation in Medieval England (1066–1377)." Ph.D. diss., Catholic University, 1930.

Fitch, W. S. *Suffolk Monasteries.* 4 vols. MSS, Suffolk Record Office, n.d.

Grace, Frank R. "The Life and Career of Thomas Howard, Third Duke of Norfolk (1473–1554)." M.A. thesis, University of Nottingham, 1961.

Jacka, H. T. "The Dissolution of the English Nunneries." M.A. thesis, University of London, 1909.

Mode, P. G. "The Influence of the Black Death on the English Monasteries." Ph.D. diss., University of Chicago, 1916.

Nichols, John. "The History and Cartulary of the Cistercian Nuns of Marham Abbey." Ph.D. diss., Kent State University, 1974.

Norris, Anthony, compiler. *A Collection of Pedigrees of Norfolk Families, Digested in Alphabetical Order, and Compiled from the Most Authentic Public Evidences, Wills, Records, Title Deeds, and Monuments.* MSS, Coleman Library. Norfolk Central Library, n.d.

Paxton, Catherine. "The Nunneries of London and Its Environs in the Later Middle Ages." D.Phil. thesis, Lincoln College, Oxford, 1992.

Ridgard, John. "The Social and Economic History of Flixton in Southelmham, Suffolk, 1300–1600." M.A. thesis, University of Leicester, 1970.

Rye, Walter. A Catalogue of Fifty of the Norfolk Manuscripts in the Library of Mr. Walter Rye at Winchester House, Putney. MSS, Coleman Library. Norfolk Central Library, 1889.

Stuckert, Howard. "Corrodies in English Monasteries." Ph.D. diss., University of Philadelphia, 1923.

Index

List of abbreviated counties:

Other Volumes in
Studies in the History of Medieval Religion

Printed in the United Kingdom
by Lightning Source UK Ltd.
123552UK00003B/85-90/A